INTRODUCTION TO
6800/68000
MICROPROCESSORS

FREDERICK F. DRISCOLL
Wentworth Institute of Technology

Breton Publishers
Boston, Massachusetts

PWS PUBLISHERS

Prindle, Weber & Schmidt • Duxbury Press • PWS Engineering • Breton Publishers •
20 Park Plaza • Boston, Massachusetts 02116

PWS Publishers is a division of Wadsworth, Inc.

Portions of this book were previously published in *Microprocessor-Microcomputer Technology* by Frederick F. Driscoll, copyright © 1983, Wadsworth, Inc., Belmont, California 94002.

Library of Congress Cataloging-in-Publication Data

Driscoll, Frederick F., 1943–
   Introduction to 6800/68000 microprocessors.
   Includes index.
  1. Motorola 6800 (Microprocessor) 2. Motorola 68000
(Microprocessor) I. Title.
QA76.8.M67D75 1987   004.165   86-24452
ISBN 0-534-07692-0

Printed in the United States of America
  2 3 4 5 6 7 8 9—91 90 89 88 87

Sponsoring editor: *George J. Horesta*
Production: *Technical Texts, Inc.*
Production editor: *Jean T. Peck*
Interior and cover design: *Sylvia Dovner*
Cover photo: *Ken Cooper/The Image Bank*
Composition: *Crane Typesetting Service, Inc.*
Cover printing: *New England Book Components, Inc.*
Text printing and binding: *The Maple-Vail Book Manufacturing Group*

For Elizabeth Maura,
my daughter and lovable sprite

Preface

The heart of a microcomputer (μC), like any other computer, is its central processing unit (CPU). The CPU fetches and executes instructions, performs arithmetic and logical operations, and establishes timing waveforms needed to carry out instructions. In a μC, the CPU is the microprocessor (μP). Advances in integrated circuit technology have allowed semiconductor manufacturers to design the μP as a single integrated circuit (IC) housed in a dual-in-line package.

There are a number of μPs on the market today fabricated by different manufacturers. Since it would be extremely difficult to cover all the μPs in one text and since most users concentrate on one particular μP family; I have selected Motorola's 6800 and 68000 μPs, memory chips, and input/output chips as the basis for this text.

Motorola introduced the 6800 μP and some memory and peripheral chips in 1974. Additional support chips have been introduced since then, and the 6800 has become a popular and widely used μP. Microprocessors are classified as to the number of bits that they can send or receive at a time (i.e., 8, 16, or 32 bits). The 6800 is an 8-bit device. Motorola has also brought out other 8-bit μPs either as enhancement of the 6800 or for unique applications. In either case, the basis for Motorola's other 8-bit μPs is the 6800.

The next major step for Motorola occurred in 1979. In that year, the company announced a new microprocessor—the 68000. Although this μP is classified as a 16-bit device, because this is how data is sent and received, it can perform arithmetic and logical operations on 8, 16, and 32 bits. It is an extremely sophisticated μP—much more than simply an enhanced version of the 6800.

A μP is not used as an isolated device; it is only one part of an entire μC system. Therefore, we need to discuss memory and input/output chips and how to interconnect them to the μP. Since any computer system requires hardware (the actual chips) and software (programs that allow the hardware to perform a useful task), we must cover both areas. Although this text does cover some general concepts, most of the book is geared toward Motorola's μP/μC products. A breakdown of the chapters follows.

General μP/μC Concepts:

1. Introduction to Digital Computers
2. Microcomputers and Microprocessors
3. Use of Codes with Microcomputers
4. Microprocessor Software
5. Basic Instructions and Addressing Modes

The first five chapters provide the reader with general knowledge and information about a μP's hardware and software. Although the chapters contain general information, the terminology is geared toward Motorola products.

6800 μP Hardware and Software:

6. 6800 Microprocessor Instruction Set
7. 6800 Microprocessor Programs
8. 6800 Microprocessor

Chapters 6 and 7 deal specifically with the software aspects of the 6800 μP. Its instructions are the topic of Chapter 6, and many of these instructions are used in Chapter 7 to write basic programs in assembly language. Chapter 8 concentrates on the 6800's hardware aspects and timing diagrams for its different addressing modes.

Introduction to Memory Chips and Systems:

9. Semiconductor Memories
10. Memory Chips and Organization

Chapter 9 discusses the way memory devices can be classified and how static and dynamic memory cells are designed. Chapter 10 shows how to interconnect memory chips to form a memory system.

Input/Output Devices:

11. Interface Devices
12. Peripheral Interface Adapter 6821
13. Asynchronous Communication Interface Adapter 6850
14. CRT Controller 6845

All general-purpose μCs have a way of communicating with peripheral equipment. Chapter 11 discusses points that are common to most I/O devices, while Chapters 12, 13, and 14 deal with three specific chips. Chapter 12 shows how a general-purpose I/O chip can be used for different applications. Many designs require a μC to send data serially to peripheral equipment; how this transmission is done is covered in Chapter 13. A display terminal is one of the most common pieces of peripheral equipment; the key device in this system is a CRT controller chip, and it is the topic of Chapter 14.

68000 μP Hardware and Software:

15. 68000 Microprocessor
16. 68000 Microprocessor Instruction Set
17. Interfacing the 68000 Microprocessor

Chapters 15, 16, and 17 concentrate on the 68000 μP. Chapter 15 lists many of the 68000's features and how it differs from the 6800 μP. Chapter 15 also deals primarily with the hardware aspects of the 68000, leaving the instructions, addressing modes, and fundamental programs for Chapter 16. The 68000 μP was designed to use the 6800 peripheral chips. How these chips are connected to the μP is shown in Chapter 17. This chapter also covers dynamic memory chips and how they are connected to the μP.

Thus, this text introduces the student or practicing engineer or technician to both the hardware and software aspects of μCs and in particular to two popular μPs—the 6800 and 68000. For students, there is enough material for an introductory course of up to two terms in length. In such a two-term sequence, the first term may concentrate on the general concepts and the 6800 μP, with an introduction to memories and I/O devices. The second term can concentrate on the design of memory systems, how particular I/O devices operate, and the 68000 μP. For the professional, this text can be used for self-study, as well as for reference because of the many practical applications. For both audiences, the answers to the odd-numbered problems should be an aid in the study of μPs and μCs.

Although the cover shows only my name, a textbook always has many behind-the-scenes contributors. Therefore, I extend a special thanks to my colleagues Professors Robert Coughlin, Robert Villanucci, John Marchand, and William Megow, who, as always, are willing to provide valuable support and assistance in the practical design phase of a μC system. Also, a thank you is extended to Dean Alexander Avtgis, Dean of the College of Engineering Technology at Wentworth for his continued support. Further thanks go to my reviewers, whose comments and suggestions aided in the preparation of the manuscript: Professor Victor A. Michael, Williamsport Area Community College; Professor Dale Pollack, Northern Illinois University; Professor Jerry Farrell, Hawkeye Institute of Technology; Professor Glen W. Jackson, Kent State University; and Professor Gerald E. Jensen, Western Iowa Technical Community College. A sincere appreciation for her work and dedication goes to an exemplary department secretary, Phyllis Wolff. Finally, I thank my wife, Jean, for her understanding of my decision to write another text and her willingness to type and retype the many pages of the manuscript on very short notice. With her, everything is possible.

Contents

6 | 6800 MICROPROCESSOR INSTRUCTION SET   79

11 | INTERFACE DEVICES   205

12 | PERIPHERAL INTERFACE ADAPTER 6821   219

13 | ASYNCHRONOUS COMMUNICATION INTERFACE ADAPTER 6850   247

1 Introduction to Digital Computers

1.0 INTRODUCTION

As human beings, we are users of many tools. Sometimes we are almost helpless without them. Tools may increase the power of our muscles or senses or help us move around. We are always trying to make tools that work better for us by redesigning or rebuilding old ones and creating new ones for future needs.

In the past few decades, one tool has been developed that has greatly improved our ability to calculate, to store information, and to control processes or the environment. This tool is the electronic computer. It has helped us to increase our knowledge by performing in seconds calculations that otherwise may take hours, weeks, or even years to do by hand. Not only is the computer fast, but also it is accurate and can do tedious jobs without becoming bored. We are then spared the drudgery of making the same calculation over and over again. Computers are machines (or tools) that solve problems for people.

Computers come in all sizes, shapes, speeds, and costs. They can be divided into two classifications: (1) analog and (2) digital. This text concentrates on digital computers, but both types will be discussed briefly to show the difference between them.

1.1 CLASSIFICATION OF COMPUTERS

1.1.1 Analog Computers

Analog computers get their name from the word *analogy*, meaning similarity or likeness. In this type of computer, an electrical circuit is designed so that it behaves electrically as some other operating system behaves. Analog computers have been designed to simulate heat transfer, liquid flow, collision between two vehicles, engine control systems, process control systems, and so on.

The first step in using an analog computer is to develop a set of equations for the original system. The next step is to use electronic components to design and build an electrical circuit that conforms to the set of equations. In the analog computer, measured quantities, usually voltage, are caused to vary in the same way that the original system would vary. In addition to voltage changes, the computer's components (resistors, capacitors, amplifiers, and so on) may be adjusted to simulate changes in the original design. For example, an inductor simulates mass, a capacitor simulates elasticity, and a resistor simulates friction. Thus, the analog computer solves the problem and gives us an output like the output of the original system. However, the majority of computers are digital rather than analog because digital computers can solve more problems faster, more easily, and with greater flexibility.

1.1.2 | Digital Computers

While an analog computer deals directly in measurable quantities (voltage, current, resistance, and so on), a digital computer deals in numbers. The term *digital* comes from the word *digit*, meaning a finger or toe, the unit humans probably used when they began counting. The numbers used in digital computers are 0 and 1, the numbers that make up the binary system. The binary system is used because electrical, magnetic, and mechanical devices that have only two states can be used to represent binary digits. For example, a lamp is either on or off.

Digital computers solve problems by carrying out instructions given to them. The set of instructions that solves a given problem is called a *program*. The person who writes such a set of instructions is referred to as a *programmer*. A digital computer is designed to recognize an instruction and to execute it. Programs are called *software*, while the electronic components and circuits that store and execute the instructions are called the computer's *hardware*.

Over the span of the last forty years, digital computer designs have evolved from using relays, to vacuum tubes, to transistors, to small-scale integration (SSI) chips, to medium-scale integration (MSI) chips, and finally to large-scale integration (LSI) chips and very large-scale integration (VLSI) chips. Today's technology of LSI and VLSI devices has revolutionized military, industrial, and commercial digital designs. In the past decade, most of the traditional equipment has become "smart" and new designs are becoming "smarter." Yet the size, weight, and power consumption of digital computers is being reduced.

The most significant LSI device that has been developed is the microprocessor, μP. It is the central processing unit, CPU, of every microcomputer, μC. Often the μP is referred to as the "heart" of a μC system because it decodes the instructions and performs all the arithmetic and logical operations. As you will learn in this text, a μC is composed of three parts: (1) the microprocessor, (2) the memory, and (3) the input/output, I/O, devices. We will examine both the hardware and software of two microprocessors, but first we will discuss some of the evolutionary process that has led to the present technology.

1.2 | HISTORY OF DIGITAL COMPUTERS

1.2.1 | Calculating Machines

The electronic digital computer is a modern tool, developed in the last few decades. However, its history may well have its origins when people first began counting using their fingers or stones. Probably the earliest digital machine is the abacus, which has been used for over five thousand years. Figure 1.1 shows an abacus. This manual calculator is made up of a rectangular frame that supports a number of parallel rods. Each rod represents a decimal place—ones, tens, hundreds, thousands, and so forth. On each rod is a number of beads that move along the rod. An operator can move the beads to add, subtract, multiply, and divide, all by hand.

Mechanical devices did not appear until the 17th century. In 1642, Blaise Pascal, a mathematician, invented a desk calculator. This machine used gears to perform addition and subtraction. Multiplication and division could only be performed by repeated additions or subtractions. Pascal's machine was improved in 1671 by another mathematician, G. W. Liebnitz. Liebnitz designed a device that could do multiplication directly. Although his machine never became practical because of mechanical difficulties, it was improved in later years by other individuals.

The next major step toward today's computers came in 1833 when Charles Babbage, an English scientist and mathematician, designed a machine that he called an analytical engine. This machine was a forerunner to the modern computer. It had a program that was stored on punched cards in a section separate from the section that performed the arithmetic operations. Unfortunately, Babbage had a history of never fully completing a design, and the design of this machine was no exception.

Between 1833 and 1930, most of the advances in the area of digital technology were with calculating machines. They were made faster and more capable of handling different applications. In 1920, the electric motor was added to calculators. Some machines of this period were called analyzers; they were designed to solve some specific problem such as a differential equation. Many analyzers of this period were mechanical machines.

FIGURE 1.1 | Chinese Abacus, a Manual Calculator Used for Thousands of Years

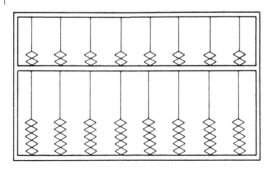

1.2.2 | Electromechanical Machines

In 1937, George Stibitz, a research mathematician at Bell Telephone Laboratories, built a binary arithmetic machine using relays, flashlight batteries, and bulbs. It is the first known machine that could do binary arithmetic. At first, it was seen as a curiosity by his colleagues and its potential was not immediately pursued. Stibitz also designed an electromagnetic calculator to multiply and divide complex numbers. This machine, known as the complex number calculator, had a high degree of reliability and was faster than comparable machines of the time. It was the first machine that could be used from a remote location.

Until the start of World War II, Bell Labs was not interested in pursuing the idea of a large-scale computer. But between 1939 and 1944, the U.S. Army asked Bell Labs to design five relay computers to aid in calculations for ballistics testing. The computers that resulted were highly reliable and had minimum downtime (breakdowns). They introduced two important new concepts: (1) a program that could be entered by tape and (2) floating point arithmetic. Both ideas are still used in today's computers. These computers, like the analyzers, were designed for a particular purpose; they are called special-purpose computers.

Also in 1937, Howard Aiken, an engineer, proposed building an automatic computing machine that would be controlled by a set of instructions. Each instruction would have its own code and the machine would perform one specific job according to the particular instruction code it was given. In addition to solving problems, the machine could produce either punched cards or typed pages. After being turned down by the Monroe Calculating Machine Company, Aiken was able to convince International Business Machines Corporation (IBM), with some financial support from the U.S. Navy and Harvard University, to build such a machine. The machine was completed in 1944 and was called the automatic sequence controlled calculator, better known as the Mark I. In the late 1940s, Aiken designed the Mark II, III, and IV. The Mark III was an all-electronic computer but it was not the first of its kind.

1.2.3 | Electronic Computers

In 1943, John Mauchly and J. Presper Eckert teamed up to design an all-electronic computer. Mauchly had written an original proposal for such a computer in 1942 but it was rejected by the U.S. Army. By 1943, the situation had changed, and the Army needed a way to get more and faster ballistic calculations. A U.S. Army lieutenant and mathematician, Herman Goldstine, reworked Mauchly's proposal and presented it again. This time it was approved. The result was the electronic numerical integrator and computer, more commonly known as ENIAC I, which was completed in 1946.

In comparison to the Mark I, the ENIAC I was a thousand times faster and could perform five thousand additions or subtractions per second. With the exception of some input and output equipment (typewriters and printers), the ENIAC I was the first computer that operated using all-electronic components. However, it was a monster of a machine, containing 18,000 vacuum tubes. Modifying a program required hours of rewiring the electronic circuits.

In 1946, John von Neumann, a professor of mathematics at the Institute of Advanced Study at Princeton University, along with Herman Goldstine and another colleague, Arthur Burks, wrote a paper describing a computer in which the program could be stored and changed without changing hardware. The first computer that worked from this principle was built by Maurice Wilkes, a computer scientist at Cambridge University. Eckert, Mauchly, and von Neumann also designed and built such a computer, called the EDVAC I, but it was not completed until 1950.

1.2.4 | Commercial Computers

During the 1930s and 1940s, only a relatively small group of mathematicians and engineers was interested in computers. Computer applications were limited to special scientific projects that required a large number of calculations. Businesses saw little purpose for such machines and committed no money for research and development. In 1950, however, Eckert and Mauchly believed that computers could be sold for commercial purposes and therefore formed their own company, which was bought by Remington Rand. In 1951, the U.S. Bureau of the Census bought the first commercial computer from Remington Rand, the UNIVAC I (universal automatic computer).

During this time, von Neumann and Goldstine had returned to Princeton and were continuing to work on experimental computers. Computer architecture designed by von Neumann became the basis of many of today's computers. In 1950, IBM began to design what it called the 701 scientific computer. Its success resulted in the company's design of the 702, intended for commercial uses.

Computers in the early 1950s were large and bulky machines. Advances in technology were needed to speed the progress of the computer industry.

1.2.5 | Second-Generation Computers

Relay and vacuum-tube computers are considered to be the first generation of digital computers. The progress of computers using this technology would have been severely limited because of size, cost, and power consumption. But two separate inventions—the transistor and the magnetic core—helped significantly to promote the growth of the computer industry and to reduce the cost of individual computers. The transistor and the magnetic core reduced the size, weight, power consumption, and thus the cost of computers. The magnetic core also allowed the computer to keep and store a program when the power was turned off. Computers developed with this technology are considered to be second generation.

1.2.6 | Third-Generation Computers

In the mid-1960s, semiconductor manufacturers were able to mass-produce a reliable package that contained ten to twenty transistors in the same area that once had contained only a single transistor. These packages are called *integrated circuits*, or ICs. This dense packaging allowed computer designers to build digital computers that were faster, more powerful, much smaller, and less costly than their predecessors. The market for these third-generation computers expanded and new uses were found for the machines. IC packages, or *chips*, are still used today and we will use some of them in this text. These first IC packages used in computers are called *small-scale integration*, or SSI, chips.

1.2.7 | Fourth-Generation Computers

Just as the transistor was replaced by SSI chips in individual computers, the many functions of the SSI package have been replaced by newer and more complex ICs. These packages are classified as *medium-scale integration*, or MSI; *large-scale integration*, or LSI; and *very large-scale integration*, or VLSI, chips. The MSI package contains from twelve to two hundred devices, the LSIs contain thousands of devices, and the VLSIs contain tens of thousands of devices. Figure 1.2 shows a typical LSI chip housed in a 40-pin dual-in-line package (DIP).

     The digital computers discussed in this text use this new technology and are called *microcomputers*, μC. In comparison to the ENIAC I of the 1940s, these fourth-generation computers have more computing power, are twenty to fifty times faster, and are thousands of times more reliable. In addition, the newest digital computers cost less, occupy less space, and consume only the smallest fraction (less than 1/10,000th) of the power needed by earlier models.

1.2.8 | LSI and VLSI Applications

LSI and VLSI chips have revolutionized military, industrial, and commercial computer designs. Traditional equipment is becoming smart and new designs are constantly emerging. An everyday example is the hand-held calculator. These chips have allowed manufacturers to cut the cost of the calculator while increasing its performance and number of functions. A few other commercial products using LSI and VLSI chips are ovens, dishwashers, gas pumps, telephones, automobiles, video games, television sets, and navigation equipment. The potential use of these chips seems endless. In each case, the new electronic designs have reduced the size, weight, and power consumption of the circuitry they have replaced while improving reliability and performance.

     The chip that has spawned most of these new designs is the *microprocessor*, μP—the central processing unit of a microcomputer. The revolution in microelectronics has brought about low-cost personal computers (μC) with enough capacity to support high-level computer languages and color graphics displays.

FIGURE 1.2 | Typical LSI Chip Housed in 40-Pin Dual-in-Line Package (DIP)

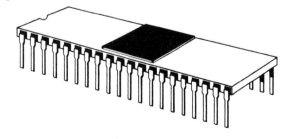

1.3 | MOTOROLA'S FAMILY OF MICROCOMPUTER PARTS

Although no one system is ideal for all applications, a designer often chooses a manufacturer who can supply a *family* of parts or subsystems. This capability allows the user the easiest way to build a complete system for a particular application. Motorola supplies an extensive line of μC components, including μPs, memory chips, peripheral devices, single-chip μCs, assembled subsystems, and complete development systems. In addition to the hardware parts, Motorola also supplies software support. This hardware and software support began with the 6800 μP and has continued through to the 68000, 68010, and 68020 μPs.

1.3.1 | Motorola's Microprocessors

Since the 6800 μP was introduced in 1974, a number of μP products have been introduced, as shown in Figure 1.3. Although this text covers the 6800 and 68000 μPs, let's list some of the key features of the other μPs. If some of the terminology describing the μPs is unfamiliar, you will come to understand it as you study the next few chapters.

6801 Microcomputer: The 6801 is a single-chip μC unit. It is compatible with the 6803. It has on-chip 128 bytes of RAM, 2048 bytes of ROM, 29 parallel I/O lines, two handshake control lines, and an internal clock generator.

6802 Microprocessor: This μP has an on-chip clock oscillator, 128 bytes of RAM, and is software compatible with the 6800. The data in the first 32 bytes of RAM can be retained by an external power source. The 6802 μP has 64K bytes address capability.

6803 Microprocessor: The 6803 is a μP version of the 6801 μC. The 6803 does not have internal ROM but is capable of addressing 64K bytes of memory. It has an expanded 6800 instruction set.

6808 Microprocessor: The 6808 μP is similar to the 6802 because it has an on-chip clock oscillator and driver, but it does not have the 128 bytes of on-chip RAM. A memory, RAM and ROM, is external to the device. The 6808 is capable of addressing 64K bytes.

6809 Microprocessor: This μP provides a major upgrade in performance from the 6800 yet is hardware compatible with it. The 6809 can perform 16-bit operations and has an 8×8 multiplier. It has been designed to handle high-level languages. In addition to using the 6800 peripherals, it has some of its own—a floating point ROM, a memory management unit, and a direct memory access (DMA) processor. A modified version of the 6809, the 6809E, can be used in multiprocessor systems.

146805 Microprocessor: The other μPs previously described are manufactured using NMOS technology. The 146805 μP and its compatible peripherals are CMOS devices. They are used in systems requiring low operating and standby power consumption, battery operation, high noise immunity, and low cooling costs.

68000 Microprocessor: The next major step in performance was the 68000 μP. When it was introduced in 1979, it was embraced primarily by the high-end system of per-

FIGURE 1.3   Performance vs. Introduction Year for 6800/68000 μPs (Redrawn with permission of Motorola Incorporated, Austin, Texas)

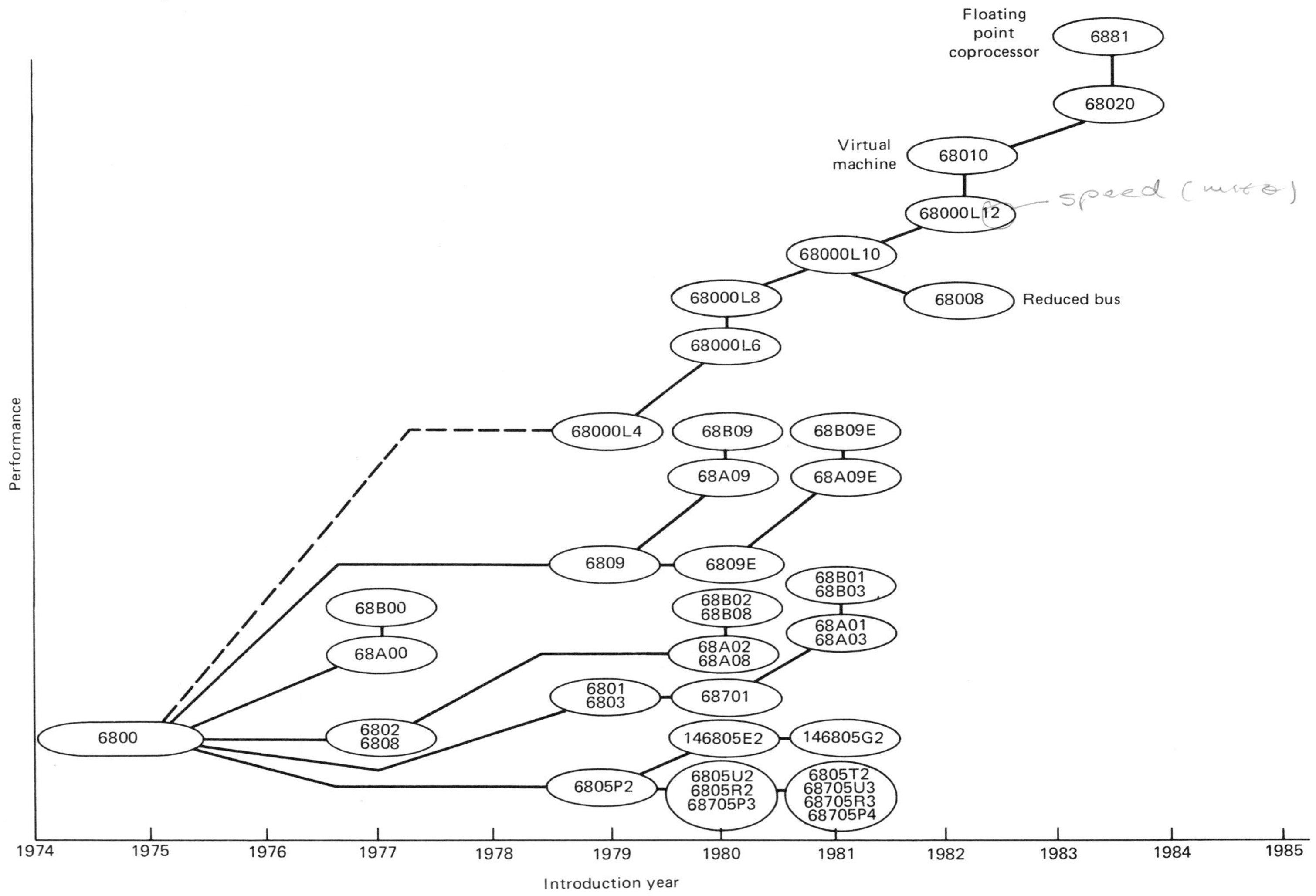

8

formance and cost. Presently, it is being introduced into more and more computer designs. Examples are Apple Computer's Macintosh; Automatix's robotic systems; Hewlett-Packard's desktop computer for science and engineering work; and Apollo Computer's engineering work station.

Similar to the way enhancements of the 6800 μP were introduced, different versions of the 68000 μP have been introduced to capture different niches of the market. The 68008 μP version has an 8-bit data bus so that it can fit easily into an 8-bit system. Internally, however, it is identical to the 68000 μP. Next came the 68010 μP. This μP is an upgraded version of the 68000 μP. It allows programmers to write very long programs because it supports virtual memory—a concept that gives a programmer unlimited memory space. The next generation, the 68020 μP, was introduced in 1984. The 68020 has a 32-bit data bus and supports virtual memory, cache, and coprocessors. A *cache* is a very fast memory system that is capable of quickly delivering data or instructions to the μP. This means the μP does not have to wait for slower memory units, and thus programs can execute faster. A *coprocessor* relieves the μP from performing specific tasks. One such coprocessor used with the 68020 μP is Motorola's MC 68881. This device performs mathematical calculations on floating point numbers.

1.3.2 | Peripheral Input/Output Chips

Motorola has designed a number of peripheral I/O devices. These LSI chips allow the user easily to interface peripheral equipment to the μP. These chips have integrated the functions of dozens of SSI and MSI chips and are programmable. As you will learn, by being able to program the devices, the user has great flexibility over how the I/O unit handles data. This program capability gives the user a way of optimizing the system's performance.

1.3.3 | Memory

All μC systems need some place to store data and instructions. This place is provided in the memory portion of the system. Some μC systems are designed to function over and over; these are called *dedicated* systems. Most often they do not require large amounts of memory (probably less than 4K bytes). Other systems, however, using high-level languages, need large amounts of memory space. Memory systems are designed by interconnecting memory chips. Later you will learn about some of the chips that are available and how they are connected to the μP.

1.3.4 | Assembled Subsystems

As previously mentioned, the building blocks of a μC system are the μP, memory, and peripheral I/O chips. They can be interconnected in a variety of ways for hundreds of different applications. An alternative approach is to purchase assembled board-level products. These products have the following advantages: (1) Boards are completely assembled and tested, (2) design time is minimized, (3) manufacturing costs are reduced, (4) the system can be expanded by purchasing additional boards, and (5) systems can be "tailored" for particular applications. A disadvantage with board-level products is that you may only need a portion of the functions designed into a board, yet the entire board has to be purchased. This disadvantage may mean that the system is physically larger and consumes more power than an in-house dedicated unit. Some system designers may use a middle-of-the-road approach, that is, purchase some assembled subsystems and design the rest.

1.4 │ SUMMARY

Computers can be classified as either analog or digital. This text deals only with the digital type—both hardware and software. Modern electronic computers have their origins in mechanical calculators of the 17th century. It was not until 1946 that an all-electronic computer, ENIAC I, was first completed. This machine was designed for military applications. Computers for commercial purposes were introduced in the early 1950s. Transistors and magnetic cores helped significantly in reducing the size, weight, power consumption, and cost of computers. The next major steps in designing more efficient computers were taken in the mid-1960s, when semiconductor manufacturers were able to mass-produce integrated circuits. These IC packages are classified as SSI, MSI, LSI, and VLSI. Although a complete microcomputer system may use all four types of ICs, the principal components are the newer LSI and VLSI chips. With the history of digital computers in mind, we are now ready to delve more deeply into the design and functions of microcomputers and their major element, the microprocessor—in particular, the 6800 and 68000.

│ PROBLEMS

1.1 Define computer.

1.2 List the two classifications of computers.

1.3 List some of the advantages of digital computers.

1.4 Define programmer.

1.5 Define software and hardware.

1.6 What was the first all-electronic digital computer?

1.7 What two inventions in the 1950s reduced the size and cost of computers?

1.8 What is the principal component in fourth-generation computers?

1.9 What are some of the advantages of assembled subsystems over in-house designs?

2 Microcomputers and Microprocessors

2.0 | INTRODUCTION

Today's digital computers fall into three categories: (1) large main-frame computers, (2) minicomputers, and (3) microcomputers. Some of the factors used to determine the category of a computer are physical size, speed, cost, and application.

The *large main-frame computers* are the fastest and most powerful—that is, they can handle a large number of instructions, and they can handle large amounts of data. Banks, insurance companies, and airlines are among the many users of large main-frame computers in which many operators have access to a common source of data. At an airline terminal, for example, airline personnel can check a reservation regardless of where the ticket was purchased or at which airport the passenger will board the airplane. Large main-frame computers are also used for inventory control, weather forecasting, and satellite calculations. The circuitry of large main-frame computers is the most complex; thus, these computers cost more than the other two types. They are designed for general purposes and can usually accept a large number of different programs.

Until the mid-1960s, most computers were of the large main-frame variety. Manufacturers then introduced computers that were slower, smaller, and designed for specific rather than general applications. These computers became known as *minicomputers*. At first, they were mainly used in laboratories and process control applications in industry. Then, the use of minicomputers grew considerably, primarily in small businesses. Minicomputers opened markets that needed computers but could not afford large main-frame machines. Both markets—large main-frame and minicomputer—continue to grow.

With fabrication processes that allowed tens of thousands of transistors to be placed in a single integrated circuit, semiconductor manufacturers were able to interconnect a few IC chips and design a new computer. These *microcomputers* are physically smaller than either main-frame computers or *minicomputers*. In most cases, they are slower and cost less, too. In a few short years, μCs have carved out their share of the computer market. They are presently being used in machine and process control; in test, scientific, and medical equipment; in traffic control; in communications equipment; and in home appliance and entertainment devices. Although the major principles of all digital computers are the same, we shall concentrate our efforts in this text on the μCs—both their hardware and their software.

Thus far we have considered how computers are classified by size, speed, cost, and application. Another way of classifying computers is by their word length.

2.1 | BIT, BYTE, AND WORD LENGTH

As previously mentioned, digital computers operate using numbers. The familiar decimal number system that we use every day is composed of ten digits (0, 1, 2, 3, 4, 5, 6, 7, 8, and 9). However, digital computers use a different number system, the *binary system*. The binary system is composed of only two digits, 0 and 1. These two digits can be used in many combinations to express not only numbers, but also letters, punctuation, special characters, and, even more importantly, computer instructions.

The major reason digital computers use the two digits 0 and 1 is that these digits can be represented by mechanical, magnetic, or electrical devices that have only two states. For example, a switch or relay can be either open or closed; a vacuum tube or transistor can be either off or on. The open, or off, state is the binary 1; the closed, or on, state is the binary 0. Although the binary digits 0 and 1 are commonly and easily used, keep in mind that these values in a number system are actually two different voltage levels inside the computer. In many digital computers, the binary digit 0 is a voltage range between 0 volts and 0.8 volt, while the binary digit 1 is a voltage range between 2.4 volts and 5 volts.

The term *binary digit* is used so often in digital work that it is commonly abbreviated to *bit*. An 8-bit pattern of binary numbers is called a *byte*. Figure 2.1A shows

FIGURE 2.1 | Examples of 8-, 16-, and 32-Bit Binary Patterns

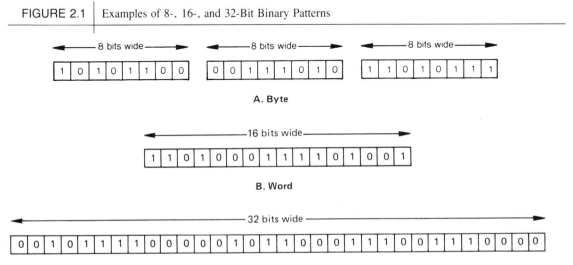

A. Byte

B. Word

C. Long Word

TABLE 2.1	Comparison of Computer Word Lengths and Their Categories

Category	Number of Binary Digits							
Micro	1	4	8	12	16	32		
Mini				12	16	32	48	
Large							48	60	64

three different examples of 8-bit binary patterns. A 16-bit pattern of binary numbers is called a *word* and a 32-bit pattern is called a *long word*. Figures 2.1B and C show examples of a binary word and a long word.

The word length or word size for microcomputers is either 8, 16, or 32 bits. The word length describes the width of the binary pattern—that is, the number of bits —that is handled at once. Large mainframe computers handle information in 64-bit binary patterns. Computers have been designed with word lengths from as small as 1 bit. These computers are usually called controllers. The commonly used lengths are 1, 4, 8, 12, 16, 32, 48, 60, and 64. Table 2.1 shows a comparison of computer word lengths and their corresponding categories.

Microcomputer programs can occupy several thousand bytes of memory. In order to eliminate writing or referring to large numbers, the symbol K is often used; it stands for 1024. Thus,

$$1K \text{ byte} = 1 \times 1024 = 1024 \text{ bytes}$$
$$4K \text{ bytes} = 4 \times 1024 = 4096 \text{ bytes}$$
$$16K \text{ bytes} = 16 \times 1024 = 16,384 \text{ bytes}$$
$$64K \text{ bytes} = 64 \times 1024 = 65,536 \text{ bytes}$$

Note: The symbol k = 1000, but the symbol K = 1024.

2.2 | MICROCOMPUTER ARCHITECTURE

A single-board μC can be simplified into three major parts, as shown in Figure 2.2. They are: (1) the central processing unit (CPU), which is the μP chip; (2) I/O ports, which connect the μC to peripheral equipment; and (3) memory, which stores data and instructions.

2.2.1 | Input/Output Ports

A μC operator must have some way of communicating with the machine—that is, some way of entering a program and obtaining the result. The operator may use a keyboard, for example, to type in a request for information. The keyboard is connected to the μC through an input port, as shown in Figure 2.3. Input/output ports are the parts of a computer that allow humans to communicate with it through *peripheral equipment* such

FIGURE 2.2 | Main Parts of a Microcomputer (μC)

as keyboards, cathode ray tubes (CRTs), card or paper tape readers, magnetic tapes, and magnetic disks.

The I/O port is an LSI chip that allows the computer either to communicate with humans or to control or be controlled by machines. It is often called a peripheral interface adapter (PIA) device. These chips can be programmed to act either as inputs to or outputs from the computer.

If the computer is being used in a process control application, then input devices called *transducers* (thermistors, thermocouples, and strain gages) are used. A transducer converts a physical analog quantity such as heat, light, or pressure into an electrical quantity. This quantity may have to be converted into a voltage or current that is usually very small. The voltage or current may first have to be amplified or otherwise processed before it is converted from an analog signal into a digital signal. For example, a thermocouple may be used as an input device to be connected with other circuitry to the I/O port, as shown in Figure 2.4. A thermocouple is used for measuring heat. Its signal,

FIGURE 2.3 | Keyboard Connected to μC through Input Port

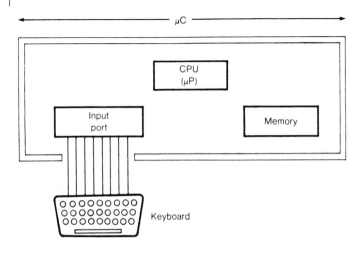

FIGURE 2.4 | Thermocouple Used as Input Device to Be Connected with Other Circuitry to I/O Port

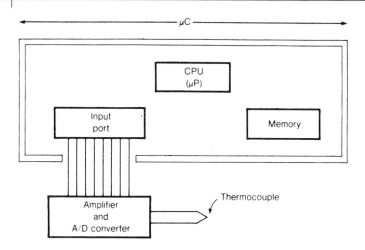

however, is small and usually requires amplification before being converted to a digital signal.

Output equipment used in process control applications may be meters, printers, or CRT displays. Other applications may have heaters, valves, relays, or solid-state switches (SCRs or triacs) as output devices to control even higher power devices such as motors that are required for operation of the process. Such systems are called *feedback control systems*. In Figure 2.5, for example, a feedback control system is shown in which the transducer monitors the pressure inside the pipe and constantly sends back data to the μC. A program is used to compare the data to a reference value stored in memory. If the pressure exceeds the reference, the μC sends out signals to close the valve and sound an alarm.

Peripheral equipment is usually slower than memory devices or the CPU. This equipment can cause the μC to waste time waiting for the equipment either to send or receive data. How peripheral equipment draws attention to itself when it wishes to communicate with the computer and how the computer responds will be discussed later. How the computer can perform many other tasks while it waits for a peripheral equipment instruction will also be considered later.

2.2.2 | Memory

Memory is that portion of the computer that stores the program and the data until they are needed. It is easiest to think of memory as groups of storage cells. Each cell can store one bit of information, either a binary 0 or 1. For example, Figure 2.6 shows a group of 8 cells or bits storing a binary pattern that represents the letter E. As shown, a combination of 0s and 1s is needed to represent the letter E. Other letters or other types of information require other combinations. Eight-bit μCs store instructions and data in groups of 8 bits (one byte). To store more than one letter, we need more than one byte. Figure 2.7 shows what a portion of memory storing the word PENCIL would look like.

FIGURE 2.5 | Feedback Control System in Which Transducer Monitors Pressure inside Pipe and Constantly Sends Back Data to μC

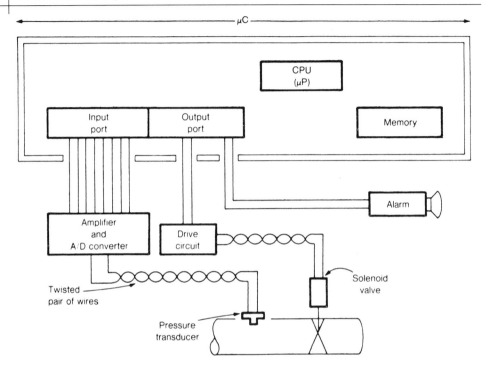

Six bytes are required, one for each letter. The binary bits that are used to represent the letters will be studied in a later chapter.

We must store each letter in a known location so that we can retrieve it. Therefore, each byte stored in memory must have an address. For example, Figure 2.8 gives the memory addresses for each letter in the word PENCIL. In this example, this word has been stored in addresses 103 through 108. Most 8-bit μCs are capable of having 65,536 addresses. The use of addresses lets the computer find quickly all information stored in memory. The terms *memory location* and *memory address* are sometimes used instead of *address*.

There are two types of memory: (1) volatile and (2) nonvolatile. A volatile memory is one that loses its information when the power is turned off. It is a temporary

FIGURE 2.6 | Letter E Stored in μC Memory as 8-Bit Binary Pattern

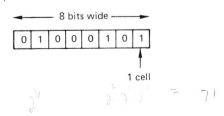

FIGURE 2.7 | Word PENCIL Stored in Memory as Six 8-Bit Binary Patterns

P =	0	1	0	1	0	0	0	0
E =	0	1	0	0	0	1	0	1
N =	0	1	0	0	1	1	1	0
C =	0	1	0	0	0	0	1	1
I =	0	1	0	0	1	0	0	1
L =	0	1	0	0	1	1	0	0

memory. A nonvolatile memory keeps its information when the power is turned off. It is permanent. Throughout this text, we will consider both types of memory and will see how each is used in a μC.

Although most 8-bit μCs on the market today are capable of having 65,536 memory locations, not all systems use this much memory. Some of the applications we will examine require less than 100 memory locations, while other applications require many more.

The nonvolatile memory chips to be discussed later are ROMs (read-only memory), PROMs (programmable read-only memories), EPROMs (erasable programmable read-only memories), and EEROMs (electrical erasable read-only memories). RAMs (random access memories), a type of volatile memory chip, also known as read/write (R/W) memories, will also be described.

2.2.3 | Central Processing Unit

The CPU is the heart of a digital computer. It decodes the instructions, controls the other parts of the machine, performs the arithmetic operations, and in many cases contains some memory (volatile or nonvolatile or both). It is this section of the computer that required tens of thousands of vacuum tubes in the ENIAC I. In today's μCs, the CPU

FIGURE 2.8 | Binary Pattern for Word PENCIL Stored in Memory Locations 103 through 108

Memory addresses								
102								
103	0	1	0	1	0	0	0	0
104	0	1	0	0	0	1	0	1
105	0	1	0	0	1	1	1	0
106	0	1	0	0	0	0	1	1
107	0	1	0	0	1	0	0	1
108	0	1	0	0	1	1	0	0
109								

2.18

is a single IC—the μP. The reader may have heard the term *computer on a chip* used to describe the μP, or may erroneously think that the terms *microprocessor* and *micro-computer* can be used interchangeably. Some of the confusion between these terms probably is caused by the fact that there are LSI chips on the market that contain I/O lines, memory, and the CPU all in a single package. These devices are μCs that are best described by the term *single-chip microcomputers*. They are used in applications such as games, entertainment, household appliances, and other specialized or dedicated control purposes. In general, however, a μC is a system made up of a small number of LSI chips. The μP is one of these chips. (In some systems, the μP is more than one IC, because everything cannot be contained in a single package. This text covers only single-chip μPs because they are the most widely used.) Most 8-bit μPs cost less than $20, and at this price it is understandable why they are so widely used.

In summary, then, the μP is the CPU of a μC. That is,

$$\mu C = \mu P + memory + I/O$$

and

$$\mu P = CPU$$

Now that we have examined the three major parts of a μC—I/O, memory, and CPU—we will see how they are connected to one another.

2.3 | SYSTEM BUS

2.19

A bus is a wire (or wires) that connects the IC chips in the computer. On a printed circuit board, they are conductor patterns. Figure 2.9 shows an I/O port, memory, and a CPU connected to a system bus. A system bus is made up of three types of buses: (1) an

---

FIGURE 2.9 | Major Parts of μC Connected to System Bus

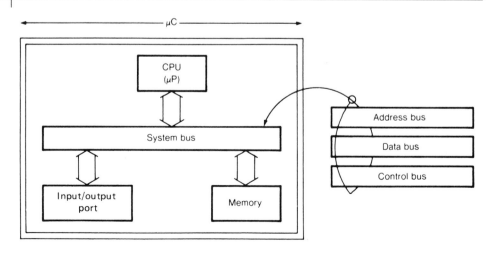

FIGURE 2.10 | Symbols for Address, Data, and Control Buses Used on Circuit Diagrams

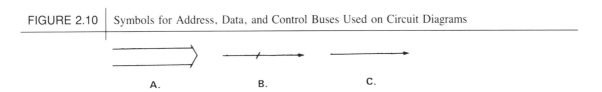

A.   B.   C.

address bus, (2) a data bus, and (3) a control bus. The *address bus* allows the CPU to address any memory location or I/O port. The *data bus* is used to transmit information (instructions or data) between the CPU and memory, between the CPU and an I/O port, or between memory and an I/O port. The *control bus* is used to transmit signals between devices that tell what is happening or should be happening. The job of the control bus is to keep everything running smoothly.

Circuit diagrams show a bus composed of more than one wire or conductor pattern as a wide double line or a single line with a slash through it. A single line with no slash indicates a single wire or conductor pattern. Figure 2.10 shows the three bus symbols used on circuit diagrams. The address and data buses are a set of parallel wires and are thus represented on circuit diagrams by the symbol given in either Figure 2.10A or Figure 2.10B. The control bus usually is made up of individual wires, and therefore each control line is most often represented by a single line as shown in Figure 2.10C.

Buses are either unidirectional or bidirectional. A unidirectional bus is one whose signals always travel in the same direction. A bidirectional bus is one in which the signals may travel in one direction at one time and in the opposite direction at another time. In circuit diagrams, arrows at the end of the bus symbols indicate which type of bus is being used. Figure 2.11 is a summary of the bus symbols used on μC diagrams.

The 8-bit μC system covered in this text has 16 address lines that are unidirectional, 8 data bus lines that are bidirectional, and 4 or 5 control lines. The 16-bit μC system covered in Chapters 15–17 has 23 unidirectional address lines, 16 bidirectional data lines, and 20 control lines. Most control lines are unidirectional.

FIGURE 2.11 | Summary of Bus Symbols Used on μC Diagrams

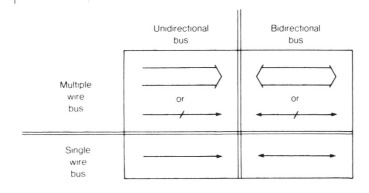

2.4 | MICROPROCESSOR ARCHITECTURE

In Section 2.2, we described the μC as having three basic parts: I/O ports, memory, and the CPU. The CPU—that is, the μP—can be described as having four basic parts: (1) registers, (2) an arithmetic and logic unit, (3) timing and control circuitry, and (4) decoding circuitry. Figure 2.12 shows these four basic parts.

A *register is* a storage location. The registers within 8-bit CPUs are either 8 bits wide or 16 bits wide. The three most widely used registers, as shown in Figure 2.12, are the *accumulator* for general-purpose use, and the *program counter* and *instruction register* for specific use. The accumulator (ACC) temporarily stores the results of an arithmetic or logic operation. The instruction register (IR) is used to store the instruction that the μP is currently operating on. The program counter (PC) stores the address of the next instruction to be operated on.

The *arithmetic and logic unit* (ALU) is that portion of the computer that actually works on the data. It performs the mathematical operations, addition and subtraction, and the logical operations, AND, OR, Exclusive OR, and complementing.

The *timing and control sections* control the internal operation of the CPU chip and are also connected to the control bus to control I/O ports and memory. A clock, part of the internal circuitry of the CPU in some μCs, sends out pulses that make the entire system work in an orderly manner. Clock pulses and circuitry are covered in later chapters.

The *decoding circuitry* of the CPU involves the process of *decoding*, by which a binary pattern is translated into an operation or sequence of operations. For example, if the binary pattern 10111001 means "add," the decoding circuitry will recognize it and send signals to all other parts of the μP to set its internal circuitry so that addition occurs.

FIGURE 2.12 | Four Basic Parts of a Microprocessor (μP)

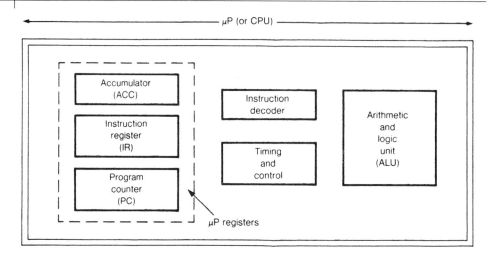

2.5 | PROGRAM EXECUTION

Assume that a computer program and data have been stored in memory and the program is ready to be executed. (In later chapters, we will discuss how the program and data got into memory.) When the computer operator presses the GO key (sometimes referred to as a run or start key), the following steps occur automatically:

1. The memory address of the first instruction of the program is loaded into the PC.
2. The PC places the memory address onto the address bus lines.
3. The address is sent to memory.
4. Memory decodes the address—that is, it finds the correct memory location.
5. Memory sends the instruction back to the µP over the data bus lines.
6. The instruction is placed in the IR inside the µP.
7. The µP decodes the instruction—that is, the instruction (by its binary pattern) tells the µP what to do.
8. The PC is incremented and the µP is now ready to receive the next piece of information, whether it is data or an instruction.

Figure 2.13 shows each of these steps, which cover the time from when the µP begins to send out an address until it sends out the next address. Steps 1 through 7 are accomplished in 0.5 to 5 microseconds (µs) because the manufacturer of the µP chip has designed into it the necessary steps to be carried out for each instruction.

Figure 2.14 shows another way to diagram the steps involved between the µP and memory. Steps 1 through 6 listed above are equivalent to the *fetch*, or read, cycle. Step 7 is the *execute*, or do, cycle. The fetch and execute cycles shown on the block diagram illustrate how a computer operates.

FIGURE 2.13 | Steps Involved from Time µP Begins to Send Out an Address Until It Sends Out Next Address

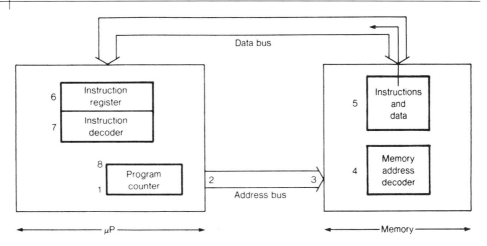

FIGURE 2.14 | Block Diagram Summarizing Steps Involved between μP and Memory

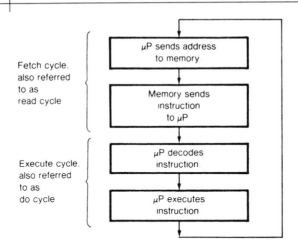

Fetch cycle,
also referred
to as
read cycle

μP sends address
to memory

Memory sends
instruction
to μP

Execute cycle,
also referred
to as
do cycle

μP decodes
instruction

μP executes
instruction

All eight steps are repeated until the μP interprets a stop, or *halt*, instruction. Sometimes an instruction tells the μP to break the normal sequence and put a new address in the PC. This instruction is called a *jump* instruction, and we will examine this instruction and applications in Chapters 6 and 7.

2.6 | SUMMARY

This chapter introduced the terms bit, byte, and word and described how computer systems are classified according to word length. A μC has three main parts: (1) I/O ports, (2) memory, and (3) the CPU, or μP. These parts are interconnected by a system bus—an address bus, a data bus, and a control bus. A brief example of how these buses are used to communicate information was given in Section 2.5. As we progress through this text, we will examine in detail the system bus and the μP architecture for two popular μPs —the 6800 and the 68000. The internal architecture of a general-purpose 8-bit μP was also described in this chapter. A μP has four basic parts: (1) registers, (2) an arithmetic and logic unit, (3) timing and control circuitry, and (4) decoding circuitry. Before we go on to the basics of μC software, we need to consider codes, why they are needed, and how they are applied to μPs and μCs.

PROBLEMS

2.1 List the three major categories of digital computers.

2.2 List the types of companies that use large main-frame computers and minicomputers.

2.3 How many digits are there in the binary system?

2.4 What is the range of voltage for a logic 1 in most μCs?

[handwritten: one digit   8 bits]

2.5 Define bit and byte.

2.6 Most μCs are designed with word lengths of how many bits?

2.7 If a μC system has 48K of memory, what is the actual number of bytes? *[handwritten: 48 × 1024]*

2.8 What are the three major parts of a μC system?

2.9 What is the function of the I/O ports? *[handwritten: Keyboard, CRT, printer, mag. disk]*

2.10 List four pieces of peripheral equipment that may be connected to a general-purpose μC.

2.11 What is the function of a transducer?

2.12 What are some typical pieces of output equipment that are used in process control applications?

2.13 What is the function of memory?

2.14 What is another name for memory location? *[handwritten: address]*

2.15 List the two general types of memory.

2.16 List the types of permanent memory chips that can be used in a μC.

2.17 Are RAMs and R/$\overline{W}$ memories used to define the same type of volatile memory?

2.18 Give a definition of μP.

2.19 Define bus.

2.20 Is the address bus unidirectional or bidirectional? *[handwritten: unidirectional]*

2.21 Is the data bus unidirectional or bidirectional? *[handwritten: Bidirectional]*

2.22 List the four major parts of a CPU. *[handwritten: register, ALU, timing and control, decoding circ.]*

2.23 What is the name of the register that stores the results of the arithmetic and logic unit in an 8-bit μP? *[handwritten: Accumulator]*

2.24 What is the name of the process by which a binary pattern is translated into an operation or sequence of operations? *[handwritten: decoding]*

3 | Use of Codes with Microcomputers

3.0 | INTRODUCTION

Digital computers operate using the binary system regardless of whether they are handling data or instructions. Data and instructions can be either numbers, words, punctuation, or special characters. We are all familiar with the decimal system and the English alphabet, but since digital circuits (hence, a computer) can only handle logic levels of 0 and 1, we have to learn a new "language," the binary system, and need to know how to convert from one system to the other.

   Reading and writing binary patterns become very cumbersome, and it is easy to make a mistake. In particular, when binary patterns of 8, 16, or 32 bits are used as they are on the μP data and address lines, mistakes can be constant. Therefore, to help reduce errors, we use codes. The code most often used with the 6800 and 68000 μPs for grouping bits is the hexadecimal code. Other codes used quite often with these μPs are the BCD (Binary Coded Decimal) and ASCII (American Standard Code for Information Interchange) codes. Each of these codes is introduced in this chapter.

3.1 | BINARY PATTERNS

As we know, the computer handles only binary bits 0 and 1. Combinations of bits are used to form instructions that the computer can interpret or to form data for the computer to work on. The data may be numbers or letters. The computer has no trouble using the binary bits 0 and 1 because they represent two distinct voltage levels, but a column of binary 0s and 1s is very tiresome for a person to look at. It is quite easy to make an error if a column has to be copied. Columns of binary bits are difficult to understand and extremely time consuming to write or to enter as a program into the computer. It is sometimes difficult to distinguish between an instruction and data. For example, the following column of binary bits is meaningless without further interpretation or explanation:

00001100

10111100

00000010

00000000

10111001

00000101

01000000

Some questions we can ask about this binary column are: Is it a set of random instructions? A program? Data? If it is a program, to which μP does it apply? (Instructions for one μP are meaningless for a different one.) The first thing we can do to make it easier to write a column of binary digits is to use codes. Codes are a shorthand notation for a group of binary digits.

3.2 | HEXADECIMAL CODE

One of the most widely used codes in μCs is the hexadecimal (or hex) code. The word *hexadecimal* means *sixteen*, which is the base of this system. It uses the digits 0 through 9 plus the letters A through F. Thus, the 16 hexadecimal symbols are as follows:

0   1   2   3   4   5   6   7   8   9   A   B   C   D   E   F

Each hex symbol represents a group of 4 binary digits. Table 3.1 shows the relationship among the decimal, binary, and hexadecimal systems.

TABLE 3.1 | Conversion Chart Showing Relationship among Decimal, Binary, and Hexadecimal Systems

Decimal	Binary	Hexadecimal
0	0000	0
1	0001	1
2	0010	2
3	0011	3
4	0100	4
5	0101	5
6	0110	6
7	0111	7
8	1000	8
9	1001	9
10	1010	A
11	1011	B
12	1100	C
13	1101	D
14	1110	E
15	1111	F

3.2.1 | Binary to Hexadecimal Conversion

The reason that the hex system is popular in μCs is that data and memory addresses are easily grouped in blocks of 4 bits. For example, the data bus lines for the 6800 μP are 8 bits wide (1 byte) and for the 68000 μP are 16 bits wide (2 bytes). Therefore, information on the 8-bit data bus can be grouped in two blocks of 4 bits and then represented by two hexadecimal symbols. As an example, assume that the binary pattern 11001001 is obtained from the data bus. To convert it into its hexadecimal equivalent, we first split the binary pattern into two groups of 4 bits:

$$11001001 = 1100 \quad 1001$$

Then, from Table 3.1, we find the hexadecimal symbol for each of the 4 bits:

$$1100 = C$$
$$1001 = 9$$

Therefore, $11001001_2 = C9_{16}$. The subscripts 2 and 16 indicate a binary number and a hexadecimal number, respectively. Sometimes, the word hex or the letter H is used instead of 16.

The column of binary bits shown in Section 3.1 is reproduced in Table 3.2 with the equivalent hex symbols. We can see how much easier the hex symbols are to look at and to check for mistakes. Keep in mind, however, that the computer only handles binary digits and that this code is for our convenience.

If the hexadecimal symbols are easier for us to use when there is an 8-bit binary pattern, we can quickly see the advantages when the binary pattern is 16 bits. This pattern occurs on the 6800's address bus lines and the 68000's data bus lines. Sixteen lines can be represented by 4 hexadecimal symbols. For example, assume that the 6800 μP puts the following bit pattern onto the address bus:

1011000010101000
B   0   A   8

TABLE 3.2 | Examples of Converting from Binary to Hexadecimal

Binary Pattern	Hex Equivalent
00001100	0C
10111100	BC
00000010	02
00000000	00
10111001	B9
00000101	05
01000000	40

TABLE 3.3 | Sixteen Bus Lines in Decimal, Binary, and Hexadecimal

Decimal	Binary		Hexadecimal
0	00000000	00000000	0000
1	00000000	00000001	0001
2	00000000	00000010	0002
3	00000000	00000011	0003
.		.	.
.		.	.
.		.	.
65,533	11111111	11111101	FFFD
65,534	11111111	11111110	FFFE
65,535	11111111	11111111	FFFF

To find the hexadecimal equivalent, we first split the pattern into groups of 4 bits:

$$1011 \quad 0000 \quad 1010 \quad 1000$$

Then, we use Table 3.1 to obtain the equivalent hex symbol for each group of 4 bits:

$$1011 = B$$
$$0000 = 0$$
$$1010 = A$$
$$1000 = 8$$

Therefore, $1011000010101000_2 = B0A8_{16}$.

A μC with 16 address bus lines has $2^{16} = 65,536$ memory locations. The first location is 0; the last address is 65,535. Table 3.3 shows a few of the possible memory addresses that a μP can have.

3.2.2 | Hexadecimal to Binary Conversion

A hexadecimal code is converted to its equivalent binary pattern by using Table 3.1. Each hex code is taken separately and converted to its binary equivalent. For example, to convert $9D_{16}$ to binary, from Table 3.1 we have:

$$9 = 1001$$
$$D = 1101$$

Therefore, $9D_{16} = 10011101_2$.

TABLE 3.4 | Examples of Counting in Hexadecimal

.	.	.	.
.	.	.	.
.	.	.	.
C	1C	9C	20FC
D	1D	9D	20FD
E	1E	9E	20FE
F	1F	9F	20FF
10	20	A0	2100
11	21	A1	2101
12	22	A2	2102
13	23	A3	2103
.	.	.	.
.	.	.	.
.	.	.	.

Similarly, we can convert the hex number 8F05 to binary by using Table 3.1:

$$8 = 1000$$
$$F = 1111$$
$$0 = 0000$$
$$5 = 0101$$

Then, $8F05_{16} = 1000111100000101_2$.

3.2.3 | Counting in Hex

Table 3.1 shows the hex count from 0 through F. But now the question arises: What is the next count? As in the decimal and binary numbering systems, the first digit repeats to 0 and the next digit is incremented, as shown by the examples in Table 3.4. Since we will be using the hexadecimal system throughout this text, we should become familiar with this system and be able to count in hex.

3.3 | MICROCOMPUTER MEMORY SPACE AND ALLOCATION

An 8-bit μP, like the 6800, that has 16 address bus lines can address 65,536 (2^{16} = 65,536) different memory locations. Table 3.3 summarizes this range in terms of decimal, binary, and hexadecimal digits. The 65,536 memory locations are called the *total memory space* in the μC. This space is divided into 256 pages labeled 00 to FF, as shown in Figure 3.1. In each page, there are 256 addresses. (As a check: 256 pages × 256 addresses per page = 65,536 addresses.)

The first two hex symbols of the address are its *page number*, while the last two hex symbols are the *line address* in that page. For example, consider the address $657A_{16}$:

FIGURE 3.1 | Total Memory Space of 65,536 Locations Divided into 256 Pages with 256 Addresses per Page

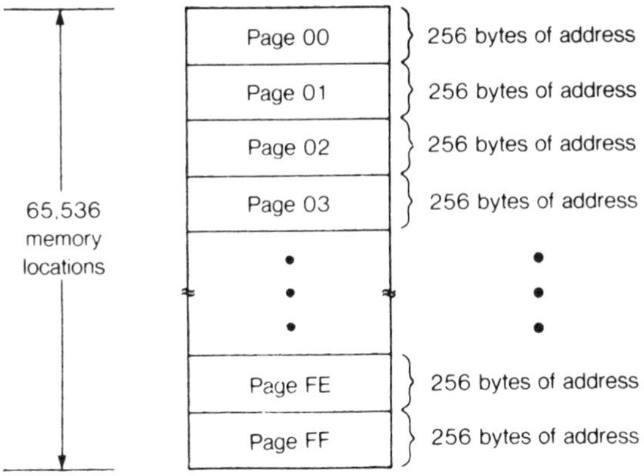

Page 00	} 256 bytes of address
Page 01	} 256 bytes of address
Page 02	} 256 bytes of address
Page 03	} 256 bytes of address
• • •	• • •
Page FE	} 256 bytes of address
Page FF	} 256 bytes of address

65,536 memory locations

65 is the page number, and 7A is the line in page 65. To summarize the interaction between the μP and memory: The μP puts onto the address bus lines a bit pattern whose hex equivalent is 657A. The memory chip or chips, and possibly external decoder chips, decode the pattern—that is, locate the address—and then send to the μP the data that is located at that address. In later chapters, we will investigate how the memory chips do their job.

Many applications do not require the μP to use all 65,536 memory locations. For example, assume that a μC application requires 1024 memory locations for data, 4096 memory locations for the main program, and 512 memory locations for input and output connections. This application thus requires only 5632 memory locations (1024 + 4096 + 512). In terms of pages, the memory locations are allocated as follows:

1024 memory locations = 4 pages

4096 memory locations = 16 pages

512 memory locations = 2 pages

Thus, a total of 22 pages is required.

One method of breaking the total memory space into pages for data, I/O, and the main program for this example is shown in Figure 3.2. The 1024 memory locations for the data have been allocated to the first 4 pages, whose hex addresses are 0000 to 03FF. The 512 locations needed for the I/O connections have been allocated to memory addresses 4000 to 41FF. The main program, which needs 4096 locations, has been given the 16 pages F000 to FFFF. This example shows two unused portions of memory space that are available for future expansion. Later we will see what chips can be used for the data, I/O, and the main program. Note that the IC chips used for the I/O connections are assigned a memory address and are addressed by the μP as is any other memory location. This type of connection results in what is called *memory-mapped I/O*. Both the 6800 and the 68000 μPs use memory-mapped I/O.

FIGURE 3.2 | Typical μC Application That Breaks Up Total Memory Space

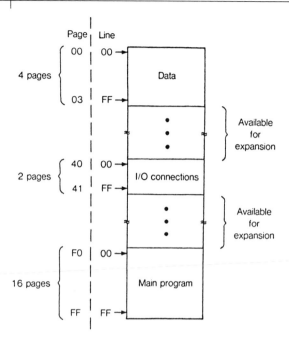

The hexadecimal code is used to represent binary patterns on the data and address buses. These codes allow us to group bits so as to reduce human errors when we work with long strings of binary digits. Therefore, 6800 and 68000 μP instructions are represented in this code.

Other codes are often used when information is going into or coming out of the μC through the I/O ports. Two of the codes widely used for this purpose are the BCD (Binary Coded Decimal) and ASCII (American Standard Code for Information Interchange) codes. The BCD code system is used only for numbers, while the ASCII code system is used for numbers, letters, punctuation marks, and control characters. Since the terms BCD and ASCII are used in the next few chapters, the next two sections of this chapter cover the basic concepts of the two code systems.

3.4 | BINARY CODED DECIMAL SYSTEM

The straight binary number system is based on positional weights (place value), as is the decimal system. For example, the decimal number 12 equals the binary number 1100. Although the μP handles straight binary numbers quite easily, we may not want to have to perform a binary to decimal conversion every time we want to know what the decimal number is. Therefore, if the μC is to receive and display only decimal information, what we are looking for is a code that produces only the decimal digits 0 through 9. Such a code is the *Binary Coded Decimal System* (abbreviated BCD). Remember that the use of the hex code is different from the use of the BCD code.

3.4.1 | Decimal to BCD Conversion

In the BCD system, each digit in a decimal number is represented by 4 binary bits. For example,

Decimal	4	3	2
BCD	0100	0011	0010

The reason that 4 binary bits are needed in the BCD system is that the decimal numbers 8 and 9 cannot be represented by 3 binary bits. That is, we run out of 3-bit binary combinations at 7 unless we add another digit. Thus,

Decimal	8	9
BCD	1000	1001

Table 3.5 shows the 4-bit BCD codes along with their decimal equivalents. Note that the binary numbers 1010, 1011, 1100, 1101, 1110, and 1111 are invalid BCD codes. We do not need these binary numbers because all the decimal numbers are already represented. These binary numbers would produce an error if they were used in the BCD

TABLE 3.5 | Conversion Chart Showing Relationship between Decimal and BCD Systems

Decimal	BCD Code	
0	0000	
1	0001	
2	0010	
3	0011	Valid
4	0100	binary
5	0101	numbers
6	0110	
7	0111	
8	1000	
9	1001	
—	1010	
—	1011	Invalid binary
—	1100	numbers in
—	1101	BCD code
—	1110	
—	1111	

system. Table 3.5 shows that only 10 of the possible 16 4-bit binary numbers are used. Other examples of decimal to BCD conversion are as follows:

$$12 = 0001 \quad 0010$$
$$47 = 0100 \quad 0111$$
$$63.5 = 0110 \quad 0011.0101$$

3.4.2 | Comparison between BCD and Straight Binary

While the straight binary system is based on the position of the bits, the BCD system converts each decimal digit into a 4-bit binary number with weights used only within each 4-bit group. Therefore, the BCD code is also known as the 8–4–2–1 code, where 8, 4, 2, and 1 are the weights of each bit in a 4-bit group.

A BCD representation of a decimal number always requires more bits than a straight binary representation. For example, convert the number 240 to straight binary and to the BCD system and compare each result:

Straight binary $240_{10} = 11110000_2$
BCD $240_{10} = 0010 \quad 0100 \quad 0000$

The straight binary number requires only 8 bits, while the BCD representation requires 12 bits. Microprocessors are able to add and subtract in both straight binary and BCD. Although μPs can do both types of addition, straight binary is more efficient because it uses fewer bits. The disadvantage is that if the μP is making all of its calculations in straight binary, a program must be included to convert straight binary to BCD before the answer can be sent to a decimal display. If the μP is making all of its calculations in BCD, a conversion program is not necessary. The disadvantage with this method, however, is that more memory space is needed to store the data, and execution of the program will be slower. In Chapter 7, we will study a conversion program.

3.5 | ASCII CODE

Today's computers are more than just calculators. In addition to numbers, they must be able to store and process data such as letters, punctuation marks, and other special characters. The computer must be capable of receiving data from a keyboard, a teletype (TTY), paper tape, magnetic tape, other external storage equipment, or even another computer. The computer must also be able to send its data to equipment such as a printer, CRT, storage equipment, or another computer. A standard code is needed for a computer to communicate easily with peripheral equipment. One of the most commonly used alphanumeric standards is the *American Standard Code for Information Interchange* (ASCII). This code uses 7 bits, which produce 128 ($2^7 = 128$) possible alphanumeric codes. Figure 3.3 lists all 128 ASCII characters.

The ASCII codes can be grouped in three major blocks. The first 32 characters (columns 0 and 1 in Figure 3.3) are machine commands that control the hardware between

FIGURE 3.3 | 7-Bit ASCII Codes

b₇	b₆	b₅	b₄	b₃	b₂	b₁	Row / Column	0	1	2	3	4	5	6	7
			0	0	0	0	0	NUL	DLE	SP	0	@	P	\	p
			0	0	0	1	1	SOH	DC1	!	1	A	Q	a	q
			0	0	1	0	2	STX	DC2	"	2	B	R	b	r
			0	0	1	1	3	ETX	DC3	#	3	C	S	c	s
			0	1	0	0	4	EOT	DC4	$	4	D	T	d	t
			0	1	0	1	5	ENQ	NAK	%	5	E	U	e	u
			0	1	1	0	6	ACK	SYN	&	6	F	V	f	v
			0	1	1	1	7	BEL	ETB	'	7	G	W	g	w
			1	0	0	0	8	BS	CAN	(	8	H	X	h	x
			1	0	0	1	9	HT	EM	)	9	I	Y	i	y
			1	0	1	0	A	LF	SUB	*	:	J	Z	j	z
			1	0	1	1	B	VT	ESC	.	;	K	[	k	{
			1	1	0	0	C	FF	FS	,	<	L	\	l		
			1	1	0	1	D	CR	GS	-	=	M	]	m	}
			1	1	1	0	E	SO	RS		>	N	^	n	~
			1	1	1	1	F	SI	US	/	?	O	—	o	DEL

Bit numbers across top: 000, 001, 010, 011, 100, 101, 110, 111 — Hex code

Hex code (left). Machine commands. Most often used. Least often used.

the μC and the peripheral equipment. Machine commands are never printed in a message. They include such commands as start, stop, and carriage return.

The next major group includes columns 2, 3, 4, and 5 in Figure 3.3. These 64 characters include the 10 decimal numbers, the 26 uppercase letters, a blank or space (SP), and common punctuation marks and printed characters.

The remaining 32 characters are listed in columns 6 and 7 in Figure 3.3. They are the lowercase letters and little-used characters.

Although the ASCII code uses 7 bits, it can be represented by the hexadecimal code. Bit 8 is usually considered to be binary 0 when the ASCII code is converted to the hexadecimal code. Figure 3.3 includes the hexadecimal code. When using Figure 3.3 to convert codes, note that the high-order bit numbers 5, 6, and 7 are given across the top of the table, while the lower-order bit numbers 1, 2, 3, and 4 are given at the left of the table. Examples of several characters in the 7-bit ASCII code and the hexadecimal code are shown in Table 3.6. The eighth bit is a logic 0.

TABLE 3.6	Examples of Converting from ASCII to Hex

Character	7-Bit ASCII	Hex
A	1000001	41
D	1000100	44
S	1010011	53
1	0110001	31
9	0111001	39
+	0101011	2B
=	0111101	3D

A μC/printer application is shown in Figure 3.4. The μC is connected to a line printer by 7 lines. Stored in memory are 4 ASCII codes. Assume that a program takes each of these ASCII codes and sends them to the printer. As each binary pattern reaches the line printer, the device interprets it and prints one character. If each of these ASCII codes is sent to the line printer in sequence, the printer will type Ohm's law: $V = IR$. Thus, the ASCII binary patterns are a standard that allows any μC to be interfaced easily to any piece of peripheral equipment that needs to send or receive data or control signals.

FIGURE 3.4	μC/Printer Application in Which ASCII Bit Pattern Is Converted into Alphanumeric Characters

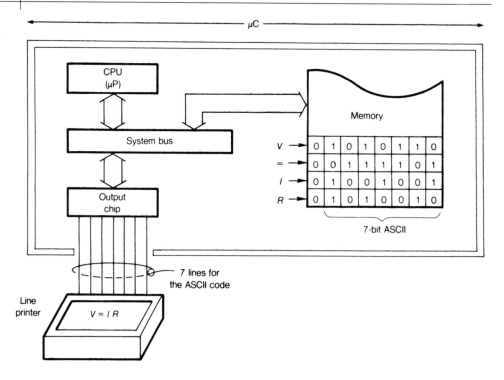

3.6 SUMMARY

In many μC systems, data is transferred among the μP, memory, and I/O devices as either 8-bit or 16-bit patterns. These binary patterns become awkward for humans to reproduce or check and increase the chance of error. Therefore, codes are needed. Each number or letter in a code represents a particular binary pattern. A code often used in μC systems is the hexadecimal code. In this chapter, this code was applied to μPs and μCs, and examples were used to show how to convert between decimal, binary, and hexadecimal. When a μC communicates with peripheral equipment such as keyboards, printers, plotters, CRT displays, and so forth, two other codes are often used, the ASCII and BCD codes.

PROBLEMS

3.1 What is the purpose of using codes? *to reduce errors*

3.2 What does the abbreviation ASCII represent? *american standard code for information Interchang*

3.3 Convert each of the following binary patterns into hexadecimal code: (a) 11000111, (b) 01101000, (c) 11110101, (d) 00111001, and (e) 10100100. *C7 68 FS 39 A4*

3.4 Convert each of the following hexadecimal codes into a binary pattern: (a) A9, (b) 17, (c) 4B, (d) 03FF, and (e) 17FA. *10101001 00010111 00101001 11111011 11 111010*

3.5 For each of the following hexadecimal codes, give the next hexadecimal value: (a) 19, (b) 7A, (c) 4F, (d) 10FF, and (e) 3FFF.

3.6 What is the maximum number of locations that a μP can address with 12 address lines? *4096 (0 - 4095)*

3.7 What are the first two hex digits of an address called? *page*

3.8 Define memory-mapped I/O.

3.9 What does the abbreviation BCD represent? *binary coded decimal*

3.10 Convert the following decimal values into BCD: (a) 59, (b) 14, (c) 27, (d) 03, and (e) 88. *01011001, 10100 00010011 1001000*

3.11 Convert the following BCD numbers into decimal: (a) 0100 0110, (b) 1001 1001, (c) 0010 0101, (d) 0110 1000, and (e) 0011 0000. *4 6 9 9 2 5 6 8 3 0*

3.12 Convert each of the following decimal numbers into straight binary and into BCD: (a) 128, (b) 64, (c) 250, (d) 76, and (e) 32. *10000000 01000000*

3.13 Write the word *microprocessor* in ASCII. Use hex code.

3.12 c = 11111 010
3.12 d = 00100110
3.12 e = 1 00000

3.13
1001101 m
1001001 i
1000011 c
1010010 r
1001111 o
1010000 p
1010010 r
1001111 o
1000011 c
1000101 e
1010011 s
s
o
r

4 | Microprocessor Software

4.0 | INTRODUCTION

In Chapter 2, we saw that a µC consists of three major parts: the µP chip, I/O chip(s), and memory chip(s). These components, along with other digital and analog components, are needed to build a complete µC system. All of these devices together with the printed circuit board, power supply, keyboard, and so forth, are called the µC's *hardware*. What is accomplished by the hardware is controlled by the µC's *software* (the program). Microcomputer users often encounter the term *firmware*; it means the software programs loaded into a portion of memory that cannot be changed during processing. This and the next chapter will introduce the general principles of µC software and hardware. Chapters 6 through 8 deal specifically with the hardware and software aspects of the 6800 µP, and Chapters 15 and 16 cover the 68000 µP.

Remember from Chapter 1 that a program is a sequence of instructions that solves a given problem. When the computer program "runs," each instruction directs the operation of the µP and the other digital circuits.

When a computer (large, mini, or micro) is being used, a change in a program usually does not require the programmer to change any components or wires (the computer's hardware). Therefore, the program is considered part of the computer's software. However, in some µC systems, a change in a program may require a change in one or more components. The following example illustrates this possibility. First, remember that a program is nothing more than a sequence of binary patterns. A change in a program is a change in one or more of the binary patterns. In a computer that has been designed for general use, a program change is made by the programmer through a keyboard. The change in the binary pattern itself occurs inside the computer and is not seen by the programmer. In a dedicated control application (where µCs are often used), the program may be stored in a PROM (programmable read-only memory). A change in the program requires a new PROM to be programmed by removing the old PROM from the system, using a PROM programmer to "burn" the new program into a new PROM, and then inserting the new PROM back into the µC system. Even though a component (the PROM) was actually changed, the term *software* still applies to describe the change.

4.1 | ASPECTS OF MICROPROCESSOR SOFTWARE

Many first-time computer users erroneously think that "computer software" refers only to the program or programs used. However, just as computer hardware is more than a few IC chips—it also includes timing, component layout, power supplies, and noise problems, for example—so software has aspects other than the program itself. Computer software includes the following steps: (1) defining the problem; (2) determining a logical solution to the problem; (3) writing the program; (4) loading, running, and debugging the program (very few programs work the first time); and (5) documenting all the steps.

4.1.1 | Problem Definition

Problem definition may seem an obvious step, but it should not be considered lightly because it can make the remaining steps easier or more difficult. If hardware and software personnel work closely to define the problem, their jobs will each be easier. They will understand each other's role, and the final product can combine the best trade-off between hardware and software. At this step, the programmer must consider all the data that will be entered, all the major processes needed to process the data, and the desired output. The programmer should allow for design flexibility, which will almost certainly be needed. Time spent clarifying problems and making sure that the programmer understands all the specifications can avoid costly errors and delays later on. For example, if at the debugging stage it is found that the problem has not been defined correctly, then a considerable amount of time, effort, and money have been wasted in a product that does not work.

4.1.2 | Logical Design

Once the problem is understood, a logical design can be created that solves the problem in the best and most efficient way. At this step, keep in mind the hardware constraints of the system such as memory space, clock frequency, number of inputs and outputs that have to be serviced, and so forth. For example, if a keyboard must be scanned every 40 milliseconds or a CRT display updated every second, then the programmer must keep these constraints in mind. During this development step, the design is broken into independent parts. Each part may be subdivided until there is enough detail to understand clearly what is to be accomplished by each subpart. The result is a step-by-step sequence for the computer to carry out. If the problem has been defined clearly, a logical design will result.

4.1.3 | Programming

After we define the problem and develop a logical design, we know what types of programs are needed. For example, we will know if we need a multiplication program, division program, square root program, timing loop program, or some other program. For each program, a specific set of rules or steps must be carried out. A set of rules or steps to solve a specific programming problem is called an *algorithm*. Computer manufacturers keep a list of algorithms that either have been written by their own staff or have been submitted to them by users. We cannot just choose an algorithm at random, however, because we must keep specific hardware constraints in mind. For example, if the μC system that we are using can contain only 8K bytes of memory, all the programming is confined to this amount of memory space.

4.1.4 | Loading, Testing, and Debugging

After the program is written, it is loaded into the μC system. Loading may occur via a keyboard or, in a dedicated control system, the program may first be entered into an EPROM (this topic is covered in Chapters 9 and 10), which is then inserted into the μC. The program is run, and the system is tested. Since few programs run the way we wish the first time, debugging will probably be necessary. Changing the program, loading the program, testing it, and debugging it will have to be done several times before the final product is ready. After the μC system is operating the way it was intended, the program can be finalized. For large-volume production, we may wish to enter the program into a maskable ROM chip (this topic is also covered in Chapters 9 and 10).

4.1.5 | Documentation

Throughout the design cycle, careful documentation of each step should be maintained. Documentation will guarantee that a design change will be remembered and will keep colleagues and supervisors informed at each point in the design. All too often documentation is left until the final product is designed, and many fine points are forgotten. Periodic documentation also avoids massive paperwork at the end of a project. Good documentation in one project can save a considerable amount of time in similar projects.

During all the steps of software design, then, we should constantly refine and document each step. All this documentation should be kept together and labeled. Documentation should always be presented clearly, but it does not have to be presented in the same way for each step. One documentation aid that is often used in trade journals, application notes, or other textbooks is a flowchart.

4.2 | FLOWCHARTS

A *flowchart* is a graphical representation, or drawing, showing the logical sequence of a problem. Many times, a complex design or program can be described more easily by a flowchart than by a statement. The following flowchart symbols are most often used in μP documentation.

Flowpath Arrows: Flowpath arrows are lines with arrowheads that indicate the path or sequence the program follows. Some examples are shown in Figure 4.1.

Terminal Symbol: At the beginning and ending points in a program flowchart is an oblong symbol representing a terminal point. Words such as start, stop, end, halt, exit, and return are usually found within this symbol. There is only one flowpath arrow associated with a terminal symbol. The arrowhead is away from the terminal at the starting point and into the symbol at the ending point, as shown in the examples in Figure 4.2.

FIGURE 4.1 | Flowpath Arrows

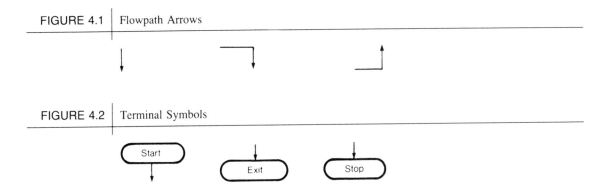

FIGURE 4.2 | Terminal Symbols

Process Symbol: The process symbol, sometimes called a *function box*, is a rectangle. Inside this box is a description of the operation the μP is to perform. A process symbol has two flowpath arrows associated with it—one entering and one leaving, as illustrated in Figure 4.3.

Decision Symbol: The power of any computer is its ability to make a decision. In hardware, decision making is accomplished when the μP checks to "see" if a flip-flop is in the logic 1 or the logic 0 state. Depending on the state of the flip-flop, the answer to all decisions is either yes or no. In a flowchart, a decision symbol is a diamond shape. A decision symbol has three flowpath arrows associated with it—one entering and two leaving. The arrows leaving a decision symbol show the path for each condition. Examples are shown in Figure 4.4.

FIGURE 4.3 | Process Symbols

FIGURE 4.4 | Decision Symbols

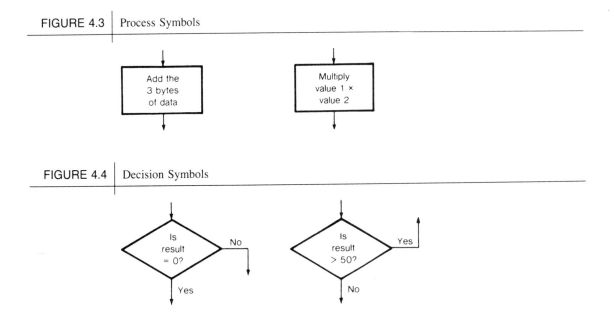

Connection Symbol: A connection symbol is a circle, and it indicates where there is entry from or exit to another part of the program. One use of a connection symbol is at the foot of a page when the flowchart is too long to fit on one page and must be continued on a second sheet. A connection symbol will also be shown at the beginning of the second sheet. In order to keep the proper page order, a letter or number is placed within the circle, as shown in the examples in Figure 4.5.

Input/Output Symbol: The I/O symbol is a parallelogram. It represents either input or output functions. For example, an input function such as when the μC reads data from a paper tape is shown on the flowchart by an I/O symbol. The symbol indicates where in the flowchart this input function happens. Likewise, an output function such as when the μC sends data to peripheral equipment is indicated by an I/O symbol. Note that on many μP flowcharts there may be a rectangular box, the same as the one used for the process symbol, instead of a parallelogram for an I/O function. Figure 4.6 shows examples of I/O symbols.

Summation Point: A summation point is where two or more arrowheads come together. On some flowcharts, the symbol is a circle or a circle with a cross in it. Some μP flowcharts use no circles at all. Examples of summation points are presented in Figure 4.7.

Additional Notes: In addition to the information within the flowchart boxes, a programmer's notes are sometimes added for better documentation. A note allows the programmer and any other user at a later time to understand quickly what should happen at

| FIGURE 4.5 | Connection Symbols |

| FIGURE 4.6 | I/O Symbols |

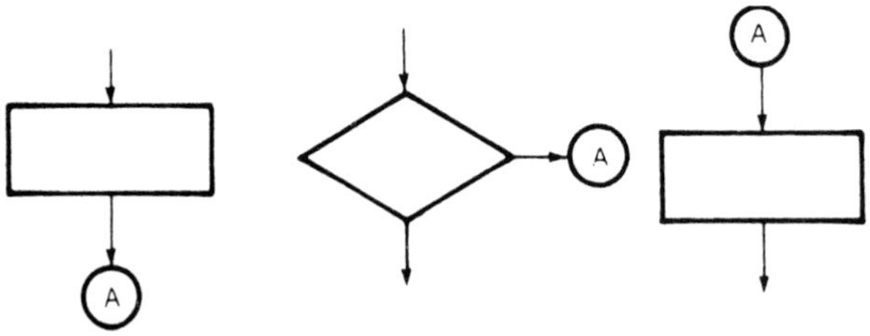

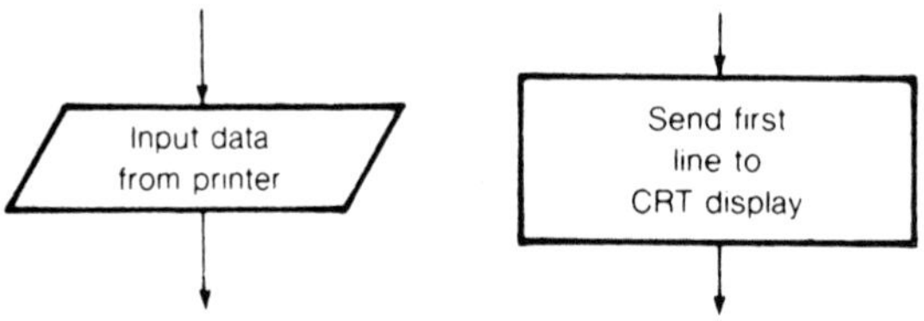

FIGURE 4.7 | Summation Points

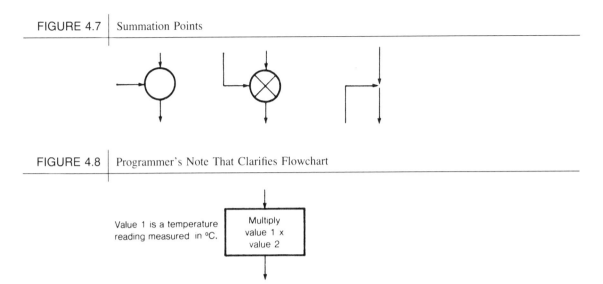

FIGURE 4.8 | Programmer's Note That Clarifies Flowchart

Value 1 is a temperature reading measured in °C.

Multiply
value 1 x
value 2

a particular point in the flowchart. Figure 4.8 shows an example of how additional notes can be helpful in clarifying a flowchart.

As an example of how the individual flowchart symbols work together to show the logical sequence of a problem, consider the flowchart in Figure 4.9. The μP software steps that are described in Section 4.1 are shown here in flowchart form. Thus, a flowchart can be used to summarize several pages of material.

4.3 | PROGRAMMING LANGUAGE LEVELS

Computer programs are written in one of three language levels: (1) machine-level language (the lowest level), (2) assembly-level language (the middle level), or (3) high-level language (the highest level). Each level has its advantages and disadvantages and often the trade-off is between programming time and memory cost. In the following subsections, we examine these advantages and disadvantages.

4.3.1 | Machine-Level Language

Machine-level language is the most basic, or lowest-level, programming language. With this language, the programmer "communicates" with the μC in binary.

Programming at this level is the most difficult because it is extremely tedious and can lead to a multitude of errors. Imagine the possibilities for error and time required to throw switches to enter a short program—one that contains only one hundred bytes of memory. Therefore, entering a program into memory using direct binary should be avoided if at all possible. Unless a person just interconnected some μC chips, he or she probably will not encounter this situation.

Most μC kits and some single-board computer systems include a PROM or ROM

FIGURE 4.9 │ Flowchart Illustrating Steps Involved in Design of Computer Software

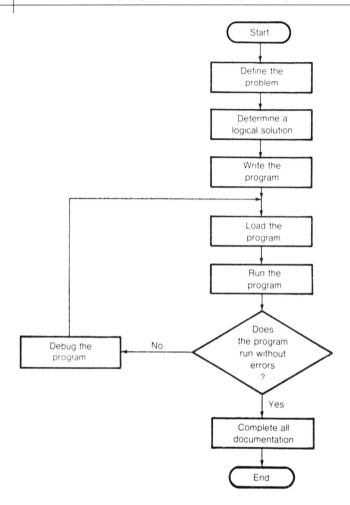

chip. This memory chip contains a monitor program. A *monitor program* is a program
4.6 that gives the μC user some basic functions once power is applied. Some of these functions
allow the user to load a program into RAM, execute, and debug it. Some μC manufacturers
include in their monitor additional programs that allow storage and retrieval of a program
from a tape cassette. The basic monitor program allows users to enter programs through
a hexadecimal or teletype keyboard.

The portion of the monitor program that converts hex code into a binary pattern
4.7 is called the *hexadecimal loader*. An illustration of this hex loader is shown in Figure
4.10. Although the hex loader makes the job of entering the program easier, it is still
time consuming and is still classified as machine-level language. Remember from Chapter
3 that the hexadecimal code is easier to write and that it is easier to find errors in a

FIGURE 4.10 | Hexadecimal Loader for Converting Hex Digits into a Binary Pattern

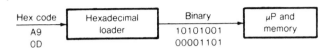

sequence of hex digits. Remember too that the μP only understands binary patterns. It is the hexadecimal loader portion of the monitor program that converts the hex code into the binary pattern. The monitor is a program that must be stored in memory and therefore requires memory space. Most monitor programs (including the hexadecimal loader) use less than 2K bytes of memory.

4.3.2 | Assembly-Level Language

The next-higher level of programming language is assembly language. This language allows a programmer to write a computer program using shorthand notations that describe the instruction. For example,

> LDA means "load the accumulator"
>
> EOR means "exclusive or"
>
> CMP means "compare"
>
> STA means "store the accumulator"
>
> SUB means "subtract"

These notations are called *mnemonics* and are often referred to as "memory joggers." By looking at the mnemonic, we can usually tell what the instruction does. Every μP manufacturer provides a list of mnemonics for its product. A computer program written using mnemonics is called an *assembly language program.* Assume that a computer program has been written in an assembly language. The program must now be loaded into the μC. One way to load it is to convert each mnemonic instruction to its hexadecimal code and enter the program using a hex keyboard. This technique is called *hand assembly.* Although the hex code is certainly easier to use than the binary code, it is still quite possible to make mistakes.

An easier way is to have the computer itself convert the mnemonics to binary patterns. A computer program that converts assembly language programs to binary patterns is called an *assembler.* In this method, the programmer uses a keyboard connected to the computer. Each instruction in the program is typed using the mnemonic notations and sent to the computer. Then the assembler takes over. When a program is written in either assembly or high-level language, it is called *source code.* Machine-level language is called *object code.* An assembler converts source code to object code, as shown in Figure 4.11. Most assemblers do more than just convert mnemonics to binary patterns. Many find the correct memory locations for different parts of the program, correct some

FIGURE 4.11 | Assembler for Converting Assembly Language Programs (Source Code) into Binary Patterns (Object Code)

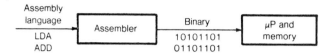

programming errors, allow the programmer to assign labels to memory locations or to input and output devices, and allow the programmer to assign sections of memory for the main program and sections for temporary data.

An assembler, like a hexadecimal loader, is a program and requires memory space. The more the assembler program can do, the more memory space it needs. The assembler translates each line of a program written in assembly language into one or more bytes of memory. A program that is 1000 lines of assembly language requires several thousand bytes of memory, because each instruction in assembly language is converted into a μP instruction and each μP instruction requires either one, two, or three (some μPs have instructions that take four) bytes of memory.

Each assembly language program is written for a particular μP. Programs written for the Motorola 6800 μP are meaningless for the Intel 8080A μP. Therefore, assembly language programs are not portable (interchangeable). Many assembly language programs will not even run on different μPs made by the same manufacturer. For example, programs written for the Motorola 6800 are not guaranteed to run using the Motorola 6809 μP and vice versa.

To some degree, writing programs in assembly language is like writing programs in machine-level language. The programmer must have a working knowledge of the μC's hardware and know which instructions affect which components. The μP and many of the I/O devices have internal registers that are programmable. The μC programmer who uses either machine- or assembly-level language must understand both the hardware and software components. The programmer must know what data is stored in the registers and what flip-flops have been set or cleared. Otherwise, errors will occur and debugging will take a considerable amount of time.

4.3.3 | High-Level Language

The next-higher computer software language is a high-level language. Some of the commonly used high-level languages associated with μCs are listed in Table 4.1.

As μC programs become longer and more sophisticated and are used in more data processing and problem solving applications, then high-level languages become more practical to use. In most cases, a program in a high-level language is approximately ten times faster and easier to write than a program in assembly language. This time is saved in actually writing the program. There is no additional time saved in the other software steps described in Section 4.1. In most high-level languages, an individual can tell from the statement what the program does, which is not true for machine or assembly languages.

Programs written in a high-level language are usually advertised as being portable. Thus, a FORTRAN program written for one computer should run on any other

TABLE 4.1 | Commonly Used High-Level Languages

Acronym	Description	Major Use
FORTRAN	FORmula TRANslation	Mathematics and engineering
BASIC	Beginner's All-purpose Symbolic Instruction Code	General purpose and time sharing
COBOL	COmmon Business-Oriented Language	Business and management information
PASCAL	Blaise PASCAL (French mathematician)	Process control

computer that has FORTRAN capability. Portability is not always guaranteed, however, and a user will have to learn each computer's idiosyncrasies. BASIC is one high-level language that seems to have so many different dialects that it can be frustrating for some users. If a program is indeed portable, a library of programs written for one computer can be used on another. The advantage is a tremendous saving in time for the programmer.

When a program is written in a high-level language, the programmer does not have to worry about the computer's internal registers, the bus structure, or any other hardware problems. In fact, the programmer need not know anything about how a computer works. However, high-level languages also have their disadvantages.

One major hurdle that has to be overcome is that the programmer has to learn the rules of the language and what can and cannot be done. If one rule is violated, the program will not run. Many high-level language programs have internal error detection. When a rule is violated, the computer prints out an error message telling the programmer where and what kind of error has occurred.

We have previously mentioned trade-offs between ease of programming and memory space. High-level languages are easier to program but use more memory space. These languages must be converted from source code into object (machine) code before execution can take place. Two programs that perform this conversion are compilers and interpreters.

4.4 | TRANSLATORS

Assemblers, compilers, and interpreters are classified as *translators*. The difference between assemblers and translators is that when a program is written in assembly language, it is the programmer who must keep track of the data contained in all the registers. When a high-level language is used, the compiler or interpreter does this job.

4.4.1 | Compilers and Interpreters

Compilers are programs that translate a high-level language into a binary code, an assembly language, or an intermediate language sometimes called *pseudo code*, or *P-code*. If the compiler generates the μP's binary pattern immediately, it is said to produce *real code*. If the compiler produces assembly language, then an assembler is needed for the final translation into machine language. Some compilers require as many as six passes through the program to complete all of the translation into the final machine language. This time constraint can easily make high-level languages and compilers unsuitable for real-time applications. (Real-time applications are applications that must be completed in the shortest possible time.)

Compilers are designed so that each statement of the program is read, analyzed, and stored (usually on a tape or disk) but *not* executed. After the compiler's translation from source code to object code is complete, the entire object code program is executed. As long as the object code program is stored, it is this program that is executed, and the compiler does not have to be used again. Modern compilers can produce very efficient object code programs that can be executed relatively quickly.

Interpreters are programs that translate each high-level language statement into object code (machine-level language) immediately, and execute it before reading the next statement. When an interpreter receives a high-level instruction, it refers to a predefined sequence of machine instructions to execute the statement. These machine instructions are stored in the computer's memory. Unlike compilers, interpreters must translate each source statement every time the program is executed. As a comparison, an interpreter may execute a source program twenty times more slowly than a compiler can execute the same program.

Like assemblers, compilers and interpreters can do more than just translation. They can list error messages and other diagnostic information. Some μC manufacturers are including modified versions of FORTRAN, BASIC, COBOL, or PASCAL in their products. They are using either compilers or interpreters that fit into 8K to 32K of memory. Remember that the more a program is to do, the more bytes of memory are needed and the less memory is available to the programmer. The maximum amount of memory space for 8-bit μPs is 64K. A compiler that translates a high-level language program into a machine-level language program probably requires at least four times more memory space than the same program written in assembly language, because high-level languages are made flexible and general enough for a wide range of problems. This flexibility produces a main disadvantage of high-level languages—longer machine-level programs. The trade-off is flexibility for memory space (programming time versus memory cost).

4.4.2 | Cross-Compilers

Although μP and μC manufacturers provide high-level languages for their products, it is usually a modified form of a general high-level language. Some manufacturers use their own version of a high-level language, such as Motorola's MPL and Intel's PL/M. Remember that compilers and interpreters for a high-level language require a large amount of memory space and that this is a limitation in most μC systems. Because compilers do take a large amount of memory, many μC users use cross-compilers. A program is written in a high-level language; then it is entered into a large or mini computer, which generates a machine-level program for their μP. Therefore, their μC system does not need a compiler program contained in its memory. When a computer uses a compiler stored in its own memory, it is called a *self-compiler*. When it uses one in another computer, it is called a *cross-compiler*. Cross-compilers do have some disadvantages. A programmer must have access to a large mainframe computer or a minicomputer with a compiler program, and the programmer may have to wait for computer time. Waiting can be very aggravating in the middle of debugging a program.

Because many high-level languages are limited to a specific μP or have been modified for a particular μC system, the user does not gain the portability or extensive program libraries that are available in larger computers. However, high-level language programming is still easier than lower-level language programming. The μP application eventually becomes the prime factor in deciding which programming language is used.

4.5 | LANGUAGE SELECTION

When we select programming language, we may be limited to machine language because the only system available is a single-board computer that contains a monitor ROM and a hexadecimal keyboard, and no additional development systems are available. If, however, the choice is between an assembly language and a high-level language, then we should be aware of the following trade-offs.

A major advantage of an assembly-level language over a high-level language is that the assembly-level language allows complete control of the steps that the μP will execute. This control, in turn, allows the programmer to minimize the number of programming steps, thus resulting in a μC system with the following benefits: (1) faster execution, (2) more data handling capability, (3) more accuracy, and (4) less hardware required. Let's consider each advantage.

Faster Execution: Some process or industrial control applications, military applications, and most communication applications require a μC to execute the program in the minimum amount of time. These applications are called real-time applications because every microsecond counts. In these applications, the result of the program is made available soon enough to influence or control the process. As we progress upward in language levels, it becomes easier to program and to understand what is happening in each program statement, but a high-level language requires more time to execute.

More Data Handling Capability: Assembly-level programming allows a program to be written in fewer possible steps. Thus, the amount of memory space required for the program is reduced, thereby saving more memory space for data. For example, a single-board computer (SBC) may only include 2K bytes of memory for the program. The more memory that is used for the program, the less is available for data. Exceeding the 2K limit at first may not seem to be a major disadvantage because the user may think that an additional memory board may simply be added to the SBC. Depending on the amount of memory added, however, the cost may be from a few hundred to several thousand dollars. Therefore, the number of units that are produced should determine whether the additional time spent on writing the program in assembly language is more cost effective than adding hardware.

More Accuracy: Programmers using assembly-level language can include additional program steps so that more accuracy is obtained. With greater accuracy, a programmer may write a new algorithm or modify an existing one for the best solution to a problem.

Less Hardware Required: Programs can be optimized to require fewer memory chips in the system and thus result in a cost saving. Remember, however, it makes no sense to save a few bytes of memory space and not reduce the number of memory chips. For example, if the memory chip being used is 2K $\times$ 8, there are 2048 bytes of memory whether or not they are all used. It also makes no sense in low-volume applications to reduce the number of memory chips if the cost of the additional development time in programming is much greater than the savings in the memory chips. By using assembly-level language, it is possible to optimize the program and save memory space. This savings could lead to the following: (1) the entire system may be built on a single printed circuit board, or (2) the program may be designed onto a single-chip μC. Single-chip μCs are very attractive for low-cost, high-volume applications, such as electronic games and household appliances. Remember that many of the benefits mentioned can be offset by the additional programming time that is required.

Assembly language programs should be considered in applications that require small to medium-size programs, need to control I/O devices, require limited data processing, and take into account memory cost as a factor. Long programs, programs that contain a lot of data processing, or programs with a lot of computation and little I/O control are the best for high-level languages.

4.6 | SUBROUTINES

Regardless of the language level used, most programs are written with one or more subroutines. A *subroutine* is a program written separately from the main program. The primary function of the subroutine is to solve a specific problem, such as a mathematical operation. As an example, if several places in the main program require multiplication, then instead of repeating the same multiplication program over and over and wasting valuable memory space, the programmer writes one multiplication program and stores it as a subroutine program. Then, whenever the multiplication operation is needed, the programmer inserts a *jump instruction* that causes the program sequence to change from the main program to the subroutine program. At the end of the subroutine program, the program sequence returns to the main program. Subroutines are extremely valuable programming tools whenever the same program is to be repeated or whenever the programmer wishes to break a larger program into more individual and manageable blocks.

Sometimes, subroutines have subroutines. This programming technique is referred to as *multilevel subroutines*, or *nesting*. Figure 4.12 shows flow lines for single and multilevel subroutines.

A *return instruction* is the last instruction in a subroutine program. It is this instruction that automatically brings the μP back to where it left off. In Figure 4.12A, there is only one subroutine program. Thus, the return instruction brings the μP back to the main program. However, in Figure 4.12B, which illustrates nested subroutines, the return instruction at the end of subroutine 2 brings the μP back to subroutine 1, not to the main program. It is the return instruction at the end of subroutine 1 that brings the μP back to the main program. Thus, the program returns to where it left off.

FIGURE 4.12 | Program Sequence Using Single and Multilevel Subroutines

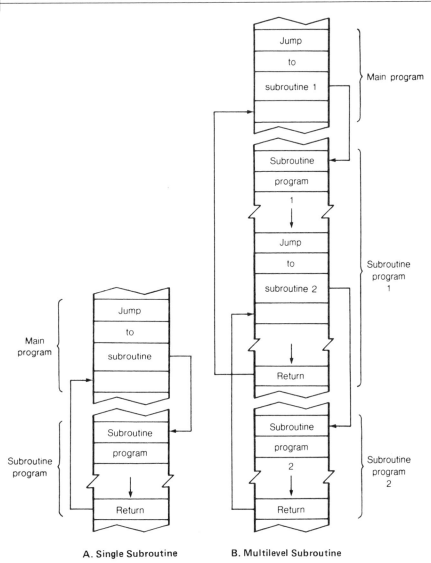

A. Single Subroutine   B. Multilevel Subroutine

Every μP has instructions that allow it to jump to and return from a subroutine. Some μP manufacturers refer to their jump to subroutine instruction as a *call instruction*.

If used properly, subroutines are a valuable programming tool; if used incorrectly, they can be a waste of memory space and time, and can be a nightmare to debug. Good documentation is a must to follow the sequence of events in subroutines.

4.7 | SUMMARY

This chapter introduced general rules of computer software that can be applied to any µP. First-time users often disregard the need for good software documentation and are troubled with problems later on, at which time they may not be able to pinpoint whether they have a hardware or software problem. In all probability, a lot of time will be wasted to track down a bug if the documentation is poor.

Although µPs are designed differently in both hardware and software, there are many similarities. One area of similarity regarding µP software is the process that involves problem definition; logical design; programming; loading, testing, and debugging; and documentation. A commonly used method of expressing a solution to a software problem is the flowchart.

Today's µC systems range from small single-boards to large multiuser, multitasking systems. To satisfy this µC range, different programming languages are needed. High-level languages use either a compiler or interpreter to translate from source code to object code. The application, cost, and µC size are some factors that are considered in choosing a programming language.

Regardless of which language level is used, most programs require subroutines. Subroutines eliminate the need for repeating an algorithm that occurs over and over again in a main program.

PROBLEMS

4.1   Define firmware.

4.2   What does computer software include?

4.3   What is a set of rules or steps to solve a specific programming problem called?

4.4   What is the graphical representation showing the logical sequence of a program called?

4.5   What are the three levels of programming languages?

4.6   What is a program that gives a µC user some basic functions once power is turned on called?

4.7   What is a program that converts hex code into a binary pattern called?

4.8   What programming language uses mnemonics?

4.9   What is the primary purpose of an assembler?

4.10 Are assembly language programs portable?

4.11 What is a difference between compilers and interpreters?

4.12 If a programmer uses a compiler stored on a computer other than the one that will run the object code, is the compiler a self-compiler or a cross-compiler?

4.13 List four advantages of assembly language programs over high-level language programs.

4.14 List three applications where assembly language programs should be considered.

4.15 What is the primary function of a subroutine?

4.16 What is another term for multilevel subroutines?

4.17 What is the last instruction of a subroutine?

5 Basic Instructions and Addressing Modes

5.0 | INTRODUCTION

Computer software personnel, especially programmers using large and mini computers, often attempt to avoid the hardware aspects of the computer. However, the μC has forced hardware and software personnel to work together to produce useful dedicated products. To utilize fully the power of a μC, it is important to understand both its hardware and its software. Even if we use a general-purpose μC system along with a high-level language, an understanding of μP architecture and other components is helpful if the system is to be expanded. Like the large and mini computers, many general-purpose μC systems are designed so that peripheral equipment (such as keyboards, CRTs, floppy disks, hard disks, and tape cassettes) is compatible and can be used to build a larger μC system. However, once we deviate from this compatibility and decide to add other I/O devices, then we must know the μC's hardware, including the internal architecture of the μP. If we write programs in either machine-level or assembly-level language, we must keep track of what data is stored in which μP register. Many μCs are used in dedicated control applications, and the programs of these applications are often written in assembly language. Without a working knowledge of the μC's hardware, it is doubtful that we can fully understand a completed system or can build a useful μP product.

In previous chapters, the basic parts of a μC were introduced, but the μP's instructions and how the instructions affect the internal registers of the μP were not discussed. The internal architecture and instructions of each μP are different, but there are certain aspects that are common to most 8-bit μPs. Although this chapter introduces some of these common points, it primarily concentrates on the architecture and instructions of the 6800 μP.

5.1 | MICROPROCESSOR ARCHITECTURE

Section 2.4 introduced μP architecture in its four basic parts: (1) registers, (2) arithmetic and logic unit, (3) timing and control circuitry, and (4) decoding circuitry. The μP has been designed so that once a binary pattern representing an instruction is fetched from memory, the pattern is automatically placed in the μP's instruction register and decoded. The binary pattern establishes the μP's timing and control for the entire time the instruction is executed. Therefore, parts 3 and 4 of the μP are affected by the instruction. Parts 1 and 2 are used by the μP to operate on data or information.

All of the μP instructions together are called its *instruction set*. The programmer arranges instructions sequentially to solve a particular problem. The instructions allow the programmer to route data or information into or out of a μP register or into the ALU. *Note:* For the 6800, the programmer does not have control of data coming out of the ALU because it is sent directly to one of two accumulators.

Each μP is unique in its architecture and its instructions. It is helpful, therefore, to visualize the basic internal architecture of a μP. A diagram, or programmer's model, of this internal architecture shows, for example, how many and what kind of registers there are. Figure 5.1 is a basic block diagram of the 6800 μP.

5.1.1 | Accumulator

The accumulators of the 6800 μP are the most often used registers. They are used to store data from memory or I/O and to send data to memory or an I/O device. They are also the registers that are closely associated with the ALU. In the 6800 μP, when an addition or subtraction instruction is executed, at least one of the numbers comes from an accumulator. The result of the arithmetic operation is automatically stored into the same accumulator. The number of bits in an accumulator often determines the μP's word size. The word size for the 6800 μP is 8 bits.

5.1.2 | Condition Code Register

The *condition code register* is 8 bits wide, although not all 8 bits are used. This register should be thought of as individual bits because the result of an instruction can either set or clear one or more of the bits. There are other instructions that can test each individual bit to see whether it is a logic 1 or a logic 0. Testing the bits allows the μP to make a decision. If the condition is true, the programmer may wish to execute one program. If the condition is false, the programmer may wish to execute a different program.

Although every μP has a condition code register, it is called different things in different μPs. Some of the names used for this register are *processor status word, processor status register, P register, status word,* or *flag register*. An individual bit is referred to as a *flag bit,* a *status bit,* or a *flag*. Three of the most common flag bits are the carry flag, the zero flag, and the sign flag. The *zero flag* is used to indicate whether the result of an instruction is 0. The *carry flag* is used in the arithmetic operations of

FIGURE 5.1 | Functional Block Diagram Showing Internal Structure of the 6800 μP (Redrawn from data sheet for MC6800 microprocessor with permission. Motorola Incorporated, Phoenix, Arizona)

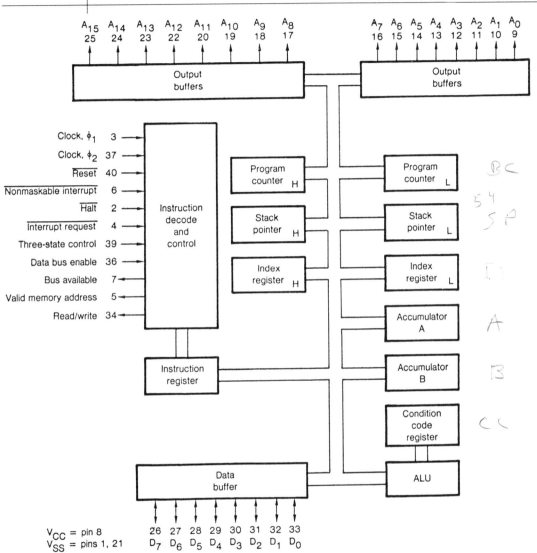

addition and subtraction to indicate whether or not there is a carry or a borrow, respectively. The *sign flag* is used to indicate whether a number is positive or negative. Of the 8 possible bits in this register, the 6800 uses 6. Note that not all bits of this register can be tested. Some bits are used by the μP to keep track of a particular condition. Each flag bit will be discussed in more detail later.

5.1.3 | Program Counter

The *program counter* (abbreviated PC) is a 16-bit register. It contains the address of the instruction being fetched from memory. Since the 6800 µP has 16 address lines, it is necessary to have a 16-bit program counter, one bit for each address line. Generally, instructions are executed sequentially from successive memory locations. When one instruction is being executed, the program counter is incremented to the address of the next instruction. The program counter can only count up. The sequential order can be changed by the use of branch or jump instructions, which will be described later.

5.1.4 | Stack Pointer

The *stack* is an area in memory (RAM) used to store temporary data. The *stack pointer* is a register in the µP that holds the memory location of the place on the stack where data can be stored or retrieved. Data is stored and retrieved sequentially from the stack. Unlike the program counter, the stack pointer is a register that can count up and down. Most µPs use what is called a "push down" and "pop up" stack. This name implies that when data is put onto the stack, the stack pointer is decremented, and that when data is retrieved from the stack, the stack pointer is incremented. This type of stack is also referred to as *last in/first out* (LIFO). Thus, the stack pointer counts down to fill the stack and counts up as the stack empties. The 6800 µP has a 16-bit stack pointer. Therefore, the stack can be located any place in memory.

5.2 | INSTRUCTION FORMAT

The 6800 µP has instructions that occupy either one, two, or three bytes of memory. Because each byte is a line in memory, when an instruction word occupies more than one byte, it must be stored in successive memory locations. Figure 5.2 shows examples of one-, two-, and three-byte µP instructions.

All instruction words have two parts, the *op code* and the *operand*. "Op code" is short for "operation code." Sometimes the op code refers to the instructional code or type of instruction. This part of the instruction is decoded by the µP and "tells" the µP what to do. The operand is the data that is operated upon. In multibyte instructions, the first byte is the op code and the remaining byte or bytes are the operand (the data) or an address (the operand address) where the data can be found. In single-byte instructions, the op code and the operand address are contained in the one 8-bit pattern. In this type of instruction, the operand address is not a memory address but rather a µP register. Since 8-bit µPs have only a few internal registers, the op code and the register where the action is to take place can be contained within 8 bits.

5.3 | BASIC INSTRUCTION SET

Each µP has instructions that are unique to it. However, most µPs usually have the same basic set of instructions, although the machine codes will usually be different. This section introduces the basic instructions and what happens when they are executed by the µP.

FIGURE 5.2 | One-, Two-, and Three-Byte μP Instructions

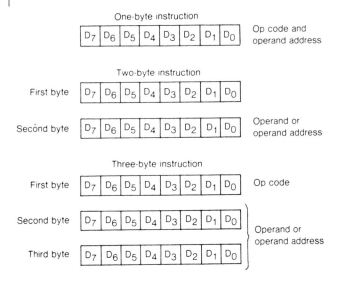

The 6800 instructions can be divided loosely into eight categories: (1) data movement instructions, (2) arithmetic instructions, (3) logical instructions, (4) compare and test instructions, (5) rotate and shift instructions, (6) program control instructions, (7) stack instructions, and (8) other machine and control instructions. (There is nothing sacred about the number of categories; other texts use more or fewer categories.) A description of what happens in each of the eight categories listed here follows.

5.3.1 | Data Movement Instructions

Data movement instructions move data from one location to another. They include instructions that move data from a memory location to a μP register, from a μP register to a memory location, from one μP register to another, and from one memory location to another. The data is moved 8 bits at a time. Therefore, all of these operations move data in a parallel fashion.

The two most fundamental instructions for the 6800 μP are the instructions to load the accumulator (the mnemonic is LDA) and the instruction to store the accumulator (the mnemonic is STA). The LDA instruction transfers a byte of data from a memory location to an accumulator. The STA instruction transfers the contents of an accumulator to a memory location. It is important to remember that when data is transferred from one register to another, the information in the first register is *not* lost. The first register is called the *source*, and the second register is called the *destination*. After a data movement instruction is completed, the source and the destination registers both contain the same data. The only way to change the data in the first (source) register is to store new data in it. Figure 5.3 shows what happens when data is moved from a source register to a destination register. The data (72) from the source register is *not* lost; the data (15) that was originally in the destination register *is* lost.

FIGURE 5.3 | Source and Destination Registers before and after Data Movement Instruction

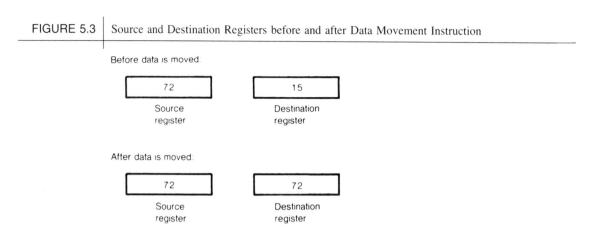

Before data is moved:

| 72 |

Source
register

| 15 |

Destination
register

After data is moved:

| 72 |

Source
register

| 72 |

Destination
register

Microprocessor instructions can be expressed by a symbolic notation. For example, the LDA instruction can be written as M→A. The direction of the arrow is from the source to the destination. Some examples of the 6800 data movement instructions are given in Table 5.1. The instructions are shown in both mnemonic form and μP notation. Although many of the following examples use accumulator A, accumulator B could have been used. More detailed examples will be given in Chapter 6.

Load Instructions: An example of what happens when the μP executes an LDA A instruction is shown in Figure 5.4. Figure 5.4A shows the situation before the execution of the instruction. The contents of the accumulator are 04_{hex}, while the contents of the memory location 1075_{hex} are 12_{hex}. After the LDA A instruction is executed, 12_{hex} from memory location 1075_{hex} is loaded into accumulator A and 04_{hex} is lost, as shown in Figure 5.4B. In assembly language, the instruction is written as LDA A 1075. Since other memory locations are not involved, their data is not transferred. Note that 12_{hex} in memory location 1075_{hex} has not been destroyed. In this example, memory location 1075_{hex} is the source and accumulator A is the destination.

TABLE 5.1 | Basic Data Movement Instructions in Mnemonic Form and Symbolic Notation

Mnemonic	Description	μP Notation	Source	Destination
LDA A	Load accumulator A	M→A	Memory	Accumulator
LDX	Load X register	M→X	Memory	X register
STA A	Store accumulator A	A→M	Accumulator	Memory
STX	Store X register	X→M	X register	Memory
TAB	Transfer contents of accumulator A to accumulator B	A→B	Accumulator A	Accumulator B
TBA	Transfer contents of accumulator B to accumulator A	B→A	Accumulator B	Accumulator A

FIGURE 5.4 | Memory and Accumulator Contents before and after Execution of LDA A Instruction

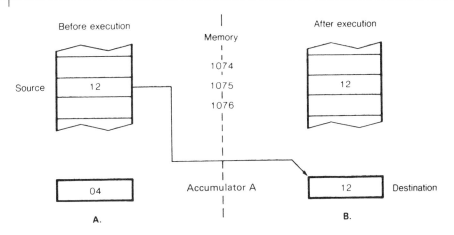

Store Instructions: Figure 5.5 shows an example of what happens when the μP executes an STA A instruction. In this example, the data in accumulator A is stored in memory location 1075_{hex}. In assembly language format, the instruction is STA A 1075. Figure 5.5A shows the contents of the accumulator and memory before the instruction is executed. The situation is the same as in Figure 5.4A. After the STA A instruction is executed, the contents of the accumulator are unchanged, but the data in memory location 1075_{hex} has been changed to 04_{hex}, as shown in Figure 5.5B. The value 12_{hex}, which was in memory location 1075_{hex}, has been lost. In this example, accumulator A is the source and memory location 1075_{hex} is the destination.

FIGURE 5.5 | Memory and Accumulator Contents before and after Execution of STA A Instruction

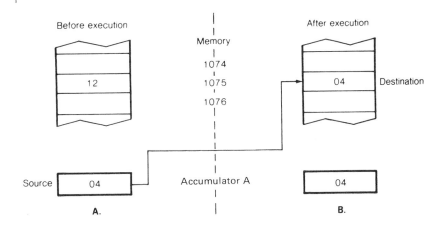

FIGURE 5.6 | Accumulator-to-Accumulator Data Transfer (A→B)

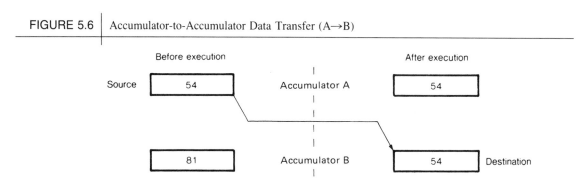

Transfer and Exchange Instructions: There are two types of instructions that move data between μP registers. The first type of instruction involves a transfer of data from one μP register to another. One register is the source and the other is the destination. The second type of instruction involves an exchange of data between two μP registers. The 6800 μP does not have an exchange instruction, but the 68000 does have it.

Figure 5.6 is an example of an accumulator-to-accumulator data transfer. The μP moves the contents of accumulator A into accumulator B. In μP notation, we can write A→B. Figure 5.6A shows two μP accumulators and their contents. In this example, accumulator A is the source and accumulator B is the destination. When an instruction to transfer accumulator A to accumulator B is executed, the result is as shown in Figure 5.6B.

An example of a register-to-register data exchange is shown in Figure 5.7. Figure 5.7A shows the situation before the exchange instruction is executed, and Figure 5.7B shows the result after execution.

FIGURE 5.7 | Register-to-Register Data Exchange

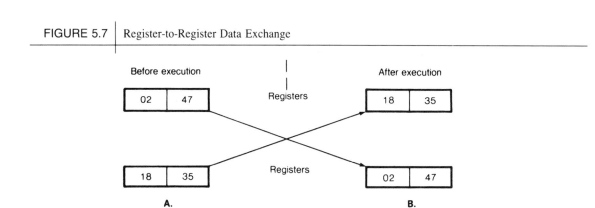

5.3.2 | Arithmetic Instructions

5.20

Arithmetic instructions use the ALU. The basic arithmetic instructions are the add, subtract, increment (add 1 to a μP register or memory location), and decrement (subtract 1 from a μP register or memory location) instructions. The arithmetic instructions and other ALU instructions are often described as the most powerful instructions in a μP instruction set. These instructions allow the μP to compute and to manipulate data. Therefore, these instructions distinguish a computer from a collection of random logic circuits. The results of many of these ALU instructions are stored automatically either in accumulator A or accumulator B.

Add Instruction: All 8-bit μPs are capable of adding two 8-bit numbers. Usually one number comes from an accumulator, while the other number comes either from a μP register or from memory. The result of the addition is automatically stored in the accumulator.

Figure 5.8A shows the contents of accumulator A and a memory location (FC41) before an add instruction is executed. Figure 5.8B shows the contents of accumulator A and the same memory location after the instruction is executed. Note that the original data (06) in accumulator A is lost and is replaced by the result (08), while the data (02) in the memory location remains unchanged. The μP notation for this example can be written as $A + M \rightarrow A$.

The example just given did not involve the carry bit. If there should be a carry from the addition, it would be stored in the carry bit of the condition code register. Microprocessors also have add instructions that include the carry bit in the addition. This type of instruction adds the contents of the accumulator, a memory location (or another μP register), and the carry bit. The result is placed in the accumulator. The μP notation for this type of addition can be written as $A + M + C \rightarrow A$.

add with carry A0cA, A0cB

FIGURE 5.8 | Memory and Accumulator Contents before and after Execution of Add Instruction $(A + M \rightarrow A)$

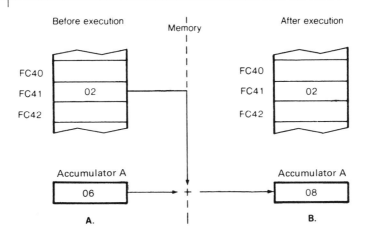

Subtract Instruction: The subtract instruction, like the add instruction, is a fundamental µP instruction. This instruction involves subtracting data in a µP register or memory location from the contents of the accumulator. The result is automatically placed in the accumulator. The µP notation for this operation is A − M→A.

Figure 5.9A shows the same conditions as in Figure 5.8A, but now we will apply the subtract instruction. The data (02) at the memory location (FC41) is subtracted from the data (06) in accumulator A. After the subtract instruction is executed, the result (04) is stored in accumulator A, as shown in Figure 5.9B.

In all µPs, subtraction is done by 2's complement arithmetic. If the result is negative, the answer is in 2's complement form. For example, if the problem is 4 − 7 = −3, the answer, −3, in 2's complement form is 11111101 (binary) or FD (hexadecimal). Microprocessors have instructions that can check the logic state of bit 7, the most significant bit of the answer. If bit 7 is a logic 0, the answer is positive; if bit 7 is a logic 1, the answer is negative. Hence, a positive or negative answer can easily be determined.

The carry bit is often referred to as the *borrow bit* when a subtract instruction is being executed. The 6800 has two types of subtract instructions—one that does not include the carry flag and another that does include it. The µP notations are A − M→A and A − M − C→A.

Increment and Decrement Instructions: The increment and decrement instructions add 1 or subtract 1 from the contents of a µP register or from the contents of a memory location. The contents of a memory location are incremented (or decremented) in the following way: (1) The data in a memory location is moved from memory to the ALU, (2) the data is incremented (or decremented), and (3) the incremented (or decremented) data is transferred back to the original memory location. This type of instruction, which involves changing the contents of a memory location, is classified as a read/modify/write

---

FIGURE 5.9 | Memory and Accumulator Contents before and after Execution of Subtract Instruction (A − M→A)

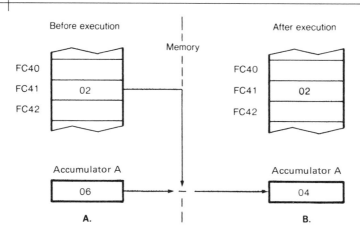

FIGURE 5.10 | Accumulators before and after Execution of Increment Instruction (A + 1→A) and Decrement Instruction (A − 1→A)

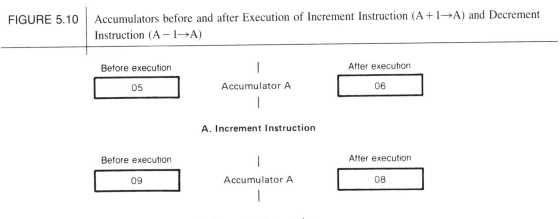

A. Increment Instruction

B. Decrement Instruction

instruction. The number of steps involved in a read/modify/write instruction makes it one of the longest instructions that a μP has to execute.

Figures 5.10A and 5.10B show examples of an increment and a decrement instruction, respectively, and the contents of the accumulator before and after the instructions are executed. The μP notation for incrementing the accumulator is A + 1→A, and for decrementing, it is A − 1→A.

Increment and decrement instructions produce a "roll-over" result. That is, if a register (or memory location) is all 1s and it is incremented, the result is all 0s and does not affect the carry flag. Likewise, if a register (or memory location) is all 0s and it is decremented, the result is all 1s and does not affect the carry flag.

5.3.3 | Logical Operations

The logical operations of AND, OR, and Exclusive OR are performed by the 6800 μP on 8 bits at a time. The contents of the accumulator and data from memory can be combined by the AND, OR, or Exclusive OR operations. Like the add and subtract instructions, these operations are performed in the ALU and the result is automatically placed in an accumulator. The 6800 logical operations in μP notation are shown in Table 5.2.

TABLE 5.2 | Symbolic Notation and Description of Logical Operations

Operation	μP Notation	Comments
AND A	$A \cdot M \rightarrow A$	Contents of accumulator A and memory location are ANDed together. Result is placed in accumulator A.
OR A	$A + M \rightarrow A$	Contents of accumulator A and memory location are ORed together. Result is placed in accumulator A.
EOR A	$A \oplus M \rightarrow A$	Contents of accumulator A and memory location are Exclusive ORed together. Result is placed in accumulator A.

FIGURE 5.11 | Memory and Accumulator Contents before and after Execution of Logical AND, OR, and Exclusive OR Instructions

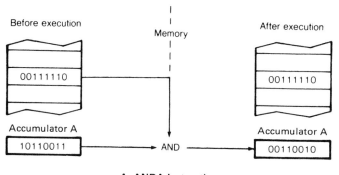

A. ANDA Instruction

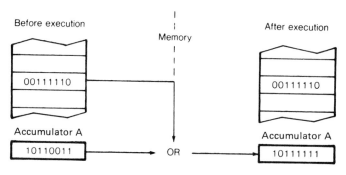

B. ORA Instruction

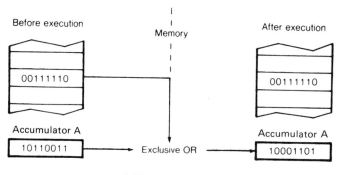

C. EORA Instruction

FIGURE 5.12	1's and 2's Complements Formed by Using Exclusive OR Instruction

11100110	← Accumulator →	11100110
11111111	← Exclusive OR → with all 1's	11111111
00011001	←1's complement→	00011001
	Increment → 2's complement→	00000001 00011010

A.   B.

Figures 5.11A, B, and C show examples of logical AND, OR, and Exclusive OR instructions, respectively. The data has been written in the binary format so that it is easy to check the answers. *Note:* Motorola uses the $+$ symbol to indicate both addition and logical OR. The user must be careful and know what operation is being executed each time the $+$ symbol is used.

Complement instructions (both 1's and 2's complements) are logical operations. Some μPs do not include these instructions, some only have a 1's complement instruction, and others can do both operations. The reason that some μP instruction sets do not include complement instructions is that complementing can be done by using other instructions. For example, the 1's complement of a number can be formed by Exclusive ORing a register with all logic 1s. An example is shown in Figure 5.12A. The 2's complement of a number may be found by first obtaining the 1's complement and then incrementing it, as shown in Figure 5.12B. The term *negative* is used for the 2's complement and the μP notation is $00 - A \rightarrow A$. The term *complement* when used alone means 1's complement. The μP notation for the 1's complement of the accumulator is $\overline{A} \rightarrow A$. The 6800 μP has instructions for doing both 1's and 2's complements.

Although μPs perform subtraction using 2's complement arithmetic, the programmer does not have to worry about obtaining the 2's complement. In the subtraction process, the 2's complement is obtained automatically by the ALU.

5.3.4 | Compare and Test Instructions

A compare instruction is a subtraction instruction. For the 6800, it involves data from an accumulator and either data from the other accumulator or data from memory. The difference between a compare instruction and a subtract instruction is that for the compare instruction the result is not stored in the accumulator or anywhere else. Therefore, the accumulator remains unchanged. What is affected is one or more of the flag bits. The instruction following a compare instruction is often an instruction to check the logic state of a flag bit (or bits) so that the μP can decide what to do next.

One purpose of a compare instruction is to allow the programmer to compare a value in memory to a value in an accumulator without changing the value of the accumulator. This instruction is often used when data is being received from peripheral

FIGURE 5.13 | Testing Individual Bit (Logic 0) by Masking Using AND Instruction

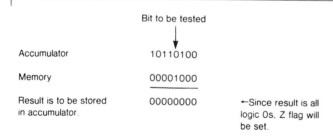

Bit to be tested

Accumulator   10110100

Memory   00001000

Result is to be stored   00000000   ←Since result is all
in accumulator.   logic 0s. Z flag will
                                         be set.

equipment. Let's consider an example. Data from peripheral equipment could have one of several values. For each different value, the program is to perform a different operation. A rapid way to determine the value of the input data is to compare it with a series of constants stored in memory. Use of a compare instruction followed by a decision-making instruction gives the programmer a quick and easy method of accomplishing this task.

Compare instructions are designed to compare bytes of data. If the programmer wishes to test the logic state of a single bit, however, there are two commonly used methods. The first is a *masking procedure*, and the second is a *bit-testing procedure*.

The masking procedure uses an AND instruction. The accumulator is ANDed with a byte of data that contains a logic 1 in the bit location (or locations) under test. If the bit being tested is not a logic 1, then the result of the AND operation is all 0s and the zero flag is set. The instruction following the AND instruction will be an instruction to check the zero flag, allowing the µP to decide what to do next. The disadvantage of this technique is that the contents of the accumulator are destroyed by the AND operation. Thus, the accumulator would have to be reloaded with the original data. To search a table for a single bit in a given position using a masking procedure would require extra programming and extra time for the instruction to be executed.

Figures 5.13 and 5.14 show bit 3 in the accumulator being tested using the masking technique. When the individual bit being checked is a logic 0, the result stored in the accumulator is zero and the Z flag is set. See Figure 5.13. When the individual bit being checked is a logic 1, the result stored in the accumulator is not zero and the Z flag is cleared. See Figure 5.14.

FIGURE 5.14 | Testing Individual Bit (Logic 1) by Masking Using AND Instruction

Bit to be tested

Accumulator   10111100

Memory   00001000

Result is to be stored   00001000   ←Since result is
in accumulator.   *not* 0s. Z flag will
                                         be cleared.

FIGURE 5.15 | Testing Several Bits by Masking Using AND Instruction

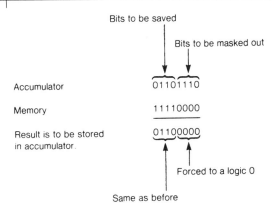

When data is being sent to or received from a peripheral device, the data often has to be modified by masking out either the least significant 4 bits or the most significant 4 bits. Figure 5.15 shows how the least significant 4 bits are masked out and the new result that is stored in the accumulator. In this figure, the Z flag is cleared because the result is not zero.

The second technique, the bit-testing procedure, also involves an AND operation, but the contents of the accumulator are not destroyed. Not all μPs have a bit-testing instruction, however, and in some of those that do, only some of the bits can be tested. Figures 5.16 and 5.17 show examples of the use of a bit-testing instruction. In Figure 5.16, the result is not stored in the accumulator, but the Z flag is set to a logic 1 because the result is zero. The result of Figure 5.17 causes the Z flag to be cleared to a logic 0 because the result is not zero. In most applications, the instruction that follows a bit-testing instruction is a conditional branch instruction. Branch instructions are program control instructions. They will be covered in Section 5.3.6.

FIGURE 5.16 | Testing Individual Bit (Logic 0) through Execution of Bit-Testing Instruction

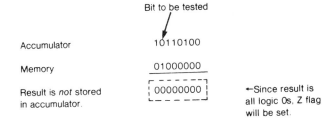

FIGURE 5.17 | Testing Individual Bit (Logic 1) through Execution of Bit-Testing Instruction

Bit to be tested

Accumulator   10111001

Memory   10000000

Result is *not* stored   10000000   ←Since result is
in accumulator.   *not* all 0s, Z flag
                                        will be cleared.

FIGURE 5.18 | Movement of Data during Execution of Rotate and Shift Instructions

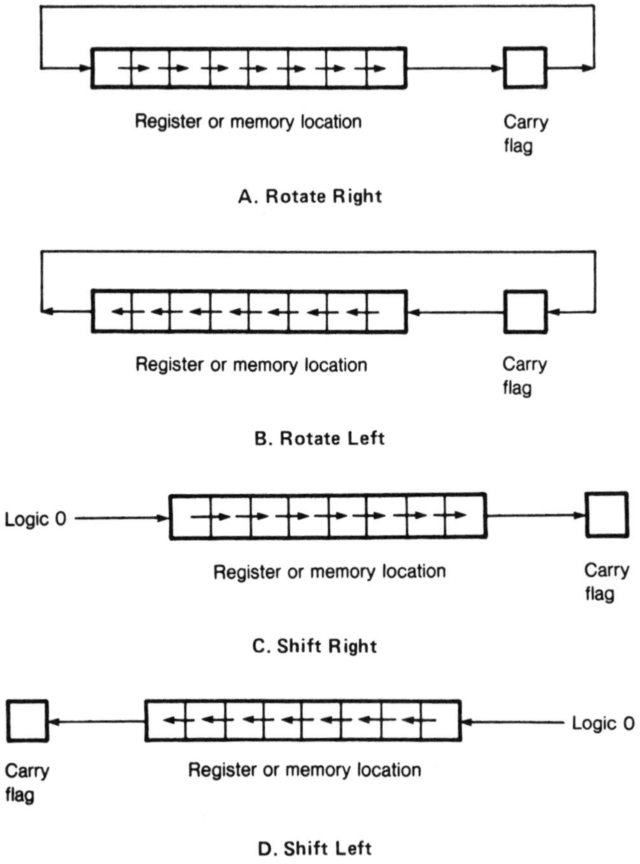

Register or memory location   Carry flag

A. Rotate Right

Register or memory location   Carry flag

B. Rotate Left

Logic 0 → Register or memory location   Carry flag

C. Shift Right

Carry flag   Register or memory location   Logic 0

D. Shift Left

5.3.5 | Rotate and Shift Instructions

Two other instructions—rotate and shift—alter the data in a register or memory location by moving the present data either right or left one bit. Both instructions involve the carry bit. The rotate instructions rotate the data through the carry bit. The shift instructions do not move the carry bit back into the register. Figure 5.18 illustrates what happens to each bit during execution of rotate and shift instructions. *Note:* Rotate instructions save the data; shift instructions destroy the data.

5.3.6 | Program Control Instructions

Program control instructions change the contents of the program counter. The μP can then skip over a number of memory locations to execute a new program or go back to an old memory location and repeat a program.

Program control instructions are either *unconditional* or *conditional* instructions. When an unconditional instruction is executed, the program counter is always changed. For the program counter to be changed when a conditional instruction is executed, the state of a flag bit (or bits) must first be checked. If the condition is true (a yes answer), the program counter is changed. If the condition is false (a no answer), the program counter is not changed and the next instruction in the program sequence is fetched and executed.

One program control instruction is used to jump to a subroutine program, and another program control instruction is used to return from the subroutine to the main program or to whichever program the user wishes to reenter. Some of the program instructions that we will discuss include the jump, branch, and return instructions. Figure 5.19 shows an example of the contents of the program counter before and after a jump instruction is executed. In this example, the μP executes a jump instruction telling it to go to memory location 8100. This instruction as written in assembly language is JMP 8100.

5.3.7 | Stack/Stack Pointer Instructions

When the μP jumps to a subroutine program, the μP must store the present contents of the program counter so that the μP can know where to return. Most μPs store the return address in random access memory (RAM). The portion of RAM that is used for this purpose is the stack. As described in Section 5.1.4, the stack pointer is a μP register that holds the stack's memory address. Remember that the stack pointer does not hold

FIGURE 5.19 | Contents of Program Counter before and after Execution of Jump Instruction

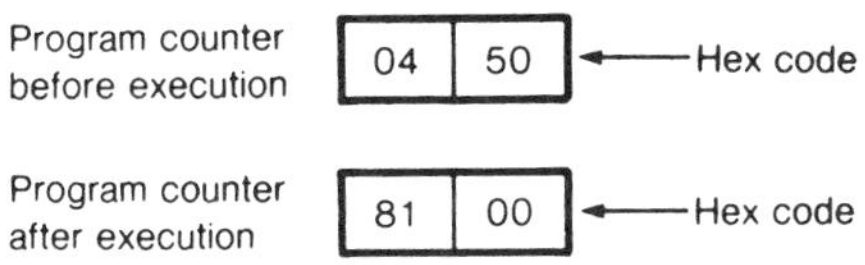

Program counter
before execution | 04 | 50 | ◀—— Hex code

Program counter
after execution | 81 | 00 | ◀—— Hex code

5.30

the actual data but, as its name implies, is a pointer to the memory location where the actual data can be stored or retrieved.

Since a subroutine program will certainly use one or more of the μP registers, the programmer may also wish to save the contents of these registers. This data can also be saved on the stack. The contents of the program counter are automatically stored on the stack when a jump to subroutine instruction is executed. However, the contents of the other μP registers must be stored on the stack by inserting specific instructions to do this job. The instruction that stores the contents of a μP register on the stack is a push instruction. The instruction that retrieves the contents of a μP register from the stack is a pull or pop instruction. When a push instruction is executed for the 6800 μP, the contents of an accumulator are stored on the stack and then the stack pointer is decremented by 1. Thus, the stack pointer is pointing to the next memory location where data can be saved. When a pull instruction is executed by the 6800 μP, the stack pointer is incremented by 1. Then this memory address is placed on the address bus and the data at that location is retrieved and moved to the proper accumulator.

5.31

Figure 5.20 shows how the 6800 μP stores the contents of its program counter on the stack. In this example, a JSR EC00 instruction tells the 6800 μP to jump to a subroutine beginning at memory location EC00. Before going to location EC00, the μP saves the contents of the program counter (507A) on the stack. XX indicates any byte of data. Other examples will be examined in later chapters.

FIGURE 5.20 | Memory and Register Contents before and after Execution of Stack/Stack Pointer Instruction

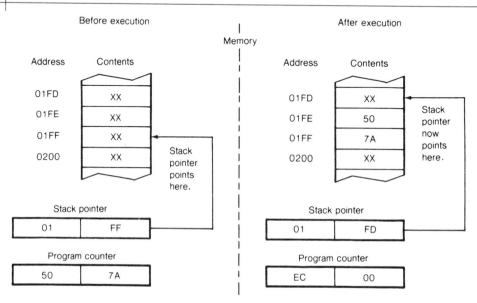

5.3.8 | Other Microprocessor Instructions

Some instructions do not fall easily into any of the previous categories. These instructions are sometimes grouped together and referred to as special-purpose instructions, miscellaneous instructions, or other μP instructions. They include instructions such as enabling or disabling the μP's interrupt lines, clearing or setting the μP's flag bits, and allowing the μP to do binary arithmetic or BCD arithmetic. They also include instructions to halt or break the program sequence.

As we study the 6800 μP, we will find that instructions do fall into one of the eight categories just discussed. Remember, some manufacturers use more categories and others use fewer, but it is only for our convenience that we group similar instructions.

5.4 | ADDRESSING MODES

Microprocessor manufacturers design into their product's instruction set a number of different ways in which the μP can retrieve data from memory. This design feature involves *addressing modes*. They allow the programmer more flexibility to write a program that can lead to faster execution, simpler operations, and less memory space.

5.32

Single-byte instructions have basically only one type of addressing mode, whereas multibyte instructions may have many different addressing modes associated with them. Thus, each instruction has as much flexibility as possible so that the μP can be used in a number of different applications. Addressing modes are an important part of a μP's architecture and instruction set, and they are often used as a selling point by μP manufacturers.

The 8-bit binary pattern of the op code includes both the type of instruction and the addressing mode. The type of instruction tells the μP what to do; the addressing mode tells the μP how to do it.

Note that not all μPs have the same addressing modes and that different manufacturers use different names to describe the same mode. To make the problem more confusing, one manufacturer may use one name for an addressing mode, while another manufacturer may use the same name for an entirely different addressing mode. These difficulties are illustrated in Table 5.3, in which each line is an equivalent addressing mode. Note that the addressing mode "Direct" means one thing to the 8080A user and something else to the 6800 user. Definitions and examples of each of the 6800's addressing modes follow.

5.4.1 | Inherent

The inherent addressing mode applies to one-byte instructions. Both the op code and the operand address are contained in a single byte (8 bits). Examples are: clear an accumulator, increment or decrement an accumulator, clear or set the carry flip-flop, clear or set the interrupt flip-flop, and shift or rotate an accumulator. When this type of instruction is decoded by the μP's instruction register, part of the 8 bits tells the μP what to do (op code) and the other part of the 8 bits tells the μP where to perform the instruction (operand

TABLE 5.3 | Addressing Modes for the 8080A, 6800, and 6502 Microprocessors

8080A	6800	6502
Register	Inherent[1]	Implied[1]
Immediate	Immediate	Immediate
Direct	Extended	Absolute
—	Direct	Zero page
—	Relative	Relative
—	Indexed[2]	Indexed[3]
		Absolute, X
		Absolute, Y
		Zero page, X
		Zero page, Y
Register	—	Memory indirect[4]
Indirect		Indirect
		Indexed indirect
		Indirect indexed

[1]This mode includes the accumulator addressing mode.

[2]The 6800 μP has one 16-bit index register.

[3]The 6502 μP has two 8-bit index registers.

[4]The 6502 μP has three types of indirect addressing modes. Each type is a memory indirect addressing mode.

address). The operand address for this instruction is always within the μP, such as an internal register or an internal flip-flop.

5.4.2 | Immediate

An immediate addressing mode instruction is a two- (or three-) byte instruction. The first byte contains the op code and the register that will receive the data. The second (and third) byte is the data that is to be placed in that register. If the register is 8 bits wide, the instruction is two bytes. If the register is 16 bits wide, the instruction requires three bytes.

This type of addressing mode is used for quickly loading data into a register or performing arithmetic or logical operations using a known or fixed value. The bytes must be stored in successive memory locations. The symbol # is used to indicate the immediate addressing mode.

For the immediate addressing mode LDA A instruction shown in Figure 5.21, the data, 05_{hex}, is part of the instruction. It is contained in the second (and sometimes third) byte. Figure 5.21A shows the mnemonic and symbol for load the accumulator immediately. After the instruction is executed, 05_{hex} is placed in accumulator A, as shown in Figure 5.21B. The data (B2) in the accumulator is lost.

FIGURE 5.21 | Memory and Accumulator Contents before and after Execution of Immediate Addressing Mode LDA A# Instruction

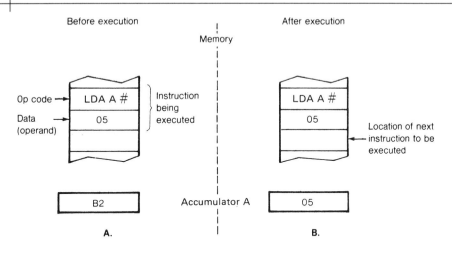

5.4.3 | Extended

The extended addressing mode instruction is a three-byte instruction. The first byte is the op code, and the second and third bytes are the address where the data can be found (operand address). For the extended addressing mode LDA A instruction shown in Figure 5.22A, the data at memory location 1450 is moved into accumulator A when the μP executes an LDA A 1450 instruction. The data (08) in the accumulator is lost. The first byte of the instruction is the address where the machine code for LDA A would be stored. The second and third bytes are the memory address of the data to be put into the accumulator. When this instruction is executed, the μP goes to memory location 1450, finds the data that is in that memory location, and places it in accumulator A, as shown in Figure 5.22B. Note for the 6800 μP, the second byte is the page address and the third byte is the line address.

5.4.4 | Direct

The direct addressing mode is a two-byte instruction. The first byte is the op code, and the second byte is the line address. The page address is understood by the μP to be page zero. Figure 5.23 shows an example of an LDA A instruction using the direct addressing mode. The accumulator is loaded with data from memory location 0075. The zero page address is understood by the μP when it decodes the instruction's op code. The previous data (01) in the accumulator is lost. Figure 5.24 shows an example of an STA A instruction using the direct addressing mode. The contents of accumulator A are stored in memory location 004E. The zero page address is understood by the μP when it decodes the instruction's op code. Any previous data (XX) in memory location 004E is lost. In the

FIGURE 5.22 | Memory and Accumulator Contents before and after Execution of Extended Addressing Mode LDA A Instruction

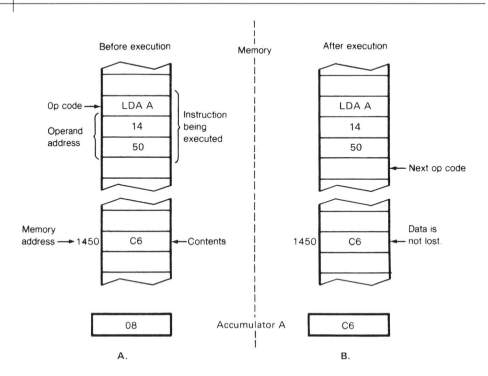

A.   B.

next two types of addressing modes to be discussed—relative and indexed—the final address, which is often called the *effective address*, must be calculated.

5.4.5 | Relative

The relative addressing mode is used by the decision-making instructions for the 6800 μP. These instructions check the condition of a flag bit and branch to a new instruction depending on the logic state of the flip-flop. Therefore, the relative addressing mode for the 6800 μP applies only to its branch instructions.

5.35

Relative addressing mode instructions use two bytes. The first byte is the op code. The second byte is called the *offset*. If the branch is to be taken, then the offset is added to the program counter and the result is the final (or effective) address of the next instruction.

Note: When the offset is added to the program counter, the result of the addition is placed back in the program counter so that the μP begins the program sequence from this new address. If the branch instruction is not taken, then the offset is not added to the program counter and the μP executes the next instruction in the program sequence.

Since the offset is the second byte of the instruction word, it has only 8 bits. Thus, the total range of addresses that can be added to the program counter is 256

FIGURE 5.23 | Memory and Accumulator Contents before and after Execution of Direct Addressing Mode LDA A Instruction

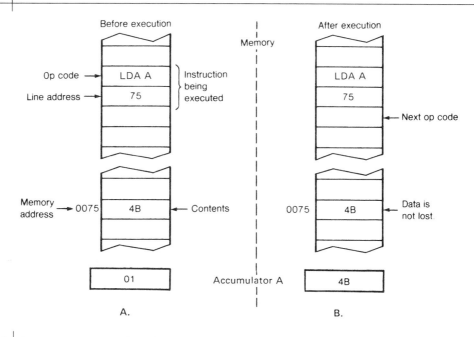

FIGURE 5.24 | Memory and Accumulator Contents before and after Execution of Direct Addressing Mode STA A Instruction

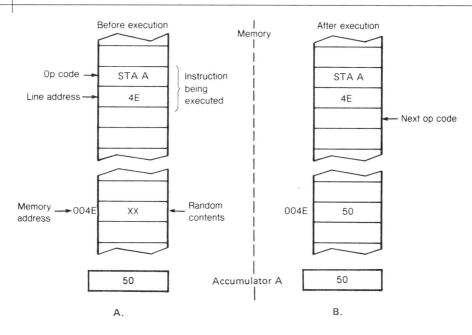

FIGURE 5.25 | Memory and PC Contents before and after Execution of Relative Addressing Mode Branch Instruction

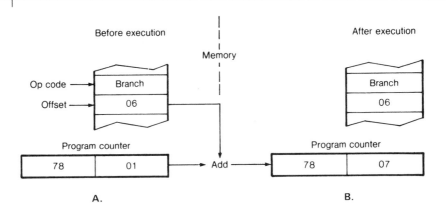

A.   B.

$(2^8 = 256)$. The range includes positive and negative offset values. This range allows the µP to branch forward and backward. All negative offset values are in 2's complement form. The maximum negative offset is -128 (1000 0000), while the maximum positive value is $+127$ (0111 1111). Although this range can be considered a limitation, it has been estimated that it satisfies 80% to 90% of branch applications.

Figure 5.25 shows an example of the relative addressing mode as applied to a branch instruction. If the branch is taken, the second byte (offset) of the instruction is added to the program counter as shown. If the branch is not taken, there is no addition and the program counter will be incremented to 7802.

5.4.6 | Indexed

The indexed addressing mode also involves an addition to obtain the final (or effective) address. Microprocessors have a special register or registers for the purpose of indexing. The 6800 has one 16-bit index register, the X register. Unlike the other types of addressing modes, the indexed addressing mode cannot be used alone, but rather it increases the capabilities of a direct addressing mode. For example, if an LDA A instruction is using an extended indexed addressing mode, the contents of the index register are added to the instruction's second byte. The result is the effective address where the data can be found. The instruction's second byte is called an *offset*. An example is shown in Figure 5.26. Here, the effective address (0107) is found by adding the instruction's offset (04) to the index register (0103). When this instruction is completed, the contents of memory location 0107 will have been moved into the accumulator.

If a µP has an index register, it also contains instructions that load, store, increment, decrement, or transfer data to or from the index register. Therefore, by controlling the contents of the index register with these instructions, the effective address can be controlled. The indexed addressing mode is especially useful in obtaining and operating on a list of data in sequential memory locations.

FIGURE 5.26 | Movement of Data during Execution of an Indexed Addressing Mode LDA A Instruction

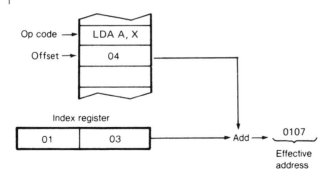

5.5 | INTERRUPTS

Until now, we have seen the μP fetch and execute instructions in a program sequentially. The only method that has been described to change the program sequence is for the μP to execute either a jump or branch instruction. Both of these instructions are capable of changing the contents of the program counter and thus the program sequence. Sometimes the jump and branch instructions are used to allow the μP to execute a subroutine program. Since instructions belong to a μP's software, we can say that the program counter has been changed because of the software. Most μPs include a feature that allows the μP to recognize a signal from an external device, stop the program that is being executed, and jump to a subroutine program. The signal is called an *interrupt signal* or an *interrupt request* because the program has been stopped or interrupted. The subroutine program is called an *interrupt service routine*. The 6800 μP receives this interrupt signal through pin 4. Figure 5.27 shows the steps that occur when a μP receives an interrupt request signal. The μP saves the address on the stack and then jumps to the interrupt subroutine. When the μP executes the return instruction, the return address is removed from the stack and loaded into the program counter. The μP is then able to continue with the program.

Let's consider a reason for incorporating this feature in the μP. If a μP could not receive an interrupt signal, the only way for an external device to signal the μP would be if the program contained a procedure for periodically stopping and checking to see whether or not an external device needed to be serviced. The problem with this technique is that an external event usually occurs asynchronously. That is, the event is not timed with the μP's internal instructions. Therefore, in all likelihood, the event would not coincide with the program, and thus the event would not be sampled until the next time the μP checked the external device. What could happen is that the external event could come and go before the μP had time to check it. Thus, external data and information could be lost. In addition to the possibility of losing data, this sampling technique wastes memory space because the programmer must insert instructions telling the μP what to do and when to do it.

Manufacturers have built into the μP a hardware feature for calling a subroutine

FIGURE 5.27 | Steps That Occur When μP Receives Interrupt Request Signal

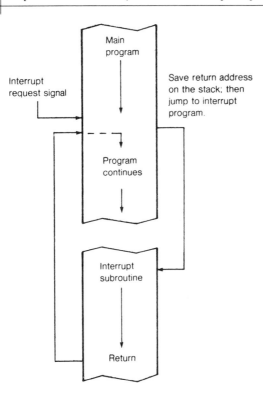

program, and this feature enables the μP to accept an interrupt request signal. This interrupt request signal transfers control of the μP to an I/O device, which, in turn, allows the programmer to write the most efficient program in terms of (1) recognizing an external signal, (2) faster program execution, and (3) overall memory space.

Although most μPs have an interrupt feature, the programmer is not at the mercy of an I/O device. Manufacturers also have included instructions to turn this feature on or off, thus allowing the μP to accept or not to accept an interrupt signal.

Some μPs, like the 6800, have two interrupt pins—*interrupt request* and *nonmaskable interrupt*. Signals on the interrupt request pin can be accepted or not at the programmer's discretion. A signal on the nonmaskable interrupt pin is always received by the μP. This pin would be connected to one device that would signal the μP only when there is an emergency, such as a power failure, an accident, or other catastrophe. In such a situation, the μP would jump to its nonmaskable interrupt service routine and could not be overridden by the programmer. Only a loss of power could stop it. Later chapters will show techniques that allow several I/O devices to use the same interrupt request pin and allow the μP to recognize each device.

5.6 | SUMMARY

In this chapter, we focused on the similarities among μPs in their architecture, instructions, addressing modes, interrupt-handling capability, package style, and pin descriptions. First, we examined the four main architectural parts of a μP: (1) registers, (2) arithmetic and logic unit, (3) timing and control circuitry, and (4) decoding circuitry. A diagram, or programmer's model, illustrated these basic parts. Such a model can help a programmer visualize what happens when an instruction is executed.

Most instructions occupy either one, two, or three bytes of memory. Instructions have two parts, the op code and the operand or operand address. Although each μP has instructions that are unique to it, most μPs have the same basic instruction set. In this text, we have divided a 6800 μP instruction set into eight categories: (1) data movement, (2) arithmetic, (3) logical, (4) compare and test, (5) rotate and shift, (6) program control, (7) stack, and (8) other machine and control instructions.

Addressing modes give an instruction flexibility by allowing the μP to read and write data in a number of different ways. In this chapter, we considered the following addressing modes: inherent, immediate, extended, direct, relative, and indexed.

PROBLEMS

5.1 List the four basic parts of a μP.

5.2 In what register inside the μP is an instruction placed?

5.3 What does the term *instruction set* mean?

5.4 Does the 6800 μP have a stack pointer register?

5.5 How many accumulators does the 6800 μP have?

5.6 What are some of the other names used for the condition code register?

5.7 What are the three most common flag bits?

5.8 What does the abbreviation PC represent?

5.9 Define stack.

5.10 Is the program counter an up-down counter?

5.11 Is the stack pointer an up-down counter?

5.12 What are the two parts of an instruction?

5.13 What part of an instruction tells the μP what to do?

5.14 List the category the following instructions fall into: (a) transfer, (b) add, (c) subtract, (d) compare, (e) push, (f) load accumulator, (g) store accumulator, (h) jump, (i) branch, (j) move data one bit to the right, (k) ANDing, (l) ORing, and (m) clear carry flag.

5.15 If data is moved from an accumulator to memory location 0100, is the data lost in the accumulator?

5.16 Refer to Problem 5.15. Is the accumulator the source or the destination?

5.17 What is the purpose of load instructions?

5.18 What is the purpose of store instructions?

5.19 Given the following registers, show what happens for each operation: (a) transfer B to C, (b) transfer A to B, and (c) exchange A and B.

5.20 Are increment and decrement instructions arithmetic instructions?

5.21 In the process of subtraction, what is the carry flag called?

5.22 If a register contains FF_{hex} and the register is incremented, what are the new contents in the register? Is the carry flag affected?

5.23 Can the 1's complement of a number be obtained by Exclusive ORing it with FF_{hex}?

5.24 What type of instruction usually follows a compare or test instruction?

5.25 What is the advantage of a compare instruction over a subtract instruction?

5.26 If you AND the following register with $0F_{hex}$, what is the result?

5.27 What is the difference between a rotate instruction and a shift instruction?

5.28 What are the two classifications of program control instructions?

5.29 What is that portion of memory called that holds the contents of the program counter when the μP is executing a subroutine program?

5.30 What is the name of the μP register that holds a stack address?

5.31 What is the name of the instruction that stores the contents of a μP register on the stack?

5.32 What is the advantage of addressing modes?

5.33 If the first byte of an instruction is the op code and the second byte is data, what type of addressing mode is being used?

5.34 If the first byte of an instruction is an op code and the second and third bytes are an address, what type of addressing mode is being used?

5.35 What is the second byte of a relative addressing mode called?

5.36 Can the programmer stop the μP from receiving (a) an interrupt request signal and (b) a nonmaskable interrupt signal?

6 | 6800 Microprocessor Instruction Set

6.0 | INTRODUCTION

Chapter 5 introduced instructions that are basic to most µPs and also their addressing modes. This chapter and Chapters 7 and 8 deal specifically with the 6800 µP. This chapter covers its instructions and addressing modes and provides examples that show the flexibility of the instruction set. Chapter 7 employs most of the instructions in a number of commonly used programs. Chapter 8 introduces the hardware aspects of the 6800 µP, such as pin designations, pin functions, and timing diagrams. Thus, Chapters 6 and 7 deal with the 6800 µP's software, while Chapter 8 deals with its hardware. Later chapters show how the 6800 can be connected to memory and peripheral devices.

The 6800 µP has 72 basic instructions. When these instructions are combined with the different addressing modes, the result is a total of 197 different op codes. These op codes comprise the entire instruction set for the 6800 µP. This instruction set gives a programmer enough flexibility to write any program for a dedicated control or a general-purpose µC application.

Chapter 5 briefly introduced some of the 6800 µP architecture and the options contained within it. Sections 6.1 and 6.2 of this chapter cover in more detail the function of the 6800's registers and describe how its condition code register works. These sections can help us visualize what happens within the µP when an instruction is fetched and executed. Since most instructions affect a bit or bits within the condition code register, knowing how the bits are affected will help us understand what the µP will do after it checks one or more of these bits.

Figure 6.1 shows the pin assignments for the 6800 µP. The function of each pin is covered in detail in Chapter 8, so this figure may be used simply for reference in this and the next chapter.

6.1 | 6800 INTERNAL ARCHITECTURE

Figure 6.2 is a functional block diagram that shows the internal architecture of a 6800 µP. The 6800 contains the basic blocks such as the arithmetic and logic unit, instruction

FIGURE 6.1 | Pin Assignments for the 6800 μP (Redrawn from data sheet for MC6800 microprocessor with permission. Motorola Incorporated, Phoenix, Arizona)

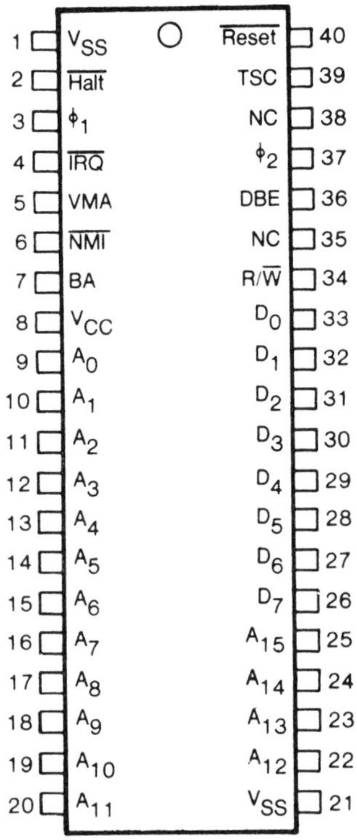

```
   1 □ V_SS        O    Reset □ 40
   2 □ Halt              TSC □ 39
   3 □ φ_1               NC  □ 38
   4 □ IRQ              φ_2  □ 37
   5 □ VMA              DBE  □ 36
   6 □ NMI               NC  □ 35
   7 □ BA              R/W   □ 34
   8 □ V_CC             D_0  □ 33
   9 □ A_0              D_1  □ 32
  10 □ A_1              D_2  □ 31
  11 □ A_2              D_3  □ 30
  12 □ A_3              D_4  □ 29
  13 □ A_4              D_5  □ 28
  14 □ A_5              D_6  □ 27
  15 □ A_6              D_7  □ 26
  16 □ A_7             A_15  □ 25
  17 □ A_8             A_14  □ 24
  18 □ A_9             A_13  □ 23
  19 □ A_10            A_12  □ 22
  20 □ A_11            V_SS  □ 21
```

register, decoding circuitry, timing and control section, address buffers, data buffers, and internal data bus. A major difference between the 6800 and most other μPs is that the 6800 has two accumulators—accumulator A and accumulator B. Both can store the results of arithmetic and logic operations. As we examine the 6800's instruction set, we will see that there are a few functions that can be done only by accumulator A. The 6800 μP has a 16-bit program counter and a 16-bit stack pointer. Since the stack pointer is 16 bits wide, the stack can be located anywhere in read/write memory. There is also a 16-bit index register. The index register is added to an instruction's operand address to calculate the final address where the μP will find the data. The 6800 μP also contains a condition code register, which we will examine in the next section.

6.2 | CONDITION CODE REGISTER

The condition code register (CCR) for the 6800 μP is also called the *program status byte*. The 6800 μP uses 6 bits of the condition code register, as shown in Figure 6.3. Bits 6 and 7 are always set to a logic 1. The carry, overflow, and interrupt flag bits can be set or cleared directly by an instruction as well as by the result of an instruction. The

FIGURE 6.2 | Functional Block Diagram Showing Internal Structure of the 6800 μP (Redrawn from data sheet for MC6800 microprocessor with permission. Motorola Incorporated, Phoenix, Arizona)

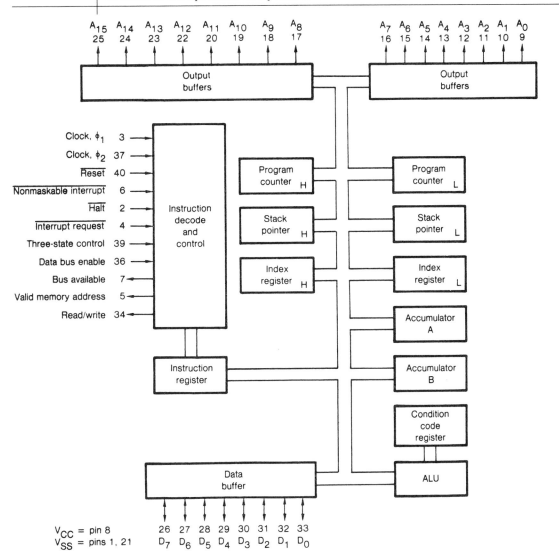

6.4

zero, negative, and half-carry flag bits are set or cleared only by the result of an instruction. Unless indicated otherwise, the results of instructions affect the flag bits in the following ways.

Carry Flag (C Flag): The carry flag bit is set to a logic 1 if there is a carry out of the most significant bit (bit 7) of the result; otherwise, $C = 0$.

FIGURE 6.3 | Condition Code Register for the 6800 μP

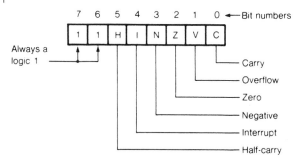

Overflow Flag (V Flag):   The overflow flag is set to a logic 1 if the result exceeds + 127 or − 128; otherwise, V = 0.

Zero Flag (Z Flag):   The zero flag is set to a logic 1 when the result is 0 (that is, each bit of the register or memory location is 0); otherwise, Z = 0. Thus, if the result is 0, then Z = 1.

Negative Flag (N Flag):   If the most significant bit of the result is a logic 1, then N = 1; otherwise, N = 0. The most significant bit of an 8-bit register or memory location is bit 7. The most significant bit of a 16-bit register is bit 15.

Interrupt Flag (I Flag):   The interrupt flag bit enables or disables the interrupt line (pin 4). This flag can be set to a logic 1 either by an external interrupt request signal or by an instruction that will be discussed in Section 6.10. This flag is cleared by a return from interrupt instruction or by a clear interrupt instruction (both of these instructions are covered in later sections).

Half-Carry Flag (H Flag):   The half-carry flag is set to a logic 1 if there is a carry from bit 3 to bit 4 of the result; otherwise, H = 0. This flag bit is only affected by three add instructions—ABA, ADD, and ADC.

6.3 | DATA MOVEMENT INSTRUCTIONS

The 6800 has three groups of instructions that move data from one location to another. They are load instructions, store instructions, and transfer instructions. The load instructions move data from a memory location to a μP register. The store instructions move data from a μP register to a memory location. The transfer instructions move data from one μP register to another.

6.3.1 | Load Instructions

The 6800 μP has three load instructions. In this section, we will consider two of these instructions; the third load instruction is used for the stack pointer and is covered in Section 6.9. The instructions that apply to the accumulator and the index register are as follows:

LDA   Load accumulator
LDX   Load index register

Table 6.1 is a listing of the 6800's load instructions. Since the 6800 has two accumulators (accumulator A and accumulator B), load instructions for both accumulators are listed in Table 6.1 along with their different addressing modes and op codes. The table also shows several examples of specific instructions.

      Load instructions affect the zero flag and the negative flag, as described in Section 6.2. The overflow is always cleared to a logic 0. A brief discussion of each load instruction follows.

LDA   Load Accumulator

The LDA instruction moves the contents of a memory location into either accumulator A or accumulator B. The contents of the memory location are not changed because it is the source location.

LDX   Load Index Register

The index register in the 6800 is 16 bits wide. Therefore, the two bytes of data have to be loaded into the index register. The LDX instruction moves data from two consecutive

| TABLE 6.1 | 6800 Microprocessor Load Instructions with Addressing Modes, Op Codes, and Examples |

Mode	Instruction	Op Code (Hex)	Example	Explanation
Immediate	LDA A #d8	86	LDA A #$07	Load accumulator A immediately with 07_{hex}.
Direct	LDA A a8	96	LDA A $07	Load accumulator A with data at memory location 0007.
Extended	LDA A a16	B6		
Indexed	LDA A d8,X	A6		
Immediate	LDA B #d8	C6		
Direct	LDA B a8	D6		
Extended	LDA B a16	F6	LDA B $80CD	Load accumulator B with data at memory location 80CD.
Indexed	LDA B d8,X	E6	LDA B $58,X	Load accumulator B with data at memory location given by X register + 58_{hex}.
Immediate	LDX #d16	CE	LDX #$1024	Load 1024 into X register, 10_{hex} into X_H and 24_{hex} into X_L.
Direct	LDX a8	DE		
Extended	LDX a16	FE		
Indexed	LDX d8,X	EE		

memory locations to the index register. The first byte of data comes from the memory location specified by the instruction and is loaded into the index register's most significant bits, X_H (bits 15–8). The second byte of data comes from the memory location following that of the first byte and is stored in the index register's least significant bits, X_L (bits 7–0).

6.3.2 | Store Instructions

The 6800 μP has three store instructions. Two of them are covered in this section; the store instruction that applies to the stack pointer is covered in Section 6.9. The instructions covered in this section are as follows:

STA   Store accumulator
STX   Store index register

Table 6.2 provides a listing of the 6800's store instructions with their addressing modes and op codes. Examples of specific instructions are also given in the table. The STA instruction includes store instructions for both accumulator A and accumulator B. Store instructions affect the zero flag and the negative flag, as described in Section 6.2. The overflow flag is always cleared to a logic 0. A brief description of each store instruction follows.

STA   Store Accumulator

The STA instruction stores the contents of an accumulator in a memory location. In this instruction, the accumulator is the source and the memory location is the destination.

TABLE 6.2 | 6800 Microprocessor Store Instructions with Addressing Modes, Op Codes, and Examples

Mode	Instruction	Op Code (Hex)	Example	Explanation
Direct	STA A a8	97	STA A $3A	Store accumulator A at memory location 003A.
Extended	STA A a16	B7		
Indexed	STA A d8,X	A7	STA A $55,X	Store accumulator A at memory location given by X register + 55_{hex}.
Direct	STA B a8	D7		
Extended	STA B a16	F7	STA B $42DC	Store accumulator B at memory location 42DC.
Indexed	STA B d8,X	E7		
Direct	STX a8	DF		
Extended	STX a16	FF	STX $AC45	Store X_H at location AC45; store X_L at location AC46.
Indexed	STX d8,X	EF		

STX   Store Index Register

The STX instruction stores the index register in two consecutive memory locations. The high-order byte, X_H (bits 15–8), is stored in the memory location specified by the instruction. The low-order byte, X_L (bits 7–0), is stored in the next memory location.

6.3.3 | Transfer Instructions

There are six transfer instructions associated with the 6800 µP. Two of these instructions are used for the stack pointer and are covered in Section 6.9, along with the other stack instructions. The remaining four transfer instructions covered in this section are as follows:

TAB   Transfer accumulator A to accumulator B
TBA   Transfer accumulator B to accumulator A
TAP   Transfer accumulator A to condition code register
TPA   Transfer condition code register to accumulator A

Table 6.3 shows these instructions with their op codes. In literature from Motorola, the condition code register is used on block diagrams to indicate the flag register within the µP, but the condition code register is also referred to as the program status byte—hence, the letter P in the mnemonics TAP and TPA.

The four instructions are single bytes and use the inherent addressing mode. The instructions TAB and TBA affect the zero flag and the negative flag, as described in Section 6.2. The overflow flag is always cleared. A brief discussion of all four instructions follows.

TAB   Transfer Accumulator A to Accumulator B

The TAB instruction transfers the contents of accumulator A to accumulator B. In this instruction, accumulator A is the source register and accumulator B is the destination register. Therefore, the contents of accumulator A are not changed, but the previous contents of accumulator B are lost.

TBA   Transfer Accumulator B to Accumulator A

The TBA instruction transfers the contents of accumulator B to accumulator A. In this instruction, accumulator B is the source register and accumulator A is the destination register. Therefore, the contents of accumulator B are not changed, but the previous contents of accumulator A are lost.

TABLE 6.3 | 6800 Microprocessor Transfer Instructions with Their Op Codes

Instruction	Op Code (Hex)
TAB	16
TBA	17
TAP	06
TPA	07

TAP   Transfer Accumulator A to Condition Code Register

The TAP instruction transfers the first 6 bits (bits 5–0) of accumulator A to the first 6 bits (bits 5–0) of the condition code register. When this transfer is executed, bits 6 and 7 of the condition code register are automatically set to a logic 1. This instruction either clears or sets the flag bits according to the data that is being transferred from accumulator A.

TPA   Transfer Condition Code Register to Accumulator A

The TPA instruction transfers the contents of the condition code register to accumulator A. Unlike the TAP instruction, this instruction transfers 8 bits of data from the condition code register to accumulator A. The first 6 bits (bits 5–0) are the flag bits. Bit 6 and bit 7 are each a logic 1.

6.4 | ARITHMETIC INSTRUCTIONS

The 6800 μP has four groups of instructions that we will classify as arithmetic instructions. They are add instructions, subtract instructions, increment instructions, and decrement instructions.

The 6800 μP has three add instructions and three subtract instructions. The 6800 μP can add two 8-bit numbers with or without the carry flag. The two accumulators of the 6800 μP can be added or subtracted.

The increment and decrement instructions add 1 or subtract 1 from a register or memory location. There are three increment and three decrement instructions associated with the 6800 μP. Two of these instructions apply to the stack pointer and will be discussed in Section 6.9.

The 6800 μP can perform addition in either straight binary or in binary coded decimal. To perform a BCD arithmetic operation requires a special instruction following the add instruction. This special instruction, which allows two decimal numbers to be added and the result to be given as a decimal number, is called a *decimal adjust instruction* and is covered in Section 6.10.

6.4.1 | Add Instructions

The 6800 μP has three add instructions:

ABA   Add accumulator A to accumulator B
ADD   Add without carry
ADC   Add with carry

Table 6.4 lists the 6800's add instructions with their addressing modes and op codes. Some specific examples of the ADD instruction and the ADC instruction are also listed in the table.

Each of the add instructions adds two 8-bit numbers in the arithmetic and logic unit and stores the result in an accumulator. The flag bits that are affected are the carry, zero, negative, overflow, and half-carry, as described in Section 6.2. A brief description of the ABA, ADD, and ADC instructions follows.

ABA   Add Accumulator B to Accumulator A

The ABA instruction adds the contents of accumulator B to the contents of accumulator A. The result is placed in accumulator A. The contents of accumulator B are not changed. This instruction does not include the carry flag in the addition. However, the carry flag may be affected by the result of the addition.

TABLE 6.4	6800 Microprocessor Add Instructions with Addressing Modes, Op Codes, and Examples

Mode	Instruction	Op Code (Hex)	Example	Explanation
Implied	ABA	1B		
Immediate	ADD A #d8	8B	ADD A #$50	Add accumulator A + 50_{hex} (result is placed in accumulator A).
Direct	ADD A a8	9B		
Extended	ADD A a16	BB		
Indexed	ADD A d8,X	AB		
Immediate	ADD B #d8	CB		
Direct	ADD B a8	DB		
Extended	ADD B a16	FB	ADD B $0375	Add accumulator B + data at location 0375 (result is placed in accumulator B).
Indexed	ADD B d8,X	EB	ADD B $48,X	Add accumulator B + data at location given by X register + 48_{hex} (result is placed in accumulator B).
Immediate	ADC A #d8	89	ADC A #$32	Add accumulator A + C flag + 32_{hex} (result is placed in accumulator A.)
Direct	ADC A a8	99	ADC A $10	Add accumulator A + C flag + data at location 0010 (result is placed in accumulator A).
Extended	ADC A a16	B9	ADC A $D400	Add accumulator A + C flag + data at location D400 (result is placed in accumulator A).
Indexed	ADC A d8,X	A9		
Immediate	ADC B #d8	C9		
Direct	ADC B a8	D9		
Extended	ADC B a16	F9		
Indexed	ADC B d8,X	E9		

ADD   Add without Carry

The ADD instruction adds the contents of an accumulator (either accumulator A or accumulator B) to the contents of a memory location. If accumulator A is used, the result goes into accumulator A. If accumulator B is used, the result goes into accumulator B. As its name implies, this instruction does not include the carry flag in the addition. The result of the addition, however, may affect the carry flag.

ADC   Add with Carry

The ADC instruction adds the contents of an accumulator (accumulator A or accumulator B) and the contents of a memory location with the carry flag. If the addition uses accumulator A, the result is placed in accumulator A. If the addition uses accumulator B, the result is placed in accumulator B. This instruction is used when a program requires multiprecision addition. Such a program will be presented in the next chapter.

6.4.2 | Subtract Instructions

There are three subtract instructions associated with the 6800 µP. They are as follows:

SBA   Subtract accumulator B from accumulator A
SUB   Subtract
SBC   Subtract with carry

Table 6.5 shows the 6800's subtract instructions with their addressing modes and op codes. Examples of the SUB and SBC instructions are also shown.

Each of the subtract instructions subtracts two 8-bit numbers in the arithmetic and logic unit. Subtraction is performed using 2's complement arithmetic. The flag bits that are affected are the carry, zero, negative, and overflow. The following discussion provides an explanation of how the carry flag is affected for each instruction. The other flag bits are affected as described in Section 6.2.

SBA   Subtract Accumulator B from Accumulator A

The SBA instruction subtracts the contents of accumulator B from accumulator A. The result is placed in accumulator A. This instruction does not involve the carry bit in the process of subtraction. However, the carry bit is affected by the result of the subtraction. The contents of accumulator B are not changed.

The carry bit is affected in the following way: $C = 1$ if the contents of accumulator B are greater than or equal to the contents of accumulator A; $C = 0$ if the contents of accumulator A are greater than the contents of accumulator B.

SUB   Subtract

The SUB instruction subtracts the contents of a memory location from an accumulator (either accumulator A or accumulator B). If accumulator A is used, the result is placed in accumulator A. If accumulator B is used, the result is placed in accumulator B. The carry bit is not included in the subtraction operation, but the result may affect the carry bit in the following way: $C = 1$ if the contents of the memory location are greater than or equal to the contents of the accumulator; $C = 0$ if the contents of the accumulator are greater than the contents of the memory location.

TABLE 6.5 | 6800 Microprocessor Subtract Instructions with Addressing Modes, Op Codes, and Examples

Mode	Instruction	Op Code (Hex)	Example	Explanation
Implied	SBA	10		
Immediate	SUB A #d8	80		
Direct	SUB A a8	90		
Extended	SUB A a16	B0		
Indexed	SUB A d8,X	A0		
Immediate	SUB B #d8	C0	SUB B #$0D	Subtract accumulator B − $0D_{hex}$ (result is placed in accumulator B).
Direct	SUB B a8	D0		
Extended	SUB B a16	F0	SUB B $2E30	Subtract accumulator B − data at location 2E30 (result is placed in accumulator B).
Indexed	SUB B d8,X	E0		
Immediate	SBC A #d8	82	SBC A #$45	Subtract accumulator A − C flag − 45_{hex} (result is placed in accumulator A).
Direct	SBC A a8	92	SBC A $2D	Subtract accumulator A − C flag − data at location 002D (result is placed in accumulator A).
Extended	SBC A a16	B2		
Indexed	SBC A d8,X	A2		
Immediate	SBC B #d8	C2		
Direct	SBC B a8	D2		
Extended	SBC B a16	F2	SBC B $2C80	Subtract accumulator B − C flag − data at location 2C80 (result is placed in accumulator B).
Indexed	SBC B d8,X	E2		

SBC   Subtract with Carry

The SBC instruction subtracts the contents of a memory location and the carry bit from an accumulator (either accumulator A or accumulator B). If the subtraction involves accumulator A, the result is placed in accumulator A. If the subtraction involves accumulator B, the result is placed in accumulator B. The result of the subtraction operation affects the carry bit in the following way: $C = 1$ if the contents of the memory location plus the carry bit are greater than or equal to the contents of the accumulator; $C = 0$ if the contents of the accumulator are greater than the contents of the memory location plus the carry bit.

6.4.3 | Increment Instructions

The 6800 μP has three increment instructions. One instruction involves the stack pointer and is included with the instructions in Section 6.9. The other two instructions are as follows:

INC   Increment
INX   Increment index register

Table 6.6 is a listing of the 6800 μP increment instructions INC and INX. Addressing modes, op codes, and examples are also provided in the table. The INC instruction applies to either accumulator or to a memory location. The contents of a memory location are incremented by a read/modify/write operation, as described in Section 5.3.2.
These increment instructions produce a "roll-over" effect. That is, if a register is all 1s and it is incremented, the result is all 0s and the carry flag is not set. A brief discussion of each increment instruction follows.

INC   Increment

The INC instruction adds 1 to the contents of either accumulator A or accumulator B or to the contents of a memory location. The INC instructions affect the N, Z, and V flags, as explained in Section 6.2.

INX   Increment Index Register

The INX instruction adds 1 to the contents of the index register. The only flag bit affected is the zero flag: Z = 1 if all 16 bits of the index register are cleared to the logic 0 state; otherwise, Z = 0.

6.4.4 | Decrement Instructions

The 6800 μP has three decrement instructions. One instruction involves the stack pointer and is covered in Section 6.9. The instructions covered in this section are the following:

DEC   Decrement
DEX   Decrement index register

TABLE 6.6 | 6800 Microprocessor Increment Instructions with Addressing Modes, Op Codes, and Examples

Mode	Instruction	Op Code (Hex)	Example	Explanation
Implied	INC A	4C		
Implied	INC B	5C	INC B	Add 1 to contents of accumulator B.
Extended	INC a16	7C	INC $507D	Add 1 to contents of memory location 507D.
Indexed	INC d8,X	6C		
Implied	INX	08		

TABLE 6.7 | 6800 Microprocessor Decrement Instructions with Addressing Modes, Op Codes, and Examples

Mode	Instruction	Op Code (Hex)	Example	Explanation
Implied	DEC A	4A	DEC A	Subtract 1 from contents of accumulator A.
Implied	DEC B	5A		
Extended	DEC a16	7A	DEC $1020	Subtract 1 from contents of memory location 1020.
Indexed	DEC d8,X	6A		
Implied	DEX	09		

Table 6.7 is a listing of the 6800's decrement instructions DEC and DEX. Addressing modes, op codes, and examples are also provided in the table. The DEC instruction applies to either accumulator or to a memory location. Like the increment instruction, the decrement instruction produces a roll-over effect. That is, a register that contains all 0s and is decremented produces a result of all 1s, but the carry flag is not affected. A brief description of the decrement instructions follows.

DEC   Decrement

The DEC instruction subtracts 1 from the contents of either accumulator A or accumulator B or from the contents of a memory location. The flag bits that are affected are Z, N, and V. The N and Z flags are explained in Section 6.2. $V = 1$ if the operation produces a 2's complement overflow; otherwise, $V = 0$. A 2's complement overflow occurs if the content of accumulator A, accumulator B, or the memory location is 80_{hex} before the instruction is executed.

DEX   Decrement Index Register

The DEX instruction subtracts 1 from the contents of the index register. The Z flag is the only flag that is affected by this instruction (see Section 6.2).

6.5 | LOGICAL INSTRUCTIONS

Like other μPs, the 6800 μP includes the basic logical instructions AND, OR, and Exclusive OR. This μP also has two other logical instructions: the 1's complement, COM, and the 2's complement, NEG. These instructions apply to both accumulators and to the contents of any memory location. Table 6.8 shows the 6800's logical instructions with their addressing modes and op codes. Specific examples are also shown for several instructions.

For the AND, OR, and Exclusive OR instructions, the flag bits affected are the N and Z flags, as described in Section 6.2. The V flag is always cleared to a logic 0. For the COM and NEG instructions, the flag bits will be discussed later. The five logical instructions are each described in the following discussion.

TABLE 6.8 | 6800 Microprocessor Logical Instructions with Addressing Modes, Op Codes, and Examples

Mode	Instruction	Op Code (Hex)	Example	Explanation
Immediate	AND A #d8	84	AND A #$02	AND accumulator A with 02_{hex} (result is placed in accumulator A).
Direct	AND A a8	94		
Extended	AND A a16	B4		
Indexed	AND d8,X	A4		
Immediate	AND B #d8	C4		
Direct	AND B a8	D4		
Extended	AND B a16	F4	AND B $FFD0	AND accumulator B with data at location FFD0 (result is placed in accumulator B).
Indexed	AND B d8,X	E4	AND B $OF,X	AND accumulator B with data at location given by X register + $0F_{hex}$ (result is placed in accumulator B).
Immediate	ORA A #d8	8A		
Direct	ORA A a8	9A	ORA A $4B	OR accumulator A with data at location 004B (result is placed in accumulator A).
Extended	ORA A a16	BA	ORA A $3F80	OR accumulator A with data at location 3F80 (result is placed in accumulator A).
Indexed	ORA A d8,X	AA		
Immediate	ORA B #d8	CA	ORA B #$47	OR accumulator B with 47_{hex} (result is placed in accumulator B).
Direct	ORA B a8	DA		
Extended	ORA B a16	FA		
Indexed	ORA B d8,X	EA		
Immediate	EOR A #d8	88	EOR A #$FF	Accumulator A is $\oplus$ with FF_{hex} (result is placed in accumulator A).
Direct	EOR A a8	98		
Extended	EOR A a16	B8		
Indexed	EOR A d8,X	A8		
Immediate	EOR B #d8	C8		
Direct	EOR B a8	D8		
Extended	EOR B a16	F8	EOR B $AA10	Accumulator B is $\oplus$ with data at location AA10 (result is placed in accumulator B).

	Mode	Instruction	Op Code (Hex)	Example	Explanation
	Indexed	EOR B d8,X	E8		
	Implied	COM A	43	COM A	Replace contents of accumulator A by their 1's complement.
	Implied	COM B	53		
	Extended	COM a16	73	COM $C400	Replace contents of location C400 by their 1's complement.
	Indexed	COM d8,X	63		
	Implied	NEG A	40		
	Implied	NEG B	50	NEG B	Replace contents of accumulator B by their 2's complement.
	Extended	NEG a16	70		
	Indexed	NEG d8,X	60		

TABLE 6.8 | continued

AND   Logical AND

The AND instruction performs the logical AND operation between each bit of an accumulator and the corresponding bit of a memory location. If the instruction involves accumulator A, the result is placed in accumulator A. If the instruction involves accumulator B, the result is placed in accumulator B.

ORA   Inclusive OR

The ORA instruction performs the logical OR operation between each bit of an accumulator and the corresponding bit of a memory location. The result is placed in accumulator A if the accumulator A instruction is used. The result is placed in accumulator B if the accumulator B instruction is used.

EOR   Exclusive OR

The EOR instruction performs the Exclusive OR operation between each bit of an accumulator and the corresponding bit of a memory location. The result is placed in accumulator A if the A instruction is used. The result is placed in accumulator B if the B instruction is used.

COM   Complement

The COM instruction takes the 1's complement of either accumulator A or accumulator B or of a memory location. Remember, the 1's complement of a binary number is formed when all 1s are changed to 0s and all 0s are changed to 1s. The flag bits affected are N, Z, V, and C. The N and Z flags are explained in Section 6.2. The V flag is always cleared to a logic 0, and the C flag is always set to a logic 1.

NEG   Negative

The NEG instruction converts the contents of either accumulator A or accumulator B or of a memory location to its 2's complement. The flag bits affected are N, Z, V, and C. Refer to Section 6.2 for an explanation of the N and Z flags. $V = 1$ if the contents of the accumulator or of the memory location are 80_{hex} as a result of the execution of this instruction; otherwise, $V = 0$. $C = 1$ if the contents of an accumulator or of a memory location are 00_{hex} as a result of the execution of this instruction; otherwise, $C = 0$.

6.6 | COMPARE AND TEST INSTRUCTIONS

Compare instructions are like subtract instructions, but the result is not put into the accumulator as it is with an ordinary subtract instruction. However, the flag bits are affected by a compare instruction. Compare instructions are used to compare the data in an accumulator with the contents of a memory location and to set or clear the appropriate flag bits. Since the data in the accumulator is not changed, this instruction is a rapid way of checking data between the accumulator and several different memory locations.

In addition to comparing data between an accumulator and a memory location, the 6800 μP instruction set also includes an instruction that allows the two accumulators to be compared. This μP also has an instruction to compare the contents of the index register with the contents of two memory locations.

The test instructions are a group of AND instructions. Again, the result is not stored in an accumulator, but the flag bits are affected. The 6800 μP has two test instructions: a bit test and a test for zero or minus. Table 6.9 is a listing of the 6800's compare and test instructions with their addressing modes and op codes. Specific examples are also listed. The instructions are briefly discussed next.

CBA   Compare Accumulators

The CBA instruction subtracts the contents of accumulator B from the contents of accumulator A. The contents of neither accumulator are affected. This instruction is a single-byte instruction, and the flag bits affected are N, Z, V, and C, as explained in Section 6.2.

CMP   Compare

The CMP instruction subtracts the contents of a memory location from either accumulator A or accumulator B. Neither the memory location nor the accumulator is changed. The flag bits affected are N, Z, V, and C, as described in Section 6.2.

CPX   Compare Index Register

The CPX instruction subtracts the contents of two consecutive memory locations from the index register. Neither the contents of the index register nor the contents of the two memory locations are changed. The contents of the first memory location are subtracted from the index register's most significant byte, X_H (bits 15–8); the contents of the second memory location, from the index register's least significant byte, X_L (bits 7–0).

The flag bits affected are N, Z, and V. $N = 1$ if the most significant bit (bit 15) of the result is a logic 1; otherwise, $N = 0$. $Z = 1$ is all the bits of the result are a

TABLE 6.9 | 6800 Microprocessor Compare and Test Instructions with Addressing Modes, Op Codes, and Examples

Mode	Instruction	Op Code (Hex)	Example	Explanation
Implied	CBA	11		
Immediate	CMP A #d8	81	CMP A #$08	Accumulator A − 08$_{hex}$.
Direct	CMP A a8	91	CMP A $B4	Accumulator A − data at location 00B4.
Extended	CMP A a16	B1		
Indexed	CMP A d8,X	A1		
Immediate	CMP B #d8	C1		
Direct	CMP B a8	D1		
Extended	CMP B a16	F1	CMP B $40A7	Accumulator B − data at location 40A7.
Indexed	CMP B d8,X	E1		
Immediate	CPX #d16	8C	CPX #$1045	X_H − 10$_{hex}$ and X_L − 45$_{hex}$.
Direct	CPX a8	9C		
Extended	CPX a16	BC	CPX $D800	X_H − data at location D800 and X_L − data at location D801.
Indexed	CPX d8,X	AC		
Immediate	BIT A #d8	85	BIT A #$0F	AND accumulator A with 0F$_{hex}$.
Direct	BIT A a8	95		
Extended	BIT A a16	B5	BIT A $48C0	AND accumulator A with data at location 48C0.
Indexed	BIT A d8,X	A5		
Immediate	BIT B #d8	C5		
Direct	BIT B a8	D5		
Extended	BIT B a16	F5		
Indexed	BIT B d8,X	E5		
Implied	TST A	4D	TST A	Determine logic state of Z and N flags according to contents of accumulator A.
Implied	TST B	5D		
Extended	TST a16	7D		
Indexed	TST d8,X	6D		

logic 0; otherwise, Z = 0. V = 1 if the subtraction from the most significant byte causes a 2's complement overflow; otherwise, V = 0.

BIT   Bit Test

The BIT instruction performs the logical AND operation on each bit of an accumulator with the corresponding bit of a memory location. Neither the accumulator nor the contents of the memory location are affected. The N and Z flags are affected, as described in Section 6.2. The V flag is always cleared to a logic 0.

TST   Test (Zero or Minus)

The TST instruction either clears or sets the Z and N flag bits according to the contents of accumulator A, accumulator B, or a memory location. Besides the Z and N flags, the C and V flag bits are always cleared.

6.7 | SHIFT AND ROTATE INSTRUCTIONS

The 6800 μP has five shift and rotate instructions associated with it. They are as follows:

ASL   Arithmetic shift left
ASR   Arithmetic shift right
LSR   Logical shift right
ROL   Rotate left
ROR   Rotate right

Table 6.10 gives the 6800's shift and rotate instructions with their addressing modes and op codes. Some examples of these instructions are also given. Each instruction can be applied to accumulator A, accumulator B, or a memory location. A brief description of the shift and rotate instructions follows.

ASL   Arithmetic Shift Left

The ASL instruction shifts the contents of accumulator A, accumulator B, or a memory location one bit to the left. The most significant bit (bit 7) is transferred to the carry flag. A logic 0 is always loaded into the least significant bit (bit 0). Figure 6.4 illustrates the ASL instruction.

   The flag bits affected are N, Z, V, and C. See Section 6.2 for explanations of the N and Z flags. V = 1 if, after the instruction is executed, either N = 1 and C = 0 or N = 0 and C = 1; otherwise, V = 0. C = 1 if, before the instruction is executed, the most significant bit (bit 7) is a logic 1; otherwise, C = 0.

ASR   Arithmetic Shift Right

The ASR instruction shifts the contents of accumulator A, accumulator B, or a memory location one bit to the right. Bit 0 is transferred to the carry flag. The contents of bit 7 are not changed. Figure 6.5 illustrates the ASR instruction.

   The flag bits affected are N, Z, V, and C. See Section 6.2 for explanations of the N and Z flags. V = 1 if, after this instruction is executed, either N = 1 and C = 0 or N = 0 and C = 1; otherwise, V = 0. C = 1 if, before the instruction is executed, the least significant bit (bit 0) is a logic 1; otherwise, C = 0.

TABLE 6.10 | 6800 Microprocessor Shift and Rotate Instructions with Addressing Modes, Op Codes, and Examples

Mode	Instruction	Op Code (Hex)	Example	Explanation
Implied	ASL A	48		
Implied	ASL B	58	ASL B	Shift contents of accumulator B left one bit.
Extended	ASL a16	78	ASL $60AD	Shift contents of location 60AD left one bit.
Indexed	ASL d8,X	68		
Implied	ASR A	47	ASR A	Shift contents of accumulator A right one bit.
Implied	ASR B	57		
Extended	ASR a16	77		
Indexed	ASR d8,X	67		
Implied	LSR A	44		
Implied	LSR B	54	LSR B	Shift contents of accumulator B right one bit.
Extended	LSR a16	74		
Indexed	LSR d8,X	64		
Implied	ROL A	49		
Implied	ROL B	59		
Extended	ROL a16	79	ROL $17D5	Rotate contents of location 17D5 left one bit.
Indexed	ROL d8,X	69		
Implied	ROR A	46		
Implied	ROR B	56		
Extended	ROR a16	76		
Indexed	ROR d8,X	66	ROR $5F,X	Rotate contents of location given by X register + $5F_{hex}$ right one bit.

FIGURE 6.4 | 6800 μP Arithmetic Shift Left (ASL) Instruction

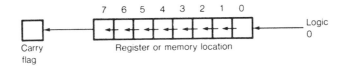

FIGURE 6.5 | 6800 µP Arithmetic Shift Right (ASR) Instruction

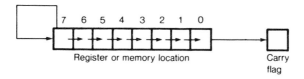

LSR   Logical Shift Right

The LSR instruction shifts the contents of accumulator A, accumulator B, or a memory location one bit to the right. A logic 0 is loaded into bit 7, and bit 0 is shifted into the carry flag, as shown in Figure 6.6.

The flag bits affected are N, Z, V, and C. The Z flag follows the rules given in Section 6.2. The N flag is always cleared to a logic 0. V = 1 if, after this instruction is executed, N = 0 and C = 1, otherwise, V = 0. C = 1 if, before this instruction is executed, the least significant bit (bit 0) is a logic 1; otherwise, C = 0.

ROL   Rotate Left

The ROL instruction shifts the contents of accumulator A, accumulator B, or a memory location one bit to the left. Bit 7 is moved into the carry flag, and the carry flag is moved into bit 0, as shown in Figure 6.7.

The flag bits affected are N, Z, V, and C. See Section 6.2 for explanations of the N and Z flags. V = 1 if, after this instruction is executed, either N = 1 and C = 0 *or* N = 0 and C = 1; otherwise, V = 0. C = 1 if, before the instruction is executed, the most significant bit (bit 7) is a logic 1; otherwise, C = 0.

FIGURE 6.6 | 6800 µP Logical Shift Right (LSR) Instruction

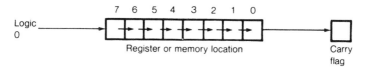

FIGURE 6.7 | 6800 µP Rotate Left (ROL) Instruction

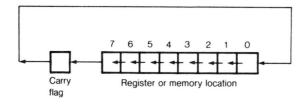

FIGURE 6.8 | 6800 μP Rotate Right (ROR) Instruction

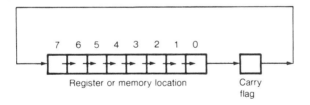

Register or memory location   Carry
                                       flag

ROR   Rotate Right

The ROR instruction shifts the contents of accumulator A, accumulator B, or a memory location one bit to the right. Bit 0 is moved into the carry flag, and the carry flag is moved into bit 7. Figure 6.8 illustrates the ROR instruction.

In addition to the carry flag, the N and Z flags are affected as described in Section 6.2. The V flag is also affected. V = 1 if, after the instruction is executed, either N = 1 and C = 0 *or* N = 0 and C = 1; otherwise, V = 0. C = 1 if, before the instruction is executed, the least significant bit (bit 0) is a logic 1; otherwise, C = 0.

6.8 | PROGRAM CONTROL INSTRUCTIONS

The 6800 μP has three groups of instructions that change the contents of the program counter and thereby change the sequential flow of the program. These instructions are jump, branch, and return instructions. There are two jump instructions, sixteen branch instructions, and two return instructions.

The jump, return, and two of the branch instructions are *unconditional* instructions. That is, these instructions always change the contents of the program counter. The remaining fourteen branch instructions are *conditional* instructions. These instructions first check the logic state of a flag bit or bits: If the condition is true (that is, if the logic state of the flag bit or bits agrees with the instruction), the branch is taken; if not, the program continues in its normal sequence.

The return instructions, as their name implies, are used to return the flow of the program back to the main program. These instructions are used as the last instruction in a subroutine program or as the last instruction in an interrupt program. Let's examine each group of instructions and the instructions that fall within that group.

6.8.1 | Jump Instructions

The two jump instructions in the 6800 μP instruction set are the following:

JMP   Jump
JSR   Jump to subroutine

Although both are unconditional instructions and both change the program counter, the JSR instruction saves a return address on the stack, while the JMP does not save a return

| TABLE 6.11 | 6800 Microprocessor Jump Instructions with Addressing Modes, Op Codes, and Examples |

Mode	Instruction	Op Code (Hex)	Example	Explanation
Extended	JMP a16	7E	JMP $8A50	Program sequence jumps to memory location 8A50.
Indexed	JMP d8,X	6E	JMP $70,X	Program sequence jumps to memory location given by X register + 70_{hex}.
Extended	JSR a16	BD	JSR $AD70	Program sequence jumps to memory location AD70. Return address saved.
Indexed	JSR d8,X	AD		

address. Table 6.11 lists the 6800 µP jump instructions with their addressing modes and op codes. Examples of the instructions are also given in the table.

JMP   Jump

The JMP instruction changes the contents of the program counter to allow the µP to execute a program in another part of memory. No flag bits are affected by this instruction.

JSR   Jump to Subroutine

The JSR instruction changes the contents of the program counter to allow the µP to execute a subroutine program. Before the subroutine is executed, this instruction stores a return address on the stack so that the µP can return to the main program. No flag bits are affected by this instruction.

6.8.2 | Branch Instructions

The 6800 µP has sixteen branch instructions. Two are unconditional and fourteen are conditional instructions. The unconditional branch instructions operate like the jump instructions in that they do not check any flag bits of the condition code register. The conditional branch instructions, however, check the logic state of one or more flag bits: If the condition is true, the branch is taken; otherwise, the program's normal sequence is executed.

All the branch instructions require two bytes of program memory. The first byte is the op code, and the second byte is the offset. Offset values are expressed in 2's complement form, which allows the µP to branch forward +127 and backward −128, the maximum range that can be obtained from eight bits when using 2's complement form.

Note: When an instruction is being executed, the contents of the program counter already contain the address of the next instruction. Therefore, when the offset is added to the program counter, the program counter does not contain the address of the branch instruction; rather, it contains the address of the instruction following the offset.

The two unconditional branch instructions are as follows:

BRA   Branch always
BSR   Branch to subroutine

These instructions are similar to the JMP and JSR instructions, respectively. The BRA instruction is like the JMP instruction using an extended addressing mode. The difference between these two instructions is that the branch instruction is two bytes of program memory and the jump instruction is three bytes. The range of the branch instruction is limited from −127 to +128. The branch instruction always takes one more cycle to execute than the jump instruction, even though it has one less byte of program memory. Therefore, if range is not a problem, the trade-off between these two instructions is memory space for time.

The BSR and JSR instructions are also similar, except that the branch instruction has a limited range, whereas the jump instruction can be directed to any memory location. The BSR instruction requires one less byte of memory than the JSR instruction (two bytes versus three), and the BSR instruction requires one less cycle to execute. Table 6.12 shows the two unconditional branch instructions with their op codes.

BRA   Branch Always

The BRA instruction adds the second byte of the instruction (the offset) to the contents of the program counter. This instruction does not store a return address on the stack. No flag bits are affected.

BSR   Branch to Subroutine

The BSR instruction adds the second byte of the instruction (the offset) to the contents of the program counter. Before the addition is done, the μP stores the contents of the program counter on the stack so that when a return from subroutine instruction is executed, the μP will return to the main program. The steps involved in executing this instruction are as follows:

1. The low-order byte (bits 7–0) of the program counter is stored in memory at the address given by the stack pointer.
2. The stack pointer is decremented by 1.
3. The high-order byte (bits 15–8) of the program counter is stored in memory at the address given by the stack pointer.
4. The stack pointer is again decremented by 1.
5. The offset is added to the program counter.
6. The μP fetches the first op code from the subroutine program.

TABLE 6.12 | 6800 Microprocessor Unconditional Branch Instructions with Their Op Codes

Instruction	Op Code (Hex)
BRA	20
BSR	8D

TABLE 6.13 | 6800 Microprocessor Conditional Branch Instructions with Their Op Codes

Condition(s)	Description	Instruction	Op Code (Hex)
C = 0 and Z = 0	Branch if higher	BHI	22
C = 1 and Z = 1	Branch if lower or same	BLS	23
C = 0	Branch if carry clear	BCC	24
C = 1	Branch if carry set	BCS	25
Z = 0	Branch if not equal to zero	BNE	26
Z = 1	Branch if equal to zero	BEQ	27
V = 0	Branch if overflow clear	BVC	28
V = 1	Branch if overflow set	BVS	29
N = 0	Branch if plus	BPL	2A
N = 1	Branch if minus	BMI	2B
N = 0 and V = 0 or N = 1 and V = 1	Branch if greater than or equal to zero	BGE	2C
N = 0 and V = 1 or N = 1 and V = 0	Branch if less than zero	BLT	2D
Z = 0 and N = 0 and V = 0 or Z = 0 and N = 1 and V = 1	Branch if greater than zero	BGT	2E
Z = 1 or N = 1 and V = 0 or N = 0 and V = 1	Branch if less than or equal to zero	BLE	2F

The 6800 μP can check the logic state of the four flip-flops (the carry, zero, negative, and overflow flags), and it also can check two or more flag bits at the same time. By doing so, the 6800 μP has fourteen conditional branch instructions, which are listed in Table 6.13.

6.8.3 | Return Instructions

The two return instructions for the 6800 μP are as follows:

RTS   Return from subroutine
RTI   Return from interrupt

A subroutine program is executed by the μP when it decodes a JSR instruction or a BSR instruction. An interrupt program is executed by the μP as a result of a high-to-low transition on either the interrupt request pin (IRQ pin, pin 4) or the nonmaskable interrupt pin (NMI pin, pin 6). The difference between the RTS and RTI instructions is the amount of information returned to the μP from the stack. The RTS instruction restores only the program counter. The RTI instruction restores the contents of all the μP registers. Table 6.14 shows the two return instructions with their op codes.

RTS   Return from Subroutine

The RTS instruction is the last instruction in a subroutine program. It restores the contents of the program counter so that the μP returns to the main program. The steps involved when this instruction is executed are as follows:

1. The stack pointer is incremented by 1.
2. The contents of the memory location given by the stack pointer are loaded into the high-order byte (bits 15–8) of the program counter.
3. The stack pointer is again incremented by 1.
4. The contents of the memory location given by the stack pointer are loaded into the low-order byte (bits 7–0) of the program counter.
5. The next instruction is fetched from the main program.

RTI   Return from Interrupt

Before the 6800 μP services an interrupt, it stores the contents of the following μP registers on the stack: the program counter, the index register, accumulator A, accumulator B, and the condition code register. Then the μP jumps to the interrupt program.

When the RTI instruction is executed, the contents of these μP registers are restored to the conditions they had before the interrupt. The memory locations holding the data are given by the stack pointer. The steps involved are as follows:

1. The stack pointer in incremented by 1.
2. The condition code register is returned.
3. The stack pointer is incremented by 1.
4. Accumulator B is returned.
5. The stack pointer is incremented by 1.
6. Accumulator A is returned.
7. The stack pointer is incremented by 1.
8. The high-order byte of the index register is returned.
9. The stack pointer is incremented by 1.
10. The low-order byte of the index register is returned.

TABLE 6.14	6800 Microprocessor Return Instructions with Their Op Codes

Instruction	Op Code (Hex)
RTS	39
RTI	3B

11. The stack pointer is incremented by 1.
12. The high-order byte of the program counter is returned.
13. The stack pointer is incremented by 1.
14. The low-order byte of the program counter is returned.
15. The μP fetches the next instruction from memory, using the returned address from the program counter.

6.9 | STACK/STACK POINTER INSTRUCTIONS

The stack pointer in the 6800 μP is 16 bits wide, which allows the programmer to have the stack located anywhere in read/write memory. There are six instructions that affect the stack pointer. They are load, store, increment, decrement, and two transfer instructions. There are also two instructions that move data between the μP and the stack. Table 6.15 shows the stack/stack pointer instructions, their addressing modes and op codes, and some examples. Now let's examine each instruction.

TABLE 6.15 | 6800 Microprocessor Stack/Stack Pointer Instructions with Addressing Modes, Op Codes, and Examples

Mode	Instruction	Op Code (Hex)	Example	Explanation
Immediate	LDS #d16	8E	LDS #$12A7	Load S_H with 12_{hex} and S_L with $A7_{hex}$.
Direct	LDS a8	9E		
Extended	LDS a16	BE		
Indexed	LDS d8,X	AE		
Direct	STS a8	9F		
Extended	STS a16	BF	STS $BF00	Store S_H at location BF00 and S_L at location BF01.
Indexed	STS d8,X	AF		
Implied	INS	31		
Implied	DES	34		
Implied	TSX	30		
Implied	TXS	35		
Implied	PSH A	36	PSH A	Put contents of accumulator A onto stack at address given by stack pointer.
Implied	PSH B	37		
Implied	PUL A	32	PUL A	Place contents of stack, at memory location given by incremented stack pointer, in accumulator A.
Implied	PUL B	33		

LDS   Load Stack Pointer

The LDS instruction moves data from memory to the stack pointer. Since the stack pointer is 16 bits wide, two bytes of data are transferred from memory to the stack pointer. These two bytes of data must be in consecutive memory locations. The first memory location contains the stack pointer's most significant byte, S_H (bits 5–8). The second memory location contains the stack pointer's least significant byte, S_L (bits 7–0).

The flag bits affected are N, Z, and V. N = 1 if the most significant bit (bit 15) of the stack pointer is a logic 1; otherwise, N = 0. Z = 1 if all bits of the stack pointer are a logic 0; otherwise, Z = 0. The V flag is always cleared by this instruction, so V = 0.

STS   Store Stack Pointer

The STS instruction stores the stack pointer in two consecutive memory locations. The most significant byte of the stack pointer, S_H, is stored in the first memory location. The least significant byte of the stack pointer, S_L, is stored in the second memory location.

The flag bits affected are N, Z, and V. N = 1 if the most significant bit (bit 15) of the stack pointer is a logic 1; otherwise, N = 0. Z = 1 if all bits of the stack pointer are a logic 0; otherwise, Z = 0. The V flag is always cleared by this instruction, so V = 0.

INS   Increment Stack Pointer

The INS instruction adds 1 to the stack pointer. Like other increment instructions, this instruction produces a roll-over effect. This instruction affects no flag bits.

DES   Decrement Stack Pointer

The DES instruction subtracts 1 from the stack pointer. Like the increment instruction, this instruction produces a roll-over effect. It does not affect any flag bits.

TSX   Transfer from Stack Pointer to Index Register

The TSX instruction transfers the contents of the stack pointer plus 1 to the index register. The contents of the stack pointer remain unchanged. This instruction allows the index register to hold the address of the last data byte put onto the stack. No flag bits are affected.

TXS   Transfer from Index Register to Stack Pointer

This TXS instruction transfers the contents of the index register minus 1 to the stack pointer. The contents of the index register remain unchanged. This instruction causes the stack pointer to operate correctly when data is pulled from the stack because, before data is removed from the stack, the stack pointer is incremented by 1. No flag bits are affected by this instruction.

PSH   Push Data onto Stack

The PSH instruction stores the contents of either accumulator A or accumulator B on the stack. The memory location at which the data is stored is given by the stack pointer. The stack pointer is then decremented by 1. The contents of the accumulator are not changed. This instruction affects no flag bits.

PUL   Pull Data from Stack

The PUL instruction increments the stack pointer by 1 and then loads either accumulator A or accumulator B with the data at the memory location given by the stack pointer. This instruction affects no flag bits.

6.10 | OTHER 6800 MICROPROCESSOR INSTRUCTIONS

In this section, we will look at condition code register instructions, two interrupt instructions, a decimal adjust instruction, a no operation instruction, and several clear instructions. These instructions and their op codes are listed in Tables 6.16 and 6.17.

6.10.1 | Condition Code Register Instructions

In Section 6.3, we discussed two transfer instructions that involve the condition code register: the TAP and TPA instructions. These instructions transfer accumulator A to the condition code register and transfer the condition code register to accumulator A, respectively. Table 6.16 lists four instructions that either set or clear an individual bit of the condition code register. All of these instructions are one-byte instructions and affect no flag bits other than the one they clear or set, as shown in Table 6.16.

Table 6.16 also shows that the interrupt flag bit can either be cleared or set, which allows the μP either to acknowledge or not to acknowledge an interrupt signal on the interrupt request pin (pin 4). The SET instruction is used, for example, when a portion of the program is of such high priority that the programmer does not wish the μP to recognize an interrupt signal. Then the SEI instruction is used at the beginning of the program. At the end of this priority program, the CLI instruction must be used; otherwise, the μP will still keep the interrupt flip-flop set and will not recognize an interrupt signal. The CLI instruction is also used, for example, after the μP has recognized an interrupt signal. Then the interrupt bit is automatically set and remains set until a return from

TABLE 6.16 | Other 6800 Microprocessor Instructions

Description	Instruction	Op Code (Hex)	Result
Clear overflow	CLV	0A	V = 0
Set overflow	SEV	0B	V = 1
Clear carry	CLC	0C	C = 0
Set carry	SEC	0D	C = 1
Clear interrupt mask	CLI	0E	I = 0
Set interrupt mask	SEI	0F	I = 1
Software interrupt	SWI	3F	
Wait for interrupt	WAI	3E	
Decimal adjust accumulator	DAA	19	
No operation	NOP	01	

TABLE 6.17	6800 Microprocessor Clear Instructions with Addressing Modes, Op Codes, and Examples

Mode	Instruction	Op Code (Hex)	Example	Explanation
Implied	CLR A	4F	CLR A	Clear accumulator A.
Implied	CLR B	5F		
Extended	CLR a16	7F		
Indexed	CLR d8,X	6F	CLR $18,X	Clear location given by X register + 18_{hex}.

interrupt (RTI) instruction is executed. However, even when an interrupt program is being executed, the user may wish the μP to be able to recognize another interrupt signal. For this type of application, one of the first instructions in the interrupt program that is being executed would be a CLI instruction.

6.10.2 Interrupt Instructions

The 6800 μP contains two interrupt instructions. They are listed in Table 6.16 with their op codes and are as follows:

SWI   Software interrupt
WAI   Wait for interrupt

These instructions allow the programmer to execute the interrupt program. The first instruction executes the interrupt program after the instruction is decoded. The second instruction places the μP in a wait state, and no instruction is executed until an interrupt signal is received by the μP on either the interrupt request pin (pin 4) or the nonmaskable interrupt pin (pin 6). Let's examine what happens when each instruction is decoded.

SWI   Software Interrupt

The following steps are executed by the μP when the SWI instruction is decoded:

1. The program counter, the index register, accumulator A, accumulator B, and the condition code register are stored on the stack.
2. The interrupt mask bit is set (I = 1).
3. The program counter is loaded with the data contained at memory locations FFFA and FFFB. The contents of memory location FFFA are loaded into the high-order byte of the program counter, and the contents of memory location FFFB are loaded into the low-order byte of the program counter.
4. The μP fetches the first instruction from the interrupt program. The last instruction from this interrupt program must be an RTI instruction so that the μP can return to its place in the main program and all the μP's registers can return to their original states.

Only the interrupt flag bit is affected (I = 1). The μP will recognize this instruction and execute the software interrupt program even if the interrupt flag bit is a logic 1.

WAI   Wait for Interrupt

When the WAI instruction is decoded, the μP executes the following steps:

1. The program counter, the index register, accumulator B, accumulator A, and the condition code register are stored on the stack.
2. The μP is placed in a wait loop until an interrupt signal is acknowledged. The μP can recognize an interrupt signal only if the interrupt flag bit is a logic 0.
3. If an $\overline{IRQ}$ signal is received, the I bit is set, and the program counter is loaded with the data contained at memory locations FFF8 and FFF9.
4. If an $\overline{NMI}$ signal is received, the I bit is set, and the program counter is loaded with the data contained at memory locations FFFC and FFFD.

If the μP is to be returned to the main program, an RTI instruction must be executed. This instruction restores all the μP registers to their original states. The only flag bit that is affected by this instruction is the interrupt bit. Since the I flag is set to a logic 1 when an interrupt occurs, the I bit is cleared to a logic 0 when the μP executes an RTI instruction.

A flowchart showing how the interrupt instructions work for the 6800 μP is given in the Appendix.

6.10.3 | Other Instructions

The 6800 μP instruction set also includes a decimal adjust instruction, a no operation instruction, and several clear instructions. These instructions are shown in Tables 6.16 and 6.17 with their op codes. A brief description of each instruction follows.

DAA   Decimal Adjust Accumulator

The DAA instruction is used in BCD addition to adjust the binary answer. It is used following an ABA, ADD, or ADC instruction. The numbers that are being added must be BCD values and not hexadecimal values.

NOP   No Operation

The NOP instruction causes the μP to go to the next instruction in sequence. No flag bits are affected.

CLR   Clear

The CLR instruction replaces the present contents of accumulator A, accumulator B, or a memory location with logic 0s. The N, V, and C flags are cleared. The Z flag is set.

6.11 | SUMMARY

This chapter grouped similar types of instructions for the 6800 μP together, as was done in Chapter 5. However, when we are writing a program and want to check (1) how an instruction works, (2) its op code, (3) its addressing mode, (4) how long it takes to execute, or (5) what flag bits are affected, a reference table is the easiest way to find the answer. Therefore, the 6800's instructions are summarized in such a table in the Appendix.

This chapter began with the 6800 μP pin assignments and internal architecture. Like many other μPs, the 6800 contains a program counter, stack pointer, index register, condition code register, and instruction register, along with the necessary buffers, latches, and control circuitry. Unlike most other μPs, however, the 6800 has two accumulators: accumulator A and accumulator B. Two accumulators give the programmer the flexibility of storing the results of an ALU operation in either accumulator. The condition code register (also called the program status register or the flag register) is the record-keeping register. There are six bits in the condition code register that are set or cleared as a result of an instruction—hence, the name record-keeping register.

In this chapter, we examined the 6800's instruction set, including the data movement, arithmetic, logical, compare and test, shift and rotate, program control, and stack/stack pointer instructions. Op codes and addressing modes were given for most of these instructions, and specific examples were provided to show the flexibility and comprehensiveness of the 6800's instruction set. The next chapter shows how these instructions are used to write programs.

PROBLEMS

All of the following problems apply to the 6800 μP.

6.1   How many basic instructions are there in the 6800 instruction set?

6.2   What is a major difference between the 6800 μP's internal architecture and the internal architecture of most other μPs?

6.3   How many 16-bit registers are there in the 6800 μP? Name them.

6.4   Name the flag bits in the 6800's condition code register.

6.5   If the result of a subtract instruction is zero, will the zero flag bit be cleared to a logic 0 or set to a logic 1?

6.6   Name the three groups of data movement instructions in the 6800 instruction set.

6.7   Explain what happens when each of the following instructions is executed (data and address values given in hex): (a) LDA A #$04; (b) LDA A $F800; (c) LDA B $50; (d) LDX #$01FF; (e) STA A $0240; (f) STA B $07,X; (g) STX $C000; (h) TBA; and (i) TPA.

6.8   What are three add instructions for the 6800 μP?

6.9   Explain the function of each of the following instructions: (a) ABA; (b) ADD A #$03; (c) ADD B $0200; (d) ADC A $15; (e) SUB A #$10; (f) SBC B #$08,X; (g) INC A; (h) INC $0150; (i) DEC B; and (j) DEX.

6.10 What are the logical instructions in the 6800 μP's instruction set?

6.11 If data from memory location 0300 is ANDed with the contents of accumulator A, where is the result stored?

6.12 Can accumulator A be ANDed with accumulator B by one instruction?

6.13 Do all of the logical operations have indexed addressing mode capability?

6.14 What flag bits are affected by the 1's complement instruction?

6.15 What flag bits are affected by the compare accumulator's instruction?

6.16 Explain what happens when each of the following instructions is executed (data and address values given in hex): (a) CMP A $57A2; (b) CMP B #$14; and (c) CPX $20.

6.17 What flag bits are affected by (a) the BIT instruction and (b) the TST instruction?

6.18 Explain what the following instructions accomplish when executed: (a) BIT A #$01; (b) TST A; (c) BIT A $4000; and (d) TST $4000.

6.19 List the five shift and rotate instructions that are in the 6800 μP instruction set.

6.20 What is the difference between the logical shift right instruction and the arithmetic shift right instruction?

6.21 Can any RAM memory location be rotated one bit to the right?

6.22 Can any ROM memory location be rotated one bit to the right?

6.23 Is the instruction ROL $0055 a read/modify/write instruction if location 0055 is in RAM?

6.24 Does the 6800 μP have an unconditional branch instruction? If your answer is yes, what are the instructions?

6.25 How many branch instructions are there in the 6800 μP instruction set?

6.26 What is the difference between the JMP instruction and the JSR instruction?

6.27 Are both the JMP and the JSR instructions unconditional instructions?

6.28 Do jump instructions have offset values?

6.29 With the JMP instruction, can the μP jump to any location in memory?

6.30 Repeat Problem 6.29 for the JSR instruction.

6.31 What is the range that a branch instruction can take?

6.32 What is the (a) advantage and (b) disadvantage of the BSR instruction over the JSR instruction?

6.33 How many conditional branch instructions are there in the 6800's instruction set?

6.34 Given the following condition of the condition code register, determine whether the branch would be taken for the following instructions: (a) BHI, (b) BCC, (c) BNE, (d) BVS, (e) BLT, and (f) BLE.

H	I	N	Z	V	C
X	X	0	1	0	1	1	0

6.35 What is the first step that the μP does after an RTS instruction is decoded?

6.36 What μP registers are returned from the stack when the 6800 μP executes an RTI instruction?

6.37 Name the instruction that affects the stack pointer.

6.38 List the different ways in which the data in the condition code register is saved on the stack.

7 | 6800 Microprocessor Programs

7.0 | INTRODUCTION

In this chapter, we will use the 6800 μP's instructions to write some commonly used programs. These programs include binary and decimal addition, binary and decimal subtraction, adding a column of numbers, checking memory for a particular value, clearing memory, transferring blocks of data between sections of memory, using the stack, using time delays, converting binary to BCD, and multiplication. These programs can be used as a basis for longer and more complex programs. The programs are written by using the 6800 mnemonics and an assembly language format. All data and addresses are given in hexadecimal code and are prefaced with a $ symbol. The first column is reserved for labels, the second column is for instructions, and the third column is for comments about the instructions. Keep in mind that the programs are general and are written to show different 6800 instructions. Also, remember that there is no unique way of writing a program, and many of these programs could have been written with fewer steps.

7.1 | ADDITION AND SUBTRACTION

In nearly every long program, there is an addition or subtraction program. Sometimes, only two 8-bit numbers are involved—single-byte operation—and in other programs multiprecision addition or subtraction is needed. The 6800 can be programmed to do both binary and decimal addition or subtraction. Remember, subtraction is done by using 2's complement arithmetic. However, the programmer does not have to worry about obtaining the 2's complement of a number; that is done automatically by the μP in the arithmetic and logic unit whenever a subtraction instruction is decoded. If the result of a subtraction is negative, the answer is in 2's complement form.

7.1.1 | Single-Byte Binary Addition

Adding two 8-bit numbers can be done in one of three ways in the 6800 μP: (1) Load accumulator A with one number and add to it a number from a memory location; (2) load accumulator B with one number and add to it another number from a memory location; or (3) add the contents of accumulator A to accumulator B. In any of the three cases, if we wish to save the result, then we must use a store instruction and move the data from an accumulator to a memory location.

Remember that augend, addend, and sum are the arithmetic terms commonly used in the process of addition. The number placed in the accumulator is the *augend*, and the number that is added to it is the *addend*. The result is the *sum*. When accumulator A and accumulator B are added, accumulator A holds the augend and accumulator B holds the addend; the sum goes into accumulator A.

The program in Example 7.1 shows single-byte addition. In the program, the data has already been stored at memory locations 0400 and 0500.

EXAMPLE

7.1 | Add the contents of memory location $0400 to the contents of memory location $0500. Store the result at memory location $0600. Use accumulator A for the addition.

Solution:

LDA A $0400	Load accumulator A with data from location $0400.
ADD A $0500	Add accumulator A + data from location $0500.
STA A $0600	Store result at location $0600.

The program in Example 7.1 does not include the carry flag in the addition. However, the result does affect the carry flag, and it is possible that the carry flag was set. If there is a carry from the most significant bit, and if we wish to save it, then additional programing steps are needed, as shown in Example 7.2.

EXAMPLE

7.2 | Repeat Example 7.1, but this time save the carry flag at memory location $0601. The carry flag should be in the least significant bit, and all other bits of location $0601 should be a logic 0.

Solution:

LDA A $0400	Load accumulator A with data from location $0400.
ADD A $0500	Add accumulator A + data from location $0500.
STA A $0600	Store result.
LDA A #$00	Clear accumulator A.
ROL A	Rotate carry flag into LSB of accumulator A.
STA A $0601	Store accumulator A (carry flag).

Remember that the symbol # stands for the immediate addressing mode.

7.1.2 | Double-Precision Addition

Double-precision addition means adding two 16-bit numbers. In the 6800 μP, this procedure requires adding the first two 8-bit numbers and storing the result, then adding the next two 8-bit numbers and storing the result. The following binary numbers show which bits are being added:

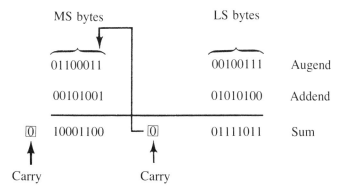

Double-precision addition requires use of the ADC instruction, because a carry from the least significant (LS) bytes must be brought forward to the most significant (MS) bytes. The program in Example 7.3 illustrates double-precision addition and the use of the ADC instruction.

Add the data at locations $0400 and $0401 to the data at locations $0500 and $0501. Store the result at locations $0600 and $0601. Use accumulator B for the addition.

Solution:

LDA B $0400	Load LS byte.
ADD B $0500	Add accumulator B + data from memory.
STA B $0600	Store result at location $0600.
LDA B $0401	Load MS byte.
ADC B $0501	Add accumulator B + carry + memory.
STA B $0601	Store result at location $0601.

The program in Example 7.3 does not save the carry flag from the most significant bytes. Example 7.2 shows the programming steps that should be included to save the carry flag in another memory location such as $0602.

7.1.3 | Multiprecision Addition

A multiprecision addition is one in which more than 8 bits are added. Therefore, double-precision addition is actually a multiprecision addition. The term *multi-* is most often applied to addition programs where more than 16 bits have to be added.

Example 7.4 shows how any number of bytes can be added. In writing a multi-precision addition program, we load one of the accumulators with a count equal to the number of times an 8-bit addition has to be performed, and we use the other accumulator for the actual addition. The program in Example 7.4 uses the index register as a pointer to memory for the augend values, addend values, and sum. The index register has to be temporarily stored in memory (page 0), because the index register is being used to hold different pointers to memory at different times, and we do not want to lose the old value. In this program, all the addend values will be lost, but this loss commonly occurs in multiprecision addition programs.

EXAMPLE

7.4

Write a multiprecision addition program that adds data in memory beginning at location $0400 to data in memory beginning at location $0500. Store the result in memory, beginning at location $0500. Use accumulator B to keep the count. Use memory locations $0020 and $0030 as temporary storage locations for the index register.

Solution:

```
                LDS  #$0400        Initialize X index register.
                STX  $20           Temporary storage 1 (location $0020).
                LDX  #$0500        Initialize X index register.
                STX  $30           Temporary storage 2 (location $0030).
                CLC                Clear carry flag.
                LDA B count        Load accumulator B with count.
MULTAD:  LDX  $20           Reload X register from temporary storage 1.
                LDA A $00,X        Load accumulator A, using X register.
                INX                Increment X register.
                STX  $20           Restore X register at temporary storage 1.
                LDX  $30           Load X register from temporary storage 2.
                ADC A $00,X        Add accumulator A + carry + memory.
                STA A $00,X        Store accumulator A, using X register.
                INX                Increment X register.
                STX  $30           Restore X register at temporary storage 2.
                DEC B              Decrement count.
                BNE MULTAD         If count ≠ 0, go to MULTAD.
                RTS                Return from subroutine.
```

The program in Example 7.4 is written so that any count can be loaded into accumulator B. If we were doing a double-precision addition, the count would be 2. If we were adding 32 bits (4 bytes), the count would be 4. Thus, the count value equals the number of bytes being added.

7.1.4 │ BCD Addition

The 6800 μP is capable of adding binary coded decimal numbers and producing a BCD result. The 6800 μP has a decimal adjust (DAA) instruction. This instruction applies only to accumulator A. Therefore, the addition should be done in accumulator A. If the addition is done in accumulator B, the result has to be transferred to accumulator A, and then the decimal adjust instruction is executed. Remember, when we do BCD addition, all numbers must be valid BCD numbers, and one byte contains two BCD numbers.

Examples 7.5, 7.6, and 7.7 show how Examples 7.1, 7.3, and 7.4 can be modified to do BCD addition. In the programs, all numbers coming from memory are valid BCD numbers. If the data coming from memory were not in a BCD format, then we would first have to do a binary-to-BCD conversion.

EXAMPLE	
7.5	Repeat Example 7.1 for BCD addition.

Solution:

LDA A $0400	Load accumulator A with data from location $0400.
ADD A $0500	Add accumulator A + data from location $0500.
DAA	Decimal adjust.
STA A $0600	Store result at location $0600.

EXAMPLE	
7.6	Modify the double-precision binary addition program of Example 7.3 to perform BCD addition.

Solution:
Since Example 7.3 used accumulator B for addition, and since the DAA instruction applies only to accumulator A, then the addition should be done in accumulator A.

LDA A $0400	Load LS byte.
ADD A $0500	Add accumulator A + data from memory.
DAA	Decimal adjust LS byte.
STA A $0600	Store result at location $0600.
LDA A $0401	Load MS byte.
ADC A $0501	Add accumulator A + carry + memory.
DAA	Decimal adjust MS byte.
STA A $0601	Store result at location $0601.

Note: The decimal adjust instruction has to be included after every addition instruction.

EXAMPLE	
7.7	What programming steps must be added to the multiprecision binary addition program of Example 7.4 to make it a multiprecision BCD program?

Solution:
Include the DAA instruction after the ADC A $00,X instruction, as shown below:

.
.
.

```
ADC A $00,X
DAA                    Decimal adjust.
STA A $00,X
```

.
.
.

7.1.5 | Single-Byte Binary Subtraction

As we saw in the previous chapter, the 6800 μP can do subtraction with and without the borrow bit (carry flag). The programs in Examples 7.8 and 7.9 use both instructions. As in addition, the 6800 μP can do three types of 8-bit subtraction. They are (1) subtract the contents of a memory location from accumulator A, (2) subtract the contents of a memory location from accumulator B, and (3) subtract accumulator B from accumulator A. The arithmetic terms commonly used in subtraction are *minuend*, the number in the accumulator; *subtrahend*, the number coming from the memory location; and *difference*, the answer. When accumulator B is subtracted from accumulator A, accumulator A holds the minuend and accumulator B holds the subtrahend. The difference is placed in accumulator A.

Remember that subtraction is done by 2's complement arithmetic. The arithmetic and logic unit automatically generates the 2's complement of the subtrahend. Example 7.8 illustrates binary subtraction.

EXAMPLE

7.8 | Subtract the contents of memory location $0850 from the contents of memory location $0800. Place the result in memory location $0900. Use accumulator A for the subtraction.

Solution:

```
LDA A $0800        Load accumulator A with minuend.
SUB A $0850        Subtract subtrahend.
STA A $0900        Store result.
```

7.1.6 | Double-Precision Binary Subtraction

Double-precision binary subtraction involves subtracting one 16-bit number (two bytes) from another. Since the 6800 μP can only do one 8-bit subtraction at one time, the subtract instruction has to be used twice. In the first subtraction, one of the least significant bytes is subtracted from the other and the result is stored. Then one of the most significant bytes is subtracted from the other and the result is stored. This procedure is similar to the procedure in double-precision binary addition.

The program in Example 7.9 shows how a loop can be set up so that the least significant bytes can be subtracted and the results stored, and then the most significant bytes can be subtracted and the results stored. This program requires the use of the index X register and a counter.

EXAMPLE	

7.9 Subtract the contents of memory locations $0020 and $0021 from the contents of memory locations $0010 and $0011. Store the result at memory locations $0050 and $0051. Use accumulator A for the subtraction, and use accumulator B as a counter.

Solution:

```
        LDX #$0000      Initialize X register with all 0s.
        LDA B #$02      Initialize accumulator B with count = 2.
        CLC             Clear carry flag.
SUBT:   LDA A $10,X     Load minuend from location $0010,X.
        SBC A $20,X     Subtract subtrahend (location $0020,X).
        STA A $50,X     Store difference at $0050,X.
        INX             Increment X register.
        DEC B           Decrement accumulator B.
        BNE SUBT        If B ≠ 0, branch to SUBT.
```

The program in Example 7.9 can be changed to a multiprecision binary subtraction by changing the count in accumulator B. The value of the count equals the number of bytes to be subtracted.

7.1.7 | Decimal Subtraction

The DAA instruction permits the 6800 μP to do decimal addition. For decimal subtraction, complements must be used. In the procedure for decimal subtraction using the 6800 μP, we first obtain the 99's complement of the subtrahend, and then we add the result to the minuend plus the carry flag. In a one-byte subtraction, the carry flag is set once; in a multibyte subtraction, the carry flag is set before the first addition. The DAA instruction follows the addition so that the answer will be the correct decimal number.

The following steps show how a multibyte decimal subtraction can be done by using the 6800 μP:

1. Initialize the index register to 0.
2. Initialize a counter to the number of bytes to be subtracted.
3. Load the accumulator with 99_{hex} (this value represents the decimal number 99).
4. Subtract the subtrahend from the accumulator (this step generates the 99's complement).
5. Temporarily store the 99's complement in memory.
6. If the 99's complement of each byte of the subtrahend has been obtained, go on. Otherwise, go back to step 3.

7. Reinitialize the index register.
8. Reinitialize the counter.
9. Set the carry flag to a logic 1.
10. Load the first byte of the minuend.
11. Add the minuend plus the carry flag plus the first byte of the 99's complement of the subtrahend.
12. Decimal adjust the answer.
13. Store the result.
14. If each byte of the minuend, the carry flag, and the 99's complement of the subtrahend has been added, the program is complete. Otherwise, go back to step 10.

Steps 1–14 show that each byte of the subtrahend is complemented, before any addition is done, so the 6800 μP programmer may use the index register. However, temporary storage of the 99's complement values is required.

Example 7.10 shows a multibyte decimal subtraction program using steps 1–14. As each byte of the subtrahend is complemented, it is stored in the memory location from which it came. Thus, the original subtrahend bytes are lost. If we wish to keep the original subtrahend values, we must choose another area of memory for temporary storage of the complemented values.

EXAMPLE

7.10 | Write a multibyte decimal subtraction subroutine program, using accumulator A for the subtraction and addition operations and using accumulator B as a counter. The subtrahend values begin at memory location $0010, and the minuend values begin at memory location $0020. Use the subtrahend area of memory for temporary storage and for the final answer.

Solution:

LDX #$0000	Initialize index register with all 0s.
LDA B # count	Use accumulator B as a counter.
COMP: LDA A #$99	Initialize accumulator A for 99's complement.
SUB A $10,X	Find 99's complement of subtrahend.
STA A $10,X	Store 99's complement temporarily.
INX	Increment index register.
DEC B	Decrement accumulator B.
BNE COMP	If B ≠ 0, branch to COMP.
LDX #$0000	Reinitialize index register.
LDA B # count	Reinitialize counter.
SEC	Set carry flag.
SUBT: LDA A $20,X	Load minuend.
ADC A $10,X	Add accumulator A + carry + 99's complement.
DAA	Decimal adjust.
STA A $10,X	Store result at location $0010,X.

INX	Increment index register.
DEC B	Decrement counter.
BNE SUBT	If B ≠ 0, branch to SUBT.
RTS	Return from subroutine.

In the program in Example 7.10, the count value is set to the number of bytes that have to be subtracted. For example, for a double-precision decimal subtraction (two bytes), the count value equals 2.

7.2 | TIME DELAYS

A program can be written so that the μP serves as a timer for control applications, for sending or receiving data, for generating waveforms, for polling peripheral devices at specified times, or for any other application in which the μP operates too fast for peripheral equipment to respond to it. Such programs are called time delays, timing loops, or delay generation.

All time delay programs have the μP repeat a set of instructions. Since each instruction requires a certain amount of time for execution, a time delay can be generated. If the μP executes the same set of instructions, a time delay loop is created, as shown in the flowchart in Figure 7.1. A counter is decremented each time the μP goes through the loop. The μP gets out of the loop when the counter equals 0. The flowchart in Figure

FIGURE 7.1 | Flowchart for Time Delay Program

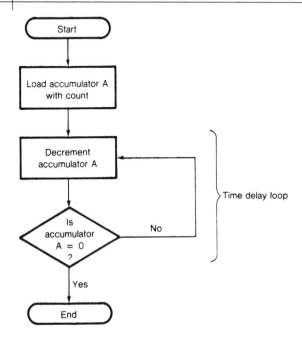

7.1 is for a time delay program that uses only accumulator A. Example 7.11 illustrates the program for the flowchart.

EXAMPLE

7.11   Write a time delay program for the flowchart of Figure 7.1. Use accumulator A.

Solution:

        LDA A, count   Initialize accumulator A with count (2 μs).
DELAY: DEC A   Decrement accumulator A (2 μs).
        BNE DELAY   If A ≠ 0, branch to DELAY (4 μs).

The times in parentheses in the program of Example 7.11 are for a 6800 μP operating from a 1 MHz clock. Equation 7.1 shows how the overall time delay can be calculated:

$$\text{Time delay} = \overbrace{2 \text{ μs}}^{\text{LDA}} + (\overbrace{2 \text{ μs}}^{\text{DEC A}} + \overbrace{4 \text{ μs}}^{\text{BNE}}) \times \text{count} \tag{7.1}$$

Example 7.12 shows how to calculate the shortest and longest time delays for the program illustrated in Example 7.11.

EXAMPLE

7.12   Determine the shortest and longest time delays possible for the time delay program of Example 7.11.

Solution:
The shortest time delay occurs when count = 01_{hex}. The shortest time delay is as follows:

$$\text{Time delay} = 2 \text{ μs} + (6 \text{ μs})(1) = 8 \text{ μs}$$

The longest time delay occurs when accumulator A is loaded with 00_{hex}. The accumulator must be decremented $256_{decimal}$ times before accumulator A is 00 again. The longest time delay is as follows:

$$\text{Time delay} = 2 \text{ μs} + (6 \text{ μs})(256) = 1538 \text{ μs}$$

The range of times in Example 7.12 is from 8 μs to 1538 μs. Therefore, we see that, by varying the count value, we can vary the overall time delay of the program. Section 7.2.1 shows how to determine the count, and Section 7.2.2 shows how to trim the program for a specified time.

7.2.1 | Calculating the Count Value

Rearranging Equation 7.1 to solve for the count value yields the following equation:

$$\text{Count} = \frac{\text{Time delay} - \text{LDA A}}{\text{DEC A} + \text{BNE}} \tag{7.2}$$

If the time delay is specified in microseconds and the 6800 μP is being driven from a 1 MHz clock, then Equation 7.2 can be written as follows:

$$\text{Count} = \frac{\text{Time delay} - 2}{6} \tag{7.3}$$

Example 7.13 illustrates an application of Equation 7.3.

EXAMPLE	
7.13	Determine the count value that has to be loaded into accumulator A of Example 7.11 for an overall time delay of 746 μs.

Solution:
Since the time delay is specified in microseconds, we use Equation 7.3:

$$\text{Count} = \frac{764 - 2}{6} = 127_{\text{decimal}} = 7F_{\text{hex}}$$

The count value in Example 7.13 is a whole number. If it had not been, the program of Example 7.11 would have had to be modified to give the correct time delay. The procedure for making these modifications is called *trimming*, a procedure we turn to next.

7.2.2 | Trimming Time Delays

If the count value of Equation 7.3 produces a whole number and a fraction, then the timing delay program must be trimmed. Trimming means adding additional program instructions (usually NOPs) to generate the correct overall time delay. Trimming is illustrated in Example 7.14.

EXAMPLE	
7.14	Write a program to generate a time delay of 1.0 ms (1000 μs).

Solution:
Begin by using Equation 7.3:

$$\text{Count} = \frac{1000 - 2}{6} = 166.333_{\text{decimal}}$$

The count value equals the whole part of the number, 166_{decimal} ($A6_{\text{hex}}$). If only the whole part of the number were considered, the time delay would be only 998 μs. This value is considered the untrimmed time delay value:

Time delay (untrimmed) $= 2~\mu s + (6~\mu s) \times 166 = 998~\mu s$

Execution of an NOP instruction takes $2~\mu s$. Therefore, adding one NOP instruction at the end of the program generates the correct overall time delay. The program is as follows:

```
         LDA A #$A6      Initialize accumulator A with count.
DELAY: DEC A             Decrement counter.
         BNE DELAY       If accumulator A ≠ 0, branch to DELAY.
         NOP             Additional 2 μs delay.
```

Therefore, the trimmed time delay is as follows:

Time delay (trimmed) $= 2~\mu s + (6~\mu s) \times 166 + 2~\mu s = 1000~\mu s = 1~ms$

7.2.3 | Nesting Time Delays

Time delays greater than $1538~\mu s$ can be generated by a time delay loop inside a time delay loop. This technique is called *nesting time delay loops*. Figure 7.2 shows a flowchart for nesting time delay loops. In this flowchart, accumulator A is cleared to give the maximum time delay for a single loop. Accumulator B is used as a second loop counter. Depending on the initial counts put into accumulator B, the overall time delay can be determined as shown in Example 7.15. *Note:* Accumulator A is loaded with 00_{hex} ($256_{decimal}$), thereby producing the maximum time delay.

EXAMPLE

7.15 | Write a time delay program by using the flowchart of Figure 7.2.

Solution:

```
         CLR A            Initialize accumulator A with 00hex (2 μs)
         LDA B count no. 2 Initialize accumulator B with count no. 2 (2 μs).
DELAY: DEC A              Decrement accumulator A (2 μs).
         BNE DELAY        If A ≠ 0, branch to DELAY( 4 μs).
         DEC B            Decrement accumulator B (2 μs).
         BNE DELAY        If B ≠ 0, branch to DELAY (4 μs).
```

The total time delay for the program in Example 7.15 is given by the following equation:

$$\text{Total time delay} = \text{Initialization} + \text{loop B} \qquad (7.4)$$

where:

$$\text{Initialization} = \underbrace{2~\mu s}_{\text{CLR A}} + \underbrace{2~\mu s}_{\text{LDA B}} = 4~\mu s$$

$$\text{Loop A} = (\underbrace{2~\mu s}_{\text{DEC A}} + \underbrace{4~\mu s}_{\text{BNE}}) \times 256_{decimal} = 1536~\mu s$$

$$\text{Loop B} = [(\overbrace{2\ \mu s}^{\text{DEC B}} + \overbrace{4\ \mu s}^{\text{BNE}}) + \overbrace{1536\ \mu s}^{\text{Loop A}})] \times \text{count no. 2}$$
$$= 1542\ \mu s \times \text{count no. 2}$$

Example 7.16 illustrates an application of Equation 7.4.

FIGURE 7.2 | Flowchart for Nesting Timing Delay Loops

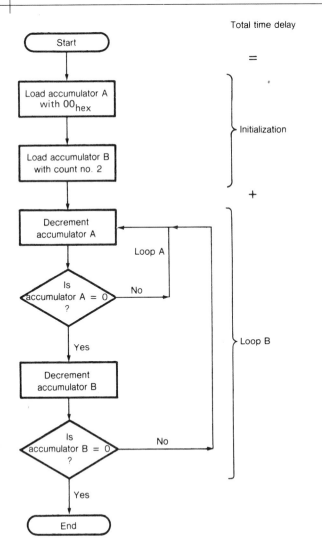

7.16 What is the shortest and the longest time delay that can be generated from the program in Example 7.15?

Solution:
The shortest time delay occurs when count no. 2 equals 1. Applying Equation 7.4 yields the result:

Total time delay $= 4 \mu s + (1542 \mu s) \times 1 = 1546 \mu s$

The longest time delay is generated when both accumulators are loaded with 00_{hex}. Applying Equation 7.4 yields the result:

Total time delay $= 4 \mu s + (1542 \mu s) \times 256 = 0.395 s$

Therefore, nesting two loops together can yield approximately a 0.4 s delay.

Since the 6800 μP has a decrement memory location instruction, we can use memory locations for additional nested time delays, thereby generating any time delay that we need. Remember, when the μP is executing a time delay program, it cannot execute any other program. Thus, time delay programs can be a considerable waste of μP time. To avoid wasting μP time, manufacturers make timing chips. The count is loaded into the timing chips, and they automatically decrement. When they equal zero, a signal can be sent to the μP on the interrupt request line so that the μP knows the count is finished. Timing chips free the μP to execute other programs.

7.3 CHECKING FOR KNOWN DATA

The compare instruction is useful when it is necessary to check memory for a specified or known value. The known value is loaded into an accumulator, and each byte of memory is compared with the accumulator value. A branch instruction follows the compare instruction so that the μP can make a decision. For example, if we want to find all the values less than or equal to 5 in a section of memory, we use the BLS instruction after the compare instruction. In program execution, every time the number from memory is less than or equal to 5, the μP will branch to another program. This new program could output the data to a CRT display or to a printer. This type of program is used when we want to check memory for a particular number, letter, or name, as shown in Example 7.17.

7.17 Write a program that checks page 4 for all values less than or equal to 5. Use accumulator A for the comparison and use accumulator B as a counter.

Solution:

LDX #$0400	Initialize X with starting address.
LDA B #$00	Initialize accumulator B as a counter.
LDA A $05	Load accumulator A with desired value.
COMP: CMP A $00,X	Compare accumulator A and memory.
BLS PRINT	Branch if memory ≤ accumulator A (branch to new program).
INX	Increment X register.
DEC B	Decrement count.
BNE COMP	If B ≠ 0, branch to COMP.

7.4 | CHECKING THE STACK

In Chapter 5, we saw that the stack is an area in memory that is used by the μP to store the contents of the program counter when a subroutine is called. Saving the present contents of the program counter before the μP jumps or branches to a subroutine program guarantees that the μP will be able to return to the program it left. Although the stack is used automatically by the μP whenever a subroutine program is called, the stack can be used at any time by the programmer. In fact, it is an ideal location for the temporary storage of data.

7.4.1 | Saving the Data of the Microprocessor Registers

When the 6800 μP executes either a jump or a branch subroutine program, only the contents of the program counter are saved. In most applications, we want to save the contents of both accumulators and the contents of the condition code register. To do so, we have to use push (PSH) and pull (PUL) instructions. Data is put onto the stack by push instructions, and it is retrieved by pull instructions. Push instructions have to be executed before the main part of the subroutine program begins. Pull instructions have to be executed at the end of the subroutine program but before the return instruction. Example 7.18 shows the use of push and pull instructions.

EXAMPLE

7.18 Write the programming steps necessary to save and return all of the data in the 6800 μP registers.

Solution:

PSH A	Save accumulator A.
PSH B	Save accumulator B.
TPA	Transfer CCR to accumulator A.
PSH A	Save accumulator A (condition code register).
.	.
.	.
.	.

Main subroutine program.

.   .
.   .
.   .

PUL A	Retrieve accumulator A (condition code register).
TAP	Transfer accumulator A to CCR.
PUL B	Retrieve accumulator B.
PUL A	Retrieve accumulator A.
RTS	Retrieve original program counter.

Note: The 6800 μP does not have a push or pull instruction for the condition code register. However, this register can be saved on the stack by transferring it to the accumulator and then using the PSH A instruction. The condition code register is retrieved from the stack by first executing a PUL A instruction and then a TAP instruction. Remember that the data has to be retrieved in the reverse order in which it was saved.

7.4.2 | Temporary Storage

The stack does not have to be reserved for subroutine programs. It can also be used at any time for temporary storage of data. Often, the stack is used to hold incoming or outgoing data temporarily. The program in Example 7.19 shows how data can be brought into the μP and put onto the stack.

Remember that the 6800 μP does not have input or output instructions. It uses memory-mapped I/O, for which a peripheral chip is wired to the system bus and appears as a memory location to the μP. For example, if a peripheral device is wired as memory location $4000, then when the μP executes a load the accumulator instruction from memory location $4000, any data that is located at this address is put into the accumulator. Peripheral devices are covered in detail in Chapters 11–14.

EXAMPLE

7.19 Write a program that brings in 10 bytes of data from an input device and stores each byte in the stack. The input device is wired as memory location $4000. Use accumulator A for bringing in the data, and use accumulator B as a counter. Use page 1 for the stack.

	LDS #$01FF	Initialize starting location of stack pointer.
	LDA B #$0A	Initialize accumulator B ($0A_{hex} = 10_{decimal}$).
INPUT:	LDA A $4000	Load accumulator A from location $4000.
	PSH A	Save data on stack.
	DEC B	Decrement counter.
	BNE INPUT	If B ≠ 0, branch to INPUT.

The program in Example 7.20 shows how the data that has been stored on the stack by the program in Example 7.19 can be added. The program uses the TSX instruction to transfer the contents of the stack pointer plus 1 (the location of the first byte of data in the stack) to the index register. Then, by using the indexed addressing mode, we can remove a byte of data from the stack and add it to the contents of the accumulator. At the end of the program, we can store the total sum in memory. The answer is to know not to exceed the contents of the accumulator. Therefore, single-byte binary addition can be used.

EXAMPLE

7.20   Write a single-byte addition program to add the data that was stored on the stack in Example 7.19. Use accumulator A for the addition, and use accumulator B as a counter. Store the result in memory location $0500.

Solution:

TSX	Transfer stack + 1 to index register.
LDA B #$0A	Initialize accumulator B ($0A_{hex} = 10_{decimal}$).
CLR A	Clear accumulator A and carry flag.
REPEAT: ADD A $00,X	Add accumulator A + data in stack.
DEC B	Decrement counter.
BNE REPEAT	If B $\neq$ 0, branch to REPEAT.
STA $0500	Store sum at location $0500.

7.5 | MULTIPLICATION

The 6800 μP does not have a multiplication instruction. Therefore, if we wish to multiply two numbers, we have to write a program to do so. The following description shows how two 8-bit positive numbers can be multiplied. When two 8-bit numbers are multiplied, the result is a 16-bit answer. Because the 6800 μP does not have any 16-bit registers, we need to use some memory locations as working registers. The memory locations in page 0 are usually used so that we can utilize the direct addressing mode.

The arithmetic terms used in multiplication are as follows:

$$
\begin{array}{rl}
42 & \text{Multiplicand} \\
\underline{35} & \text{Multiplier} \\
210 & \left.\vphantom{\begin{array}{c}1\\1\end{array}}\right\} \\
\underline{126} & \text{Partial product} \\
\hline
1470 & \text{Product}
\end{array}
$$

The values shown above are decimal numbers.

Before the multiplication program begins, the multiplicand and the multiplier have to be stored in memory. Remember that the product is eventually going to consist of 16 bits. The low-order 8 bits are referred to as the least significant (LS) byte of the product and the high-order 8 bits are referred to as the most significant (MS) byte.

The steps involved in multiplication are as follows:

1. Check the least significant bit of the multiplier. If it is 0, rotate both bytes of the product one bit to the right. If it is 1, add the multiplicand to the most significant byte of the product, and then rotate both bytes of the product one bit to the right.
2. Have all bits of the multiplier been checked? If yes, then the program is finished. Jump to step 3. If no, rotate the multiplier one bit to the right and then repeat step 1.
3. Store the result.

Table 7.1 shows how 42 is multiplied by 35, using the binary number system and the steps just described. Note in the multiplication that the shift operation is done by rotate right instructions. Since the multiplier is represented by 8 bits, step 1 has to be done 8 times. A counter keeps track of the number of times step 1 has been done. The count is shown in column 1 in Table 7.1. Column 2 shows the logic state of the multiplier for each test, starting with the least significant bit. Column 3 describes what is happening. Column 4 shows the addition that is done in the accumulator. Column 5 shows the contents of a working register, which holds the contents of the LS byte of the partial product. After the last rotation, the accumulator contains the MS byte of the product, and the working register holds the LS byte. Example 7.21 illustrates a program for 8-bit multiplication for positive numbers.

TABLE 7.1 | Steps Involved in Binary Multiplication of Two 8-Bit Numbers (42 × 35 = 1470)

Count	Multiplier Logic State	Comments	Accumulator	Working Register
Start			00000000	00000000
8	1	Add multiplicand	00101010	00000000
		Shift right	00010101	00000000
7	1	Add multiplicand	00111111	00000000
		Shift right	00011111	10000000
6	0	Shift right	00001111	11000000
5	0	Shift right	00000111	11100000
4	0	Shift right	00000011	11110000
3	1	Add multiplicand	00101101	11110000
		Shift right	00010110	11111000
2	0	Shift right	00001011	01111100
1	0	Shift right	00000101	10111110
			(MS byte of product)	(LS byte of product)

Note: 42 = 00101010 is the multiplicand; 35 = 00100011 is the multiplier.

TABLE 7.2	Memory Locations to be Used in Example 7.21

Memory Location (Hex)	Purpose
0020	Count
0021	Multiplicand
0022	Multiplier
0023	MS byte of product
0024	LS byte of product

EXAMPLE

7.21

Write an 8-bit multiplication program using the steps outlined above and the memory locations in page 0, shown in Table 7.2, as working registers.

Solution:

	LDA A #$08	Load accumulator A with number of bits to be multiplied.
	STA A $20	Store count in location $0020.
	CLR A	Clear accumulator A and carry flag.
	LDA B $21	Load accumulator B with multiplicand.
MULT:	LSR $22	Shift multiplier right (bit 0 into carry).
	BCC ROTATE	If carry = 0, branch to ROTATE.
	ABA	Add multiplicand to accumulator A.
ROTATE:	ASR A	Shift accumulator A.
	ROR $24	Rotate location 0024.
	DEC $20	Decrement count.
	BNE MULT	If location 0020 ≠ 0, branch to MULT.
	STA A $23	Store MS byte in location 0023.

Note: Motorola's *Application Manual* (pages 2-12 to 2-21 of the *Manual*) describes how the 6800 μP can be programmed to multiply two 16-bit numbers. This multiplication generates a 32-bit product.

7.6 | SUMMARY

In this chapter, we saw many of the 6800 μP instructions used in a number of different programming applications. As in previous chapters, the memory locations were chosen at random. Also, the programs could have been inserted into a main program or written as a subroutine. If programs are written as a subroutine, remember that the last instruction has to be an RTS instruction. If they are written as an interrupt subroutine program, the last instruction has to be an RTI instruction.

Section 7.1 showed how binary and decimal addition and subtraction can be accomplished using the 6800 μP. When two 8-bit numbers are being added or subtracted, the operation is a single-byte operation. A multiprecision program is needed when the numbers to be added or subtracted are longer than 8 bits. If two 16-bit numbers (2 bytes) are being operated upon, the multiprecision program is a double-precision program.

Section 7.2 showed the μP can be programmed for time delays. In the event that a time delay loop does not generate the exact delay, a time delay program can be trimmed, as described in Section 7.2.2.

A program that searchers through memory for a particular value was illustrated in Section 7.3. The stack can be a very efficient area in memory for storing data temporarily. Several examples of how to use the stack instructions were given in Section 7.4.

Like most μPs, the 6800 has to be programmed to do multiplication. Section 7.5 showed a program for multiplying two 8-bit positive numbers. This multiplication program produces a 16-bit answer. Therefore, the product requires two memory locations to store the answer.

PROBLEMS

All of the following problems apply to the 6800 μP.

7.1 Write a program that adds the contents of location $0150 to the contents of location $0160. Store the result at memory location $0160. Use accumulator B.

7.2 Continue the program of Problem 7.1 so that the carry flag is saved at memory location $0161.

7.3 Does the following program add a column of five numbers at locations $0400 to $0404 and store the result at location $0030? The result does not produce a carry.

```
              CLC
              LDA B #$05
              LDX #$0400
              LDA A #$00
COLADD:       ADC A $00,X
              INX
              DEC B
              BNE COLADD
              STA A $0030
```

7.4 What would be the count value in Example 7.4 for a 24-bit addition program?

7.5 Can a decimal adjust be made for accumulator B?

7.6 Repeat Problem 7.1 for BCD addition.

7.7 Repeat Problem 7.1 for binary subtraction.

7.8 What instruction or instructions have to be modified so that the program in Example 7.9 subtracts the contents of locations $0020 to $0023 from the contents of locations $0010 to $0013?

7.9 If accumulator A in Example 7.11 is initialized with 48_{hex}, what time delay will be generated?

7.10 With what value must accumulator A in Example 7.11 be initialized for a time delay for 842 μs?

7.11 What time delay would be generated in Example 7.14 if the NOP instruction were accidentally inserted between the DEC instruction and the BNE instruction?

7.12 Refer to Example 7.15. If accumulator A $= 00_{hex}$ and count no. $2 = 80_{hex}$, what time delay is generated by the program?

7.13 What data will be lost if the programming steps of Example 7.18 are written as follows?

.

.

.

TPA

PHA

PHB

PHA

.

.

.

7.14 Modify Example 7.19 for 20 bytes of data.

7.15 Continue Example 7.19 so that, after 10 bytes of data have been stored on the stack, the μP will add the column of numbers in BCD. Use accumulator A for the addition, use accumulator B for a counter, and store the result at location $0750. Use the PUL A instruction.

8 | 6800 Microprocessor

8.0 | INTRODUCTION

This chapter deals with the 6800 μP's pin descriptions, timing diagrams, events that occur when an instruction is fetched and executed, events that occur when power is applied, and procedure for handling interrupts.

The 6800 μP is a central processing unit around which an entire μC system can be built. It is fabricated using NMOS technology and is housed in a 40-pin dual-in-line package. The 6800 requires an external circuit to generate the two-phase nonoverlapping clock pulses. Figure 8.1 shows the 6800 μP along with a 6870A clock generator circuit. The 6800 μP needs an external clock driver, such as the MC6870A, to generate the ϕ_1 and ϕ_2 nonoverlapping clock pulses. The 6870A provides not only the clock signals for the μP, but also a ϕ_2 clock pulse that is TTL compatible and other control signals.

8.1 | PIN DESCRIPTIONS

The following paragraphs briefly describe the functions of the 6800's pins. Figure 8.2 shows the pin designations for this μP.

Address Bus (A_0–A_{15}): There are 16 address bus pins that allow the 6800 μP to address 64K bytes. Each pin is capable of driving one standard TTL load and 130 pF. All the lines have three-state drivers that allow this μP to perform direct memory access (DMA) operations.

Data Bus (D_0–D_7): There are eight bidirectional data bus pins that allow the μP to communicate with memory and peripheral chips. When the μP is sending data, the output buffers are capable of driving one standard TTL load and 130 pF. Each pin has three-state capability.

Power Pins: The 6800 μP is a +5 V (pin 8) device. It does, however, require two ground connections (pins 1 and 21).

FIGURE 8.1 | 6800 μP with 6870A Clock Generator Circuit

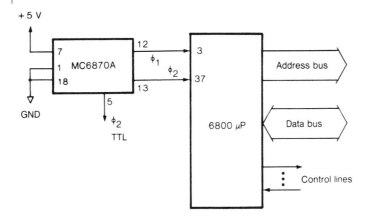

FIGURE 8.2 | 6800 μP Pin Designations (Redrawn with permission of Motorola Incorporated, Austin, Texas)

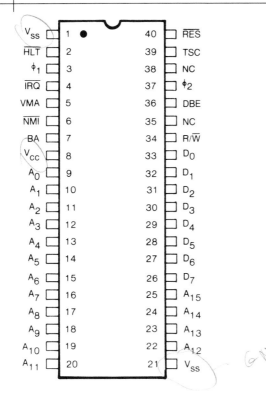

Clock Pins: The 6800 μP requires two nonoverlapping clock signals—ϕ_1 (pin 3) and ϕ_2 (pin 37). These clock signals must be generated externally to the μP from a clock generator and driver circuit, such as the MC6870A or MC6871.

The 6800 μP has six input control lines ($\overline{\text{HLT}}$, $\overline{\text{IRQ}}$, $\overline{\text{NMI}}$, DBE, TSC, and $\overline{\text{RES}}$) and three output control lines (VMA, BA, and R/$\overline{\text{W}}$). The bar over a pin designation means that this line's active state is low. A brief description of the function of each control pin follows.

$\overline{\text{HLT}}$ (Pin 2):   In normal operation, the logic level on pin 2 is high. When the logic level goes low, the μP finishes the instruction it is executing and then halts (no more instructions are fetched and executed). This permits an external signal to control the execution of the program. This feature is often used during program debugging. When the $\overline{\text{HLT}}$ line goes low, the bus available pin goes high, the valid memory address line goes low, and all other three-state lines go to their three-state condition.

$\overline{\text{IRQ}}$ (Pin 4):   The abbreviation IRQ stands for *interrupt request*. When the logic level on this line goes low, the μP finishes the instruction it is executing and jumps to the interrupt service routine, provided that the μP's interrupt flag bit is not set. The μP returns to the program it left after decoding a return from interrupt instruction.

$\overline{\text{NMI}}$ (Pin 6):   This pin is the nonmaskable interrupt request pin. This interrupt cannot be disabled by the programmer or by the μP. When pin 6 receives a low logic level, the μP finishes executing its present instruction and then always jumps to its nonmaskable interrupt service program. The μP returns to its normal operation after decoding a return from interrupt instruction.

DBE (Pin 36):   The abbreviation DBE stands for *data bus enable*. When there is a high logic level input on this line, the μP's data bus buffers are enabled. This signal permits the μP to send data out onto the data bus during a write cycle. In most applications, the DBE signal comes from the ϕ_2 clock cycle.

TSC (Pin 39):   TSC stands for *three-state control*. A high logic level on this line causes the μP's address lines and the R/$\overline{\text{W}}$ line to go into their high impedance state. The VMA and BA lines go low. The ϕ_1 and ϕ_2 clock inputs go high and low, respectively. *Caution:* Since the μP is a dynamic device, the input on this line cannot be held high for longer than 4.5 μs, or the data in the μP will be lost.

$\overline{\text{RES}}$ (Pin 40):   This pin is the reset pin. It is used to initialize the program counter after power is first turned on. If the reset pin is held low for at least 8 clock cycles and is brought back high, the μP retrieves data at location FFFE and then the data at FFFF. The data stored at these two successive memory locations should be the starting address of the main program.

VMA (Pin 5):   The abbreviation VMA stands for *valid memory address*. When this line goes high, it is a signal to all other devices that there is a valid address on the address bus lines.

BA (Pin 7): The abbreviation BA stands for *bus available*. When the µP is controlling the system, the logic level on this pin is low. When this line goes to a high logic level, the µP address and data bus are in the high impedance state. This line goes high under two conditions: (1) when the µP receives a $\overline{\text{HLT}}$ signal or (2) if the µP decodes a wait for interrupt instruction.

R/$\overline{\text{W}}$ (Pin 34): The read/write line indicates whether the µP is receiving data or sending data. When this line is high, the µP is reading (receiving) data from memory or an I/O device. When this line is low, the µP is writing (sending) data to memory or an I/O device.

8.2 | φ₁ AND φ₂ CLOCK SIGNALS

Figure 8.3 shows typical φ₁ and φ₂ clock signals for the 6800 µP. The electrical characteristics are given in Table 8.1. The frequency range for the 6800 is from 100 kHz to 1 MHz. This frequency range causes a range of cycle times from 1.0 µs to 10 µs. The minimum pulse width high times are specified as $\text{PW}_{\phi H}$. The high input clock voltage level is given by V_{IHC} and the low input clock voltage level is given by V_{ILC}. The overshoot voltage is V_{OS} (see Figure 8.3). The value t_{ut} is the total up time. It is used by a designer to guarantee that the required access times for memory and peripheral chips are met. Time t_{d} is the delay or separation time measured at a maximum overlap voltage, V_{OV} (see Figure 8.3). This separation time ensures that the nonoverlapping requirement is met.

FIGURE 8.3 | Clock Timing Waveform (Redrawn with permission of Motorola Incorporated, Austin, Texas)

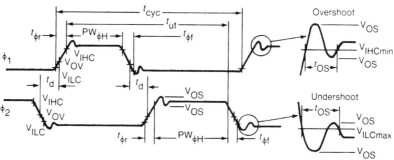

$V_{\text{OV}} = V_{\text{SS}} + 0.5$ V (Clock overlap measurement point)

TABLE 8.1 | Electrical and Timing Characteristics for ϕ_1 and ϕ_2 Clock Pulses

DC ELECTRICAL CHARACTERISTICS ($V_{CC} = 5.0$ Vdc, $\pm 5\%$, $V_{SS} = 0$, $T_A = T_L$ to T_H unless otherwise noted)

Characteristic		Symbol	Min	Typ	Max	Unit
Input High Voltage	Logic	V_{IH}	$V_{SS} + 2.0$	–	V_{CC}	V
	$\phi 1, \phi 2$	V_{IHC}	$V_{CC} - 0.6$	–	$V_{CC} + 0.3$	
Input Low Voltage	Logic	V_{IL}	$V_{SS} - 0.3$	–	$V_{SS} + 0.8$	V
	$\phi 1, \phi 2$	V_{ILC}	$V_{SS} - 0.3$	–	$V_{SS} + 0.4$	
Input Leakage Current						
($V_{in} = 0$ to 5.25 V, $V_{CC} = $ Max)	Logic	I_{in}	–	1.0	2.5	μA
($V_{in} = 0$ to 5.25 V, $V_{CC} = 0$ V to 5.25 V)	$\phi 1, \phi 2$		–	–	100	
Three-State Input Leakage Current	D0-D7	I_{IZ}	–	2.0	10	μA
($V_{in} = 0.4$ to 2.4 V, $V_{CC} = $ Max)	A0-A15, R/$\overline{W}$		–	–	100	
Output High Voltage						
($I_{Load} = -205 \mu A$, $V_{CC} = $ Min)	D0-D7	V_{OH}	$V_{SS} + 2.4$	–	–	V
($I_{Load} = -145 \mu A$, $V_{CC} = $ Min)	A0-A15, R/$\overline{W}$, VMA		$V_{SS} + 2.4$	–	–	
($I_{Load} = -100 \mu A$, $V_{CC} = $ Min)	BA		$V_{SS} + 2.4$	–	–	
Output Low Voltage ($I_{Load} = 1.6$ mA, $V_{CC} = $ Min)		V_{OL}	–	–	$V_{SS} + 0.4$	V
Internal Power Dissipation (Measured at $T_A = T_L$)		P_{INT}	–	0.5	1.0	W
Capacitance						
($V_{in} = 0$, $T_A = 25°C$, $f = 1.0$ MHz)	$\phi 1$		–	25	35	
	$\phi 2$	C_{in}	–	45	70	pF
	D0-D7		–	10	12.5	
	Logic Inputs		–	6.5	10	
	A0-A15, R/$\overline{W}$, VMA	C_{out}	–	–	12	pF

CLOCK TIMING ($V_{CC} = 5.0$ V, $\pm 5\%$, $V_{SS} = 0$, $T_A = T_L$ to T_H unless otherwise noted)

Characteristic		Symbol	Min	Typ	Max	Unit
Frequency of Operation	MC6800		0.1	–	1.0	
	MC68A00	f	0.1	–	1.5	MHz
	MC68B00		0.1	–	2.0	
Cycle Time	MC6800		1.000	–	10	
	MC68A00	t_{cyc}	0.666	–	10	μs
	MC68B00		0.500	–	10	
Clock Pulse Width	$\phi 1, \phi 2 - $ MC6800		400	–	9500	
(Measured at $V_{CC} - 0.6$ V)	$\phi 1, \phi 2 - $ MC68A00	$PW_{\phi H}$	230	–	9500	ns
	$\phi 1, \phi 2 - $ MC68B00		180	–	9500	
Total $\phi 1$ and $\phi 2$ Up Time	MC6800		900	–	–	
	MC68A00	t_{ut}	600	–	–	ns
	MC68B00		440	–	–	
Rise and Fall Time (Measured between $V_{SS} + 0.4$ and $V_{CC} - 0.6$)		t_r, t_f	–	–	100	ns
Delay Time or Clock Separation						
(Measured at $V_{OV} = V_{SS} + 0.6$ V@$t_r = t_f \leq 100$ ns)		t_d	0	–	9100	ns
(Measured at $V_{OV} = V_{SS} + 1.0$ V@$t_r = t_f \leq 35$ ns)			0	–	9100	

Source: Reprinted with permission of Motorola Incorporated, Austin, Texas. Copyright © 1980 by Motorola Incorporated.

8.3 | TIMING DIAGRAMS FOR THE ADDRESS AND DATA BUSES

Figures 8.4 and 8.5 show the timing diagrams for a read and write operation, respectively. Table 8.2 gives the names and specifications for all the times. A cycle starts when the ϕ_1 clock signal rises to 0.3 V. The address, R/$\overline{W}$ signal, and VMA signal are stable after

FIGURE 8.4 | Timing Diagram for Reading Data from Memory or Peripherals (Redrawn with permission of Motorola Incorporated, Austin, Texas)

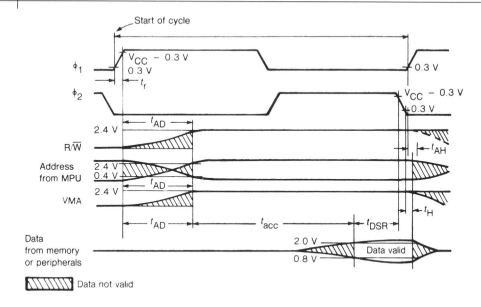

t_{AD}, address delay time. The read access time is t_{acc}, followed by the data setup time, t_{DSR}. The data coming into the μP is latched at the end of the ϕ_2 clock signal. To guarantee that the μP latches the data, the data on the data bus is held there for an additional hold time, t_H.

When the 6800 μP writes data, the address bus, R/$\overline{W}$, and VMA signals are stabilized by the end of the address delay time, t_{AD}. The data bus enable (DBE) pin must be brought high. After a data delay write time, t_{DDW}, the data on the data bus is valid. In most systems, the DBE is connected to the ϕ_2 clock signal. Figure 8.5 shows the timing diagrams when DBE = ϕ_2 and when DBE ≠ ϕ_2.

8.4 | CYCLE-BY-CYCLE OPERATION

The 6800 μP has 72 different types of instructions and seven addressing modes. This section gives a cycle-by-cycle description of what happens on the address and data buses when an instruction is fetched and executed by the μP. The section is subdivided according to addressing modes. In the following examples, a clock cycle is t_{cyc}, the time for a complete ϕ_1 and ϕ_2 clock pulse. The memory locations have been chosen at random.

8.4.1 | Immediate Addressing Mode

The immediate addressing mode is an addressing technique in which the first byte of the instruction is the op code and the second byte is the data (operand). Exceptions to this

FIGURE 8.5 | Timing Diagram for Writing Data to Memory or Peripherals (Redrawn with permission of
Motorola Incorporated, Austin, Texas)

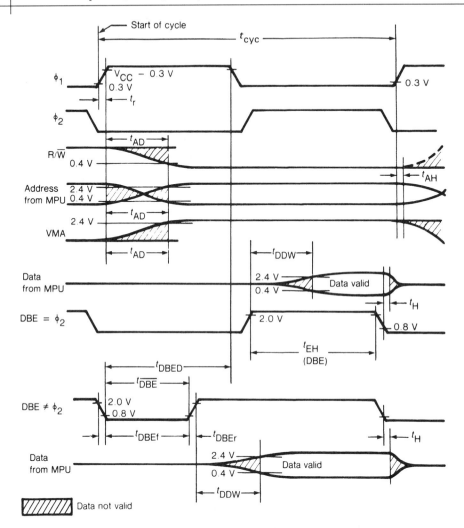

are the CPX, LDS, and LDX instructions, which have the operand in the second and
third bytes of the instruction.

Figure 8.6 shows a timing diagram for the immediate addressing mode. Data
buses for a two-byte and a three-byte instruction are illustrated. Referring to Figure 8.6,
we see that, during the first half of cycle 1, the program counter's (PC) current address
is put on the address bus, the R/$\overline{\text{W}}$ line goes high designating a read operation, and VMA
goes high designating that the current address is a valid memory address. The PC is
incremented on the falling edge of ϕ_1. During the second half of cycle 1, the op code is
put on the data bus from memory and loaded into the μP. The new value in the PC goes

TABLE 8.2 | Read and Write Timing Characteristics

Characteristic	Symbol	MC6800			MC68A00			MC68B00			Unit
		Min	Typ	Max	Min	Typ	Max	Min	Typ	Max	
Address Delay C = 90 pF C = 30 pF	t_{AD}	– –	– –	270 250	– –	– –	180 165	– –	– –	150 135	ns
Peripheral Read Access Time $t_{acc} = t_{ut} - (t_{AD} + t_{DSR})$	t_{acc}	605	–	—	400	–	—	290	–	—	ns
Data Setup Time (Read)	t_{DSR}	100	–	–	60	–	–	40	–	–	ns
Input Data Hold Time	t_H	10	–	–	10	–	–	10	–	–	ns
Output Data Hold Time	t_H	10	25	–	10	25	–	10	25	–	ns
Address Hold Time (Address, R/$\overline{W}$, VMA)	t_{AH}	30	50	–	30	50	–	30	50	–	ns
Enable High Time for DBE Input	t_{EH}	450	–	–	280	–	–	220	–	–	ns
Data Delay Time (Write)	t_{DDW}	–	–	225	–	–	200	–	–	160	ns
Processor Controls Processor Control Setup Time Processor Control Rise and Fall Time Bus Available Delay Three-State Enable Three-State Delay Data Bus Enable Down Time During φ1 Up Time Data Bus Enable Rise and Fall Times	t_{PCS} t_{PCr}, t_{PCf} t_{BA} t_{TSE} t_{TSD} t_{DBE} t_{DBEr}, t_{DBEf}	200 – – – – 150 –	– – – – – – –	– 100 250 40 270 – 25	140 – – – – 120 –	– – – – – – –	– 100 165 40 270 – 25	110 – – – – 75 –	– – – – – – –	– 100 135 40 220 – 25	ns

Source: Reprinted with permission of Motorola Incorporated, Austin, Texas. Copyright © 1980 by Motorola Incorporated.

out on the address bus and the operand, which is usually data, is loaded into the μP at the end of cycle 2. The PC has been incremented again. The op code of the next instruction is fetched on the next cycle if the immediate addressing mode instruction was two bytes long. For the CPX, LDS, and LDX instructions, cycle 3 is needed for the μP to receive the third byte of the instruction. A summary of instructions and cycle-by-cycle operation for the immediate addressing mode is given in Table 8.3. Examples 8.1 and 8.2 illustrate determinations of the number of clock cycles needed for certain program listings.

EXAMPLE

8.1 Show the clock cycles needed to load accumulator A immediately with data 00_{hex}.

Program Listing	Memory Listing
C400 LDA A #$00	C400 86 Op code
	C401 00 Data

Solution:

Clock Cycle	Address Bus	Data Bus	Internal Operation
1	C400	86	Fetch op code; increment PC to C401.
2	C401	00	Decode op code 86; increment PC to C402; latch data 00 into μP.
3	C402	Next op code	

FIGURE 8.6 | Timing Diagram for Immediate Addressing Mode

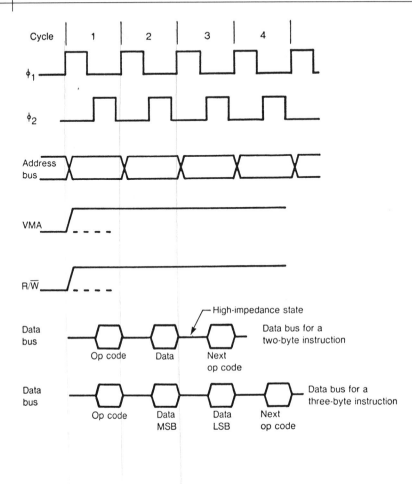

TABLE 8.3 | Summary of Immediate Addressing Mode Instructions

Instructions	Cycles	Cycle #	VMA Line	Address Bus	R/W Line	Data Bus
ADC EOR ADD LDA AND ORA BIT SBC CMP SUB	2	1	1	Op Code Address	1	Op Code
		2	1	Op Code Address + 1	1	Operand Data
CPX LDS LDX	3	1	1	Op Code Address	1	Op Code
		2	1	Op Code Address + 1	1	Operand Data (High Order Byte)
		3	1	Op Code Address + 2	1	Operand Data (Low Order Byte)

Source: Reprinted with permission of Motorola Incorporated, Austin, Texas. Copyright © 1980 by Motorola Incorporated.

The LDA A immediate instruction takes two clock cycles because on the third clock cycle, the next op code is being fetched by the μP. The data at the end of clock cycle 2 is latched into the μP.

<table>
<tr><td>EXAMPLE</td><td></td></tr>
</table>

8.2 Show the number of clock cycles needed to load the X index register immediately with data 0010_{hex}. Remember, the X register is a 16-bit register.

Program Listing	Memory Listing		
F850 LDX #$0010	F850	CE	Op code
	F851	00	Data (high byte)
	F852	10	Data (low byte)

Solution:

Clock Cycle	Address Bus	Data Bus	Internal Operation
1	F850	CE	Fetch op code; increment PC to F851.
2	F851	00	Decode op code (CE); increment PC to F852; latch data 00 into X register.
3	F852	10	Increment PC to F853; latch data into X register.
4	F853	Next op code	Fetch next op code; increment PC to F584.

8.4.2 | Direct Addressing Mode

The direct addressing mode for the 6800 μP is a two-byte instruction. The first byte is the op code and the second byte is the low byte of the operand address. The high byte is understood by the μP to be in page zero. This addressing mode allows the user to address directly the lowest 256 bytes in memory (locations 0 through 255). This allows faster execution times by storing or retrieving data in these locations. In most configurations, these locations should be a random access memory. The 6800 μP has 16 instructions that can use the direct addressing mode. Although all of them are two bytes long, their execution times may require three, four, or five clock cycles, depending on the instruction. A summary of instructions and cycle-by-cycle operation for the direct addressing mode is given in Table 8.4. Example 8.3 illustrates the clock cycles needed in a program listing.

Figure 8.7 shows the timing diagram for a load the accumulator instruction using the direct addressing mode. The address in the program counter is put on the address bus and the LDA op code is loaded into the μP during cycle 1. The PC is incremented. During cycle 2, 8 bits for the address low (ADL) byte are received by the μP. The upper 8 bits are forced to all zeros. In cycle 3, the new address is put on the address bus and

TABLE 8.4 | Summary of Direct Addressing Mode Instructions

Instructions	Cycles	Cycle #	VMA Line	Address Bus	R/W̄ Line	Data Bus
ADC EOR ADD LDA AND ORA BIT SBC CMP SUB	3	1	1	Op Code Address	1	Op Code
		2	1	Op Code Address + 1	1	Address of Operand
		3	1	Address of Operand	1	Operand Data
CPX LDS LDX	4	1	1	Op Code Address	1	Op Code
		2	1	Op Code Address + 1	1	Address of Operand
		3	1	Address of Operand	1	Operand Data (High Order Byte)
		4	1	Operand Address + 1	1	Operand Data (Low Order Byte)
STA	4	1	1	Op Code Address	1	Op Code
		2	1	Op Code Address + 1	1	Destination Address
		3	0	Destination Address	1	Irrelevant Data
		4	1	Destination Address	0	Data from Accumulator
STS STX	5	1	1	Op Code Address	1	Op Code
		2	1	Op Code Address + 1	1	Address of Operand
		3	0	Address of Operand	1	Irrelevant Data
		4	1	Address of Operand	0	Register Data (High Order Byte)
		5	1	Address of Operand + 1	0	Register Data (Low Order Byte)

Source: Reprinted with permission of Motorola Incorporated, Austin, Texas. Copyright © 1980 by Motorola Incorporated.

the operand is loaded in the μP. Example 8.4 illustrates the clock cycles needed for a store instruction. This store instruction requires four clock cycles. On the fifth clock cycle, the 6800 μP fetches the next op code.

A STA instruction is handled in the same manner as an LDA instruction, except that there is an additional cycle for the STA instruction, due to the μP's architecture. This additional cycle is required to move the accumulator internally, and it occurs during clock cycle 3 in Example 8.4. During this clock cycle, the data bus is in an indeterminate

EXAMPLE

8.3 | Show the clock cycles needed for loading accumulator B with data from page 00.

Program Listing	*Memory Listing*	*Data at Location 0700*
0400 LDA B $70	0400 D6 Op code	85
	0401 70 ADL	

Solution:

Clock Cycle	*Address Bus*	*Data Bus*	*Internal Operation*
1	0400	D6	Fetch op code; increment PC to 0401.
2	0401	70	Decode op code D6; increment PC to 0402.
3	0070	85	Latch data (85) into μP.
4	0402	Next op code	Fetch next op code; increment PC to 0403.

FIGURE 8.7	Timing Diagram for Loading Accumulator B with Data from Page 00

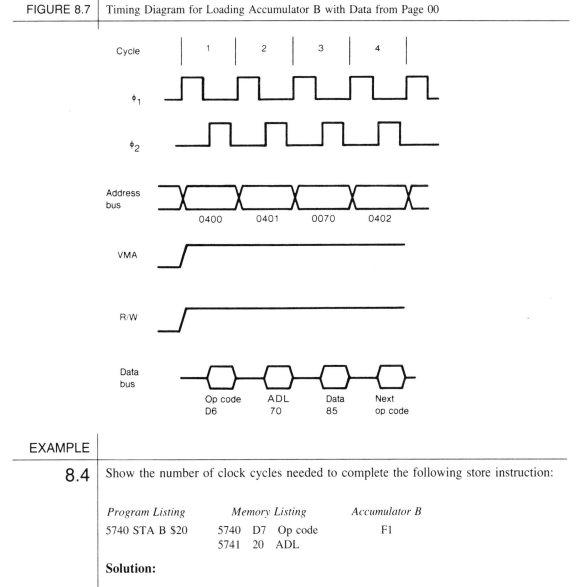

8.4	Show the number of clock cycles needed to complete the following store instruction:

Program Listing	Memory Listing		Accumulator B
5740 STA B $20	5740 D7	Op code	F1
	5741 20	ADL	

Solution:

Clock Cycle	Address Bus	Data Bus	Internal Operation
1	5740	D7	Fetch op code; increment PC to 5741.
2	5741	20	Decode op code D7; increment PC to 5742; latch ADL (20).
3	0020	Data (irrelevant)	Bring R/$\overline{\text{W}}$ line low.
4	0020	F1	Data F1 from accumulator B is sent to location 0020.
5	5742	Next op code	Fetch next op code; increment PC to 5743.

FIGURE 8.8 | Timing Diagram for Storing Data in Page 00

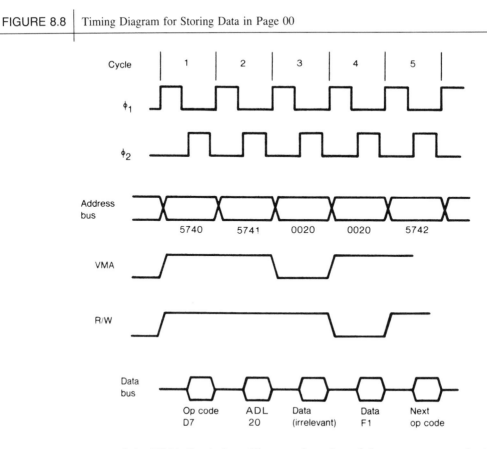

state and the VMA line is low. The actual storing of data occurs on cycle 4. The next instruction follows on the next clock cycle. Figure 8.8 shows the timing diagram for an STA instruction. Example 8.5 shows what happens on each clock cycle when the μP executes an STX instruction.

This instruction requires one more clock cycle than the instruction in Example 8.4 because two bytes of data have to be stored in memory. If we continue Example 8.5, the contents of the program counter (C202) that has been held since clock cycle 2 are placed on the address bus on the next clock cycle. Figure 8.9 shows a timing diagram for the instruction in this example.

EXAMPLE

8.5 | Show the number of clock cycles needed to store the following data in the X register at an address in page 00:

Program Listing	Memory Listing			X Register
C200 STX $80	C200	DF	Op code	471E
	C201	80	ADL	

Solution:

Clock Cycle	*Address Bus*	*Data Bus*	*Internal Operation*
1	C200	DF	Fetch op code; increment PC to C201.
2	C201	80	Decode op code DF; increment PC to C202; latch ADL.
3	0080	Data (irrelevant)	VMA line is low; bring $\overline{R/W}$ line low for next cycle.
4	0080	47	Send high byte of X register to location 0080; increment address to 0081.
5	0081	1E	Send low byte of X register to location 0081.
6	C202	Next op code	Fetch next op code; increment PC to C203.

FIGURE 8.9	Timing Diagram for Storing Contents of Index Register in Page 00

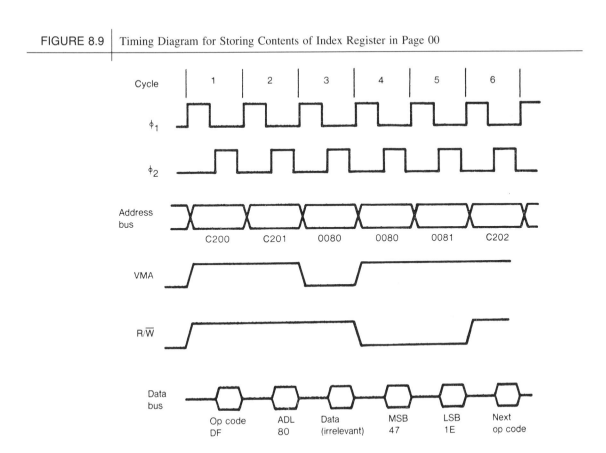

8.4.3 | Indexed Addressing Mode

An indexed addressing mode instruction is a two-byte instruction. The first byte is the op code, and the second byte is an offset value. The address contained in the second byte of the instruction is added to the lowest 8 bits of the index register. This result is then used to address memory. The modified address is held in a temporary address register, so there is no change to the index register or the program counter.

In the first two cycles of an LDA indexed address instruction, the op code is loaded into the μP, followed by the index offset. In the third cycle, the low-order byte of the index register is added to the offset; the carry propagates during cycle 4. The VMA goes low during these two cycles, while the μP is preparing the indexed address. The new address then goes on the address bus during cycle 5.

The STA indexed instruction is handled in the same manner as the LDA instruction; however, an additional cycle is required for the STA indexed instruction, due to the μP's architecture. VMA is held low, then, for three bytes for the STA instruction instead of two for the LDA instruction. The 6800 μP's indexed addressing mode instructions and cycle-by-cycle operations are summarized in Table 8.5. Example 8.6 and Figure 8.10 show the steps involved for an STA indexed instruction. The contents of the index register and the offset value are added to produce the final address.

EXAMPLE

8.6   Show the number of clock cycles needed to store accumulator A using the indexed addressing mode.

Program Listing	Memory Listing			X Register	Accumulator A
D900 STA A $10,X	D900	EF	Op code	3050	E4
	D901	10	Offset		

Solution:

Clock Cycle	Address Bus	Data Bus	Internal Operation
1	D900	EF	Fetch op code; increment PC to D901.
2	D901	10	Decode op code EF.
3	3050	Data (irrelevant)	Add 50 + 10 = 60 (no internal carry).
4	3060	Data (irrelevant)	Add 30 + internal carry = 30.
5	3060	Data (irrelevant)	Bring R/$\overline{\text{W}}$ line low for next clock cycle.
6	3060	E4	Send out data E4 to location 3060.

TABLE 8.5 | Summary of Indexed Addressing Mode Instructions

Instructions	Cycles	Cycle #	VMA Line	Address Bus	R/W̄ Line	Data Bus
JMP	4	1	1	Op Code Address	1	Op Code
		2	1	Op Code Address + 1	1	Offset
		3	0	Index Register	1	Irrelevant Data
		4	0	Index Register Plus Offset (w/o Carry)	1	Irrelevant Data
ADC EOR ADD LDA AND ORA BIT SBC CMP SUB	5	1	1	Op Code Address	1	Op Code
		2	1	Op Code Address + 1	1	Offset
		3	0	Index Register	1	Irrelevant Data
		4	0	Index Register Plus Offset (w/o Carry)	1	Irrelevant Data
		5	1	Index Register Plus Offset	1	Operand Data
CPX LDS LDX	6	1	1	Op Code Address	1	Op Code
		2	1	Op Code Address + 1	1	Offset
		3	0	Index Register	1	Irrelevant Data
		4	0	Index Register Plus Offset (w/o Carry)	1	Irrelevant Data
		5	1	Index Register Plus Offset	1	Operand Data (High Order Byte)
		6	1	Index Register Plus Offset + 1	1	Operand Data (Low Order Byte)
STA	6	1	1	Op Code Address	1	Op Code
		2	1	Op Code Address + 1	1	Offset
		3	0	Index Register	1	Irrelevant Data
		4	0	Index Register Plus Offset (w/o Carry)	1	Irrelevant Data
		5	0	Index Register Plus Offset	1	Irrelevant Data
		6	1	Index Register Plus Offset	0	Operand Data
ASL LSR ASR NEG CLR ROL COM ROR DEC TST INC	7	1	1	Op Code Address	1	Op Code
		2	1	Op Code Address + 1	1	Offset
		3	0	Index Register	1	Irrelevant Data
		4	0	Index Register Plus Offset (w/o Carry)	1	Irrelevant Data
		5	1	Index Register Plus Offset	1	Current Operand Data
		6	0	Index Register Plus Offset	1	Irrelevant Data
		7	1/0 (Note 2)	Index Register Plus Offset	0	New Operand Data
STS STX	7	1	1	Op Code Address	1	Op Code
		2	1	Op Code Address + 1	1	Offset
		3	0	Index Register	1	Irrelevant Data
		4	0	Index Register Plus Offset (w/o Carry)	1	Irrelevant Data
		5	0	Index Register Plus Offset	1	Irrelevant Data
		6	1	Index Register Plus Offset	0	Operand Data (High Order Byte)
		7	1	Index Register Plus Offset + 1	0	Operand Data (Low Order Byte)
JSR	8	1	1	Op Code Address	1	Op Code
		2	1	Op Code Address + 1	1	Offset
		3	0	Index Register	1	Irrelevant Data
		4	1	Stack Pointer	0	Return Address (Low Order Byte)
		5	1	Stack Pointer − 1	0	Return Address (High Order Byte)
		6	0	Stack Pointer − 2	1	Irrelevant Data
		7	0	Index Register	1	Irrelevant Data
		8	0	Index Register Plus Offset (w/o Carry)	1	Irrelevant Data

Source: Reprinted with permission of Motorola Incorporated, Austin, Texas. Copyright © 1980 by Motorola Incorporated.

FIGURE 8.10 | Timing Diagram for STA Indexed Instruction

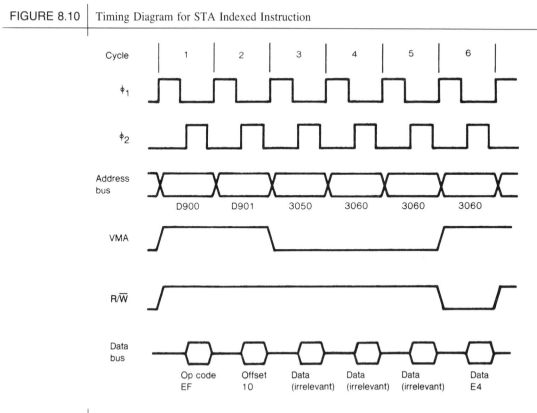

8.4.4 | Extended Addressing Mode

All extended addressing mode instructions are three-byte instructions. The first byte is the op code, the second byte is the 8 high-order address bits. The third byte of the instruction contains the low-order 8 bits of the address. Table 8.6 gives a summary of the instructions for the extended addressing mode. Notice in Table 8.6 and in Examples 8.7 and 8.8 that the VMA line is low for some instructions. This is again due to the internal architecture of the μP. When the VMA line is low, it signifies that the data bus is in an indeterminate state and the data is considered to be irrelevant. Examples 8.7 and 8.8 show what happens on each clock cycle for loading and storing data in the accumulator using the extended addressing mode.

EXAMPLE |

8.7 | Show the number of clock cycles that are needed for loading accumulator A using the extended addressing mode.

Program Listing	Memory Listing			Data in Memory
0350 LDA A $4712	0350	B6	Op code	4712 1D
	0351	47	ADH	
	0352	12	ADL	

TABLE 8.6 | Summary of Extended Addressing Mode Instructions

Instructions	Cycles	Cycle #	VMA Line	Address Bus	R/W̄ Line	Data Bus
STS STX	6	1	1	Op Code Address	1	Op Code
		2	1	Op Code Address + 1	1	Address of Operand (High Order Byte)
		3	1	Op Code Address + 2	1	Address of Operand (Low Order Byte)
		4	0	Address of Operand	1	Irrelevant Data
		5	1	Address of Operand	0	Operand Data (High Order Byte)
		6	1	Address of Operand + 1	0	Operand Data (Low Order Byte)
JSR	9	1	1	Op Code Address	1	Op Code
		2	1	Op Code Address + 1	1	Address of Subroutine (High Order Byte)
		3	1	Op Code Address + 2	1	Address of Subroutine (Low Order Byte)
		4	1	Subroutine Starting Address	1	Op Code of Next Instruction
		5	1	Stack Pointer	0	Return Address (Low Order Byte)
		6	1	Stack Pointer 1	0	Return Address (High Order Byte)
		7	0	Stack Pointer 2	1	Irrelevant Data
		8	0	Op Code Address + 2	1	Irrelevant Data
		9	1	Op Code Address + 2	1	Address of Subroutine (Low Order Byte)
JMP	3	1	1	Op Code Address	1	Op Code
		2	1	Op Code Address + 1	1	Jump Address (High Order Byte)
		3	1	Op Code Address + 2	1	Jump Address (Low Order Byte)
ADC EOR ADD LDA AND ORA BIT SBC CMP SUB	4	1	1	Op Code Address	1	Op Code
		2	1	Op Code Address + 1	1	Address of Operand (High Order Byte)
		3	1	Op Code Address + 2	1	Address of Operand (Low Order Byte)
		4	1	Address of Operand	1	Operand Data
CPX LDS LDX	5	1	1	Op Code Address	1	Op Code
		2	1	Op Code Address + 1	1	Address of Operand (High Order Byte)
		3	1	Op Code Address + 2	1	Address of Operand (Low Order Byte)
		4	1	Address of Operand	1	Operand Data (High Order Byte)
		5	1	Address of Operand + 1	1	Operand Data (Low Order Byte)
STA A STA B	5	1	1	Op Code Address	1	Op Code
		2	1	Op Code Address + 1	1	Destination Address (High Order Byte)
		3	1	Op Code Address + 2	1	Destination Address (Low Order Byte)
		4	0	Operand Destination Address	1	Irrelevant Data
		5	1	Operand Destination Address	0	Data from Accumulator
ASL LSR ASR NEG CLR ROL COM ROR DEC TST INC	6	1	1	Op Code Address	1	Op Code
		2	1	Op Code Address + 1	1	Address of Operand (High Order Byte)
		3	1	Op Code Address + 2	1	Address of Operand (Low Order Byte)
		4	1	Address of Operand	1	Current Operand Data
		5	0	Address of Operand	1	Irrelevant Data
		6	1/0	Address of Operand	0	New Operand Data

Source: Reprinted with permission of Motorola Incorporated, Austin, Texas. Copyright © 1980 by Motorola Incorporated.

Solution:

Clock Cycle	Address Bus	Data Bus	*Internal Operation*
1	0350	B6	Fetch op code; increment PC to 0351.
2	0351	47	Decode op code B6; increment PC to 0352.
3	0352	12	Hold ADH (47); increment PC to 0353.
4	4712	1D	Latch incoming data.
5	0353	Next op code	Fetch next op code; increment PC to 0354.

EXAMPLE

8.8 Show the number of clock cycles needed to store accumulator A in the following program:

Program Listing	Memory Listing	Accumulator A
8450 STA A $27FA	8450 B7 Op code	11
	8451 27 ADH	
	8452 FA ADL	

Solution:

Clock Cycle	Address Bus	Data Bus	Internal Operation
1	8450	B7	Fetch op code; increment PC to 8451.
2	8451	27	Decode op code B7; increment PC to 8452.
3	8452	FA	Hold ADH (27); increment PC to 8453.
4	27FA	Data (irrelevant)	VMA line is low; bring R/$\overline{\text{W}}$ line low for next clock cycle.
5	27FA	11	Send out data (11) from accumulator A to 27FA.
6	8453	Next op code	Fetch next op code; increment PC to 8454.

Figure 8.11 shows the timing diagram for a load the accumulator instruction using the extended addressing mode. The contents (1D) of memory location 4712 are being transferred to accumulator A. Figure 8.12 shows the timing diagram for a store the accumulator instruction using this mode. The contents (11) of accumulator A are stored at memory location 27FA.

FIGURE 8.11 | Timing Diagram for Loading Accumulator A Using Extended Addressing Mode

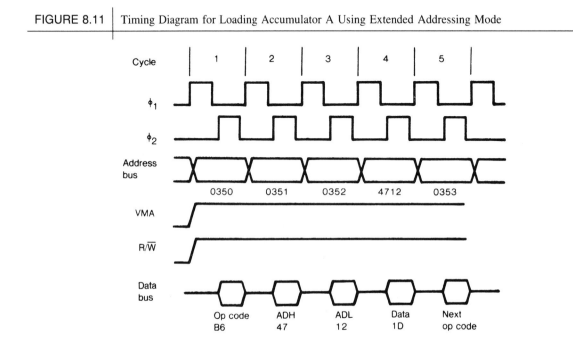

FIGURE 8.12 | Timing Diagram for Storing Accumulator A Using Extended Addressing Mode

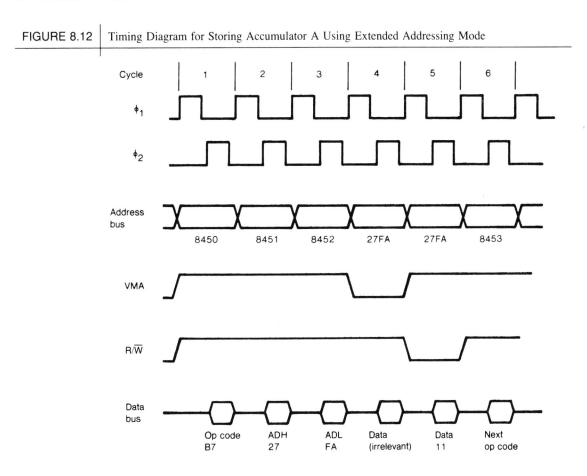

8.4.5 | Inherent Addressing Mode

For the 6800 μP, the inherent addressing mode is divided into two addressing modes—implied and accumulator. Both types are one-byte instructions.

Implied Addressing Mode: There are two types of implied addressing mode instructions—those that require an operand address and those that do not. An example of an instruction that does not is the TBA instruction. This instruction causes the μP to move the contents of accumulator B to accumulator A. The binary patterns on the address and data buses are valid only on the first cycle of the instruction. For those instructions that do require an address, the address is held by an internal μP register such as the stack pointer. Thus, no additional data is required from memory to develop an address. An example of this type of instruction is PSH.

Accumulator Addressing Mode: In accumulator only addressing, either accumulator A or accumulator B is specified. An example is ASL A (arithmetic shift left on the A accumulator).

TABLE 8.7 | Summary of Inherent Addressing Mode Instructions

Instructions	Cycles	Cycle #	VMA Line	Address Bus	R/W̄ Line	Data Bus
ABA DAA SEC ASL DEC SEI ASR INC SEV CBA LSR TAB CLC NEG TAP CLI NOP TBA CLR ROL TPA CLV ROR TST COM SBA	2	1	1	Op Code Address	1	Op Code
		2	1	Op Code Address + 1	1	Op Code of Next Instruction
DES DEX INS INX	4	1	1	Op Code Address	1	Op Code
		2	1	Op Code Address + 1	1	Op Code of Next Instruction
		3	0	Previous Register Contents	1	Irrelevant Data
		4	0	New Register Contents	1	Irrelevant Data
PSH	4	1	1	Op Code Address	1	Op Code
		2	1	Op Code Address + 1	1	Op Code of Next Instruction
		3	1	Stack Pointer	0	Accumulator Data
		4	0	Stack Pointer − 1	1	Accumulator Data
PUL	4	1	1	Op Code Address	1	Op Code
		2	1	Op Code Address + 1	1	Op Code of Next Instruction
		3	0	Stack Pointer	1	Irrelevant Data
		4	1	Stack Pointer + 1	1	Operand Data from Stack
TSX	4	1	1	Op Code Address	1	Op Code
		2	1	Op Code Address + 1	1	Op Code of Next Instruction
		3	0	Stack Pointer	1	Irrelevant Data
		4	0	New Index Register	1	Irrelevant Data
TXS	4	1	1	Op Code Address	1	Op Code
		2	1	Op Code Address + 1	1	Op Code of Next Instruction
		3	0	Index Register	1	Irrelevant Data
		4	0	New Stack Pointer	1	Irrelevant Data
RTS	5	1	1	Op Code Address	1	Op Code
		2	1	Op Code Address + 1	1	Irrelevant Data
		3	0	Stack Pointer	1	Irrelevant Data
		4	1	Stack Pointer + 1	1	Address of Next Instruction (High Order Byte)
		5	1	Stack Pointer + 2	1	Address of Next Instruction (Low Order Byte)

Source: Reprinted with permission of Motorola Incorporated, Austin, Texas. Copyright © 1980 by Motorola Incorporated.

Accumulator addressing mode instructions are one-byte, two-cycle instructions, and the address and data buses are active only during the first cycle of the instruction when the operator is being loaded from memory. During the second cycle, the machine performs the operation and VMA is high.

Table 8.7 gives a summary of the instructions and a cycle-by-cycle timing description for the 6800 μP's inherent addressing mode. Example 8.9 shows the cycle-by-cycle operation for a one-byte accumulator addressing mode instruction. Example 8.10 shows what happens for a two-byte accumulator addressing mode instruction.

TABLE 8.7 | continued

Instructions	Cycles	Cycle #	VMA Line	Address Bus	R/W̄ Line	Data Bus
WAI	9	1	1	Op Code Address	1	Op Code
		2	1	Op Code Address + 1	1	Op Code of Next Instruction
		3	1	Stack Pointer	0	Return Address (Low Order Byte)
		4	1	Stack Pointer – 1	0	Return Address (High Order Byte)
		5	1	Stack Pointer – 2	0	Index Register (Low Order Byte)
		6	1	Stack Pointer – 3	0	Index Register (High Order Byte)
		7	1	Stack Pointer – 4	0	Contents of Accumulator A
		8	1	Stack Pointer – 5	0	Contents of Accumulator B
		9	1	Stack Pointer – 6	1	Contents of Cond. Code Register
RTI	10	1	1	Op Code Address	1	Op Code
		2	1	Op Code Address + 1	1	Irrelevant Data
		3	0	Stack Pointer	1	Irrelevant Data
		4	1	Stack Pointer + 1	1	Contents of Cond. Code Register from Stack
		5	1	Stack Pointer + 2	1	Contents of Accumulator B from Stack
		6	1	Stack Pointer + 3	1	Contents of Accumulator A from Stack
		7	1	Stack Pointer + 4	1	Index Register from Stack (High Order Byte)
		8	1	Stack Pointer + 5	1	Index Register from Stack (Low Order Byte)
		9	1	Stack Pointer + 6	1	Next Instruction Address from Stack (High Order Byte)
		10	1	Stack Pointer + 7	1	Next Instruction Address from Stack (Low Order Byte)
SWI	12	1	1	Op Code Address	1	Op Code
		2	1	Op Code Address + 1	1	Irrelevant Data
		3	1	Stack Pointer	0	Return Address (Low Order Byte)
		4	1	Stack Pointer – 1	0	Return Address (High Order Byte)
		5	1	Stack Pointer – 2	0	Index Register (Low Order Byte)
		6	1	Stack Pointer – 3	0	Index Register (High Order Byte)
		7	1	Stack Pointer – 4	0	Contents of Accumulator A
		8	1	Stack Pointer – 5	0	Contents of Accumulator B
		9	1	Stack Pointer – 6	0	Contents of Cond. Code Register
		10	0	Stack Pointer – 7	1	Irrelevant Data
		11	1	Vector Address FFFA (Hex)	1	Address of Subroutine (High Order Byte)
		12	1	Vector Address FFFB (Hex)	1	Address of Subroutine (Low Order Byte)

Although the instruction in Example 8.9 is listed as requiring only two clock cycles, the actual transfer takes place during the third clock cycle. This internal operation does not interfere with other operations, so the instruction is considered to need only two clock cycles.

In Example 8.10, although the contents (70) of accumulator A are actually stored on the stack by the end of the third clock cycle, the 6800 μP takes an additional clock cycle (clock cycle 4) to decrement the stack pointer. This leaves the stack pointer holding the next available address where data can be stored. Figure 8.13 shows the timing diagrams for a push instruction.

EXAMPLE

8.9   Show the clock cycles needed for transferring the contents of accumulator B to accumulator A.

Program Listing   *Memory Listing*
  0200 TBA   0200   17

Solution:

Clock Cycle	*Address Bus*	*Data Bus*	*Internal Operation*
1	0200	17	Fetch op code; increment PC to 0201.
2	0201	Next op code	Decode op code (17); increment PC to 0202.
3	0202	Next byte from memory	Transfer the contents of accumulator B to accumulator A; increment PC to 0203.

EXAMPLE

8.10   Show the clock cycles needed for the following push instruction:

Program Listing	*Memory Listing*	*Accumulator*	*Stack Pointer*
B460 PSH A	B460 36 Op code	70	02FF

Solution:

Clock Cycle	*Address Bus*	*Data Bus*	*Internal Operation*
1	B460	36	Fetch op code; increment PC to B461.
2	B461	Next op code (to be ignored)	Decode op code 36; ignore incoming op code; hold PC at B461.
3	02FF	70	Data (70) is sent from accumulator A to stack.
4	02FF	70	Stack pointer is decremented at this time; VMA = 0, R/$\overline{\text{W}}$ = 1.

8.4.6 | Relative Addressing Mode

This addressing mode is the addressing mode for the branch instruction. Remember from Chapter 6 that branch instructions are two-byte instructions. The first byte is the op code and the second byte is the offset.

When a branch instruction is executed, the sequence of events is as follows:

FIGURE 8.13 | Timing Diagram for Push Instruction

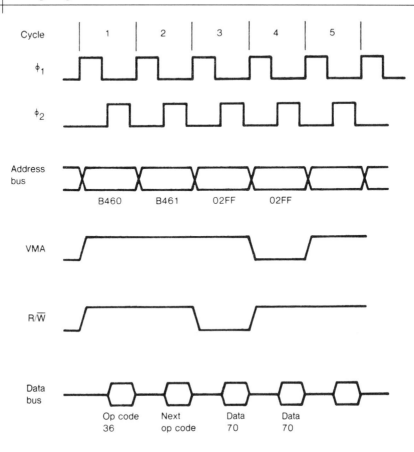

1. The op code is fetched from the memory and stored in the instruction register during cycle 1.
2. The offset is loaded into the μP during cycle 2.
3. The offset is added to the low-order bits of the program counter in cycle 3 and the carry is propagated during cycle 4.
4. During cycles 3 and 4, the VMA line goes low while the μP is operating on the offset.
5. The next instruction is loaded during cycle 5.

Table 8.8 is a cycle-by-cycle description of what happens during a relative addressing mode. Figure 8.14 shows the timing diagram for a branch instruction using the relative addressing mode. The following four examples, Examples 8.11, 8.12, 8.13, and 8.14, show what happens during each clock cycle for different situations that could occur when the μP is executing a branch instruction.

TABLE 8.8 | Summary of Relative Addressing Mode Instructions

Instructions	Cycles	Cycle #	VMA Line	Address Bus	R/W̄ Line	Data Bus
BCC BHI BNE BCS BLE BPL BEQ BLS BRA BGE BLT BVC BGT BMI BVS	4	1	1	Op Code Address	1	Op Code
		2	1	Op Code Address + 1	1	Branch Offset
		3	0	Op Code Address + 2	1	Irrelevant Data
		4	0	Branch Address	1	Irrelevant Data
BSR	8	1	1	Op Code Address	1	Op Code
		2	1	Op Code Address + 1	1	Branch Offset
		3	0	Return Address of Main Program	1	Irrelevant Data
		4	1	Stack Pointer	0	Return Address (Low Order Byte)
		5	1	Stack Pointer − 1	0	Return Address (High Order Byte)
		6	0	Stack Pointer − 2	1	Irrelevant Data
		7	0	Return Address of Main Program	1	Irrelevant Data
		8	0	Subroutine Address	1	Irrelevant Data

Source: Reprinted with permission of Motorola Incorporated, Austin, Texas. Copyright © 1980 by Motorola Incorporated.

FIGURE 8.14 | Timing Diagram for Branch Instruction Using Relative Addressing Mode

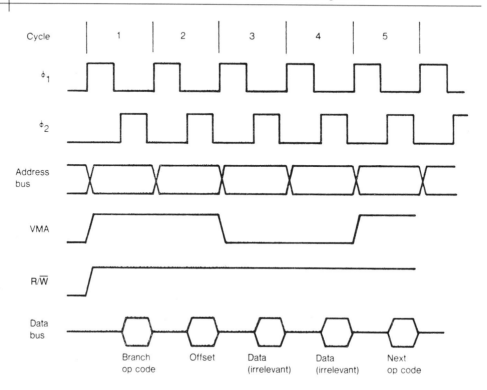

EXAMPLE

8.11 Show the clock cycles needed to execute the following branch on minus instruction. The offset value is positive ($04 = +4$) and there is no page crossing.

Program Listing	Memory Listing			Negative Flag
1586 BMA $04	1586	2B	Op code	1
	1587	04	Offset	

Solution:

Clock Cycle	Address Bus	Data Bus	Internal Operation
1	1586	2B	Fetch op code; increment PC to 1587.
2	1587	04	Decode op code 2B; increment PC to 1588.
3	1588	Data (irrelevant)	Check N flag; add 88 + 04 = 8C (no internal carry).
4	158C	Data (irrelevant)	Add 15 + internal carry (15 + 0 = 15).
5	158C	Next op code	Bring VMA line back high; fetch new op code; increment the new PC to 158D.

        Since the N flag is a logic 1, then the branch is taken. The branch address is put on the address bus on the fifth clock cycle.

EXAMPLE

8.12 Repeat Example 8.11, but this time use an offset value of $-9 = F7_{hex}$.

Program Listing	Memory Listing			Negative Flag
1586 BMI $F7	1586	2B|F7	Op code	1
	1587	F7	Offset	

Solution:

Clock Cycle	Address Bus	Data Bus	Internal Operation
1	1586	2B	Fetch op code; increment PC to 1587.
2	1587	F7	Decode op code 2B; increment PC to 1588.
3	1588	Data (irrelevant)	Bring VMA line low; check N flag; add 88 + F7 = 7F with no internal borrow.
4	157F	Data (irrelevant)	Subtract 15 − 0 = 15.
5	157F	Next op code	Bring VMA line back high; fetch new op code; increment the new PC to 1580.

EXAMPLE

8.13   Repeat Example 8.11 with a positive offset of 7C. This offset value causes a page crossing.

Program Listing	Memory Listing		Negative Flag
1586 BMI $7C	1586 2B	Op code	1
	1587 7C	Offset	

Solution:

Clock Cycle	Address Bus	Data Bus	Internal Operation
1	1586	2B	Fetch op code; increment PC to 1587.
2	1587	7C	Decode op code 2B; increment PC to 1588.
3	1588	Data (irrelevant)	Bring VMA line low; check N flag; add 88 + 7C = 04 with an internal carry.
4	1504	Data (irrelevant)	Add 15 + 1 = 16.
5	1604	Next op code	Bring VMA line back high; fetch new op code; increment new PC to 1605.

EXAMPLE

8.14   Show the clock cycles needed for the following negative branch. The offset value EC causes a page crossing in the negative direction.

Program Listing	Memory Listing		Negative Flag
1536 BMI $EC	1536 2B	Op code	1
	1537 EC	Offset	

Solution:

Clock Cycle	Address Bus	Data Bus	Internal Operation
1	1536	2B	Fetch op code; increment PC to 1537.
2	1537	EC	Decode op code 2B; increment PC to 1538.
3	1538	Data (irrelevant)	Bring VMA line low; check N flag; add 38 + EC = 24 with an internal borrow.
4	1524	Data (irrelevant)	Subtract 15 − 1 = 14.
5	1424	Next op code	Bring VMA line back high; fetch new op code; increment PC to 1425.

8.5 | INTERRUPTS

The 6800 μP has four different types of interrupts: reset ($\overline{\text{RST}}$), nonmaskable ($\overline{\text{NMI}}$), software (SWI), and interrupt request ($\overline{\text{IRQ}}$). Three of these interrupts ($\overline{\text{RST}}$, $\overline{\text{NMI}}$, and $\overline{\text{IRQ}}$) are hardware interrupts because they are activated by signals external to the μP. The fourth interrupt (SWI) is a software interrupt because it is initiated when the μP decodes the SWI instruction. Regardless of which type of interrupt occurs, the μP fetches the starting address of the interrupt service program from memory. The starting address (not the program) must be stored in the following locations:

Reset ($\overline{\text{RST}}$)	FFFE	FFFF
Nonmaskable interrupt ($\overline{\text{NMI}}$)	FFFC	FFFD
Software interrupt (SWI)	FFFA	FFFB
Interrupt request ($\overline{\text{IRQ}}$)	FFF8	FFF9

These eight addresses are called *vectors* or *vector addresses* because they contain information that points the μP to an interrupt service routine. Let's consider the timing diagrams for each type of interrupt.

8.5.1 | Reset

A reset signal is used to initialize the μP after power is turned on or to reinitialize the μP at any time. If the reset line goes low for at least eight clock cycles and then goes high, the μP resets itself. The following conditions occur after eight clock cycles:

1. The interrupt mask bit is set. This is the I bit of the condition code register.
2. The address bus contains FFFE.
3. The R/$\overline{\text{W}}$ line is high (read condition).
4. The VMA line goes low.
5. The data bus lines are in their high impedance state.
6. The BA line goes low.

Note: Although the address bus line contains an address (FFFE), neither memory chips nor peripheral devices respond to it because the VMA line is low. The VMA line goes high after the reset line goes high. Figure 8.15 shows the timing diagram for the reset condition.

8.5.2 | $\overline{\text{NMI}}$, SWI, and $\overline{\text{IRQ}}$

The 6800 μP handles the $\overline{\text{NMI}}$, SWI, and $\overline{\text{IRQ}}$ interrupts similarly, except that each has its own vector address. For the nonmaskable interrupt ($\overline{\text{NMI}}$) and the interrupt request ($\overline{\text{IRQ}}$), the μP completes the instruction in progress before beginning the interrupt sequence. For the software interrupt (SWI), after this instruction is decoded, the μP begins the interrupt sequence. Before the vector address is fetched, the μP stores on the stack the contents of the program counter, the index register, accumulator A, accumulator B,

FIGURE 8.15 | Timing Diagram for Reset Condition (Redrawn with permission of Motorola Incorporated, Austin, Texas)

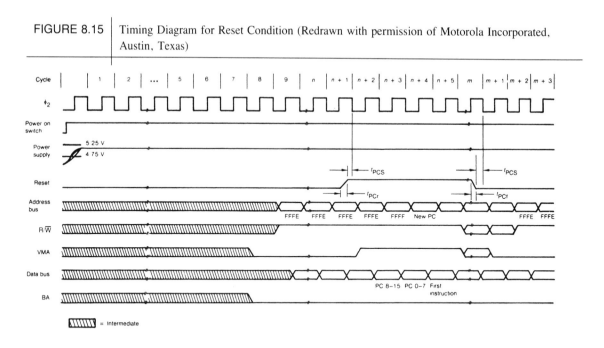

FIGURE 8.16 | Saving Status of μP in Stack (Redrawn with permission of Motorola Incorporated, Austin, Texas)

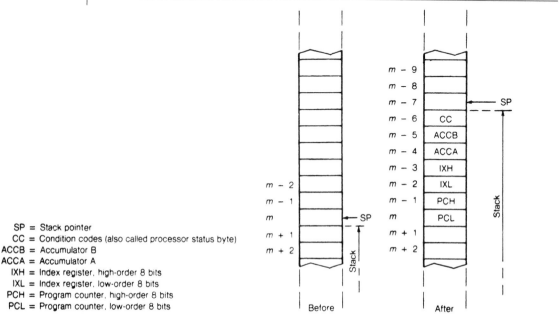

SP = Stack pointer
CC = Condition codes (also called processor status byte)
ACCB = Accumulator B
ACCA = Accumulator A
IXH = Index register, high-order 8 bits
IXL = Index register, low-order 8 bits
PCH = Program counter, high-order 8 bits
PCL = Program counter, low-order 8 bits

FIGURE 8.17 | Timing Diagram for $\overline{\text{NMI}}$ and $\overline{\text{IRQ}}$ Interrupts (Redrawn with permission of Motorola Incorporated, Austin, Texas)

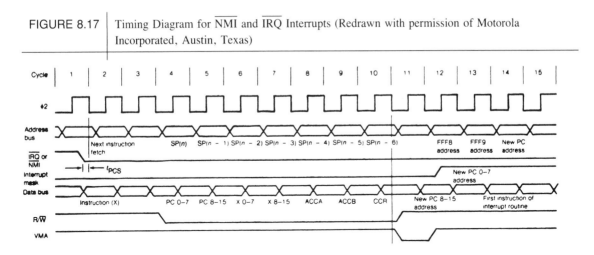

and the condition code register. Figure 8.16 shows this data being stored on the stack. Figure 8.17 shows the timing diagram for the $\overline{\text{NMI}}$ and $\overline{\text{IRQ}}$ interrupts.

Remember from Chapter 5 that the difference between an interrupt request and a nonmaskable interrupt is that the μP can be stopped from recognizing an interrupt request signal but it cannot be stopped from recognizing a nonmaskable interrupt request signal. If the I bit in the condition code register is set, the μP will not recognize an interrupt request. The I bit is set in one of the following ways:

1. By a reset condition,
2. With an SEI (set interrupt flag) instruction,
3. By recognizing an interrupt request signal,
4. By recognizing a nonmaskable interrupt signal,
5. By recognizing an SWI (software interrupt).

The CLI (clear interrupt flag) instruction resets the I bit to a logic 0.

8.6 | WAIT FOR INTERRUPT

In Chapter 6, we saw that the 6800 μP has a WAI (wait for interrupt) instruction. This instruction suspends all μP operation so that the μP does not fetch and execute any more instructions. After a WAI instruction has been executed, the μP stores the contents of the program counter, the index register, accumulator A, accumulator B, and the condition code register on the stack. The μP's address, data, and R/$\overline{\text{W}}$ lines go to their high impedance state. The VMA line goes low and the BA line goes high. These conditions remain until the μP receives an $\overline{\text{IRQ}}$ or an $\overline{\text{NMI}}$ signal. Remember, however, that if the I bit is set, the μP can never recognize an $\overline{\text{IRQ}}$ signal. If the I bit is set, the μP can only recognize a nonmaskable interrupt or reset signal. The μP recognizes a reset condition at any time. A reset overrides any operation. The timing diagram for the WAI instruction is shown in Figure 8.18.

FIGURE 8.18 | Timing Diagram for Wait Instruction (Redrawn with permission of Motorola Incorporated, Austin, Texas)

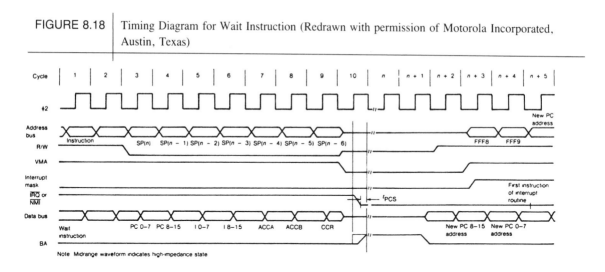

Note Midrange waveform indicates high-impedance state

8.7 | HALT AND SINGLE-INSTRUCTION EXECUTION

The $\overline{\text{HLT}}$ line allows an external signal to stop the μP from fetching and executing any more instructions. Controlling the μP in this way is primarily used for two purposes: (1) DMA (direct memory access) operation and (2) single-instruction execution.

In normal operation, the $\overline{\text{HLT}}$ line is high and the μP fetches and executes the program instructions. When the $\overline{\text{HLT}}$ line goes low, the μP stops all activity. As a response, the μP brings the bus available (BA) line high. This is a signal from the μP that the address bus, data bus, and R/$\overline{\text{W}}$ lines have gone to their high impedance states. The μP is said to be "floating" because it no longer controls the buses. So that no memory chip or peripheral device is falsely activated, the VMA line goes low. When the μP is in this condition, data can be quickly transferred between memory and peripheral equipment because the data does not have to go through the μP. This condition is called *direct memory access* (DMA). In order to do DMA operations, a special peripheral device called a DMA controller is needed.

The second purpose of using the $\overline{\text{HLT}}$ line is to allow debugging of a program by execution of one instruction at a time. When the $\overline{\text{HLT}}$ line goes low, the μP completes the instruction it is executing and then stops all activity. The $\overline{\text{HLT}}$ line must go low before the trailing edge of the ϕ_1 clock pulse of the last cycle of an instruction. Point A of Figure 8.19 shows this condition. The minimum time in Figure 8.19 is shown as t_{PCS}.

If either a nonmaskable interrupt or interrupt request signal occurs while the μP is halted, the signal is latched into the μP. However, the μP will not respond to the interrupt until the $\overline{\text{HLT}}$ line goes back high. If a rest signal occurs while the μP is halted, the following conditions occur:

1. VMA line remains low.
2. BA line goes low.
3. Data bus remains in its high impedance state.

FIGURE 8.19 | Halt and Single-Instruction Execution for System Debugging (Redrawn with permission of Motorola Incorporated, Austin, Texas)

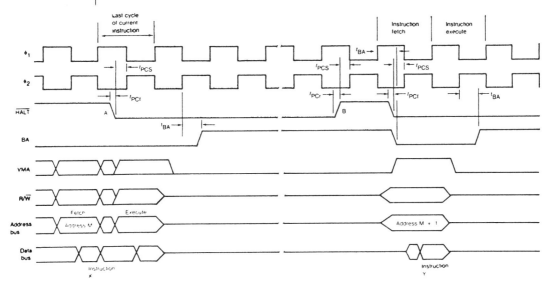

4. R/$\overline{\text{W}}$ line goes high.
5. Address bus contains the address FFFE.

As long as the $\overline{\text{HLT}}$ line remains low, conditions 1–5 hold. When the $\overline{\text{HLT}}$ line goes high, the µP addresses the reset vector location (FFFE and FFFF) and the reset program is executed.

In order to do single-step execution, the $\overline{\text{HLT}}$ line must be brought high for one µP cycle and then returned low, as shown by point B in Figure 8.19. This condition allows the µP to execute one instruction and then halt. Each time we want to execute an instruction, the $\overline{\text{HLT}}$ line must be brought high and then low again. The right half of Figure 8.19 shows the timing diagram for a one-byte, two-cycle instruction, such as an inherent addressing mode instruction.

8.8 | SUMMARY

This chapter covered the hardware aspects of the 6800 µP from its pin descriptions to how it handles an interrupt request, including its clock signals, timing diagrams, cycle-by-cycle operations, and interrupts. Remember that the number of clock cycles required to execute an instruction depends on the type of instruction and the addressing mode. Therefore, choice of the right addressing mode allows the µP and µC system to operate most efficiently by storing the program in the fewest number of bytes or by executing an instruction with the fewest number of clock cycles. As an example, Section 8.4 showed examples and timing diagrams for different 6800 instructions and addressing modes. Several examples compared the 6800's extended addressing mode with its direct addressing mode.

Section 8.5 covered the 6800's hardware and software interrupts. The hardware interrupts are reset ($\overline{\text{RST}}$), nonmaskable interrupt request ($\overline{\text{NMI}}$), and interrupt request ($\overline{\text{IRQ}}$). There is one software interrupt request instruction (SWI). Each interrupt request has its own pair of vector addresses.

The 6800 μP has a WAI instruction. This instruction permits the μP to stop fetching and executing any more instructions until an interrupt request signal is received.

In Section 8.7, we saw how an external signal can be used to halt the μP from fetching and executing any more instructions. This method of halting the μP can be used to debug programs when it is used as a single-step feature.

PROBLEMS

8.1 Does the 6800 μP require an external circuit to generate the two-phase nonoverlapping clock pulses?

8.2 What are the power requirements for the 6800 μP?

8.3 Name the input and output control lines.

8.4 When the $\overline{\text{HLT}}$ pin goes low, does the μP finish executing the present instruction before halting?

8.5 What do the following abbreviations stand for? (a) $\overline{\text{IRQ}}$, (b) $\overline{\text{NMI}}$, (c) DBE, (d) TSC, (e) $\overline{\text{RES}}$, (f) VMA, and (g) BA.

8.6 What does the line over the control symbols represent?

8.7 For a 1 MHz system, what is the minimum pulse width time?

8.8 When is the data coming into the μP latched?

8.9 How many clock cycles are needed for an LDX immediate addressing mode instruction?

8.10 When, during the clock cycle, is the program counter incremented to the next memory location?

8.11 Does the direct addressing mode for the 6800 μP apply only to page zero?

8.12 What is the advantage of using the direct addressing mode?

8.13 How many bytes is the indexed addressing mode instruction?

8.14 During what clock cycle(s) in an indexed addressing mode are the index register and the offset value added?

8.15 When the 6800 μP's VMA line is low, what does it signify?

8.16 Does the VMA line go low in all extended addressing mode instructions?

8.17 Are all inherent addressing mode instructions one-byte instructions?

8.18 What are the two groups of inherent addressing mode instructions?

8.19 How many clock cycles are required by a PSH B instruction? What is accomplished on the last clock cycle?

8.20 Does the relative addressing mode apply only to the branch instructions?

8.21 Examples 8.11 to 8.14 show that, when a branch is taken, the 6800 μP requires four clock cycles. Does the 6800 μP also require four clock cycles if the branch is not taken? If yes, during what clock cycle(s) is the VMA line low?

8.22 List the four different types of interrupts for the 6800 μP.

8.23 What are the interrupt vectors for each type of interrupt?

8.24 Why does the μP set the interrupt flag bit during a reset operation?

8.25 Name two reasons for using the $\overline{\text{HLT}}$ line.

8.26 What does the term *floating* mean?

9 | Semiconductor Memories

9.0 | INTRODUCTION

In Chapter 2, we examined the three major parts of a μC system: the μP, memory, and input/output ports. In Chapters 6–8, we dealt with the hardware and software aspects of the 6800 μP. We saw that the μP fetches and executes instructions that are stored in memory. In this chapter, we will look at the memory devices that are most often used in μC systems. Chapter 10 will cover specific memory chips and show how to connect them to the 6800 μP.

Memories store information. The information may be instructions, alphanumeric data, punctuation marks, special characters, and so forth. There are many different ways and devices for storing information, so let's first consider the different memory categories.

9.1 | MEMORY CLASSIFICATIONS

Memories may be classified in a number of different ways. Some are (1) material used —semiconductor versus magnetic; (2) retention of information when power is turned off—volatile versus nonvolatile; and (3) access to data—serial versus random. Let's look at each classification.

9.1.1 | Semiconductor versus Magnetic

Memory IC chips are manufactured using either bipolar or MOS technology. These devices are called *semiconductor memories*. They use either the principle of a flip-flop to store a logic 1 and a logic 0, or a charge on a capacitor for a logic 1 and no charge for a logic 0.

Another method of storing logic 1s and logic 0s uses magnetic materials. Before 1970, the most popular type of memory unit was the ferrite core. These doughnut-shaped rings were magnetized in one direction for a logic 1 and in the other direction for a logic 0. Although ferrite cores are seldom used now, they enabled computers to store large amounts of data in a relatively small area. Their disadvantages were high cost, large power consumption, low speed, and low density. Although the ferrite core is seldom used today, the principle of storing binary information on magnetic material is still used with μC systems in the form of tape cassettes, floppy disks, hard disks, and bubble memories. The emphasis in this text, however, is on semiconductor memories because they are used in every system, both dedicated control and general-purpose μC systems.

9.1.2 | Volatile versus Nonvolatile

A *volatile memory* is one that loses its information when power is turned off or if there is a power failure. In other words, power must be kept on to retain the information in memory. Sometimes the word *temporary* is used in place of volatile.

A *nonvolatile memory* is one that retains its information when power is turned off or if there is a power failure. This type of memory is also known as *permanent* memory. Magnetic memories are nonvolatile. Semiconductor memories may be either volatile or nonvolatile.

9.1.3 | Serial versus Random

This classification deals with the way information can be written to or retrieved from memory. Each instruction or piece of data is stored at a memory address. On magnetic tape, all information is stored in sequence. Therefore, if we want to go to a new address, the tape must be moved forward or backward to that address. For example, if the tape is at address 0100_{hex} and we wish to go to 0200_{hex} (256 addresses away), the tape must be moved forward from address 0100 to address 0200 before the data can be accessed. All the data between these two addresses must pass by the tape head before the new address is reached. Thus, all the data is in series. This type of memory is also called *sequential access memory*.

Even with high-speed tape drives, sequential access memories are slow. Tapes do have their advantages, however, in that they can store large amounts of data in a small area, and they are inexpensive.

Random access memories are the fastest because any memory location can be addressed directly. Therefore, reading or writing data is very fast because we do not have to pass sequentially through many locations. Semiconductor memories used in μC systems use the principle of random access.

Let's consider a comparison to the example just given for access to a magnetic tape memory. If the μP is to access location 0100_{hex}, the following steps occur:

1. The μP puts 0100 onto the address bus.
2. The address is decoded by external decoders, the memory chip(s), or both.
3. Information is either sent to or received from the μP across the data bus.

If the μP wishes to access location 0200_{hex}, steps 1–3 are repeated, except that address 0200 is put onto the address bus. Therefore, information at every location can be obtained in the same amount of time.

The term *random access memory* is used in two ways: (1) for the way a μP can address a memory location or (2) for a type of semiconductor memory. We have just used the first definition to compare sequential access with random access. Let's now consider the second definition.

As previously mentioned, a semiconductor memory can be either volatile or nonvolatile. A volatile semiconductor memory is also known as a *random access memory* (RAM) device. A nonvolatile semiconductor memory is known as a *read-only memory* (ROM) device. Every address in each type of memory chip (both RAM and ROM) can be accessed by the μP in the same amount of time. Hence, every memory location in either a RAM or ROM chip uses the random rather than the sequential method of accessing data.

9.2 | SEMICONDUCTOR MEMORY TECHNOLOGY

Semiconductor memories can be subdivided according to the technology used in their manufacturing process, either bipolar technology or metal-oxide semiconductor (MOS) technology. In bipolar technology, manufacturers have most often used transistor-transistor logic (TTL), Schottky TTL, and emitter-coupled logic (ECL). In MOS technology, memory devices have been manufactured using P channel MOS (PMOS), N channel MOS (NMOS), and complementary MOS (CMOS). These technologies allow manufacturers to improve or trade off speed, density, and power consumption. Trade-offs have been made in all digital logic circuits, including the μP chip itself. For example, the fastest memories are bipolar, particularly those using ECL technology. The trade-off is that as speed increases, so does power consumption.

Semiconductor manufacturers have shifted from making PMOS memory devices to making NMOS memory devices because the latter allow increased speed and packaging density. CMOS devices consume the least power but are slightly more expensive.

Manufacturers have increased the speed of NMOS devices so that their access times approach—and in some cases overlap—the access times of TTL bipolar memories, and, depending on the operating speed, they may consume less power than TTL devices. NMOS memories are the backbone of μC memory systems. If speed is the primary consideration, then a designer usually chooses ECL memories. To improve speed, manufacturers are now using a high-speed NMOS device, called an HMOS. Most memory devices (both RAMs and ROMs) in μC systems use NMOS technology. To allow the μP memory and peripheral devices to be interconnected easily, all the voltage levels are TTL compatible. We will now consider the different types of RAMs and ROMs that are available.

9.3 | RANDOM ACCESS MEMORIES (RAMS)

As previously mentioned, the term *random access memory* refers to a volatile memory. A RAM device allows the μP to read data from or write data to the device. Therefore, RAMs are also referred to as read/write (R/$\overline{\text{W}}$) memories. The term *read/write memory* is often more descriptive than random access memory because we can visualize the μP receiving (reading) and sending (writing) data to memory. The term *random access memory* is more descriptive when we study a timing diagram because every address can be accessed in the same amount of time. There are two types of RAMs—static and dynamic. We now look at each type in more detail.

A *static* RAM is a memory device that stores information in a flip-flop. As long as power is applied, the information is held. Remember, however, that if the power is lost, the information is lost.

A *dynamic* RAM is a memory device that stores data on a capacitor. With time, the capacitor loses its charge, and therefore even when power is applied, the charge on the capacitor must be refreshed periodically to maintain the data. Most dynamic RAMs require a refresh signal every 2 ms, and some can go as long as 4 ms between refresh signals. In order to provide this refresh signal, some additional circuitry is required. Let's consider some of the advantages and disadvantages of each type of RAM.

The obvious advantage of the static RAM is that it is easier to use because it requires no additional circuitry. Static RAMs are also faster than dynamic RAMs and consume less power than dynamic RAMs. Static RAMs are available in bit-wide, byte-wide (8 bits), or half-byte-wide (4 bits) formats. This flexibility allows memory systems to be built quite rapidly. For example, a popular static RAM is the 2114. It is organized as 1024 words × 4 bits. Therefore, two of these chips give the user 1K × 8 bits of memory in two ICs.

Although dynamic RAMs require periodic refreshing, they have a lower cost per bit and are available in denser packages than the static RAMs. A denser package means that there are more bits per package. Dynamic RAMs only come one bit wide. Some of the commonly used dynamic RAMs are 4K × 1, 16K × 1, 32K × 1, 64K × 1, and 256K × 1. Soon there will be on the market a 1M × 1 dynamic RAM. As technology improves, the speed of dynamic RAMs is decreasing, and more of the external circuitry is either put into the memory chip or contained in a single IC. Earlier dynamic RAMs required three power supplies, +12 V and ±5 V, but the newer dynamic RAMs, including the 64K and 256K dynamic RAMs, require only a single supply, +5 V.

9.4 | STATIC NMOS RAM DEVICES

In many systems, the static NMOS RAM is the backbone of the memory system. Table 9.1 gives data for some of the static NMOS RAMs manufactured by Motorola.

All input and output lines of NMOS RAMs are TTL compatible. All output data lines are also three-state, except in the 2125A and the 2125H devices. Their output lines are open collector, not three-state.

The automatic power down column in Table 9.1 indicates those static RAMs that draw less current from the power supply when the device is not selected. For example, the 2148, when it is selected, draws a maximum current of 140 mA. But when the device is not selected, it draws only a maximum of 30 mA. This feature is different from the low-power version. For example, the 2114, with a maximum current of 100 mA, is also available in a low-power version, the 21L14, which has a maximum current of only 70 mA. These devices do not have an automatic power down, which means that their maximum current could be drawn whether the device is selected or not. Low-power versions usually cost more and, therefore, the additional cost has to be taken into con-

TABLE 9.1 | Motorola Static NMOS RAMs

Part Number	Organization	Access Time (ns max.)	Number of Pins	Low-Power Version Available	Automatic Power Down Capability
MCM2114	1024×4	200–450	18	Yes	No
MCM2115A[1]	1024×1	45–70	16	Yes	No
MCM2115H[2]	1024×1	20–35	16	No	No
MCM2125A	1024×1	45–70	16	Yes	No
MCM2125H	1024×1	20–35	16	No	No
MCM2147	4096×1	55–100	18	No	Yes
MCM2147H	4096×1	35–55	18	No	Yes
MCM2148	1024×4	70–85	18	No	Yes
MCM2148H	1024×4	45–55	18	No	Yes
MCM2149H	1024×4	45–55	18	No	No
MCM2167	$16,384 \times 1$	55–100	20	No	Yes
MCM4016	2048×8	20–200	24	No	Yes
MCM6641	4096×1	200–450	18	Yes	No
MCM6810	128×8	250–450	24	No	No

[1]A indicates an improved version with lower access times. In many cases, only the A version is now being manufactured.

[2]H stands for high speed.

sideration when a system is being designed. The trade-off is the cost and, possibly, the size of the power supply versus the cost of the memory chips.

9.5 | STATIC NMOS RAM CELL

The two types of MOS static RAMs that are primarily used in µC systems are the NMOS and CMOS devices. An NMOS device is faster and costs less than a CMOS device. However, CMOS devices have the advantage of low power, and they are used in many portable µP-controlled instruments. The design of the basic memory cell is similar for both devices.

Figure 9.1 shows a basic NMOS memory cell. It is a static cell because it requires no additional clock signals to refresh the data. Q_1 and Q_2 are used as high-resistance loads. Q_3 and Q_4 form a flip-flop. Q_5 and Q_6 act as switches to allow the memory cell to be read from and written to. The circuit in Figure 9.1 shows only one address line, X. X and Y address lines will be discussed in Section 9.5.3.

9.5.1 | Circuit Operation

Voltage V_{DS_3} is the drain-to-source voltage of Q_3. It is also the gate-to-source voltage of Q_4 because of the cross-coupling nature of the flip-flop. Voltage V_{DS_4} is the drain-to-source voltage of Q_4 and is also the gate-to-source voltage of Q_3. If Q_3 is on—that is,

FIGURE 9.1 | Six-Transistor Static RAM Cell

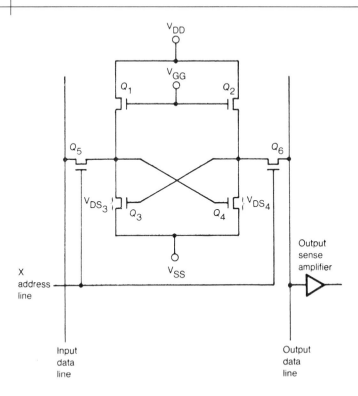

if the drain-to-source of Q_3 is conducting current—then V_{DS_3} is very small. This low voltage causes Q_4 to be off. When Q_4 is off, its drain-to-source voltage is large, so that V_{DS_4} is approximately V_{DD}. The large voltage of V_{DS_4} keeps Q_3 on.

9.5.2 | Switching Action

To change the state of the flip-flop, a positive signal is applied on the X address line and on the input line. This positive input signal increases V_{DS_3}. As V_{DS_3} increases, Q_4 begins to conduct, which in turn reduces V_{DS_4}. As V_{DS_4} decreases, the current to Q_3 decreases, thus increasing V_{DS_3} further. This process keeps repeating until Q_3 is cut off and Q_4 is conducting. Thus, the state of the flip-flop has changed, so that Q_3 is off and Q_4 is on.

If we want to change the state of the flip-flop back to Q_3 on and Q_4 off, the steps are as follows: (1) Bring the X address line high, and (2) bring the input data line low. The gate-to-source voltage of Q_4 will then be low, which cuts off Q_4. When Q_4 is off, Q_3 will conduct and will remain on. Although the circuit on Figure 9.1 shows the output data line to be the complement of the input data line, RAM cells have an additional inverter so that the input and output polarities are the same. A block diagram for this static memory cell is shown in Figure 9.2.

FIGURE 9.2 | Block Diagram for Static Memory Cell

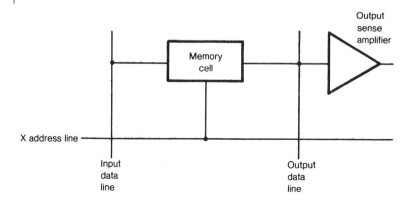

9.5.3 | Memory Array

Figure 9.3 shows a 2 × 2 memory array using four of the memory cells of Figure 9.1. This circuit uses both X and Y address lines. The X address line chooses a particular row and the Y address line chooses a particular column of cells. A particular memory cell is chosen only when there is a logic 1 on both a row line and a column line. For example, if we want to address memory cell 1,1 then a logic 1 has to be placed on the X_1 line and on the Y_1 line. A logic 1 placed on the X_1 line addresses all of the memory cells of the first row. A logic 1 placed on the Y_1 line addresses all the memory cells of the first column. Remember, only one row line at a time can be a logic 1 and only one column line at a time can be a logic 1. When the Y_1 line is a logic 1, Q_A and Q_B conduct and all the data lines of the first column are connected to the drain of Q_{in}. The logic 1 on the Y_1 line also causes all of the output data lines of the first column of memory cells to be connected to the drain of Q_{out}.

The read/write (R/$\overline{W}$) line is used by the μP either to read data from a memory cell or to write data to a memory cell. If the R/$\overline{W}$ line is high, the μP is reading data from a memory cell. When this line is high, it causes Q_{in} to be off and Q_{out} to be on. In the circuit shown in Figure 9.3, the output data line contains the complemented logic state of the addressed memory cell. This complement can be corrected by another inverter at the output.

If the R/$\overline{W}$ line is low, the μP is writing data to a memory cell. When this line is low, it causes Q_{in} to on and Q_{out} to be off. Now the logic level on the data input line is directed to the addressed cell.

The circuit of Figure 9.3 shows how each individual memory cell can be addressed by the μP. This is how a one-bit-wide static RAM device could be arranged. In static RAM devices that are organized as half-byte-wide (4 bits) or full-byte-wide (8 bits) devices, as shown in Figure 9.4, the Y address lines select four memory cells or eight memory cells at a time. Obviously, these devices have four or eight input and output lines, respectively. In Figure 9.4, each block contains four memory cells. When a particular row and column are selected, the four cells associated with that block are connected

FIGURE 9.3 | 2 × 2 Static Memory Array

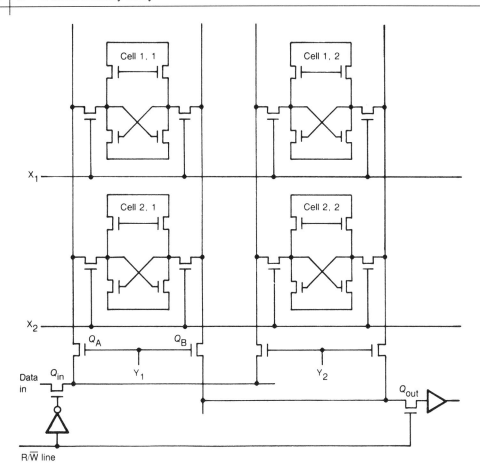

to the data lines. The logic level on the R/W̄ line (not shown) determines whether data is being received or sent.

9.6 | DYNAMIC RAMS

Dynamic RAMs store data as a charge on a capacitor instead of in a flip-flop, as in a static RAM. The capacitor is referred to as a *parasitic capacitor* because it is not a separate element but, rather, is the gate capacitance of a MOS transistor. Figure 9.5 is a diagram of a three-transistor RAM cell showing the parasitic capacitance (C_S) from gate to source (Q_2). In order to emphasize the presence of the parasitic capacitance, it is drawn as a separate element on circuit diagrams, as shown in Figure 9.5. As with any capacitor, this capacitor eventually loses its charge and therefore must be periodically refreshed. Most devices require every cell to be refreshed within 2 ms. Some dynamic

FIGURE 9.4 | Static RAM Device Half-Byte (4 Bits) or Full Byte (8 Bits) Wide

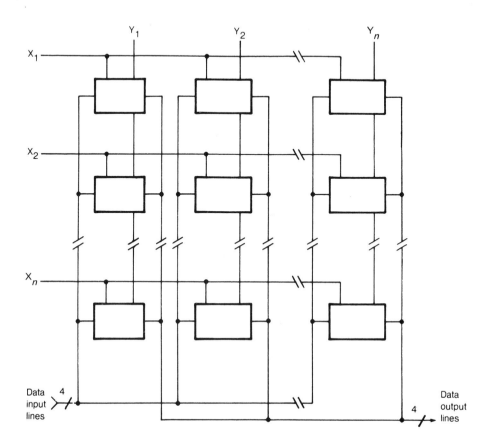

RAMs, such as Texas Instruments' TMS 4164, can go as long as 4 ms without being refreshed. As previously mentioned, dynamic RAMs require additional circuitry to provide the refreshing, and this is a disadvantage. Much of the additional circuitry has been incorporated into either the RAM chip itself, or into the μP (not the 6800) or into a single IC controller chip. Therefore, dynamic RAMs are becoming easier to use. Remember, the advantages of dynamic RAMs over static RAMs are as follows:

1. More bits per device (denser packaging),
2. Less cost per bit,
3. Less power consumed per bit, both active and standby.

The reason manufacturers can fabricate dynamic RAMs with more bits per IC is that these RAMs require fewer transistors per cell than do static RAMs; therefore, they are less expensive to make and consume less power per bit.

FIGURE 9.5 | Parasitic Capacitance (C_S) for Dynamic RAM Cell

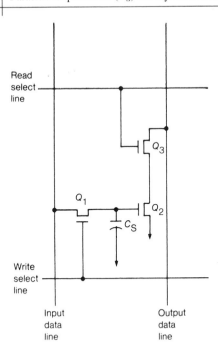

Read
select
line

Q_3

Q_1

Q_2

C_S

Write
select
line

Input
data
line

Output
data
line

9.6.1 | Cell Design

Dynamic cell designs, like other devices, have changed over the past few years. Earlier dynamic RAMs used three transistors per memory cell, although some manufacturers did experiment with four transistors per cell in a configuration similar to a static RAM cell. To increase package density, all of the newest dynamic RAMs now use a single transistor per cell. These devices include the $16{,}384 \times 1$, $32{,}768 \times 1$, $65{,}536 \times 1$, and $262{,}144 \times 1$ memory chips. The break between the three-transistor and single-transistor devices occurred in the 4096×1 device. Some 4K devices use three transistors, while others are designed with a single transistor. Three-transistor cells tend to be more temperature stable and need less internal sense circuitry. Single-transistor cells allow more bits to be packaged in the same area.

9.6.2 | Three-Transistor Dynamic Memory Cell

The circuit in Figure 9.6 shows a three-transistor dynamic memory cell. It requires two select lines (read and write) and two data lines (input and output). This is the basic storage cell used in the 1103 dynamic RAM. The device was first introduced in 1970, and it became instrumental in the increased use of semiconductor memory rather than core memory.

FIGURE 9.6 | 1103 Dynamic Memory Cell

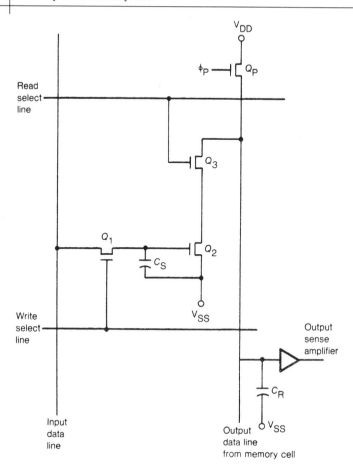

Write Operation: Data is written into the three-transistor cell by the following steps (refer to Figure 9.6):

1. Data is put onto the input data line.
2. The write select line is brought to a logic 1, turning on Q_1.
3. C_S charges or discharges to the logic level on the data line.
4. After sufficient time ($\sim$ 115 ns) to allow C_S to charge or discharge, the write select line can go low to turn off Q_1.

Note: The 115 ns in step 4 is not the total cycle time but rather is the minimum time the data has to be stable. The total access time has to be greater than 580 ns.

Read Operation: Data is read from the three-transistor cell by the following steps (refer to Figure 9.6):

1. The precharge transistor, Q_P, is turned on by a signal ϕ_P. This is called a precharge signal.
2. The reference capacitor, C_R, is charged to a logic 1 when Q_P is turned on.
3. The precharge signal is removed, causing Q_P to turn off and C_R to remain charged.
4. The read select line goes to a logic 1, which turns on Q_3.
5. Capacitor C_R remains charged or discharges, depending on the logic level on C_S: If C_S is at a logic 0, then Q_2 remains off and C_R cannot discharge. If C_S is at a logic 1, then Q_2 is turned on and C_R can discharge through Q_2 and Q_3.
6. The sense amplifier reads the logic state of C_R, which is the complement of C_S. The data output line of the 1103 is complemented.

Refresh Operation: The charge on C_S is refreshed by a modified read and write operation. Each cell in a row is refreshed at the same time, as shown in Figure 9.7. The steps for refreshing are as follows:

1. The precharge transistor, Q_P, is turned on and capacitor C_R is initially charged. Then Q_P is turned off.

FIGURE 9.7 | Refresh Operation

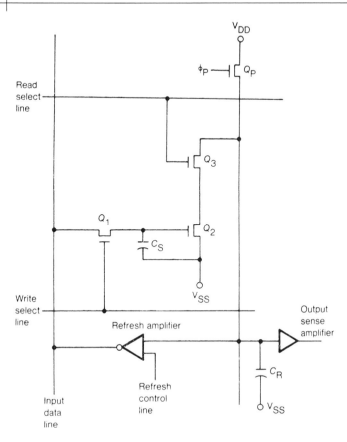

2. The read select line is brought to a logic 1 and Q_3 is turned on. Capacitor C_R can remain charged or can discharge in the same manner as in the read operation, step 5. The read select line is turned off.
3. The control line on the refresh amplifier is activated.
4. The logic level on C_R is the input to the refresh amplifier.
5. The refresh amplifier inverts the signal and puts it onto the input data line.
6. The write select line is activated and the storage capacitor, C_S, is refreshed.

Steps 1–6 would take place even if C_S initially had no charge on it. This procedure would guarantee that C_S remained uncharged and that no stray charge "leaked" onto it. The refresh amplifier is a sense amplifier with an inverter.

9.6.3 | Single-Transistor Dynamic Memory Cell

In order to fabricate more dynamic memory cells on a substrate, manufacturers have turned to the single-transistor memory cell, which is shown in Figure 9.8. Transistor Q_1 acts as a switch so that data can be read from or written to the storage capacitor, C_S. The row select line is used for both reading and writing. The data line is used for both reading data and writing data. The cell shown in Figure 9.8 requires additional internal circuitry to direct the input signal to C_S and to sense the voltage on C_S.

FIGURE 9.8 | Single-Transistor Memory Cell

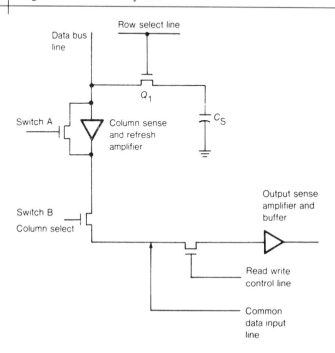

Write Operation: The following steps are used to write data into the single-transistor cell:

1. The row select line is brought to a logic 1, turning on Q_1.
2. Switches A and B are turned on.
3. The logic level on the data line either charges or discharges the storage capacitor, C_S.
4. Switches A and B and the row select line are returned to a logic 0, turning off switches A and B and Q_1, allowing C_S to holde the data.

Read Operation: The steps involved in reading data from the single-transistor cell are as follows:

1. The row select line is brought to a logic 1, to turn on Q_1 and to put the charge held by C_S on the data line.
2. Switches A and B are put into the read and data output positions, respectively.
3. The sense amplifier senses the signal placed on the data line by C_S, amplifies the signal so that the output is at a "clean" logic 1 or logic 0 state, sends the amplified signal to the memory's output amplifier and buffers, and returns the amplified signal to the data line so as to recharge or discharge C_S to its initial logic state.
4. Switches A and B are returned to their off state and Q_1 is turned off.

Refresh Operation: The refresh operation is similar to the read operation. The steps are as follows:

1. The row select line is brought to a logic 1 and the charge on C_S is placed on the data line.
2. Switch A is placed in the read position; switch B is left in the off position.
3. The sense amplifier works in the same way as in the read operation, step 3.

There are several ways of doing the refresh operation. In some cases, the output buffers are left open in their high impedance state; in other cases they are not, and the data appears on the output lines. There is one sense amplifier per column and each memory cell in a row is refreshed at the same time. Therefore, if a dynamic memory has 128 rows, then refreshing requires 128 refresh cycles. There are some exceptions to this rule because some memory chips allow two rows to be refreshed at the same time. In this case, only 64 refresh cycles would be required.

9.6.4 | Need for Sense/Rewrite Amplifier

Unlike the three-transistor dynamic memory cell, the single-transistor cell is a destructive memory cell. This means that the charge on C_S is partially lost during a read operation. For this reason, the data must be rewritten into the cell on every read operation. Let's examine why.

FIGURE 9.9 | Sense/Rewrite Amplifier

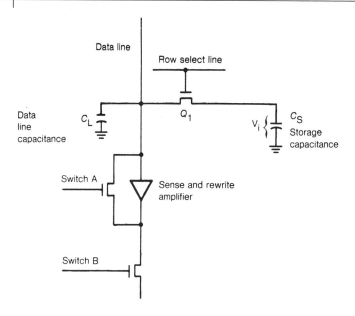

Figure 9.9 illustrates why the sense/rewrite amplifier is needed. Every memory cell in a column is connected to the same data line; this adds capacitance to the line. In fact, the line capacitance, C_L, in Figure 9.9, may be ten to twenty times the capacitance of a single storage cell. When the transistor Q_1 is turned on, there is a voltage division between C_L and C_S and a loss of charge on C_S. Voltage V_i is reduced. Therefore, the sense/rewrite amplifier does not receive all of the voltage that was on C_S and any loss of charge must be replaced.

The voltage received by the sense/rewrite amplifier is given by the voltage division law for capacitors:

$$V_{S/R} = \frac{C_S}{C_S + C_L} V_i \tag{9.1}$$

where: $V_{S/R}$ = Input voltage to sense/rewrite amplifier

C_S = Value of storage capacitance

C_L = Value of data line capacitance

V_i = Initial voltage on C_S

EXAMPLE

9.1 | Some typical values of voltage and capacitance are $C_S = 0.05$ pF, $C_L = 1.0$ pF, and $V_i = 10$ V. Calculate the input voltage to the sense/rewrite amplifier.

Solution:
Applying Equation 9.1 yields

$$V_{S/R} = \frac{0.05 \text{ pF}}{0.05 \text{ pF} + 1.0 \text{ pF}} \times 10 \text{ V} \cong \frac{1}{20} \times 10 \text{ V} = 500 \text{ mV}$$

The voltage $V_i = 10$ V indicates that the capacitor C_S is initially charged to a logic 1. A logic 0 would be stored as 0 V. In this example, the amplifier must be capable of detecting 500 mV as a logic 1. (Most dynamic memory devices use amplifiers that are capable of detecting at least 200 mV as a logic 1.) The amplifier amplifies the 500 mV back to 10 V and reapplies it to the data line, thereby recharging C_S.

9.6.5 | Charge on C_S

The equation for capacitance in terms of charge, Q, and voltage, V, is as follows:

$$C = \frac{Q}{V} \tag{9.2}$$

When the storage cell's capacitance is initially charged to a voltage V_i, then the charge stored on the plates of C_S is given by Equation 9.3:

$$Q_i = C_S \times V_i \tag{9.3}$$

When the cell is being read, V_i changes to $V_{S/R}$, a final voltage, and the charge on C_S at this time is given by Equation 9.4:

$$Q_f = C_S \times V_{S/R} \tag{9.4}$$

Q_f and $V_{S/R}$ represent the charge and voltage, respectively, on C_S before it is recharged by the sense/rewrite amplifier during a read operation.

EXAMPLE

9.2 | Using the values in Example 9.1, calculate Q_i and Q_f.

Solution:
From Example 9.1, $C_S = 0.05$ pF, $V_i = 10$ V, and $V_f = 500$ mV. Therefore:

$$Q_i = 0.05 \text{ pF} \times 10 \text{ V} = 500 \times 10^{-15} \text{ coulombs}$$

and

$$Q_f = 0.05 \text{ pF} \times 500 \text{ mV} = 25 \times 10^{-15} \text{ coulombs}$$

Example 9.1 has C_S storing a logic 1 represented by $V_i = 10$ V. If C_S had stored a logic 0, then V_i would be 0 V and Q_i and Q_f would be 0. This is actually the ideal case, because some charge could "leak" onto C_S and therefore Q_i would not be 0. Even if C_S were an ideal capacitor and Q_i were 0, Q_f would not be 0 because of the presence of noise on the data line. For these reasons, the sense/rewrite operation is needed to ensure that a logic 0 remains stored in the memory cell.

9.7 | NONVOLATILE MEMORIES

As previously mentioned, semiconductor RAMs (either static or dynamic) are volatile memories—the programs and data are lost when the power is turned off. There are many applications, however, when it is necessary to save information in a nonvolatile memory after power is turned off. A semiconductor device is needed so that it can be mounted on a printed circuit (PC) board. The nonvolatile memory should also have fast access time and enough bits to store a program of reasonable size (at least 1K words). Obviously, we do not want to go back to large and bulky core memories, and disk or magnetic tape systems are impractical and too expensive for many applications such as consumer products—microwave ovens, dishwashers, games, and so on. Even in systems in which general-purpose programs are entered through a keyboard or from disks or tapes, there is a program stored in the computer that allows the user to enter a program and operate the system.

Hence, there is a need to provide nonvolatile memory storage for μCs. Although magnetic disks and tapes are nonvolatile storage, here we will consider only nonvolatile semiconductor memories. There are six types of nonvolatile semiconductor memories that are often used with μPs:

1. ROM, maskable read-only memory;
2. PROM, programmable read-only memory;
3. EPROM, erasable (using ultraviolet light) and reprogrammable read-only memory, sometimes referred to as UV PROM;
4. EEPROM, electrically erasable programmable read-only memory, also abbreviated as E^2PROM, and sometimes referred to as EAROM (electrically alterable read-only memory), EEROM, or E^2ROM;
5. Battery backup for RAM devices;
6. MBM, magnetic bubble memory.

No one μC system uses all of the memory methods. The first five are used most often. Magnetic bubble memories are being used more often now, but they are still few and far between. Let's concentrate on the first four devices.

9.7.1 | ROM

A read-only memory, ROM, chip is permanently programmed at the factory by the semiconductor manufacturer. This IC device is sometimes referred to as a maskable ROM to distinguish its programming method from that of other ROM chips. In the last (or last two) manufacturing step, the binary pattern is entered by a technique called *masking*. Usually manufacturers will make ROMs only in lots of hundreds, thousands, or tens of thousands. Obviously, ROMs are used in high-volume products such as microwave ovens, games, and so forth. The program sent to the ROM manufacturer must be correct. Otherwise, the factory will produce hundreds or thousands of worthless devices. There is a method of working around errors that exist in a maskable ROM chip. The technique is called *patching*. However, this method requires another chip, and the system has to have been designed to take the additional chip. Most consumer products are not designed with this additional flexibility. Therefore, in most cases, ROMs that have an error are worthless devices. Although the cost of an error in a ROM chip is high, the cost of the ROM chip on a per-bit basis is the lowest of all the permanent memory chips.

9.7.2 | PROM

ROM chips are not suitable for many μC applications. Instead, μC users usually need a nonvolatile storage device that satisfies one or more of the following criteria:

1. A piece of equipment that is not designed for high-volume production;
2. A nonvolatile memory chip with the same pin configuration as ROM, to use until ROM chips are delivered;
3. A nonvolatile memory chip that can be programmed in the field or laboratory for last-minute design modifications.

Semiconductor manufacturers have responded to these demands with the programmable read-only memory, PROM. These devices can be programmed only once. They are designed with fusible links that can be "blown" or not, depending on the binary pattern of the program. New PROMs, with all the fuses intact, are called clean PROMs.

In order to "burn" or blow the fusible links to enter the program into a PROM, the user needs a PROM programmer (a piece of equipment, not a person). Commercially available PROM programmers are easy to use because they are complete packages containing socket(s), power supply, additional working memory (buffer memory), serial or parallel keyboard interface, hex keyboard, seven-segment display readout of address and data, and, most important of all, the correct voltage levels and proper timing pulses.

Like ROMs, there is no margin for error in the use of PROMs. Once a fusible link has been blown, it cannot be changed. Therefore, once a PROM is programmed, it cannot be reprogrammed, and it is essential to be sure the program is correct before a PROM is programmed. An error is not as costly, however, as it is with a ROM device. An error wastes only one PROM, not hundreds or thousands of them. The cost per bit of a PROM is more than the cost per bit of a ROM, but in many cases it is well worth the extra money.

9.7.3 | EPROM

Both the ROM and PROM chips can only be programmed once. During design development stages, and in some low-volume production of μC applications, designers need a memory device in which the program can be erased and the device can then be reprogrammed. Two devices are presently being marketed that are reprogrammable nonvolatile memories: (1) the erasable programmable read-only memory, EPROM, and (2) the electrically erasable programmable read-only memory, EEPROM or E^2PROM. This section introduces the EPROM and Section 9.7.4 covers the EEPROM.

The reprogrammable memory device most often used today is the EPROM or UV PROM. Like the PROM, EPROMS are usually programmed using a PROM programmer. The EPROMS are erased by placing them under an ultraviolet lamp (hence UV PROM) for a specified amount of time. Typically, erasure times are from 15 minutes to 1 hour.

The major advantage of EPROMs is that they can be erased and reprogrammed. Other advantages are that these devices operate from a single $+5$ V power supply. This is not the programming voltage, but the operating voltage in the µC system. Many manufacturers have a ROM chip that is pin compatible with the EPROM. Therefore, when a design is finalized and it is going to be used in a large volume item, a ROM chip can be ordered and inserted into the same PC board without any modifications.

Disadvantages of the EPROM are the following:

1. It must be removed from the circuit to be erased.
2. It requires a long time for erasure.
3. It has a limited life cycle (100 to 1000 erasures and reprogrammings).
4. The entire device is erased (block erasure), not just an individual byte.

There are some development systems that place the erasure unit on the PC board so that the EPROM does not have to be removed for erasure. There are not many of these systems, however, because the entire system has to be stopped while the EPROM is erased. Therefore, most development is done by using a zero insertion socket in the PC board and inserting and removing the EPROM when necessary. When a programming bug(s) is to be corrected, the EPROM is removed and placed under the ultraviolet lamp, and a blank EPROM is programmed using a PROM programmer (usually requiring 1 to 2 minutes) and inserted into the PC board socket. The new program can be tested while the old EPROM is being erased. Therefore, a separate erasure unit, PROM programmer, and extra EPROMs are the quickest and most convenient method of using EPROMs.

9.7.4 | EEPROM

The electrically erasable programmable read-only memory, EEPROM or E^2PROM, is a nonvolatile reprogrammable memory chip. This device is sometimes referred to as an electrically alterable read-only memory, EAROM. The EAROM is actually an older version, and the way each cell is made is different from the way the cells are made in the EEPROM. Most manufacturers refer only to EEPROMS.

Like the PROM and EPROM, the EEPROM is purchased blank and is programmed by the user. Remember that PROMs cannot be erased, but EPROMS can be erased by using an ultraviolet lamp. EEPROMs are erased and programmed using an electrical pulse. This feature allows both erasing and programming to be done right on the PC board without removing the EEPROM.

Some EEPROMs have only block erasure (all bits are cleared), but others allow the user to erase one byte at a time. Byte erasure is a convenient feature because usually the user only needs to change one byte or at most a few bytes at a time when debugging a program. Devices that can be debugged on a per-byte basis are usually slower than block erasure devices.

Although the operating voltage for these devices is +5 V, the erasing and programming voltage is usually +17 V to +20 V. To leave the EEPROM in the circuit and have the μP do the erasing and programming, additional support logic is required as well as the +17 V to +20 V.

Although binary patterns can be written into EEPROMs by the μP using the additional circuitry, EEPROMs are not intended to be used as read/write memories, but rather they are intended to be used as read-mostly memory (RMM). Manufacturers' specifications list the data retention time as between 10 and 20 years. The more often these devices are erased and reprogrammed, the shorter their lifespan becomes. Most users probably do not have to worry about this problem, however, because many EEPROMs can be programmed tens of thousands of times without any deterioration.

9.8 | NONVOLATILE MEMORY DEVICES IN SYSTEM DEVELOPMENT

Before a program is finalized and ready to be placed in a μC system, it has gone through a number of programming and reprogramming steps to get all of the bugs out of it. If the final program is to be stored in a PROM or ROM chip, it has usually gone through several stages using the different nonvolatile memory chips. Most μP programs are designed by the use of a RAM-to-ROM procedure. This is a multistep procedure resulting in a finalized program. First, the program is entered into RAM, where it is run, tested, and debugged. This step may take weeks or even months. After the programmer is satisfied that the program and the system are operating correctly, the program can be transferred to an EEPROM. Since this chip is a nonvolatile memory, the system may be turned off and on at different times to see if it responds as it should. If any additional errors are found or if other program modifications have to be made, they can be made on the EEPROM almost as easily as on the RAM chips. The next step after the EEPROM would be an EPROM. Using a PROM programmer, the designer could insert the chip into the final PC board. Last-minute modifications can still be made by removing the EPROM, easing it, and reprogramming it. When all of the bugs are removed and the system is operating correctly, the program is ready to be burned into a PROM chip for low-volume applications or into a ROM chip for high-volume applications.

Users of ROM chips have to plan for the semiconductor manufacturer's turn-around time. That is, the time between when the manufacturer receives a program and when the user receives the ROM chips has to be included in the schedule for design development. In most cases, 4 to 6 weeks should be allowed for delivery. While the user is waiting for the ROM chips, many manufacturers will begin shipping products containing PROM chips.

9.9 | MEMORY SPEED

Most 8-bit μPs operate on frequencies between 1 MHz and 2 MHz. This means the μP's clock cycle time is from 500 ns to 1 μs. So that the μP does not wait for data coming from memory, the memory chip should be fast enough to respond to the μP. This means we have to consider the memory chip's access time and cycle time.

Access time is the time interval between the instant at which the memory chip receives a valid address and the instant at which the output data is valid. For writing data into a memory chip, access time is the time between the instant at which the memory chip receives a valid address and the instant at which the storage is completed. In fully static ROMs, PROMs, EPROMs, and RAMs, the access time and the cycle time are equal. In dynamic RAMs and in some dynamic ROMs, cycle time and access time are not the same.

Cycle time is the time required to complete an entire memory cycle. It includes the access time, regeneration time, and any additional time until the memory chip can receive the next address. Many dynamic RAMs have destructive readouts—that is, when the data is read out, it is also destroyed. Therefore, the chip must regenerate or refresh the storage cell. Refreshing takes additional time, and this added time is why the cycle time is not equal to the access time.

Some ROM chips are fully static, while others are edge enabled. In the fully static ROM, access time and cycle time are the same. In the edge-enabled ROM, additional time is needed to precharge the support circuitry. The advantage of these devices is that they consume less power when the chip is not selected. The disadvantage, however, is that the chip enable line must go to the high state and then back to the low state every time a new address is selected.

9.10 | ALLOWING ENOUGH TIME FOR DATA TO BE RECEIVED

First-time users of a μP may think that only the access time or cycle time of the memory chip must be considered to have the μP receive valid data from memory. Let's look at an example in which the access time and the cycle time are each equal to 450 ns, a typical access time for a static RAM. In Figure 9.10, typical ϕ_1 and ϕ_2 clock cycles are shown for the 6800 μP operating at 1 MHz. The clock cycle time is 1 μs. The μP manufacturer guarantees that 300 ns after the ϕ_1 clock signal goes high, the address on the address bus is valid. Therefore, for the worst possible case, 300 ns could be wasted while the μP places a valid address on the address bus. Let's consider negligible time for the memory chip to receive this valid address. If the memory chip's access time is 450 ns, then a total of 750 ns (300 ns + 450 ns) is the time used before the data is valid on the data bus. This leaves 250 ns for the μP to receive the data, which is plenty of time. See Figure 9.10.

If the μP's clock frequency is changed to 2 MHz (this corresponds to the μP's cycle time of 500 ns), let's see what could happen. The manufacturer states that the address from the μP is valid 150 ns after the ϕ_1 clock signal goes high. Although this time has been reduced from 300 ns to 150 ns, the memory chip's access time has not

FIGURE 9.10 | Relationship of Data to ϕ_1 and ϕ_2 Clock Pulses

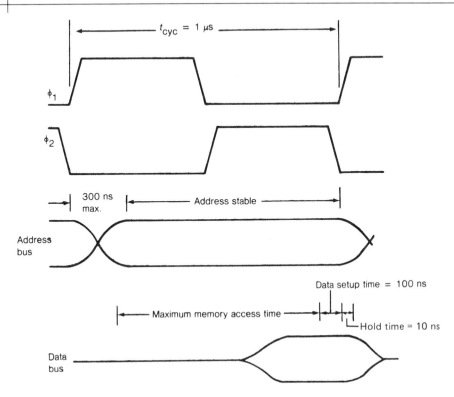

been reduced; it is still 450 ns. Therefore, the total time is 600 ns (150 ns + 450 ns). This means that the μP has entered the next cycle before the memory has been able to respond. If the μP has not been placed in a wait state, it will never receive valid data and the system will never work. We see, then, that running the μP at a faster frequency without considering the access and cycle times of the memory chips will lead to disaster.

9.11 | SUMMARY

All computers require memory to store programs and data. In this chapter, we examine the different classifications of memories: (1) semiconductor versus magnetic, (2) volatile versus nonvolatile, and (3) serial versus random.

Two of the most commonly used semiconductor memories in μC systems are RAMs and ROMs. RAM devices are either static or dynamic. Static devices are easier to use and are faster. However, dynamic RAMs can be manufactured with greater density. The disadvantage most often cited for dynamic RAMs is the need for periodic refreshing of the individual bits. Section 9.6 shows different cell designs that are used for dynamic

RAMs. Nonvolatile memories that are found in μC systems are ROMs, PROMs, EPROMs, and EEPROMs.

Regardless of the type of memory chip used, access time or cycle time must be considered when a system is designed. This is to ensure that the μP receives or sends data to the right memory location. Section 9.10 discusses the factors that must be considered when memory chips are added to a μC system. The next chapter focuses on how these memory chips are interconnected to form a workable memory system.

PROBLEMS

9.1 What is the primary function of memories?

9.2 List the different classifications of memories.

9.3 What are the principal semiconductor technologies used for memory devices?

9.4 Define (a) volatile memory and (b) nonvolatile memory.

9.5 Is a volatile memory device a temporary or a permanent memory?

9.6 In most applications, are serial access memory devices faster or slower than random access memories?

9.7 What are the two ways the term *random access* is used?

9.8 Is the data in a ROM chip accessed as a random memory?

9.9 Of semiconductor technologies mentioned in this text, which is the fastest?

9.10 What is the advantage of CMOS memory devices?

9.11 What are the two types of random access memories?

9.12 What is the principal storage element for (a) static memories and (b) dynamic memories?

9.13 List the advantages of static RAMs over dynamic RAMs.

9.14 Refer to Figure 9.1 and consider that Q_3 is on and Q_4 is off. What steps are required to switch the state of the memory cell?

9.15 Refer to Figure 9.3 and consider that memory cell 2,2 is to store a logic 0. What steps are required?

9.16 What is the name of the capacitor in a dynamic memory cell?

9.17 What are the advantages of dynamic RAMs?

9.18 Does the capacitor in a dynamic cell need a refresh signal to maintain a logic 0? Explain your answer.

9.19 List six types of nonvolatile memories.

9.20 What are some applications for maskable ROM chips?

9.21 Are PROM devices reusable?

9.22 What is the difference between erasing an EPROM chip and erasing an EEPROM chip?

9.23 Do EPROMs have block erasure or byte erasure?

9.24 Define access time.

10 Memory Chips and Organization

10.0 | INTRODUCTION

Chapter 9 dealt with the different types of memories that are available. In this chapter, we will look at some of the more commonly used memory chips and see how they are connected to the 6800 μP. Although a designer may choose a specific μP, the choice of a memory is more general because memory chips from one manufacturer usually can be used with any μP. Some semiconductor manufacturers specialize in making only memory chips.

One of the first decisions that must be made concerns the number of bytes of temporary and permanent memory that are to be included in the system. Then, a decision must be made about the type of temporary memory—static or dynamic—and the type of permanent memory—ROM, PROM, EPROM, or EEPROM—to be used. In this chapter, we will see how to connect static RAMs and EPROMs into a system using a 6800 μP. These two devices cover a wide range of 8-bit applications. Although many 8-bit μP systems do require dynamic RAMs, these memory devices are used more frequently with 16-bit μPs. Therefore, dynamic RAMs are covered in Chapter 18.

10.1 | 2114 STATIC RAM

The 2114 static RAM and its low-power version, the 21L14, are read/write memory devices that are often used. Both devices are housed in an 18-pin dual-in-line package and both have the same pin designations. The pin designations are shown in Figure 10.1. The device requires only +5 V. It contains 4096 static memory cells organized as 1024 words × 4 bits. Therefore, two packages are required for 1K of memory in an 8-bit μC system. All lines are TTL compatible, which simplifies the interconnections. Besides the low-power version, this device can also be purchased with different maximum access times (200 ns, 250 ns, 300 ns, and 450 ns). Sections 10.1.1 and 10.1.2 show how to wire this memory chip to the 6800 μP.

FIGURE 10.1 | Pin Designations for 2114 or 21L14 Static RAM

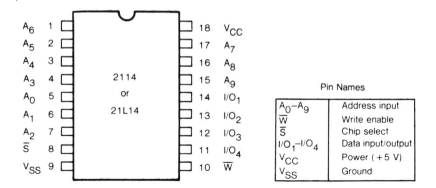

Figure 10.1 shows that this device has 10 address lines, labeled A_0 to A_9. These lines allow the μP to address any one of 1024 words ($2^{10} = 1024$). The I/O lines are connected to the data bus so that the μP can read and write data. The write enable ($\overline{W}$) line is connected to the μC system's read/write line.

10.1.1 | 1K of Memory Using the 2114

Figure 10.2 shows how two 2114 packages can be arranged for 1K $\times$ 8 bits of memory. The address lines are connected either directly to the μP or through address buffers to the μP. In either case, the address lines are labeled to correspond to the μP terminology. Line A_0 eventually goes back to pin A_0 on the μP, line A_1 to pin A_1 on the μP, and so forth.

The connections to the data bus are not quite as straightforward as they are for the address bus. One package is chosen to hold the least significant four bits of data and the other package to hold the most significant four bits. In Figure 10.2, the package on the right contains the least significant four bits and is wired to data bus lines D_0 to D_3. The package on the left is wired to data bus lines D_4 to D_7 and contains the most significant four bits. Each 2114 package contains four data input/output lines, labeled I/O_1 to I/O_4. When the memory chip is being wired to the data bus, the I/O_1 pin must be connected to the data bus line with the lowest number in the group of four. Pin I/O_4 must be connected to the data bus line with the highest number in the group of four. Figure 10.2 shows to which data bus line each I/O pin must be connected.

The $\overline{W}$ pin is the read/write enable pin. When the logic level on this line is high, the μP is reading (receiving) data from the memory chips. When the $\overline{W}$ line goes low, the μP is writing (sending) data to memory. This line must be held high until the address information is stable so as to prevent the μP from erroneously writing data to a memory location. Section 10.3 shows the necessary circuitry needed between the μP and the $\overline{W}$ pin to prevent false data from reaching the memory chips.

The chip select pin ($\overline{S}$) enables or disables the I/O pin circuitry. When the chip select line goes high, the I/O pins are in their high impedance state. When this line goes

FIGURE 10.2 | Two 2114 Packages for 1K of Memory

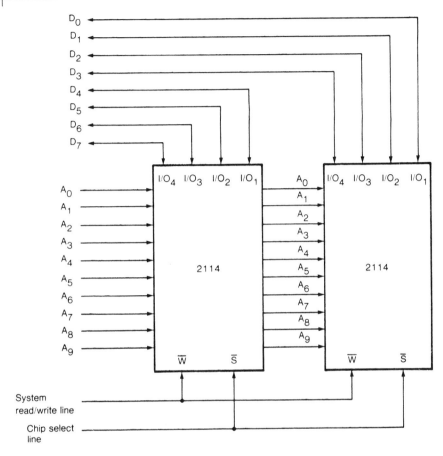

$V_{CC} = +5 \text{ V}$ V_{SS} = ground

low, the I/O circuitry is enabled either as input latches or as output buffers. Which condition exists depends on the logic level on the read/write line. If the R/$\overline{\text{W}}$ line is low, the input latches are enabled and the memory chips will trap the data on the data bus at the falling edge of the ϕ_2 clock cycle. When the $\overline{\text{S}}$ line is low and the R/$\overline{\text{W}}$ line is high, the memory chip's output buffers are enabled. The memory chips will put the data on the data bus at the end of the memory chips' access time. Remember from Chapter 9 that access time is measured from the instant when the memory chip receives a stable address, as illustrated in Figure 9.10.

The chip select line is wired either directly to a μP address line, such as A_{14} or A_{15}, or to a decoder chip. Since the 64K of memory are divided between RAM, ROM, I/O, and future expansion, decoder chips are used much more often than a μP address line. Section 10.4 shows how decoder chips can be used to subdivide the total memory space.

10.1.2 | 2K of Memory Using the 2114

Figure 10.3 shows how four 2114 memory chips can be interconnected to yield 2048 bytes $\times$ 8 bits of RAM memory. The 10 address lines (A_0-A_9) and the system read/write line ($R/\overline{W}$) are wired to each memory chip. The chips are grouped so that the high four bits of RAM 0 and RAM 1 are next to each other and the low four bits are together. The reason for this is so that the printed circuit board can be laid out with few or no crossovers on the data bus lines. Microcomputer boards normally are double sided and many are multilayer boards.

The two packages that make up RAM 0 must be wired so they have the same chip select line. The $\overline{S}$ pins of RAM 1 must also be connected together. Therefore, there is a chip select line for every two packages. These lines go back to other μP address lines or to decoder chips, as discussed in Section 10.4.

Although the 2114 can be used to expand memory even further, there are some hardware problems that should be considered, and another memory chip might be a better choice. Let's consider what goes into the decision.

FIGURE 10.3 | Four 2114 Packages for 2K of Memory

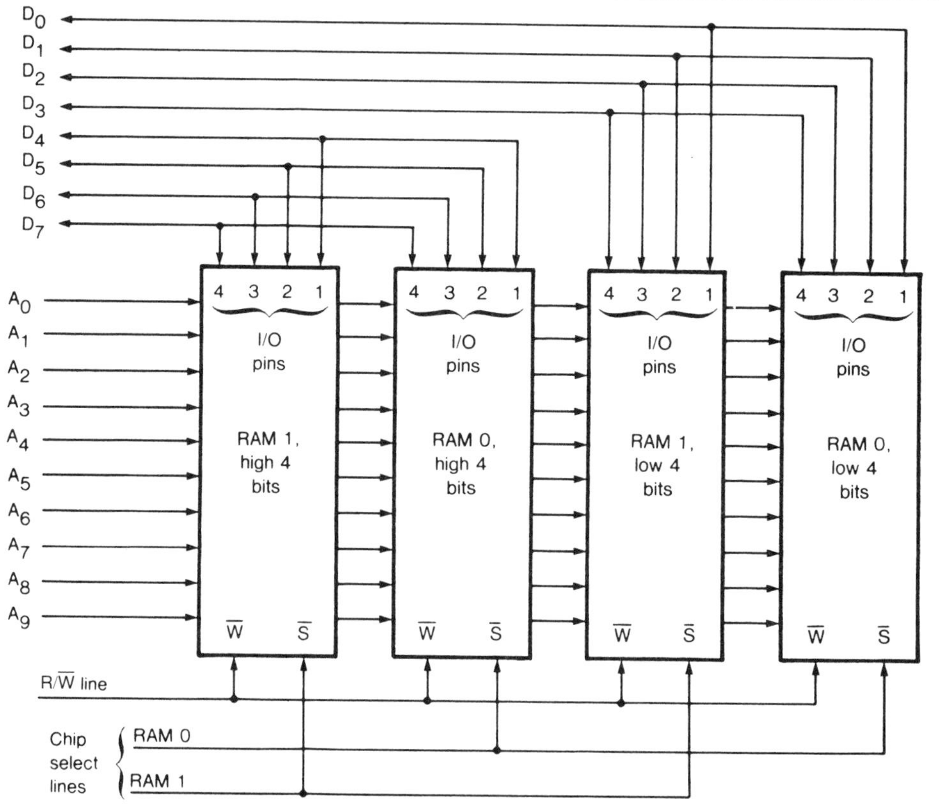

10.2 | MEMORY EXPANSION

When a µC system requires 4K, 8K, 16K, 32K, or more bytes of temporary memory, the 2114 may not be the best choice. The loading effect on each data bus line should be considered. Look at Figure 10.3 again, and note that each data bus line is connected to two 2114 packages. This means that the loading effect on each line is 2. Another way of stating this is to say that when the 2114 memory chip is used, the loading on each line equals the following expression:

$$\frac{\text{Number of bytes}}{K} \qquad (10.1)$$

Applying Equation 10.1 to Figure 10.3 yields the next equation:

$$\frac{2K}{K} = 2$$

Figure 10.4 shows how 4K of memory can be connected to the µP. Each data bus line is connected to four packages, producing a loading effect of 4. Although most µC systems need data bus buffers, the loading effect on each line should still be taken into consideration so that no limitations are exceeded. Let's now look at how the loading effect, not the package count, can be reduced.

FIGURE 10.4 | Eight 2114 Packages for 4K of Memory

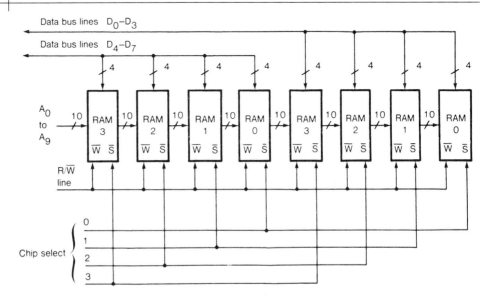

10.2.1 | 2147 Static RAM

The 2147 is a 4096-bit static random access memory organized as 4096 words × 1 bit. This device has automatic power down, which means that when the device is not selected there is a considerable saving of power. The pin designations for the 2147 are shown in Figure 10.5.

The 2147 is housed in an 18-pin dual-in-line package. Twelve pins are used for the address lines A_0–A_{11}. The μC system's read/write line is connected to the write enable pin, $\overline{W}$. The chip selected pin is labeled $\overline{E}$, which stands for chip enable. Power, +5 V, is applied to the V_{CC} pin and ground to the V_{SS} pin. The 2147 has an input data pin, D, and an output data pin, Q. Thus, the 2147 can be used in systems that have separate input and output data bus lines. The majority of μC systems, however, have only eight common data bus lines. Therefore, each data bus line is used for inputting and outputting data. The 2147 allows the D and Q pins to be wired together for such systems.

10.2.2 | 4K of Memory Using the 2147

Since the 2147 is a 4K × 1-bit memory device, a system requires eight 2147 packages to produce a 4K × 8-bit static RAM, as shown in Figure 10.6. This memory system requires the same number of packages as the system in Figure 10.4, but the loading effect on each data bus line is different. In the system of Figure 10.4, there are four packages connected to each data bus line. In the memory system of Figure 10.6, however, there is only one package connected to each data bus line, thus reducing the loading effect by a factor of 4.

FIGURE 10.5 | Pin Designations for 2147 Static RAM

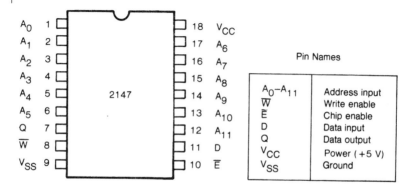

FIGURE 10.6 | Eight 2147 Packages for 4K of Memory

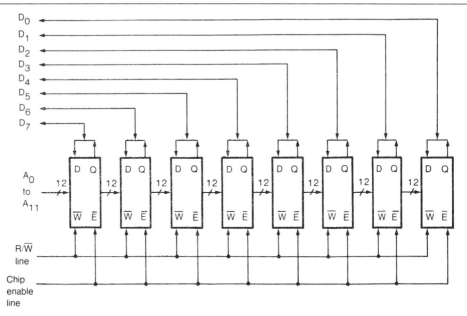

10.3 | SYSTEM READ/WRITE LINE

Manufacturers' data sheets for RAM chips specify that the write enable line must be held high until the binary pattern on the address bus is stable. This specification is not a problem if the μP is going to read data from memory, but when the μP is going to write data, this specification must be taken into account. The write enable line cannot go low until the address bus is stable.

In a 6800 system, the μP's valid memory address (VMA) line can be used in conjunction with an address line wired to the memory chip select pin or with the μP's R/$\overline{\text{W}}$ line wired to the write enable pin on the memory package.

A way of using the VMA line with the address bus connections is to have the VMA line control the enable pin of a chip decoder. (Although the topic of decoding is covered in the next section, an example of enabling memory chip select pins would be to wire the VMA line to G_1 of the 74LS138 in Figure 10.10.) Another way to keep the read/write line high until the address bus is stable is shown by the circuit of Figure 10.7A. The timing diagrams are shown in Figures 10.7B and 10.7C. In the case of a write operation, the system read/write line will not go low until the ϕ_2 clock pulse goes high. Remember the ϕ_2 clock pulse goes high well after the address bus is stable. The circuit of Figure 10.7 can be used as is, either for the 6502 μP or the 6800 μP. If we want to use this circuit and the 6800's VMA line, then we must replace the ϕ_2 line from the μP with the VMA line.

FIGURE 10.7 | Digital Circuit for Keeping R/W Line High Until Address Bus Is Stable

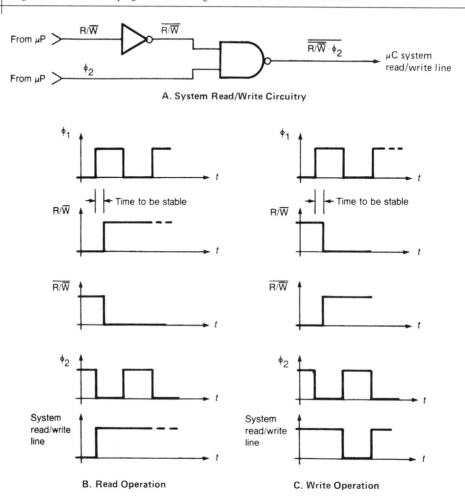

A. System Read/Write Circuitry

B. Read Operation   C. Write Operation

10.4 | DECODING THE MEMORY SPACE

At some point in the design of a μC system, a decision has to be made about how much temporary memory, permanent memory, and I/O are to be included. Next, a decision has to be made about where in the total memory system everything will be placed. Let's consider that a system is to have 4K of RAM, 2K of EPROM, and 16 bytes of I/O. RAM is to be located from page 00 to page 0F. ROM is to be located at the highest memory locations from page F8 to FF. The 16 bytes of I/O are to be wired at memory locations 4000 to 400F. Figure 10.8 is a memory map that shows where everything is to be placed in the total memory space.

FIGURE 10.8 | Typical Memory Map

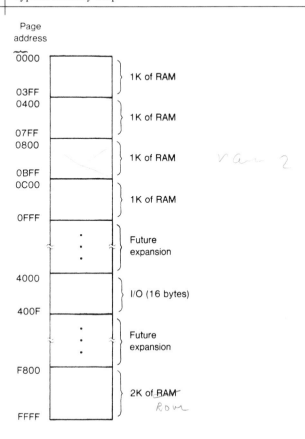

In this example, the two most significant address lines (A_{15} and A_{14}) can be used to identify RAM, ROM, and I/O, but we shall use a 4-to-16 decoder chip (74154). The 16 outputs provided by this chip divide the address space into 4K blocks (64K/16 = 4K). For our applications we need only three of the 16 outputs, as shown in Figure 10.9.

If the 4K of RAM are built using the 2147 memory chips, then the RAM output line from the 74154 decoder chip is wired directly to the chip enable line of the array in Figure 10.6. However, if the 4K of RAM are built using the 2114 memory chips, then another decoding network is needed. This decoding circuit must be capable of selecting a pair of RAM chips labeled 0, 1, 2, or 3 in Figure 10.4. A 74LS138 can be used for this decoding application, as shown in Figure 10.10. The figure also shows which address bus lines must be decoded and where the RAM output line of the memory map decoder is connected. Output line 0 from the memory map decoder is used to enable or disable the chip decoder. When the memory map line is high, the 4 chip select lines are high, regardless of the logic levels on address lines A_{10} and A_{11}. When the RAM memory map

FIGURE 10.9 | 74154 Decoder for Decoding Memory Map of Figure 10.8

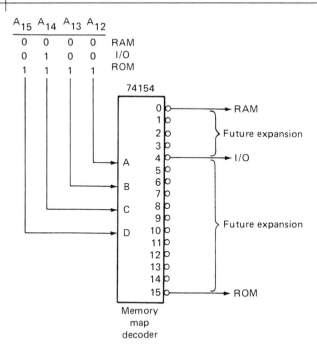

line is low, then the logic levels on lines A_{10} and A_{11} determine which chip select line goes low. This allows the µP to communicate with one pair of memory chips.

Four address lines produce 16 possible outputs ($2^4 = 16$). Although a 4-to-16 decoder chip, such as the 74154, is available, there are some reasons for not using it:

1. It is housed in a 24-pin package. This means that this may be the only chip of its size on the PC board, and it may require special handling and insertion.
2. It is usually the only 4-to-16 decoder being used. Thus, the user must order, handle, store, and check an extra part. (Also, it won't be possible to buy it in large quantities to obtain maximum discount.)
3. The 74154 is available only as a standard TTL or low-power chip, not in a low-power Schottky, LS, version, A standard TTL input has twice the input loading effect as does an LS version. Therefore, a standard TTL input loads the bus lines more than an LS input.

To overcome these problems, system designers try to use an LS package in as many places as possible. As previously mentioned, the 74LS138 IC is a popular and commonly used decoder chip. Figure 10.10 showed one application of how it can be used. Two 74LS138 ICs can be interconnected to produce a 4-to-16 decoder, as shown

FIGURE 10.10 | 74LS138 Decoder for Selecting RAM Chips

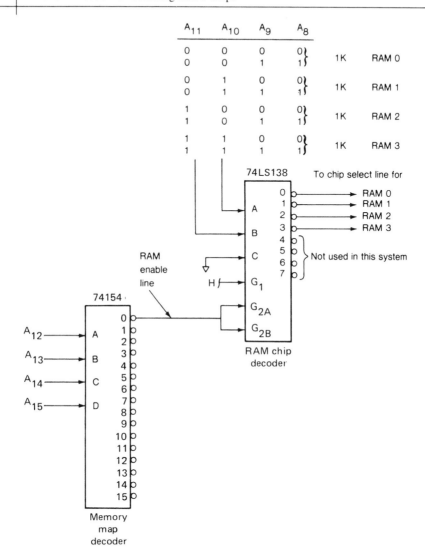

in Figure 10.11. Certainly there are disadvantages with this circuit; one is that two decoder packages are needed, which means that additional drill holes and another package to which V_{CC} and ground must be connected are needed. These are some of the things that must be considered by the system designer.

Although Figure 10.11 shows that address lines A_{12}, A_{13}, A_{14}, and A_{15} are used, any four address lines could be used. Note, in Figure 10.11, the numbers 0 to 15 on the outside of the packages are the 16 output lines.

FIGURE 10.11 | 4-to-16 Decoder Using Two 74LS138 Chips

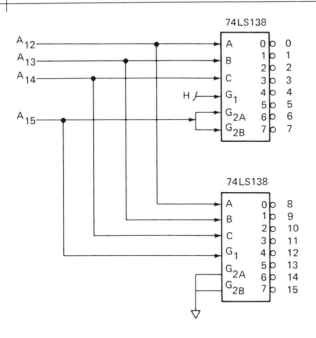

10.5 | 2716 EPROM

The 2716 IC is an ultraviolet erasable programmable read-only memory (UV EPROM). It is a 16,384-bit device organized as 2048 bytes × 8 bits. A transparent lid on the top of the package allows the entire device to be erased by ultraviolet light. An erase operation causes every bit to go to the logic 1 state. When the device is programmed, only the bits that contain logic 0 change state.

Figure 10.12 shows the pin designations for the 2716. This device is housed in a 24-pin dual-in-line package. There are 11 address pins, A_0 to A_{10}, that enable the device to address 2048 bytes (2^{11} = 2048). The eight DQ pins, DQ_0 to DQ_7, are pins connected to the data bus. They are also used to input data during programming. One of the reasons that this device is so popular is that it requires only $+5$ V for the read operation. This voltage is not the programming voltage, which is $+25$ V.

10.5.1 | Programming the 2716

The 2716 is set up in the programming mode under the following conditions:

$$V_{CC} \text{ (pin 24)} = +5 \text{ V}$$

$$\overline{G} \text{ (pin 20)} = V_{IH}$$

$$V_{PP} \text{ (pin 21)} = +25 \text{ V}$$

FIGURE 10.12 | Pin Designations for 2716 EPROM

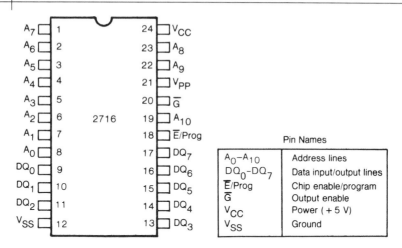

$A_0–A_{10}$	Address lines
$DQ_0–DQ_7$	Data input/output lines
$\overline{E}/Prog$	Chip enable/program
$\overline{G}$	Output enable
V_{CC}	Power (+ 5 V)
V_{SS}	Ground

Pin Names

The data is entered in 8-bit words through the DQ pins. Remember, only 0s will be programmed when 0s and 1s are entered. After the address and data lines are set up, a program pulse is applied to the $\overline{E}$/Prog pin (pin 18). The recommended program pulse is a low-to-high pulse, V_{IL} to V_{IH}, with a pulse width of 2 ms. Therefore, the 2716 cannot be programmed by a DC signal.

10.5.2 | Read Operation

After the address is stable and at the end of the access time, data is valid at the DQ pins. The 2716 has a standby mode to reduce power dissipation when the device is not selected. The 2716 is in the standby mode when the $\overline{E}$/Prog pin is high, V_{IH}. In this mode, the output pins are in their high impedance state.

10.5.3 | Erase Operation

The 2716 is erased by exposure to ultraviolet light. The recommended wavelength is 2537 angstroms. Like all EPROMs, when this device is erased, all the bits are erased. This procedure is called *block erasure*. An erased bit is a logic 1 for the 2716.

10.5.4 | Wiring the 2716 into the System

The 2716 is actually easier to wire into a μC system than the 2114 or the 2147 static RAMs. The reason is that the 2716 EPROM is not split between two or more chips and, therefore, the 8 data pins are connected directly to the data bus.

Figure 10.13 shows how the 2716 can be connected to a system. The 11 address lines, $A_0–A_{10}$, are wired directly back to the μP. In many systems, address buffers are connected between the μP and memory to reduce loading effects on the μP's lines. Their input pins are connected to the μP, and the corresponding output pin is connected to a memory line.

FIGURE 10.13 | 2716 EPROM Wired into a μC System

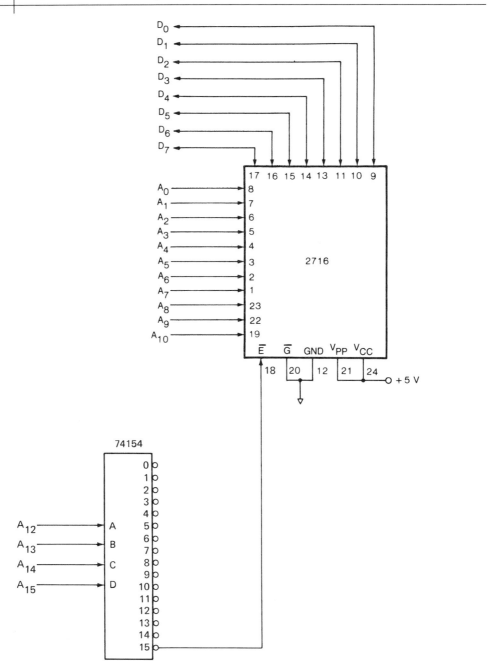

The 8 data bus lines, DQ_0–DQ_7, are connected to the μP's corresponding data bus lines. Like the address lines, data lines often require buffering.

After the 2716 is programmed and inserted into a system, the V_{PP} cannot be left floating; it must be tied to V_{CC}. When the $\overline{G}$ pin is high, the output lines are disabled. This means that the output data lines remain in their high impedance state regardless of the logic state of the $\overline{E}$/Prog pin. Therefore, for normal operation, the $\overline{G}$ pin is tied to ground.

The chip is selected or deselected by the $\overline{E}$/Prog pin, pin 18. As shown in Figure 10.13, this pin is connected to the memory map decoder. When address lines A_{12} to A_{15} go to a logic 1 state, output line 15 of the decoder goes low. This low logic level is the signal to the 2716 that the μP is selecting it and wishes to receive data from it. An EPROM does not need a read/write line because data can only be read from it.

10.6 | SUMMARY

This chapter showed how static and EPROM chips can be interconnected to form the memory portion of a μC. The popular 2114 static RAM is organized as 1024 words × 4 bits, so two of these devices yield 1K of memory. In Section 10.2, the 2147 static RAM, organized as 4096 words × 1 bit, was discussed. We found that comparisons can be made among the different types of static memory chips that are available.

The 2716 EPROM is one of the most widely used UV EPROMs. This device gives the user 2048 words × 8 bits of permanent memory. Once programmed, it is easily connected to a system and operates from +5 V.

Dynamic RAMs need additional support circuitry, such as a multiplexer and a dynamic memory controller. In Chapter 12, we will look at some of the problems encountered when dynamic memories are used.

PROBLEMS

10.1 What is the word size of a 2114 static RAM?

10.2 How many 2114 memory chips are required in a 3K × 8 system?

10.3 How many address pins are there on the (a) 2114 and (b) 2147 memory chips?

10.4 When the $\overline{W}$ pin on the 2114 chip goes low, is the memory chip receiving or sending data?

10.5 Why must the $\overline{W}$ pin be high until the address information is stable?

10.6 What is the function of the $\overline{S}$ pin on the 2114?

10.7 When does the memory chip put data on the data bus?

10.8 In a 3K × 8 memory system using the 2147, how many chip select lines are there?

10.9 For the memory system of Problem 10.8, what is the loading factor on each data bus line?

10.10 What does the expression *automatic power down* mean? Which memory chip has this feature?

10.11 Which pin is the chip select pin on the 2147?

10.12 Are both the 2114 and the 2147 +5 V devices?

10.13 What is an advantage and a disadvantage of the 2147 memory chip over the 2114 memory chip?

10.14 Why does the circuit of Figure 10.7 also prevent any unwanted glitches from occurring on the system read/write line?

10.15 Refer to Figure 10.9. What section of the total memory space does output line 3 decode?

10.16 Consider that a system is to have 5K of RAM using the 2114 chip. What changes must be made in the circuit of Figure 10.10 so the circuit will be able to decode the next 1K of RAM?

10.17 Consider that another 2716 EPROM has to be connected to the memory space outlined in Figure 10.8. What locations should the device occupy to avoid adding another decoder chip? (*Hint:* See Figure 10.9.).

10.18 When a 2716 EPROM is erased, what is the logic state of each bit?

11 | Interface Devices

11.0 | INTRODUCTION

In Chapter 2, we looked at the μC system's three main building blocks: the μP, memory, and interface devices (also called interface chips). Interface devices allow the μP to communicate with peripheral equipment such as keyboards, printers, plotters, CRT displays, storage devices, solid-state switches, relays, transducers, or even other computers. Semiconductor manufacturers have designed into a single IC package the circuitry the μP needs to interface with commonly used peripheral equipment. They have also designed some general-purpose interface devices that can be used for a wide variety of applications. These ICs use LSI technology, and they can replace 50 to 100 SSI packages. The interface devices are also programmable; that is, they are under the programmer's control. Although many interface chips have been designed for a specific function, the manufacturer has designed into the chip the usual methods of doing the same job, such as the rate at which data is transmitted or received. The programmer chooses the method by having the μP send a specific binary pattern to the interface device. By changing the binary pattern, the programmer chooses another method.

General-purpose interface devices are also programmable and allow the user great flexibility in design. In addition, the programmer may change the way the device does a job at any time. For example, the programmer may wish to receive data from peripheral equipment at one rate for part of a program and change the rate for another part of the program.

Although interface devices are designed for general or specific applications, they have many points in common. In this chapter, we will study these common points, and in the following chapters we will examine some of the commonly used interface chips. With this chapter as a background, the reader will be able to study other peripheral chips easily.

The list that follows contains the interface IC devices most often used with Motorola μPs:

MC6821   Peripheral Interface Adapter (PIA)
MC6828   Priority Interrupt Controller (PIC)

MC6840	Programmable Timer Module (PTM)
MC6843	Floppy Disk Controller (FDC)
MC6844	Direct Memory Access Controller (DMAC)
MC6845	CRT Controller (CRTC)
MC6846	ROM–I/O–Timer
MC6847	Video Display Generator (VDG)
MC6850	Asynchronous Communication Interface Adapter (ACIA)
MC6852	Synchronous Serial Data Adapter (SSDA)
MC6854	Advanced Data Link Controller
MC6860	0–600 bps Digital Modem
MC6862	2400 bps Digital Modulator
MC68488	General-Purpose Interface Adapter

Many of these devices are also built by other IC manufacturers. Although the Motorola interface devices normally are used with their own μPs, they can be used with other 8-bit or 16-bit μPs.

11.1 | PIN ASSIGNMENTS

The interface devices in the list just given are housed in either a 24-, a 28-, or a 40-pin dual-in-line package. Most devices can be purchased in either a plastic package or in a ceramic package for better heat dissipation.

FIGURE 11.1 | Typical μP System, Including Interface Device

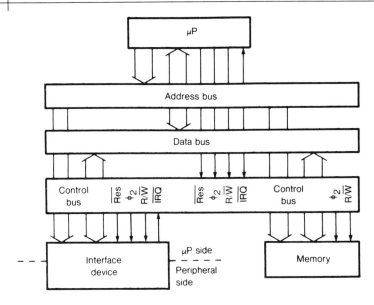

FIGURE 11.2 | Pin Designations for MC6821 Peripheral Interface Adapter (Redrawn from data sheet for
            MC6821 PIA with permission. Motorola Incorporated, Phoenix, Arizona)

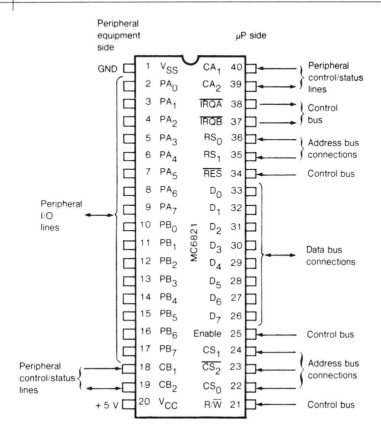

An interface device is the link between the μP and peripheral equipment, so the device may be visualized as having a μP side and a peripheral side, as shown in the logic diagram of Figure 11.1. On the μP side are the pins that are connected to the address bus, data bus, and control bus. On the peripheral side are the input and output (I/O) lines. The I/O lines are either for general-purpose applications or for a specific purpose, depending on the device.

Many interface devices have all the μP pins arranged on one side and the I/O lines on the other side of the device. This allows for easy PC board layout. Figure 11.2 shows the pin assignments for Motorola's 6821 peripheral interface adapter, which is a general-purpose interface device. The MC6821 device has all of the μP connections on one side of the chip and all but two (CA$_1$ and CA$_2$) of the peripheral lines on the other. Pins 1 and 20 are the power supply pins. Pins 2–19 and pins 39 and 40 are for the peripheral equipment. Pins 21–38 are to be connected to the μP bus lines. Figure 11.2 shows that this device can easily be wired to the μP's bus lines and connected to peripheral equipment. More detailed discussion of the MC6821 is found in Chapter 12.

11.2 | CONNECTIONS TO THE MICROPROCESSOR

An interface device has pins that are to be connected to the μP's address bus, data bus, and control bus. Let's look at the pins in each group.

11.2.1 | Address Bus Connections

Chip Select: Interface devices have one or more chip select (CS) lines. In small systems, these lines are, or may be, connected directly to the μP's address lines, as shown in Figure 11.3A. In larger systems, interface devices (as well as memory) are connected to decoder chips, as shown in Figure 11.3B. Remember, from Chapter 10, that decoder chips allow more or all of the total memory space to be used.

In devices with only one chip select line, the active state of the line is usually low. That is, when either the μP's address line or the output of the decoder, wired to the chip select line, goes low, the interface device is enabled and can communicate with the μP. Devices with two or more chip select lines must have the correct logic state applied to all chip select lines to enable the device. All chip select lines must be used; they cannot be left floating. Devices with multiple chip select lines usually will have at least one of the lines with an active low state. Since the output lines of decoder chips are active low states, they can be directly connected to the chip select line. Figure 11.4 illustrates four possible connections to chip select lines. An interface device's chip select pins can be connected directly to the μP, as in Figure 11.4A, or indirectly through a decoder chip, as in Figure 11.4B.

FIGURE 11.3 | Connections for Chip Select (CS) Lines

A. Small System

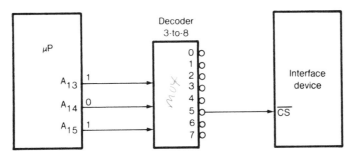

B. Large System

FIGURE 11.4 | Four Possible Connections to Chip Select Lines

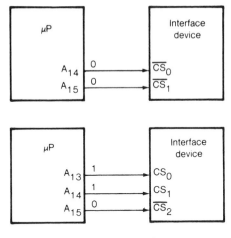

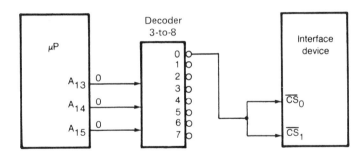

A. Direct Connection

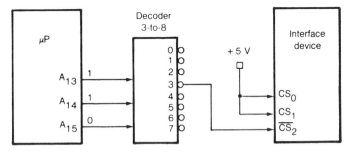

B. Using Decoder Chip

Register Select: Besides the chip select pins, interface devices have one or more additional pins connected to the address bus. This line (or lines) is the register select line. It is used by the μP to communicate with a particular register within the interface device.

Register select lines are usually connected to the lowest-numbered address lines of the μP. For example, if the interface device has only one register select pin, it should be connected to the μP's A_0 address line. If there are two register select pins, they should be connected to the μP's A_0 and A_1 address lines.

Unlike the chip select lines, which may be connected to a decoder chip, register select pins are always connected directly to the address lines, as shown in Figure 11.5.

Some manufacturers, such as Intel, do not call this pin (or pins) "register select." Instead, they use the name of the actual register that is being addressed. Since the name of the register may be different for different interface devices, the name of the pin is not always the same. In either case, there should be no problem because it is important to be familiar with manufacturers' data sheets for any device and to learn the function of each pin and each internal register before using the device.

11.2.2 | Data Bus Connections

Interface devices have eight bidirectional data lines that connect directly to the μP's data bus lines. Figure 11.6 shows that pin D_0 of the interface device is connected to D_0 of the μP, D_1 is connected to D_1, and so forth. These lines allow the interface device to send and receive one byte (8 bits) of data at a time from the μP. The actual wiring pattern of the data bus is shown in Figure 11.6A. Simplified circuit drawing are shown in Figures 11.6B and 11.6C.

FIGURE 11.5 | Register Select Line Connections

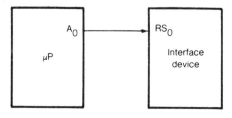

A. Single Register Select Line

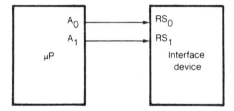

B. Two Register Select Lines

FIGURE 11.6 | Data Bus Connections

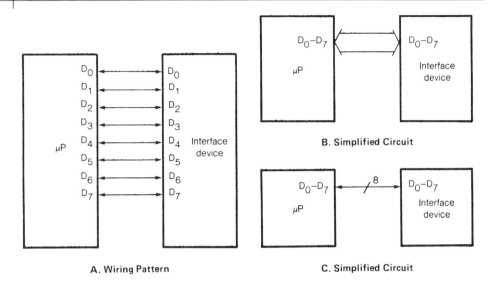

A. Wiring Pattern

B. Simplified Circuit

C. Simplified Circuit

11.2.3 | Control Bus Connections

The number of control bus lines connected to an interface device depends on the device. Most chips, however, have from three to six pins that are wired to the control bus lines. Most interface chips have a read/write pin (or pins), a ϕ_2 clock pin, and an interrupt request pin. Many interface devices also have a reset pin. Let's examine the purposes of these control pins.

Read/Write: Motorola devices have one read/write pin that is wired to the system read/write line. Remember, the terms *read* and *write* always refer to whether the μP is reading (receiving) or writing (sending) data, and not to the interface device.

When the interface device is selected (by the correct binary pattern on the chip select pins) and the read/write line is high, the μP is reading (receiving) data from the interface device. The binary pattern on the register select lines determines which register within the interface device is sending data to the μP.

If the interface device is selected and the read/write is low, then the μP is writing (sending) data to the interface chip. The binary pattern on the register select lines determines which register within the interface device is receiving the data.

Enable: The enable input pin is used to receive the ϕ_2 clock signal so that all data transferred to and from the interface device is synchronized with the μP. This clock signal is used by many interface devices to generate their own internal timing signals. When the 6800 μP is used, the ϕ_2 (TTL) line must be ANDed with the μP's VMA (valid memory address) line. The output of the AND gate is then connected to the interface device's enable pin. Figure 11.7 shows how the enable signal is obtained for the 6800. Chapter 17 shows how to connect these peripherals to a 68000 μP.

FIGURE 11.7 | Generating the Enable Signal

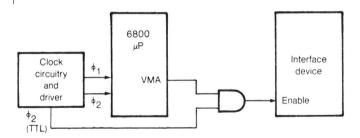

On some Motorola data sheets, the term *clock* may be used, but it is intended for a clock signal other than the ϕ_2 clock signal. Thus, it is important to check the data sheet for each interface device carefully before using it.

Interrupt Request: Interface devices usually have one or more interrupt request pins. An interrupt request is a signal from an interface device to the μP. The signal indicates that the interface device needs servicing from the μP. Since the 6800 μP has only one interrupt request pin (not counting the nonmaskable interrupt pin), then all interrupt request lines from interface devices must be wired together, as shown in Figure 11.8. In order to be able to tie a number of interface interrupt request pins together, manufacturers have used open drain circuitry on this pin. Therefore, a pull-up resistor is needed on the interrupt request line, and that is the function of the 3.0 kΩ resistor in Figure 11.8.

If a number of interrupt request lines are tied together, then the μP needs to have a way of determining which interrupt needs servicing. This is done by a program called an interrupt polling routine. The μP checks the status of the interrupt request line of each interface device. The order in which they are checked is determined by the writer of the polling routine program. Obviously, this technique takes time, especially if a number of interrupt request lines are tied together.

Another technique for determining which I/O device is signaling the μP is a hardware approach. All interrupt request lines are wired to an interrupt controller chip. The function of this chip is to determine the order in which interrupt request lines need servicing and also to send one signal to the μP. The μP checks the controller chip to find out which interface device needs servicing.

Reset: Some interface devices have a reset pin that is connected to the system's master reset line. A 6800 μP system has active low reset lines. That is, when the reset line goes to its active state, all devices wired to it set their internal registers to a predetermined logic state. In most cases, that state is a logic 0.

Some interface devices do not have a reset pin. The internal registers of these devices go to a predetermined logic state (usually logic 0) by circuitry within the device that senses the voltage level of the power supply line (the V_{CC} line). The term *predetermined logic state* means that the logic state is determined by the manufacturer, not by the user.

FIGURE 11.8 | Interface Connections for Interrupt Request Pins

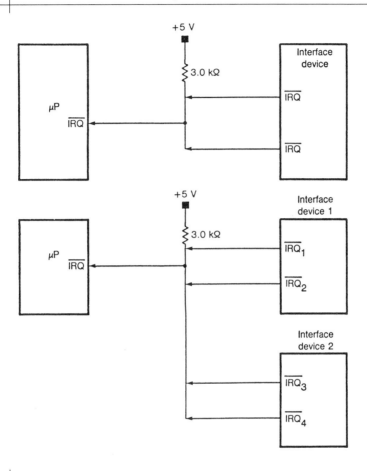

11.3 | INTERNAL BLOCK DIAGRAMS

The internal block diagram for each peripheral device is different because of the different functions the devices perform. However, there are many common points, and Figure 11.9 shows some block diagrams and terms that are applicable to many interface devices.

11.3.1 | Address Decoding

Chip Select: Like memory chips, interface devices have internal circuitry that enables them. In other words, this circuitry "tells" the device whether or not the μP wishes to communicate with it. For the three chip select lines shown in Figure 11.9, the circuit is a three-input AND gate. The output of this gate activates the timing and control section.

FIGURE 11.9 | General Block Diagram of Interface Device

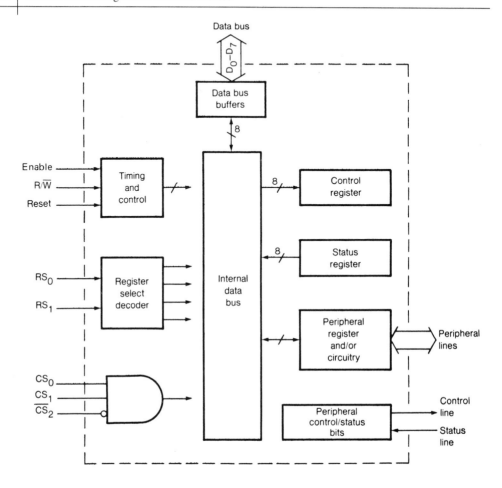

Register Select: Besides the chip select circuitry, the interface device must have circuitry to decode the particular register that is going to communicate with the μP. As with any decoder, the number of output lines equals 2^n, where n equals the number of input lines. Figure 11.9 shows two register select input lines and four ($2^2 = 4$) output lines. Therefore, the μP is able to communicate with four internal registers of the interface device. In general, the number of register select lines determines the number of registers that can communicate with the μP. As we study some interface devices, however, we will see that manufacturers sometimes use other techniques.

Manufacturers may show the chip and register select circuitry as a single block or in a block with the device's timing and control circuitry.

11.3.2 | Timing and Control

The function of this block is to receive the enable signal, the read/write signal, and the reset signal (if the device has a reset pin), and to generate the internal timing and control pulses to allow data to flow from one internal interface register to another, from an interface register to the μP or from the μP to an interface register.

The direction of data to and from the μP is determined by the logic state of the read/write line. This logic state, in conjunction with circuitry of the timing and control section, determines what happens in the data bus buffer section.

11.3.3 | Data Bus Buffers

The data bus buffers allow the transfer of data between the μP and the interface device. The circuitry in this block has output drivers that are three-state devices. When the interface chip is not selected, the drivers are in their high impedance (off) state. When the μP has selected the interface chip and is going to read data from it, the output drivers are turned on and are TTL compatible. Remember, when the μP is reading data, the interface device is sending it.

When the μP is writing (sending) data to the interface chip, the output drivers are turned off and the data is received through this block and either transferred to the appropriate register or captured in an input data latch network (not shown in Figure 11.9).

11.3.4 | Internal Bus Structure

Eight-bit interface devices move data between registers 8 bits (one byte) at a time. Therefore, each device has an 8-bit internal data bus. In addition, interface devices also have internal control lines.

Control lines originate at the control and timing block and go to the appropriate registers. Other signal lines are sometimes needed between registers so that the logic state of a bit (or bits) can be monitored.

The internal structure of interface devices is not considered to have an address bus. An address is decoded, as previously mentioned, and a control signal is sent to the appropriate register telling it to be ready to send or receive data.

11.3.5 | Control Register

Large-scale-integration (LSI) interface devices are programmable devices. That is, a binary pattern sent to these devices determines how they will operate. For example, a binary pattern to an interface adapter chip determines which line (or lines) is input and which is output. An asynchronous interface chip uses a binary pattern to know at what rate to transmit and receive data. A timer interface chip uses a binary pattern to determine the time interval between the pulses that it generates. Some interface chips can perform different functions or the same function at different speeds, or can disable or enable the interrupt request line, or can perform several other operations. Therefore, by changing the binary pattern, the user can make use of a number of options for the best overall system performance.

Most interface devices have what is known as a *control register.* The binary pattern loaded into this register programs how the interface chip will do a job, and in some cases the binary pattern programs the choice of job. The binary pattern that the μP sends to this register is often referred to as the *control word.* The control register in some interface devices is a register to which the μP can only write data. For these devices, the μP cannot read data from the control register. Other interface devices allow the μP to read and write data to and from the control register. Each bit of the control register has a specific function in determining how the interface device will operate.

11.3.6 | Status Register

As data or control signals are transferred between the μP and an internal register, between registers, or between the interface device and peripheral equipment, the interface chip must keep a "record" of these transfers so that the μP can periodically check the record and know that everything is operating correctly. This record-keeping register is most often referred to as the *status register.* As with other registers, this is an 8-bit register. Each bit is a record of a different function. Status registers are read-only registers; that is, the μP can read data from the register but cannot write data to it. Once the μP has read the data, it can check the logic state of each bit and make a decision about what to do next.

Some interface devices do not need an 8-bit control register and an 8-bit status register. In these chips, there may be one control/status register. Part of the register is used for control and the remaining part for status. When the μP sends an 8-bit binary pattern to this type of dual function register, the data will enter only those bits that are the control bits. All other bits are ignored. When the μP reads this type of register to find out the logic state of the status bit(s), the control bits are often sent too. However, the program can be written to ignore the control bits and concentrate only on the status bits.

11.3.7 | Peripheral Registers, or Circuitry

The registers, or circuitry, that are connected to the peripheral lines are usually labeled for the specific function that they perform. For example, in the CRT (cathode ray tube) controller chip, the circuitry that controls the video is labeled the video output. In an asynchronous interface chip, the register that is used to send data to peripheral equipment is labeled the transmit shift register, while the register that receives the data is labeled the receive shift register. General-purpose interface adapter chips refer to the register that is connected to the I/O lines as either a peripheral register or as a port.

11.3.8 | Peripheral Status/Control Logic

In addition to the peripheral lines, many interface devices are designed to send or receive control signals from peripheral equipment and act on these signals. Depending on the interface device, these signals may be used by the device without disturbing the μP. In other cases, the μP must be notified of what is happening, and for those cases an interrupt request signal is sent to the μP.

The circuitry in the control block works with the status and control registers. Some differences are: There are usually only one or two bits associated with this block and the μP does not have access to it. The μP has access only to the status and control registers. Therefore, if the logic state of the peripheral control block is to be interpreted by the μP, it is interpreted through the status register. Likewise, if an interface device has a peripheral control logic circuit, then its logic state is usually set by the μP through the control register. This procedure allows two or more bits of the control register to determine the logic state for a single control line.

11.4 SUMMARY

Microprocessor manufacturers have designed a number of general-purpose and specific-purpose interface devices. Although they have been built to do many different jobs, there are many similarities among interface devices. In this chapter, we examined the common points from pin designations to internal architecture.

As the link between the μP and peripheral equipment, the interface device can be visualized as having a μP side and a peripheral side. On the μP side, the pins are connected to the address, data, and control buses. On the peripheral side, the interface device's I/O lines are connected to the external equipment.

Some of the common points of the internal architecture are shown in Section 11.3. They are: address bus decoding circuitry; timing and control circuitry; data bus buffers; control, status, and peripheral registers; and peripheral status/control logic. The next three chapters focus on three popular interface chips, how they are connected to the buses, and how they are programmed to send or receive data between the μP and peripheral equipment.

PROBLEMS

11.1 What is the purpose of an interface device?

11.2 Why are interface devices programmable?

11.3 Are interface devices connected to the μP's address, data, and control buses?

11.4 What pins on the interface device are used by the μP to indicate that the μP wants to communicate with it?

11.5 Can unused chip select lines be left "floating"?

11.6 What is the purpose of the register select lines?

11.7 To what bus lines should the register select lines be connected?

11.8 Are register select lines connected to decoder chips or directly to the μP?

11.9 How are the interface chip's data lines connected to the μP?

11.10 What are the most common control bus connections?

11.11 What is the purpose of the enable pin on the interface device?

11.12 On the interface device, is the interrupt request line an input or output control line?

11.13 What is the name of the program used to identify the interrupt that needs servicing?

11.14 What is the function of a reset pin?

11.15 List the internal blocks that are common to many interface devices.

11.16 For most peripheral devices, if there are two register select lines, with how many internal registers can the µP communicate?

11.17 When a device is not selected, what state are the data lines in?

11.18 Which register receives the binary pattern that programs the device? What is the binary pattern called?

11.19 Which register keeps a ''record'' of what is happening in the interface device?

12 Peripheral Interface Adapter 6821

12.0 | INTRODUCTION

The 6821 peripheral interface adapter (PIA) is a general-purpose programmable input/output chip housed in a 40-pin dual-in-line package, as shown in Figure 12.1. Although this interface chip has been designed by and for Motorola's μP products, it can be used with other μPs. For example, users of 6502 μPs often use this chip. The purpose of any I/O chip is to simplify the problem of connecting the μP to peripheral equipment. Peripheral equipment could be connected to the μP by using logic gates and combinational logic circuits. This technique usually requires a large number of components, however, thus defeating one of the major advantages of a μC system—a design requiring few ICs. Like other peripheral devices, the 6821 eliminates many individual components and it is programmable. It has 16 I/O lines in two groups, port A and port B. The user has control over all 16 I/O lines. For example, the programmer may choose two lines of port A to be input lines and the remaining six lines of port A to be output lines. At the same time, any number of lines of port B may be programmed as input lines and the remaining lines as output lines. Hence each I/O line of each port can be programmed independently.

12.1 | MICROPROCESSOR AND PIA CONNECTIONS

The μP and the PIA are interconnected by the data bus, address bus, and control bus, as shown in Figure 12.2. These connections include an 8-bit bidirectional data bus, three chip select lines, two register select lines, two interrupt lines, a read/write line, an enable line, and a reset line. Let's examine the function of each line or group of lines.

12.1.1 | Data Bus

The eight bidirectional data lines (D_0–D_7) allow the transfer of data between the μP and the PIA. Each line has a three-state output driver. These devices remain in the high impedance (off) state except when the μP selects the PIA *and* the μP is reading (receiving) data from the PIA. For the μP to read data from the PIA, the R/$\overline{\text{W}}$ line must be in the read (high) state.

FIGURE 12.1 | Pin Assignments for Peripheral Interface Adapter 6821 (Redrawn from data sheet for MC6821 PIA with permission. Motorola Incorporated, Phoenix, Arizona)

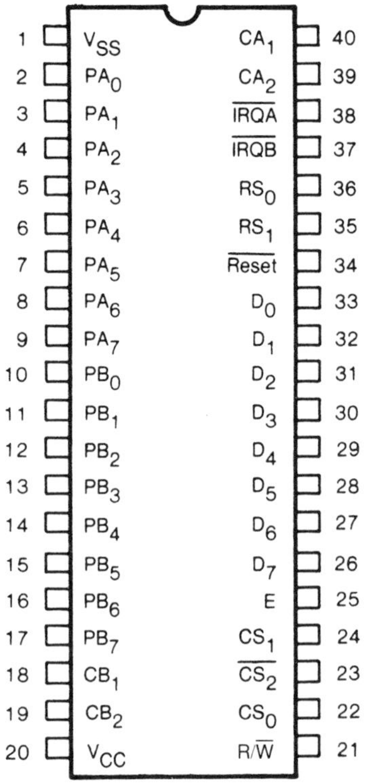

12.1.2 | Address Bus

11.3

The 6821 has five pins that are connected to the address bus lines. Although the user could choose any combination of the 16 address bus lines, we will look at one or two wiring diagrams that yield a good solution to most problems. The five pins on the PIA are grouped into chip select lines and register select lines.

Chip Select Pins (CS_0, CS_1, and $\overline{CS_2}$):   These three pins are used by the μP to select the PIA. They may be connected directly to three address bus lines, or one pin may be wired to a decoder chip while the other pins are wired to their appropriate logic states, as shown in Figures 12.3A and B. In order for the device to be selected, both CS_0 and CS_1 must be high and $\overline{CS_2}$ must be low. The voltage levels on the chip select pins must be stable whenever the μP is reading or writing data to the PIA.

Register Select Pins (RS_0 and RS_1):   The two register select pins should be connected to address bus lines A_0 and A_1, as shown in Figure 12.3C. The logic levels on these pins are used to select the various registers inside the PIA. Like the chip select pins, the voltage levels on the register select pins must be stable whenever the μP is reading or writing data to the PIA. The reason that these pins are wired to address bus lines A_0 and

FIGURE 12.2 | 6821 PIA Connected between μP Bus Lines and Peripheral Equipment

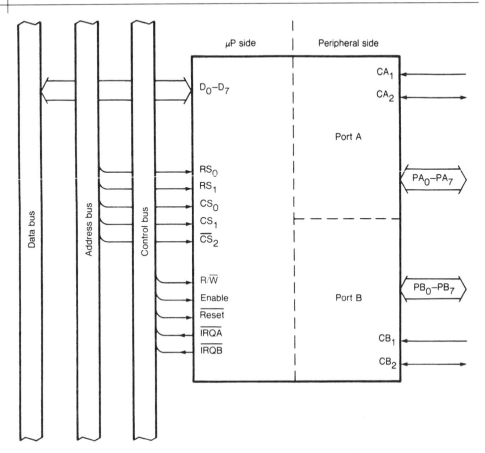

A_1 is that the PIA's internal registers will be in four consecutive address locations. For the connections shown in Figure 12.3B, the locations can be 4000, 4001, 4002, and 4003.

12.1.3 | Control Bus

The 6821 has five pins that are connected to four control bus lines. The reason that five PIA pins need only four control lines is that two of the pins ($\overline{IRQA}$ and $\overline{IRQB}$) are wired together to one line, as shown in Figure 12.4. A brief description of each control line follows.

Reset: This pin is connected to the μC system's reset line. Whenever this line is brought low, all register bits within the PIA are cleared to a logic 0. This allows the designer of a system to know the logic state of the PIA registers whenever the system's master reset button is pressed. On the diagrams in Figures 12.1 and 12.4, the line over the word "reset" indicates that the active state of this pin is a logic 0.

FIGURE 12.3 | Wiring Diagrams for Chip Select Pins (CS_0, CS_1, and $\overline{CS_2}$) and Register Select Pins (RS_0 and RS_1)

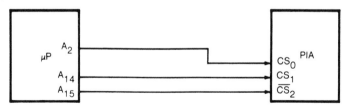

A. Chip Select Direct Connection

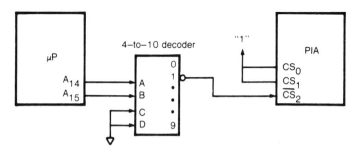

B. Chip Select Decoder Connection

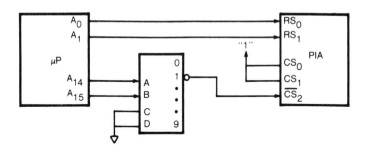

C. Register Select Connection

Enable (E):   The enable pin is the only pin on the PIA that receives a timing signal. The timing of all other signals and data transfers is controlled by either the leading or trailing edge of the enable pulse. If a 6821 is used with a 6502 μP, then the enable pin should be connected to the ϕ_2 clock signal line. If a 6821 PIA is used with a 6800 μP, then the ϕ_2 clock signal should be ANDed with the μP's VMA signal, as shown in Figure 12.4.

Interrupt Request ($\overline{IRQA}$ and $\overline{IRQB}$):   The interrupt request lines ($\overline{IRQA}$ and $\overline{IRQB}$) are used to send an interrupt signal to the μP. The lines may be tied directly to the μP's $\overline{IRQ}$ pin, as shown in Figure 12.4. The $\overline{IRQA}$ and $\overline{IRQB}$ lines are ''open drain'' lines (there is no internal load device on the chip) and are capable of sinking 1.6 mA. The open connection permits all PIA interrupt request lines to be ORed together.

FIGURE 12.4 | Wiring Diagram for 6800 μP Connected to 6821 PIA

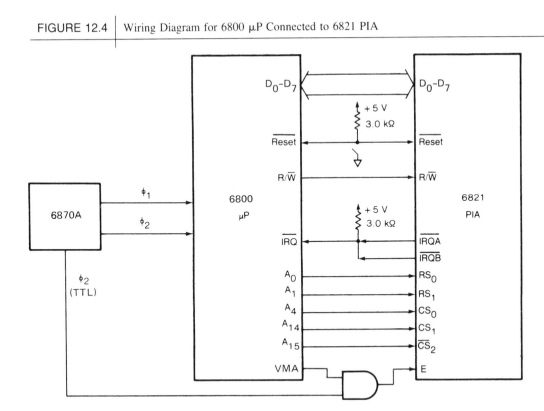

Each interrupt request line on the PIA has two flag bits that cause the line to go low. Each flag bit is associated with a peripheral control line. For port A, the peripheral control lines are labeled CA_1 and CA_2. For port B, the peripheral control lines are CB_1 and CB_2. A simplified drawing is shown in Figure 12.5. The 6821 can be programmed so that one or more of the peripheral control lines can be disabled.

In Section 12.6, we will look at a program that allows the μP to read and test the PIA flag bits to determine which peripheral interrupt line is signaling the μP. These flag bits are cleared to a logic 0 when the μP reads the data from the correct port or when the reset line goes low.

FIGURE 12.5 | Status Information Bits (Bits 6 and 7) of Control Register

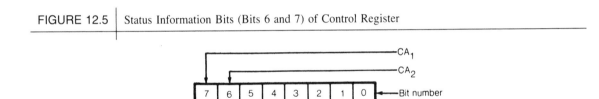

Control lines CA_2 and CB_2 have a dual function. Each can be programmed either as an input interrupt request line, as just described, or as an output line to control peripheral equipment.

12.2 | PERIPHERAL INTERFACE LINES

The 6821 PIA has two ports, and each port has eight bidirectional I/O lines. Associated with each port are two interrupt/control lines. Although the port lines are described as bidirectional I/O lines, note that each line can be programmed as either an input line or an output line, but not both at the same time.

12.2.1 | Port A

Each peripheral data line of port A can be programmed either as an input line or as an output line. This is accomplished by loading a binary pattern into a data direction register for port A (DDRA). This register is inside the PIA and can be addressed by the μP. If a logic 1 is loaded into a bit of the data direction register, the corresponding port line becomes an output line. If a logic 0 is loaded into a bit of the data direction register, the corresponding port line becomes an input line. This register and how to program it are covered in Section 12.4. When a line is programmed as an output line, it is capable of driving two TTL loads. When it is programmed as an input line, it is the equivalent of one TTL load.

12.2.2 | Port B

Like port A, each peripheral data line of port B can be programmed either as an input line or as an output line. Unlike the output lines of port A, the output buffers of port B have three-state capability. Those of port A are only TTL compatible. When a peripheral data line of port B is programmed as an input line, the output buffer associated with that line enters its high impedance state. When a peripheral data line of port B is programmed as an output line, data on this line (or lines) can be read back to the μP correctly even if the voltage on a line drops below 2.0 V for a logic 1. As output lines, port B lines are compatible with standard TTL and may also be used as drivers for the base of a transistor switch because they can deliver 1.5 mA at 1.5 V.

Like port A, the binary pattern stored in the data direction register of port B (DDRB) determines which is an input and which is an output line. A logic 0 in a bit of the DDRB makes the corresponding bit in port B an input line. A logic 1 in a bit of DDRB makes the corresponding bit in port B an output line. Remember, the binary pattern in the data direction register only sets up the port lines as input or output lines; the pattern is not the data that is sent to or received by the port. The μP has to write or read the data to the port as a separate set of instructions.

12.2.3 | Interrupt Lines (CA_1 and CB_1)

Lines CA_1 and CB_1 can be used only as input interrupt lines. These lines set the interrupt flag bit (bit 7) of the control register. The PIA can be programmed so that either a low-to-high or a high-to-low transition can be recognized on these peripheral lines.

12.2.4 | Interrupt/Control Line (CA$_2$)

The peripheral interrupt/control line, CA$_2$, can be programmed either as an input line or as an output line. As an input line, CA$_2$ is used as an interrupt line. When programmed as an output line, CA$_2$ is used as a control or handshake signal line from the PIA to peripheral equipment. This line is TTL compatible.

12.2.5 | Interrupt/Control Line (CB$_2$)

Like CA$_2$, peripheral line CB$_2$ can be programmed as an input interrupt line or as an output control line. As an output, it is compatible with TTL and may be used as a source of up to 1 mA and 1.5 V to drive a transistor.

12.3 | INTERNAL OPERATION

Each 6821 PIA has two peripheral sides, side A and side B. Each side has a peripheral interface register (also called a port), a data direction register, and a control register. Therefore, there are a total of six registers within the 6821 that can be addressed by the μP: two peripheral interface registers (port A and port B), two data direction registers (DDRA and DDRB), and two control registers (CRA and CRB). Figure 12.6 shows the internal block diagram for the 6821 PIA.

Although there are six addressable registers, a 6821 chip requires only four address locations. Two registers on each side—the port and the data direction register —have the same address. In this section, we will see how the μP distinguishes one register from another. In the next section, we will focus on how to program the 6821.

12.3.1 | Peripheral Interface Registers

Inside the PIA, the peripheral interface register or port is the addressable register that allows the μP to send and receive data over the I/O lines. If the lines are programmed as input lines, the μP takes in the data by executing a load instruction at the port address. The μP sends data to a port and then to lines programmed as output lines by having the μP execute a store instruction. The port register, as with all the PIA registers, should be treated as any other address location. Therefore, all the instructions that a μP contains to process data in a memory location can be used for the PIA registers.

12.3.2 | Data Direction Registers (DDRA and DDRB)

The two data direction registers (DDRA and DDRB) allow the user to program the corresponding peripheral lines as either input lines or output lines. A logic 0 in a data direction bit causes the corresponding peripheral line to be an input line; a logic 1 causes the corresponding peripheral line to be an output line. The binary pattern in a DDR only programs the peripheral lines as input or output; the pattern is not the data on the lines. An analogous situation is shown in Figure 12.7. The bit in the DDR controls the position of the switch; it does not determine the data that the μP can receive or send. A logic 1 in a bit of the DDR is similar to the switch in position A in Figure 12.7A. The μP can only send data on this line. A logic 0 in a bit of the DDR is similar to the switch in

FIGURE 12.6 | 6821 PIA Internal Block Diagram (Redrawn from data sheet for MC6821 PIA with permission. Motorola Incorporated, Phoenix, Arizona)

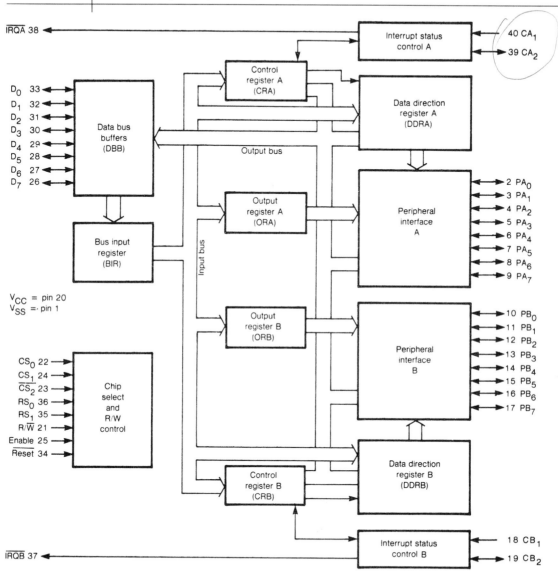

position B in Figure 12.7B. The μP can only receive data when the switch is in this position.

Each line of port A and each line of port B in the 6821 PIA is programmed individually. For example, two lines on port A can be programmed as input lines while the remaining lines of port A are output lines. Port B can also be programmed in any fashion. Figure 12.8 shows several examples of binary patterns in a data direction register and the corresponding I/O lines.

FIGURE 12.7 | Switch Position for Output and Input Lines Controlled by Data Direction Register (DDR)

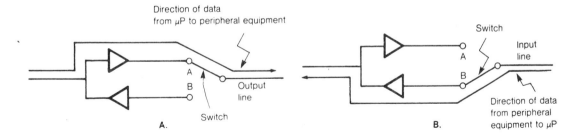

12.3.3 | Control/Status Registers (CRA and CRB)

The 6821 has two control/status registers. They are most often referred to as simply the control register. Both the A and B portions contain such a register. Bits 0 through 5 are the control bits and can be written to by the μP. Bits 6 and 7 are the status bits and can only be read by the μP.

The binary pattern in the control bits determines how the μP will work with the PIA and the peripheral equipment. For example, the binary pattern determines (1) whether CA_2 (or CB_2) is an input or output control line; (2) whether CA_1 (or CB_1) and CA_2 (or CB_2) respond to low-to-high or high-to-low transitions; and (3) whether the μP communicates with a port or a DDR. Figure 12.9 shows the word format of the control register. Remember, the word format is a binary pattern that programs how the PIA will

FIGURE 12.8 | Examples of Binary Patterns in DDR and Corresponding I/O Lines

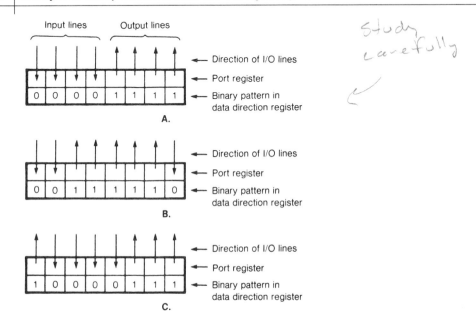

operate. Although the μP sends an 8-bit binary pattern, only bits 0 to 5 are loaded into the control register. Bits 6 and 7 are read-only locations, and the data on lines 6 and 7 never reaches bits 6 and 7 of the control/status register. Let's examine the function of each control bit.

Control Bits 0 and 1:   Bits 0 and 1 of both control registers determine how lines CA_1 and CB_1 are to operate. Bit 0 in control register A enables or disables the $\overline{IRQA}$ line. Bit 0 of control register B does the same for the $\overline{IRQB}$ line. Bit 1 of each register determines whether the PIA's CA_1 (or CB_1) line recognizes a high-to-low transition or a low-to-high transition. Table 12.1 summarizes the binary patterns for the first two control register bits.

Control Bit 2:   Bit 2 of the control/status register selects whether the μP addresses the DDR or the port. This bit is needed because the port and the DDR have the same memory address. If bit 2 of the control register is a logic 0, the μP is communicating with the DDR. If bit 2 is a logic 1, the μP is communicating with the port. The addresses for the 6821 may be confusing to the first-time user. For both the A and B portions, the port and DDR have the same address, while the control/status register has the next memory address. In most applications, however, the DDR is addressed only once, and that is during initialization. The advantage is that several 6821 chips can be connected to the system and be easily decoded, as we will see in Section 12.5. Remember, each 6821

| FIGURE 12.9 | Word Format of Control Register |

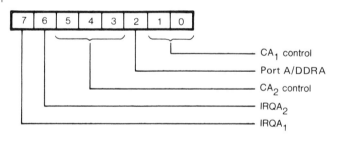

A.

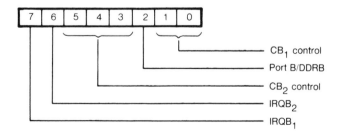

B.

TABLE 12.1 | Control of Interrupt Inputs CA_1 and CB_1

CRA-1 (CRB-1)	CRA-0 (CRB-0)	Interrupt Input CA1 (CB1)	Interrupt Flag CRA-7 (CRB-7)	MPU Interrupt Request IRQA (IRQB)
0	0	↓ Active	Set high on ↓ of CA1 (CB1)	Disabled — IRQ remains high
0	1	↓ Active	Set high on ↓ of CA1 (CB1)	Goes low when the interrupt flag bit CRA-7 (CRB-7) goes high
1	0	↑ Active	Set high on ↑ of CA1 (CB1)	Disabled — IRQ remains high
1	1	↑ Active	Set high on ↑ of CA1 (CB1)	Goes low when the interrupt flag bit CRA-7 (CRB-7) goes high

Notes: 1. ↑ indicates positive transition (low to high)

2. ↓ indicates negative transition (high to low)

3. The Interrupt flag bit CRA-7 is cleared by an MPU Read of the A Data Register, and CRB-7 is cleared by an MPU Read of the B Data Register.

4. If CRA-0 (CRB-0) is low when an interrupt occurs (interrupt disabled) and is later brought high, IRQA (IRQB) occurs after CRA-0 (CRB-0) is written to a "one".

Source: Reprinted with permission of Motorola Incorporated, Austin, Texas.

gives the user 16 I/O lines and four peripheral control lines, and takes only four memory addresses. These memory addresses are wired to be four consecutive locations, such as the following:

4000 (port A and DDRA)

4001 (control/status register A)

4002 (port B and DDRB)

4003 (control/status register B)

Section 12.4 gives the programming steps needed to use a 6821 PIA.

Control Bits 3, 4, and 5: Bits 3, 4, and 5 of both control registers are used to program peripheral control lines CA_2 and CB_2. When bit 5 is a logic 0, the control line is programmed as an interrupt input line. When bit 5 is a logic 1, the line is programmed as an output control line. When programmed as output, control lines CA_2 and CB_2 have different characteristics. Tables 12.2, 12.3, and 12.4 summarize how the control bits 3, 4, and 5 control CA_2 and CB_2.

Status Bits 6 and 7: Bits 6 and 7 of the control register are the interrupt flag bits. Bit 7 indicates the status of the peripheral interrupt line CA_1 (or CB_1). This bit is set to a logic 1 when there is an active transition on the peripheral interrupt line. When line CA_2 (or CB_2) is programmed as an input line, then bit 6 of the control/status register is the interrupt

TABLE 12.2 | Control of CA$_2$ and CB$_2$ as Interrupt Inputs [CRA-5 (CRB-5) low]

CRA-5 (CRB-5)	CRA-4 (CRB-4)	CRA-3 (CRB-3)	Interrupt Input CA2 (CB2)	Interrupt Flag CRA-6 (CRB-6)	MPU Interrupt Request IRQA (IRQB)
0	0	0	↓ Active	Set high on ↓ of CA2 (CB2)	Disabled — IRQ remains high
0	0	1	↓ Active	Set high on ↓ of CA2 (CB2)	Goes low when the interrupt flag bit CRA-6 (CRB-6) goes high
0	1	0	↑ Active	Set high on ↑ of CA2 (CB2)	Disabled — IRQ remains high
0	1	1	↑ Active	Set high on ↑ of CA2 (CB2)	Goes low when the interrupt flag bit CRA-6 (CRB-6) goes high

Notes: 1. ↑ indicates positive transition (low to high)

2. ↓ indicates negative transition (high to low)'

3. The Interrupt flag bit CRA-6 is cleared by an MPU Read of the A Data Register and CRB-6 is cleared by an MPU Read of the B Data Register.

4. If CRA-3 (CRB-3) is low when an interrupt occurs (Interrupt disabled) and is later brought high, IRQA (IRQB) occurs after CRA-3 (CRB-3) is written to a "one".

Source: Reprinted with permission of Motorola Incorporated, Austin, Texas.

TABLE 12.3 | Control of CB$_2$ as Output (CRB-5 high)

CRB-5	CRB-4	CRB-3	CB2 Cleared	Set
1	0	0	Low on the positive transition of the first E pulse following an MPU Write "B" Data Register operation.	High when the interrupt flag bit CRB-7 is set by an active transition of the CB1 signal.
1	0	1	Low on the positive transition of the first E pulse after an MPU Write "B" Data Register operation.	High on the positive edge of the first "E" pulse following an "E" pulse which occurred while the part was deselected.
1	1	0	Low when CRB-3 goes low as a result of an MPU Write in Control Register "B"	Always low as long as CRB-3 is low. Will go high on an MPU Write in Control Register "B" that changes CRB-3 to "one".
1	1	1	Always high as long as CRB-3 is high. Will be cleared when an MPU Write Control Register "B" results in clearing CRB-3 to "zero".	High when CRB-3 goes high as a result of an MPU Write into Control Register "B".

Source: Reprinted with permission of Motorola Incorporated, Austin, Texas.

TABLE 12.4 | Control of CA$_2$ as Output (CRA-5 high)   *E = enable*

CRA-5	CRA-4	CRA-3	CA2	
			Cleared	Set
1	0	0	Low on negative transition of E after an MPU Read "A" Data operation.	High when the interrupt flag bit CRA-7 is set by an active transition of the CA1 signal.
1	0	1	Low on negative transition of E after an MPU Read "A" Data operation.	High on the negative edge of the first "E" pulse which occurs during a deselect.
1	1	0	Low when CRA-3 goes low as a result of an MPU Write to Control Register "A".	Always low as long as CRA-3 is low. Will go high on an MPU Write to Control Register "A" that changes CRA-3 to "one".
1	1	1	Always high as long as CRA-3 is high. Will be cleared on an MPU Write to Control Register "A" that clears CRA-3 to a "zero".	High when CRA-3 goes high as a result of an MPU Write to Control Register "A".

Source: Reprinted with permission of Motorola Incorporated, Austin, Texas.

flag bit for this line. These bits can only be read by the μP. They are cleared to the logic 0 state when the μP reads the data from the port or when the reset line goes low.

Remember, the term *active transition* means that lines CA$_1$, CA$_2$, CB$_1$, and CB$_2$ can be programmed to recognize either a low-to-high transition or a high-to-low transition.

12.3.4 | Reset Line

When the reset line goes low, it causes all I/O lines to become input lines and all bits of the other registers to be cleared to the logic 0 state. Peripheral lines CA$_2$ and CB$_2$ become input lines. Therefore, any time the reset line is activated (goes low), the PIA must be reprogrammed as the user wants it. Programming steps for the data direction registers and the control registers are given in the next section.

12.4 | PROGRAMMING THE 6821 PIA

One of the first programming steps in any μC system is to initialize all the I/O ports when the power is applied. In most applications, once a line is programmed as either an input or output line, it is left in that state. Occasionally, however, the user may wish to reprogram one or more of the I/O lines or a control line. The following examples show the programming steps necessary to initialize the 6821 for different uses. Example 12.1 shows how to program both port A and port B. Example 12.2 shows how to program port A and its control lines.

EXAMPLE | *may be useful for   Lab I*
--------|

12.1 Write the programming steps necessary to satisfy the following conditions:

1. All lines of port A are to be input lines.
2. All lines of port B are to be output lines.
3. Control lines are not used.
4. The PIA is wired at locations 4000–4003.

Solution:

The first two memory locations (4000 and 4001 in this example) always apply to the A side. The third and fourth locations (4002 and 4003 in this example) always apply to the B side. From Section 12.3.3, we have the following:

A side 4000   (port A and DDRA)
        4001   (control register A)
B side 4002   (port B and DDRB)
        4003   (control register B)

The programming steps must include the following functions:

1. Load bit 2 of each control register with a logic 0 so the μP communicates with the data direction registers.
2. Load DDRA with all logic 0s, making port A all input lines.
3. Load DDRB with all logic 1s, making port B all output lines.
4. Reload bit 2 of each control register with a logic 1, allowing the μP to communicate with the port at a future time.

The programming steps to satisfy the preceding conditions are as follows:

LDA A #$00 ⎫
STA A $4001 ⎬   Clear bit 2 of each control register.
STA A $4003 ⎭
STA A $4000   DDRA loaded with 0s.
LDA A #$FF ⎫
STA A $4002 ⎭   DDRB loaded with 1s.
STA A $4001 ⎫
STA A $4003 ⎭   Reset bit 2 of each control register.

The control lines in this example were not going to be used. Therefore, we are not concerned with the logic state of control bits 0, 1, 3, 4, and 5.

EXAMPLE	

12.2   Write the programming steps necessary to initialize a 6821 PIA to meet the following conditions:

1. Port line A_0 is to be an output line and all other lines of port A are to be input lines.
2. Interrupt input line CA_1 is to be receiving a high-to-low transition signal and the PIA should be capable of sending an interrupt request signal to the µP.
3. Line CA_2 is to be an output control line and is to be able to send a low-to-high signal to peripheral equipment after the CA_1 signal is received.
4. Port B is not being used.
5. The PIA is wired at locations 8000–8003.

Solution:
Although port B is not being used, the device is connected as follows:

A side 8000   (port A and DDRA)
        8001   (control register A)
B side 8002   (port B and DDRB)
        8003   (control register B)

From Tables 12.1 and 12.4, we know that the final binary pattern that must be stored in control register A is as follows:

7 6	5 4 3	2	1 0
X X	1 0 0	1	0 1
Don't care	CA_2 from Table 12.4	Port A	CA_1 from Table 12.1

The following programming steps satisfy the preceding conditions:

LDA A #$00 ⎱
STA A $8001 ⎰   Clear bit 2 and temporarily disable the $\overline{IRQA}$ line.
LDA A #$01 ⎱
STA A $8000 ⎰   Port A_0 is an output line; all other lines are input.
LDA A #$25 ⎱
STA A $8001 ⎰   Control register is loaded with final binary pattern.

In this example, the "don't care" conditions are considered to be a logic 0. If logic 1s are to be sent on data lines 6 and 7, then the last two steps are as follows:

LDA A #$E5
STA A $8001

Remember, the logic levels on data lines 6 and 7 never reach bits 6 and 7 because these bits are the status bits.

12.5 CONNECTING SEVERAL PIAS TO THE SYSTEM

Each PIA has six registers (two ports, two DDRs, and two control registers) that can communicate with the μP. However, the port and the data direction register have the same address. Therefore, four memory locations are needed to address one PIA completely. The use of the same address for the port and data direction register may seem confusing at first. The register with which the μP communicates depends on bit 2 of the control register. As the previous programming examples showed, the control register may have to be addressed twice. The first time is to clear bit 2 so the μP can load data into a DDR. The second time is to set bit 2 so the μP can read or write data to the port. What appears to be an awkward arrangement becomes an easy interface to the μP as more PIAs are added to the system.

Figure 12.3A showed how one PIA chip could be connected directly to a μP. However, when several PIAs are being used, decoder chips are needed. Using only four memory locations to identify a PIA makes maximum use of the decoder chips and thus creates an efficient system. Let's consider a μC system that is to have four PIAs wired between memory locations 4000 and 400F. This is the same memory allocation that was given to I/O in Chapter 10, as shown in Figure 10.9. As we will see, the decoder line, line 1 of Figure 10.9, will be wired to each PIA chip. A low on this line indicates that the μP wants to communicate with one of the PIAs. We still have to identify which PIA and which register within the PIA are to send or receive data. These two functions can be carried out by the lowest four address lines. Figure 12.10 shows all the binary combinations that can exist on four address lines. Thus, all memory locations between 4000 and 400F are included.

Figure 12.10 also shows how a 74LS138 decoder chip can be used to decode address lines A_2 and A_3. Address lines A_0 and A_1 are wired to all the PIAs. From Figure 12.10, we see that lines A_2 and A_3 remain at the same logic state for four counts (four address locations). Hence, maximum use is made of each address line, creating a very efficient system.

If more PIAs are to be connected to the system, address line A_4 would be wired to the C input on the 74LS138 chip. This connection would permit four more PIAs to be connected to the system.

The 74LS138 has three enable input pins—G_1, G_{2A}, and G_{2B}. For the 74LS138 to decode the binary pattern on its A, B, and C inputs, the enable inputs must be at the logic levels shown in Figure 12.10. If one or more of the enable inputs is at a different logic level, then all of the outputs are high. Thus the enable pins are control inputs for the '138. How the '138 can be controlled is shown in Figure 12.11. When the 74154 decoder chip in Figure 12.11 decodes an address beginning with 0100 (binary 4), output number 4 goes low. This low logic level enables the 74LS138. Depending on the binary pattern on address lines A_2 and A_3, a particular PIA is thus selected.

FIGURE 12.10 | Binary Combinations on Four Address Lines

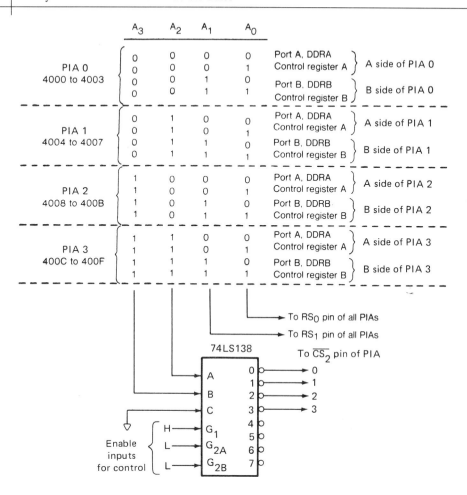

12.6 | A SOFTWARE POLLING TECHNIQUE

The 6800 μP has one interrupt request pin. It is designed to be an open-drain device so that several PIA interrupt request lines can be tied to it through a 3.0 kΩ pull-up resistor. However, when several PIA interrupt request lines are used in a system, the μP must be able to distinguish one interrupt request signal from another. The schematic of Figure 12.12 shows how the interrupt request lines of the four PIAs of Figure 12.11 can be tied to a 6800 μP. Each interrupt request line coming from the PIA represents two possible interrupt signals. (See either Figure 12.5 or PIA 1 of Figure 12.12.)

FIGURE 12.11 Typical PIA Decoding

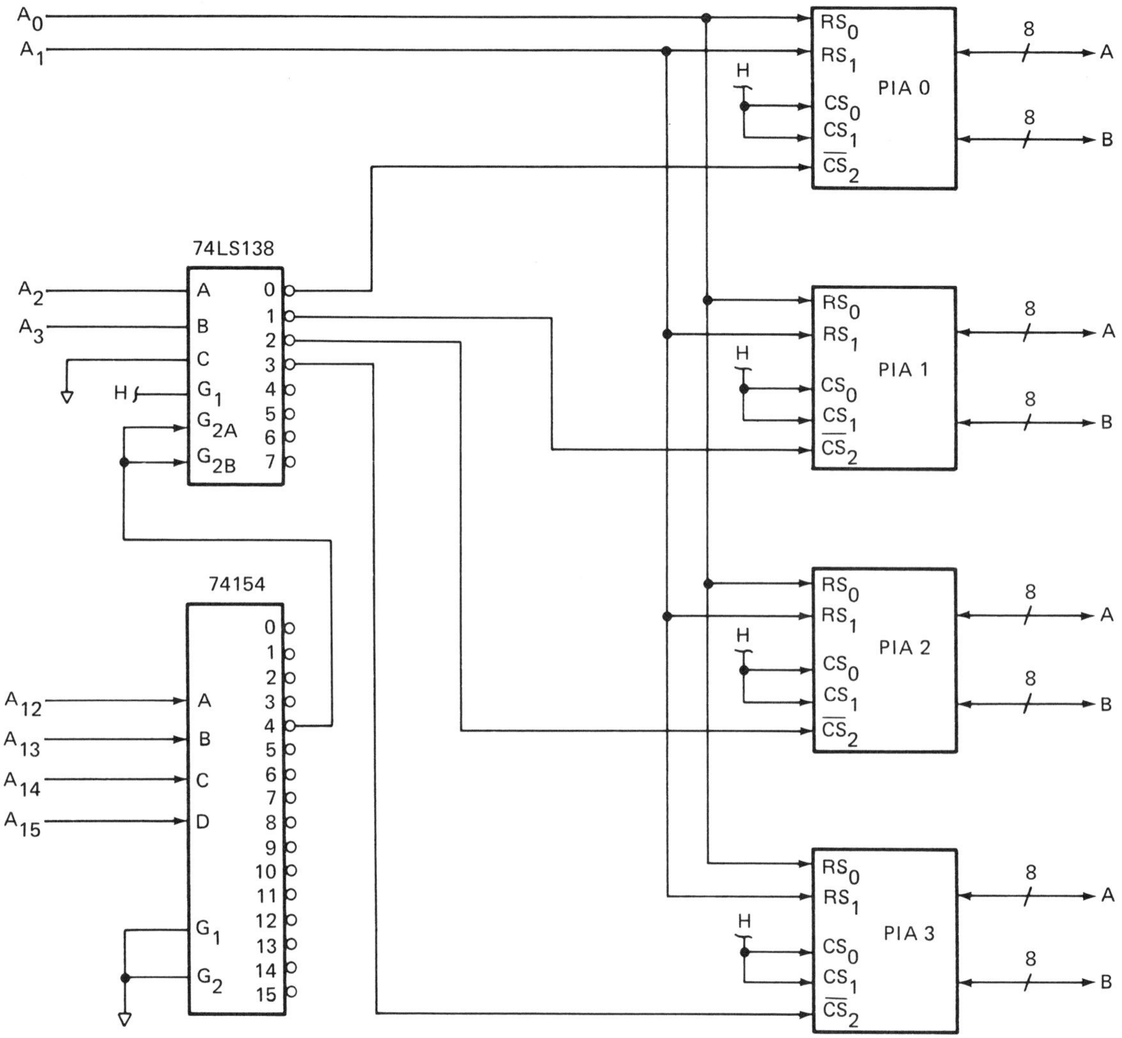

FIGURE 12.12 | PIA Interrupt Request Lines Tied to μP's $\overline{\text{IRQ}}$ Pin through 3.0 kΩ Pull-up Resistor

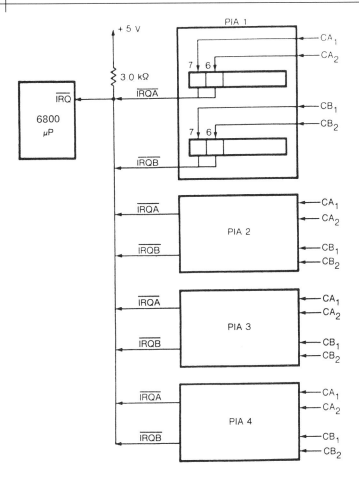

When the μP receives an interrupt request signal, it must determine which PIA and which peripheral interrupt line (CA_1, CA_2, CB_1, or CB_2) on the PIA need servicing. If a program is used to do this, it is called a *software polling technique*. The programmer chooses the priority of servicing by determining which control register and which bit (either 7 or 6) is tested first. If the four PIAs are wired between locations 4000 to 400F, then Table 12.5 gives the address of each control register.

The following programming steps show how each control register and each interrupt request bit can be checked. The offset (P_1, P_2, and so on) for each branch instruction would direct the μP to a program to service that particular interrupt. The software polling program is as follows:

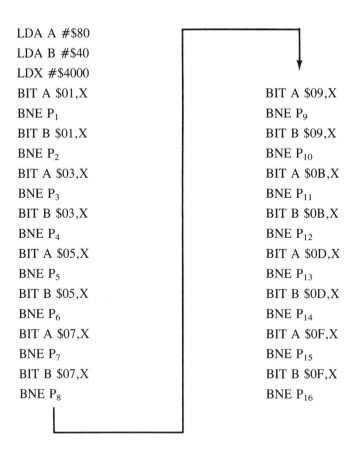

```
LDA A #$80
LDA B #$40
LDX #$4000
BIT A $01,X          BIT A $09,X
BNE P₁               BNE P₉
BIT B $01,X          BIT B $09,X
BNE P₂               BNE P₁₀
BIT A $03,X          BIT A $0B,X
BNE P₃               BNE P₁₁
BIT B $03,X          BIT B $0B,X
BNE P₄               BNE P₁₂
BIT A $05,X          BIT A $0D,X
BNE P₅               BNE P₁₃
BIT B $05,X          BIT B $0D,X
BNE P₆               BNE P₁₄
BIT A $07,X          BIT A $0F,X
BNE P₇               BNE P₁₅
BIT B $07,X          BIT B $0F,X
BNE P₈               BNE P₁₆
```

TABLE 12.5 | Address of Control Register

Control Register	PIA Number	Location
A	0	4001
B	0	4003
A	1	4005
B	1	4007
A	2	4009
B	2	400B
A	3	400D
B	3	400F

12.7 | INTERFACING A PIA WITH AN ALPHANUMERIC PRINTER

As previously mentioned, the MC6821 is a general-purpose interface device. In this section, it is used as the link between the μP and an alphanumeric printer.

12.7.1 | Printer Description

The printer is a Gulton Model AP–20, a self-contained alphanumeric thermal printer. All its electronics, including a RAM memory buffer, a character generator ROM, a power supply, and control circuitry, are enclosed in the printer's case. The print format is 20 characters per line. Each character is a 5 × 7 dot matrix, as shown in Figure 12.13. The printer is designed to accept 64 ASCII characters. (Figure 3.3, columns 2, 3, 4, and 5, lists the most frequently used characters.)

Data is sent from the PIA to the printer one character at a time. The data is stored in a RAM buffer. When 20 characters have been stored, or when a carriage return code or an end-of-line code has been received, the printer begins printing the data. The print head contains 100 thermal print dots so that an entire row of character dots is printed at one time. The bottom row of dots is printed first, as shown in Figure 12.13. After one entire line is complete, the paper is automatically advanced one or more lines.

12.7.2 | PIA–Printer Connections and Operation

The PIA of Figure 12.14 uses peripheral lines PB_0 to PB_6 to transmit a 7-bit ASCII character. Peripheral line PB_7 and control lines CB_1 and CB_2 are used for handshake signals.

Line CB_2 is used as a clock signal to the printer. The inverter gate on this line is needed because the printer's external clock line (pin 18 on the printer) requires a positive-going pulse. By using the CB_2 line in this fashion, the data sent to port B from the μP will have enough time to stabilize on the peripheral lines before it is clocked into the printer.

The printer also requires a positive pulse on its load data line (pin 19 on the printer). This pulse is sent by the μP through the port B_7 line (pin 17 on the PIA). The inverter gate is needed because the μP is sending a 7-bit ASCII character with a logic 0 on the eighth data bus line. In this system, the load data line goes high on the first character and the data is transmitted when the external clock line goes high.

FIGURE 12.13 | 5 × 7 Dot Matrix of Printer

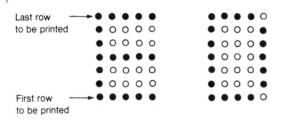

Last row to be printed

First row to be printed

FIGURE 12.14 | 6821 Used as Interface Link between μP and Alphanumeric Printer

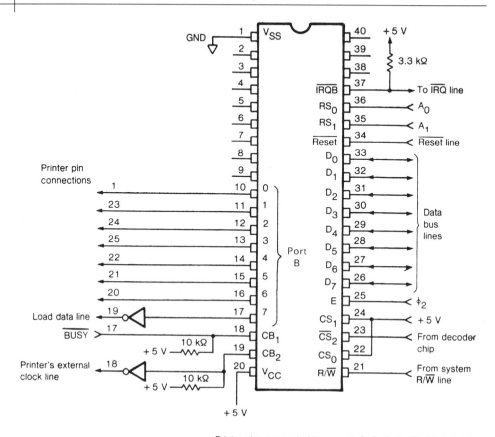

Printer pins connected to ground: 5, 6, 7, 8, 10, 12, 14, 16

When the printer decodes a carriage return command or an end-of-line signal, or when the 20-character RAM buffer is full, the $\overline{BUSY}$ line goes low. This signal is sent back to the PIA's CB_1 pin indicating that a line of data is being printed. When the $\overline{BUSY}$ line goes low, the PIA sends an interrupt request signal back to the μP on the $\overline{IRQB}$ line. The μP recognizes the interrupt request and jumps to an interrupt subroutine that is a time delay program. The printer then has enough time to print one line before the μP begins sending the printer the next line of data. Figure 12.15 shows how the CB_2 and $\overline{BUSY}$ handshake signals operate.

12.7.3 | Programming the PIA

In order to satisfy the handshake signals, the B side of the PIA must meet the following criteria:

1. All peripheral lines of port B must be programmed as output lines.
2. Control line CB_1 must be programmed to send an interrupt request signal to the μP when it receives a high-to-low transition.
3. Control line CB_2 must be programmed as an output line and the line must go low when the μP writes data to port B.
4. After the μP initializes the data direction register of port B, the μP must always be able to communicate with the peripheral lines.

To meet these specifications, we need to use data in Tables 12.1 and 12.3. The final binary pattern stored in control register B is shown in Figure 12.16.

FIGURE 12.15 | Operation of CB_2 and $\overline{BUSY}$ Handshake Signals

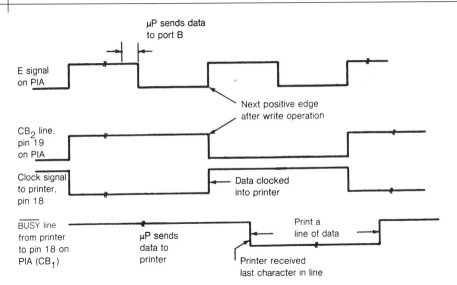

FIGURE 12.16 | Binary Pattern Stored in Control Register B

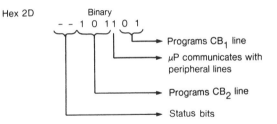

EXAMPLE

12.3 Consider the PIA to be wired at memory locations 8000, 8001, 8002, and 8003. After the $\overline{\text{reset}}$ line is activated and released, program the B side of the PIA to meet criteria 1–4.

Solution:

After $\overline{\text{reset}}$, all lines are input lines and all register bits contain a logic 0. Using the 6800 assembly language mnemonics, we have the following:

$$\left.\begin{array}{l}\text{LDA A } \#\$FF \\ \text{STA A } \$8002\end{array}\right\} \quad PB_0\text{--}PB_7 \text{ are programmed as output lines.}$$

$$\left.\begin{array}{l}\text{LDA A } \#\$2D \\ \text{STA A } \$8003\end{array}\right\} \quad \text{Programming control register B.}$$

Now any data stored at port B by the μP will be sent to the printer on the next clock signal.

12.8 | SWITCH CLOSURE APPLICATION

Figure 12.17 shows two applications of the PIA—switch closure and vacuum pump control. These two applications use the A side of the PIA shown in Figure 12.14. This section covers the switch closure, and Section 12.9 deals with the vacuum pump.

FIGURE 12.17 | PIA Application in Switch Closure and Vacuum Pump Control

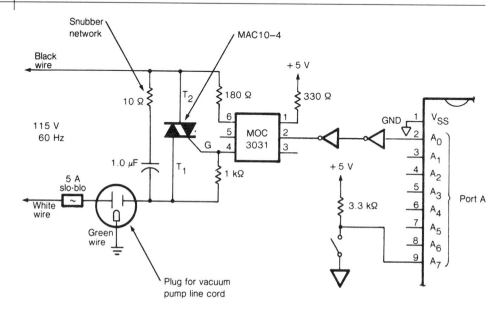

A switch and a pull-up register are wired to PIA line A_7. Consider that once the μP recognizes that this switch is closed, the μP jumps to another program and does not need to monitor PA_7 again until the program is finished. Figure 12.18 is a flowchart showing how the 6800 μP can monitor bit 7 (port line A_7) of memory location 8000. The 50 ms time delay program guarantees that the μP will not recognize any noise on the line or switch bounce. The time delay program is referred to as a subroutine in the following program. Using 6800 assembly language mnemonics, we can write the programming steps necessary to satisfy the flowchart steps:

```
        LDA A #$80      Initialize accumulator A.
LOOP:   BIT A $8000     Monitor PA₇.
        BNE LOOP        Loop if A₇ = 1 (switch not closed).
        JSR TDELAY      Jump to delay subroutine.
        LDA A #$80      Reinitialize accumulator A.
        BIT A $8000     Retest PA₇.
        BNE LOOP        Loop if A₇ = 1 (there was not a true switch closure).
```

FIGURE 12.18 | Flowchart for 6800 μP Monitoring Bit 7

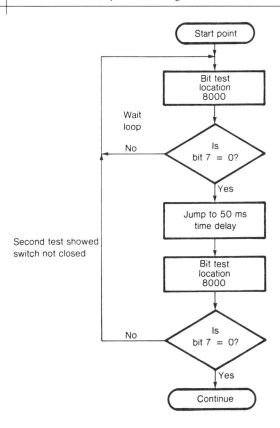

12.9 | CONTROLLING A VACUUM PUMP

One peripheral line and some additional external interface circuitry allow the μP to control a 1/6 hp vacuum pump, as shown in Figure 12.17. When the μP outputs a logic 0 on the PA_0 line, the vacuum pump is turned on. Since a PIA's output line is a latch network, the vacuum pump remains on until the μP stores a logic 1 at PA_0.

The MOC3031 is a zero-voltage-crossing, optically isolated, triac driver manufactured by Motorola, Inc. This device consists of a gallium arsenide infrared-emitting diode, optically coupled to a photo triac containing a zero-crossing circuit. Figure 12.19 shows a schematic for the coupler. To guarantee that the emitting diode triggers the photo triac, a diode current of 10–15 mA must flow. Since this current is greater than that which can be sinked by PA_0, a TTL buffer is needed.

The maximum rms current that can flow between pins 6 and 4 of the MOC3031 is 100 mA. Since the vacuum pump draws several amps during normal operating conditions, a heat-sinked power triac is needed. The optically coupled triac turns on the power triac, applying power to the plug. The vacuum pump's line cord is inserted into this plug, and thus the μP controls power to the pump. The snubber network ensures that the power triac does not have a false turn-on. (For more information on optical couplers, power triacs, heat sinks, and snubber networks, see *Solid State Devices and Applications*, by Frederick F. Driscoll and Robert F. Coughlin, Prentice-Hall, Inc., Englewood Cliffs, N.J., 1975.)

The arrangement shown in Figure 12.17 allows the interface circuitry to be mounted near the μP and the vacuum pump a short distance away.

After the μP turns on the vacuum pump, the μP should jump to a 5 s time delay program. This delay would allow the pump to come up to pressure before any other program starts.

The following program initializes the A side of the PIA and keeps the pump off until it is to be turned on later in the main program. The A side addresses are 8000 and 8001.

```
LDA A #$01 ⎫
STA A $8000 ⎬   Set only vacuum pump line PA₀ as an output line.
LDA A #$04 ⎫
STA A $8001 ⎬   Set bit 2 of control register A.
LDA A #$01 ⎫
STA A $8000 ⎬   Output line PA₀ is latched high to keep the pump off.
```

12.10 | SUMMARY

The 6821 peripheral interface adapter is a general-purpose I/O device. Although this chip was designed primarily for the 6800 μP, it is often used with other μPs. The 6821 has two ports, A and B. Each port has eight peripheral lines; each line can be programmed as either an input or an output line. In addition to these I/O lines, the 6821 has other peripheral lines for "handshaking." Like other peripheral devices, the 6821 is easily

FIGURE 12.19 | Schematic of MOC3031

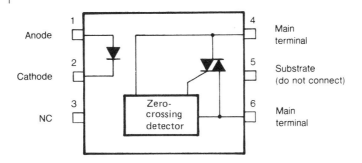

connected to the μP's address, data, and control buses. It is capable of sending an interrupt request signal back to the μP either from peripheral side A or peripheral side B.

Sections 12.3 and 12.4 show how to program the 6821's peripheral lines and control (handshake) lines. Section 12.5 shows how decoder chips are used to connect several PIAs to a μP. When a μP is capable of receiving an interrupt request from several PIAs, a software polling technique, as shown in Section 12.6, can be used to identify which PIA is requesting service. Sections 12.7, 12.8, and 12.9 show three applications of how the PIA is used as the interface device between the μP and peripheral equipment.

PROBLEMS

12.1 How many ports does the 6821 have?

12.2 Can the I/O lines be programmed independently?

12.3 How many pins on the 6821 are connected to the address bus?

12.4 What are the logic levels on the chip select pins?

12.5 Is the active state of the reset pin high or low?

12.6 What is the function of the enable pin?

12.7 What is the difference between the I/O lines of port A and the I/O lines of port B?

12.8 The binary pattern in what register determines whether an I/O line is programmed as input or output?

12.9 What lines are the peripheral interrupt lines?

12.10 Which two registers within the 6821 have the same address?

12.11 The following binary pattern is stored in data direction register A:

7 6 5 4 3 2 1 0   Bit number

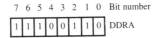

Which lines are programmed as input lines and which are output lines?

12.12 How many bits of the control register are used for status information?

12.13 What is the function of bit 2 of the control register?

12.14 When the $\overline{\text{reset}}$ line is activated, are the lines automatically programmed as input or output lines?

12.15 The following binary pattern is stored in control register A:

```
7  6  5  4  3  2  1  0   Bit number
X  X  1  0  0  1  0  0   Control register A
```

(a) Will the μP communicate with the port or with the data direction register? (b) What is the active transition on the CA_1 line? (c) Is CA_2 programmed as an interrupt or a control line?

12.16 The PIA is wired at locations 4000–4003. Write the programming steps necessary to satisfy the following conditions: (a) All lines of port A are output lines; (b) All lines of port B are input lines; (c) CA_1 and CA_2 are not used; (d) CB_1 is an interrupt request line with high-to-low active transition; and (e) CB_2 is an output control line with low-to-high active transition when the CB_1 signal is received.

12.17 Refer to Figures 12.10 and 12.11. If two more PIAs have to be added to the system, how should they be decoded?

13 Asynchronous Communication Interface Adapter 6850

13.0 | INTRODUCTION

Digital data is transferred either serially over a single line or in parallel over many lines. In *serial transmission*, the binary data is sent down a single wire one bit at a time. In *parallel transmission*, each bit has its own wire and all the data is sent at the same time. Figure 13.1 shows examples of serial and parallel transmission of 8 bits of data (10110110).

Parallel transmission obviously is faster because all bits are sent at once. Therefore, parallel transmission is used within the computer, for functions like transferring data between the CPU and memory, between the CPU and I/O devices, and between memory and I/O devices. However, multiple wires become extremely cumbersome, costly, and susceptible to noise if parallel transmission is used between computers or between a computer and its peripheral equipment (such as keyboards, CRT displays, and printers). Therefore, an I/O device is needed that is capable of converting the CPU's parallel data to serial format and transmitting it. Likewise, the I/O device must be capable of receiving serial data and converting it to a parallel format to be put into the μC's data bus. An I/O device that is capable of transmitting and receiving serial data is Motorola's MC6850 asynchronous communication interface adapter (ACIA).

In some systems, circuitry in addition to the ACIA is needed. For example, the distance between a computer and its peripheral equipment may become so great that the only convenient link is a telephone line. In order to use a telephone to send and/or receive digital data, a modem is required. The term *modem* comes from the words *modulator* and *demodulator*. The modulator portion converts the serial data from an ACIA to a signal suitable for telephone transmission. The demodulator section converts the telephone signals to logic 1s and 0s and sends the serial data to an ACIA. Figure 13.2 shows three applications of ACIAs. Also included in this figure is an RS232C interface block. RS232C is an interface standard used in many computer systems.

FIGURE 13.1 | Examples of Data Transmission

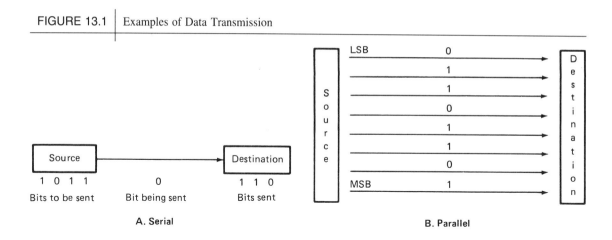

A. Serial

B. Parallel

Figure 13.2A illustrates how a keyboard and CRT display can be connected to a μP through an ACIA. This application assumes that the μP and peripheral equipment are fairly close—usually less than 50 ft. If a telephone line is used to connect the keyboard and CRT display, then an ACIA and modem system is needed at both ends of the communication link, as shown in Figure 13.2B. The dashed line around the ACIA and modem circuitry in Figure 13.2B indicates that it has been designed as a unit on a single PC board. However, most often you will find μC systems with one or more serial I/O ports that are RS232C compatible, as shown in Figure 13.2C. This compatibility allows you to use modems and other peripheral equipment from different manufacturers with your system. Most modems and other peripheral equipment designed for μCs are RS232C compatible.

13.1 | SYNCHRONOUS AND ASYNCHRONOUS COMMUNICATION

The transfer of serial data is either synchronous or asynchronous. Synchronous communication is used for high-speed data transmission. Usually this type of communications is needed between a group of mini or large mainframe computers. This communication link constantly transmits data or synchronization (sync) bits when no data is being transmitted. The sync bits ensure that the receiver is always "locked onto" the rate at which the data is being sent and when the data is coming. High-speed data transmission is not always needed and, in particular, usually is not needed in μC systems. These systems use slow-speed peripheral equipment and usually do not have to transfer data at high rates. For μCs, asynchronous communication is the best choice and, therefore, this chapter only covers this type.

FIGURE 13.2 | Three Applications Using the MC6850 ACIA

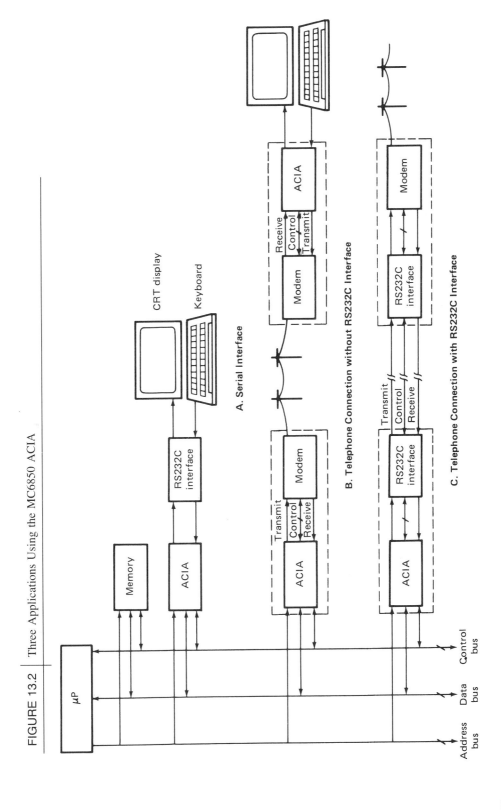

A. Serial Interface

B. Telephone Connection without RS232C Interface

C. Telephone Connection with RS232C Interface

13.2 | ASYNCHRONOUS CHARACTER FORMAT

Early teleprinters used the condition that an idle line (no data being sent) is one in which current is flowing. In these teleprinter systems, data was transmitted when the current was interrupted. The idle state became known as the "1" state or *mark* condition. The absence of current on the line was called the *space* condition or "0" state. Most of today's data transmission systems rely on voltage changes. However, the terms *mark* and *space* are still used. For TTL levels, a logic 1 is the mark condition and a logic 0 is the space condition.

Asynchronous transmission begins when the line is brought from mark to space. This first bit is called the *start* bit. The start bit is immediately followed by the data bits. Depending on the format chosen, there are between 5 and 8 data bits. A parity bit is often used, and this bit follows the data bits. Each character in asynchronous transmission ends with a stop bit or bits. Figure 13.3 illustrates the character format for asynchronous communication.

In order for the transmitter and receiver to interpret the data correctly, both systems agree on a data code. The most widely used code today is the ASCII code (American Standard Code for Interface Interchange) covered in Chapter 3. Example 13.1 shows a serial pulse train for an ASCII character.

EXAMPLE

13.1

Draw the character format for the capital letter E. Use a 7-bit data format, even parity, and one stop bit.

Solution:
From Figure 3.3, we find:

$$E = 45_{hex} = \boxed{1000101}$$

MSB   LSB

The waveform of this format is shown in Figure 13.4. The parity bit is a logic 1, so the total number of 1s in the data plus the parity bit is an even number.

Note: ASCII characters are stored in memory as 8 bits. The eighth bit may be a don't-care condition. However, all 8 bits are sent by the μP to the ACIA. As you will see, the ACIA may be programmed to send only the first 7 bits. At this time, don't worry about the start, parity, or stop bit(s); these are all inserted by the ACIA.

Another characteristic of asynchronous communication is that each group of data bits is "framed" by a start bit and stop bit(s). In synchronous communication, blocks of data are sent between sync bits. For this reason, asynchronous communication is called *character framed* and synchronous communication is called *block framed*. Framing each character wastes at least 20% of the transmission time. The advantage of asynchronous communication is the simplicity of design; the receiver is required only to sense the start bit and this format has a relatively stable clock.

In any asynchronous communication link, the transmitter and receiver must be

FIGURE 13.3 | Character Format for Asynchronous Communication

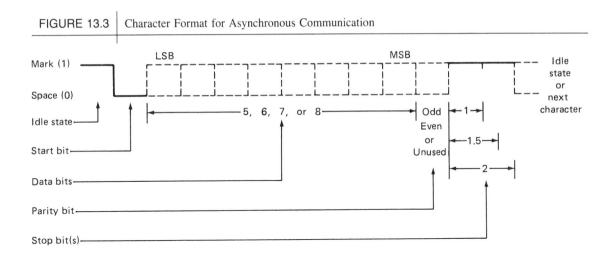

FIGURE 13.4 | Character Format for the Letter E Using One Stop Bit

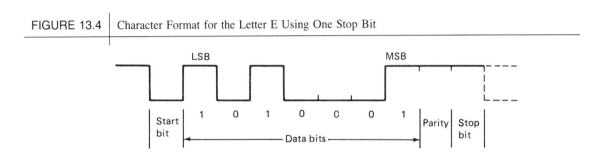

set not only for the same character format but also for the same rate of transfer. The rate at which data is transferred is referred to as the baud rate.

13.3 | BAUD RATE

The time to transmit (or receive) a bit is known as *bit time* or time per bit, as shown in Figure 13.5. The reciprocal of the bit time is *baud rate*. In equation form, this is expressed as:

$$\text{Baud rate} = \frac{1}{\text{Bit time}} \tag{13.1}$$

Other relationships for asynchronous communication are as follows:

$$\text{Character time} = \text{Total number of bits in a character} \times \text{Bit time} \tag{13.2}$$

$$\text{Characters per second} = \frac{1}{\text{Character time}} \tag{13.3}$$

$$\text{Data bits per second} = \frac{\text{Data bits}}{\text{Character}} \times \frac{\text{Characters}}{\text{Second}} \tag{13.4}$$

Example 13.2 shows how Equations 13.1 to 13.4 apply to Figure 13.4.

EXAMPLE	

13.2   If the bit time in Figure 13.4 is 9.09 ms, determine the (a) baud rate, (b) time to transmit one character, (c) number of characters per second, and (d) number of data bits per second.

Solution:

a. Applying Equation 13.1 yields the result:

$$\text{Baud rate} = \frac{1}{9.09 \text{ ms}} = 110 \text{ baud}$$

b. In Figure 13.4, we see that the character contains 10 bits (1 start bit, 7 data bits, 1 parity bit, and 1 stop bit). Using Equation 13.2 yields the result:

$$\text{Character time} = 10 \text{ bits} \times 9.09 \text{ ms} = 90.9 \text{ ms}$$

c. Applying Equation 13.3 yields the result:

$$\text{Characters/second} = \frac{1}{90.9 \text{ ms}} = 11 \text{ characters/s}$$

d. In Figure 13.4, we see there are 7 data bits. Using Equation 13.4, we obtain the following:

$$\text{Data bits/s} = (7 \text{ bits/character}) \times (11 \text{ characters/s}) = 77 \text{ bits/s}$$

FIGURE 13.5	Comparison of Bit Time and Character Time

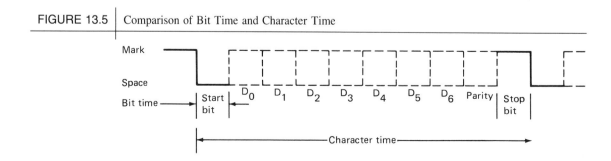

Baud rate refers to the total number of bits being transmitted (or received) in one second. In Example 13.2, the baud rate is 110, but only 77 bits actually carried data. The remaining 33 bits (110 − 77) are overhead. Remember that this overhead is a disadvantage of asynchronous communication. The advantages are that the hardware and software designs are easier than for synchronous communication.

Tables 13.1 and 13.2 list the characteristics of the most commonly used baud rates. Table 13.1 is for a character format of 1 start bit, 7 data bits, 1 parity bit, and 1 stop bit. Table 13.2 is similar to Table 13.1, except that each character has 2 stop bits.

TABLE 13.1 Comparison of Different Baud Rates Using 10 Bits per Character (1 Start Bit, 7 Data Bits, 1 Parity Bit, 1 Stop Bit)

Baud Rate	Bit Time (ms)	Character Time (ms)	Characters/s	Data Bits/s
110	9.09	90.9	11	77
150	6.66	66.6	15	105
300	3.33	33.3	30	210
600	1.66	16.6	60	420
1200	0.833	8.33	120	840
2400	0.416	4.16	240	1,680
4800	0.208	2.08	480	3,360
9600	0.104	1.04	960	6,720
19.2K	0.052	0.52	1,920	13,440
38.4K	0.026	0.26	3,840	26,880

TABLE 13.2 Comparison of Different Baud Rates Using 11 Bits per Character (1 Start Bit, 7 Data Bits, 1 Parity Bit, 2 Stop Bits)

Baud Rate	Bit Time (ms)	Character Time (ms)	Characters/s	Data Bits/s
110	9.09	100	10	70
150	6.66	73.3	13.6	95.2
300	3.33	36.6	27.3	191.1
600	1.66	18.3	54.6	382.2
1200	0.833	9.2	108.7	761.4
2400	0.416	4.6	217.4	1,521.8
4800	0.208	2.3	434.8	3,043.6
9600	0.104	1.1	909	6,363
19.2K	0.052	0.55	1,818.2	12,727.4
38.4K	0.026	0.28	3,571.4	24,999.8

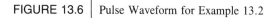

FIGURE 13.6 | Pulse Waveform for Example 13.2

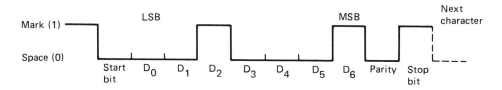

EXAMPLE

13.3   Refer to Figure 13.6 and determine the (a) data bit pattern, (b) ASCII character, and (c) type of parity.

Solution:

a. From Figure 13.6, we see that the data bits are 0010001. Since the least significant bit (LSB) is the first bit sent after the start bit, the bit pattern must be reversed to conform to convention. Therefore, the data bit pattern is 1000100.

b. Now use Figure 3.3 to find that this binary pattern is 44_{hex} or the capital letter D in ASCII.

c. Since the total number of 1s in the data bits and parity bit is an even number, the character format has even parity.

13.4 | THE MC6850 ACIA

As mentioned earlier, Motorola's serial I/O device is called an asynchronous communication interface adapter (ACIA) and is numbered MC6850. This device permits a μP to send and receive serial data asynchronously. Like other peripheral interface devices, this device is programmable and its internal registers are addressable. We will now study how this device is connected to a μP, how its internal registers operate, and what programming steps are necessary to send and receive data.

13.5 | PACKAGE STYLE

The 6850 ACIA is housed in a 24-pin dual-in-line package, as shown in Figure 13.7. The device is designed so that it can be connected directly to the μP's address, data, and control buses. The pins that are connected to the peripheral lines of the device allow it to transmit and receive data asynchronously. Other peripheral pins are for control functions when this device is used with a modem.

Since most of the pins are connected to internal registers, the names and purposes of these registers will be covered first along with the general operation of the ACIA. This

FIGURE 13.7 | Pin Assignments for the MC6850 ACIA (Redrawn with permission of Motorola Incorporated, Austin, Texas)

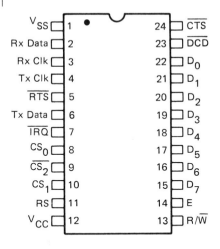

will make it easier to understand (1) the purpose of each pin, (2) how to connect the device to the μP, (3) which registers can communicate with the μP, and (4) how the ACIA sends and receives data from peripheral equipment.

13.6 | BLOCK DIAGRAM

Figure 13.8 shows an internal block diagram of the ACIA. It consists of a number of registers, including a transmit data register, transmit shift register, status register, control register, receive data register, and receive shift register. In addition to these registers, the device has chip select, read/write control circuitry, data bus buffers, peripheral control circuitry, parity generation, and parity checking circuitry.

With all of this circuitry, however, there are only four registers that can be addressed by the μP. They are the transmit data register, status register, control register, and receive data register. All of these are 8-bit registers. The transmit data and control registers are *write-only* registers, while the status and receive data registers are *read-only* registers. *Note:* The μP does not directly address either the transmit shift or the receive shift register. Their operation and how data flows into and out of them is controlled by the internal circuitry of the ACIA.

The bits of the control register determine how the 6850 is programmed to operate. By changing the binary pattern sent to this register, the programmer can choose to operate the device in a number of different modes. The function of each bit or group of bits of the control register is given in Section 13.11.

Each bit in the status register keeps a record of a particular function so that the μP can check it and know what is happening. The name and function of each status bit is covered in Section 13.12.

FIGURE 13.8 | Block Diagram of the MC6850 ACIA (Reprinted with permission of Motorola Incorporated, Austin, Texas)

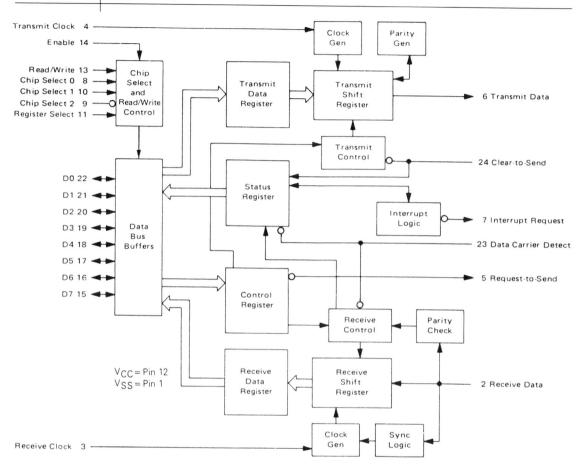

13.7 | PRINCIPLES OF OPERATION

Before giving a detailed function of each register, we shall discuss the basic operation of the 6850 ACIA.

13.7.1 | Transmitter Operation

In a typical transmitting sequence, data is sent to the *transmit data register* by the μP. The internal circuitry of the ACIA transfers the data to the *transmit shift register*. The data is then sent out serially on the *transmit data line*.

Before the μP actually sends the data to the transmit data register, the μP must know if the register is empty. The μP can find out that the register is empty in one of two ways: (1) by receiving an interrupt request signal, or (2) by first checking a bit in the status register that keeps track of whether the transmit data register is full or empty. Both methods are discussed in more detail later in this chapter.

The transmit shift register is a parallel-to-serial shift register. The internal circuitry of the ACIA transfers the data from the data register to the shift register in a parallel fashion. Then the data is transmitted out serially.

The reason for using two registers is that the μP can write new data to the data register while the ACIA is transmitting an old character from the shift register. This technique is called *double buffering*. It allows the μP to continue to execute a program while the ACIA handles the transmission of data.

Since the 6850 is designed to transmit and receive data asynchronously, the ACIA automatically generates the start bit. It can also be programmed to generate a parity bit (either even or odd) and either one or two stop bits.

The start, data, parity, and stop bits are shifted out of the transmit shift register on the negative edge of the transmit clock signal. The start bit is transmitted first, followed by the least significant data bit (that bit that came in on the D_0 line). Bits D_1 through D_6 or D_7, the parity bit, and the stop bit(s) are then shifted out. The rate at which data is transmitted is determined by an external transmit clock signal (this is not the ϕ_2 clock signal) and by a bit pattern written into two bits of the control register. Since this control register also determines how the receiver section of the ACIA operates, we will study how the receive operation works before studying the control register.

13.7.2 | Receiver Operation

Data is received serially by the ACIA on the *receive data line*. As each bit is received, it is shifted into the *receive shift register*. When the start bit, the data bits, the parity bit, and the stop bit(s) have been received, the ACIA automatically transfers the data bits in parallel to the *receive data register*. *Note:* Only the data bits are transferred to the receive data register. The start, parity, and stop bits are not transferred; they are said to be "stripped away." The μP receives the data bits by reading the receive data register.

Before the data bits are transferred from the shift register to the data register, the ACIA has been designed to detect three types of errors—framing error, overrun error, and parity error. The record of whether an error has occurred or not is kept in the status register (Section 13.12).

The μP can find out if the receive data register is full of current data in one of two ways: (1) by receiving an interrupt request signal, or (2) by checking bit 0 of the status register. This bit is called the receive data register full bit. In either case, before the μP reads the data, the program first should check the status register to "see" if an error has occurred.

If an error has occurred, the programmer may wish to jump to an error program. If no error has occurred, the μP then can read the receive data register. A flowchart that shows how to check the status register and how to read the receive data register is covered in Section 13.13.2.

Like the transmitter portion of the ACIA, the receiver portion is double-buffered by having a receive shift register and a receive data register. This allows the μP to receive data, process it, and return to the main program while new data is being shifted into the ACIA.

The reason why the μP can return to a program while the ACIA is sending or receiving data is that the μP executes its instructions in microseconds while serial data is sent and received in milliseconds (the fastest rate at which most peripheral equipment can operate). Thus the ACIA "frees" the μP from the task of waiting for new data to be sent or received.

13.8 | PIN FUNCTIONS

The 6850 interfaces directly to a μP with an 8-bit bidirectional data bus, three chip select lines, a register select line, an interrupt request line, a read/write line, and an enable line. These lines allow the μP to control and communicate with the ACIA.

On the peripheral side, there is a serial output line (transmit data), a serial input line (receive data), and three peripheral control lines (clear-to-send, data carrier detect, request-to-send). There are also two power supply pins (V_{DD} = +5 V and V_{SS} = gnd) and two clock lines (transmit clock and receive clock).

13.8.1 | Address Bus Connections

Chip Select Pins (CS_0, CS_1, and $\overline{CS_2}$):   The 6850 has three chip select pins that are high input impedance and TTL compatible. The device is selected by the μP whenever CS_0 and CS_1 are high and $\overline{CS_2}$ is low. The select pins may be wired either directly to the μP's address lines or to a decoder chip. The direct connection is often used in dedicated control systems that require only a small amount of memory (usually less then 4K) and only a few peripherals. If a decoder chip(s) is used, a convenient wiring pattern is to permanently tie CS_0 and CS_1 high and let one output line of the decoder chip drive the $\overline{CS_2}$ line. Figure 13.9 shows two ways of connecting an ACIA device to a 6800 μP. Unused chip select lines cannot be left "floating"; they must be tied to their appropriate logic levels (see CS_0 and CS_1 in Figure 13.9B). In both applications of Figure 13.9, the ACIA is selected when the μP addresses location 6000.

Register Select (RS):   The 6850 has one RS line. The device uses the logic level on this line *along with* the logic level on the read/write line to determine which of four internal registers communicates with the μP. Figure 13.10 summarizes which ACIA register communicates with the μP for the different logic combinations of the RS and the $R/\overline{W}$ lines. The RS line should be wired to the address bus line, A_0, so that the internal registers are in sequential locations (such as 6000 and 6001). *Note:* Each location has the potential of addressing two registers; which register communicates with the μP depends on the logic level on the $R/\overline{W}$ line.

Read/Write ($R/\overline{W}$):   The logic state of the read/write determines whether the μP is receiving (reading) or sending (writing) data to the ACIA. When the $R/\overline{W}$ line is high, the μP is reading data from one of the ACIA's internal registers—either the status register or the receive data register. When the $R/\overline{W}$ line is low, the μP is writing data to one of the ACIA's internal registers—either the control register or the transmit data register.

FIGURE 13.9 | Examples of Wiring the 6850 ACIA to the 6800 μP

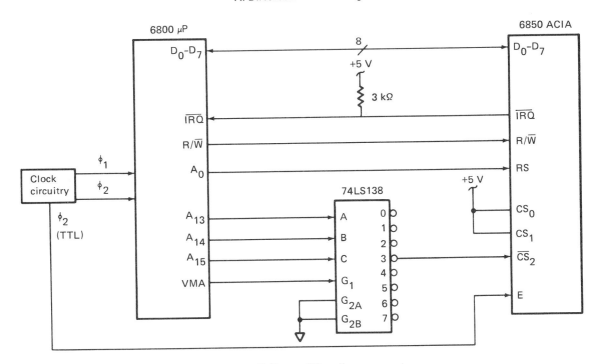

A. Direct Address Decoding

B. External Decoding

FIGURE 13.10 | Truth Table for the ACIA's Register Select and Read/Write Lines

Logic state of RS line	Logic state of R/$\overline{W}$ line	Communication with ACIA register
L	L	μP sends data to the control register.
L	H	μP receives data from the status register.
H	L	μP sends data to the transmit data register.
H	H	μP receives data from the receive data register.

As previously stated, the R/$\overline{W}$ line works in conjunction with the register select line to determine which ACIA register is communicating with the μP. (Once again, this information is summarized in Figure 13.10.)

13.8.2 | Data Bus Connections

As with other interface devices, the 6850's data bus lines (D_0–D_7) connect directly to the system's data bus, as shown in Figure 13.9. When the device is not selected, the data bus output drivers go to their high impedance state, thereby removing the ACIA from the data bus.

13.8.3 | Control Bus Connections

Enable (E): The logic level on this pin enables the ACIA's input/output data buffers. All data transfers between this device and the μP occur on the negative-going edge of the ϕ_2 clock signal.

When this device is used with the 6800 μP, the enable pin is connected either to the ϕ_2 clock signal line or to a VMA·ϕ_2 line.

Interrupt Request ($\overline{IRQ}$): The $\overline{IRQ}$ pin is connected to the μP's interrupt request line. This pin allows the ACIA to signal the μP either to send or receive data. Which condition occurs depends on the logic state of certain bits within the ACIA's control and status registers.

As with other interface devices, there is no internal pull-up register. This allows the ACIA's $\overline{IRQ}$ line to be wire ORed to other $\overline{IRQ}$ lines with other interface devices. The $\overline{IRQ}$ line to the μP remains low as long as the cause of the interrupt is present.

Clock Inputs (Tx Clk and Rx Clk): There are two input clock lines—transmit clock (Tx Clk) and receive clock (Rx Clk). These lines are *not* the ϕ_2 clock signal that is wired to the enable pin. The ϕ_2 signal is used to transfer data between the μP and the ACIA or between internal registers of the ACIA. The transmit and receive clock inputs provide the clocking signals for the data that is to be transmitted or received on the transmit data and receive data lines, respectively. If data is to be transmitted and received at the same baud rate, then the clock lines can be connected together as will be shown in Section 13.14.

The clock frequencies are set at 1, 16, or 64 times the data rate. The 6850 has an internal divider.

The transmitter sends data on the negative transition of the clock-signal. The receiver samples data on the positive transition of the receive clock signal.

The receive clock signal is used for the synchronization of data that is coming into the ACIA on the receive data line.

13.9 | SERIAL DATA LINES

Transmit Data Line (Tx Data): The transmit data (Tx Data) output line is a single line that is used to transmit data serially from the ACIA to a modem or other peripheral equipment. Data rates up to 500K bits per second (bps) may be transmitted. Usually this device is used to transmit data at a slower rate, such as the baud rates given in Tables 13.1 and 13.2.

Receive Data Line (Rx Data): The receive data (Rx Data) input line is the line through which the serial data is received. The incoming data is synchronized internally with the receive clock signal when clock rates of 16 and 64 times the bit rate are used. When a clock rate of 1 is used, external synchronization is needed. The receive data line has a high-impedance TTL compatible input.

13.10 | PERIPHERAL AND MODEM CONTROL LINES

The 6850 permits limited control of a modem or other peripheral equipment. The control pins are clear-to-send ($\overline{\text{CTS}}$), request-to-send ($\overline{\text{RTS}}$), and data carrier detect ($\overline{\text{DCD}}$). As indicated by the bar over the letters, these lines have active low states.

Request-to-Send ($\overline{\text{RTS}}$): The $\overline{\text{RTS}}$ line is an output line used most often with a modem. This line allows the μP to send a signal to a modem indicating that the μP is ready to send data. The logic level of this line is set by bits in the ACIA's control register, as we will study in Section 13.11.

Clear-to-Send ($\overline{\text{CTS}}$): The $\overline{\text{CTS}}$ line is used by the ACIA to receive a control signal from a modem. In this application, the signal indicates that the modem is ready to receive data from the ACIA and send the data over a telephone line. If this line is not used, it must be wired low.

Data Carrier Detect ($\overline{\text{DCD}}$): The $\overline{\text{DCD}}$ line, like the $\overline{\text{CTS}}$ line, is an input line to the ACIA from a modem. This line is used to signal the ACIA that the modem's carrier signal has been lost. If the receive interrupt enable bit in the control register (Section 13.11) is set, a low-to-high transition on the $\overline{\text{DCD}}$ line initiates an interrupt to the μP. This is how the μP "learns" that the modem's carrier signal has been lost. If the $\overline{\text{DCD}}$ line is not used, it must be wired low.

13.11 | CONTROL REGISTER

The ACIA's control register (CR) is an 8-bit write-only register. The binary pattern sent to this register by the μP controls how data is transmitted and received by the ACIA. The control register is addressed by the μP selecting the ACIA (using lines CS_0, CS_1, and $\overline{CS_2}$) and bringing the register select (RS) and the read/write ($R/\overline{W}$) lines low. Each group of bits of the control register is labeled in Figure 13.11 and described in the following discussions.

Bits 0 and 1—Clock Divide/Master Reset Bits: The binary pattern in these two bits determines the divide ratios used by both the transmitter and receiver sections. These two bits also are used as a master reset. Shown in Table 13.3 are the bit patterns and their functions.

Let's first study what the master reset function is and how it is used. After power is applied from either power-on or a power fail/restart network, the ACIA's internal circuitry senses the power-on transition and holds the chip in a reset condition to prevent erroneous output transitions. This reset condition must be released in order to use the 6850. That is, the μP first has to set CR_0 and CR_1 to a logic 1 before programming the entire control register.

Therefore, to initialize the device, the μP has to write to the ACIA at least twice—once to release the power-on reset logic and the second time to initialize the entire

FIGURE 13.11 | Control Register with Bit Names for the 6850 ACIA

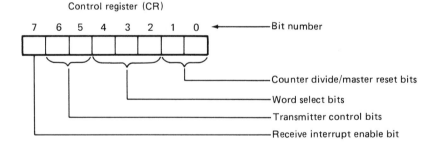

TABLE 13.3 | Clock Divide/Master Reset Bits

Control Bits		
CR_1	CR_0	*Function*
0	0	÷ 1
0	1	÷ 16
1	0	÷ 64
1	1	Master reset

control register. The first write instruction to the control register can be of the following form:

7　6　5　4　3　2　1　0　← Control bit number

x　x　x　x　x　x　1　1　← Control word

where x can be either a logic 0 or a logic 1. If the ACIA is wired so that the control register is at address 6000, as shown in Figure 13.9, then the following programming steps would clear the internal power-on reset logic:

LDA A #$03

STA A $6000

When power is applied, all the status bits in the ACIA, except the $\overline{CTS}$ and $\overline{DCD}$ bits, are cleared to a logic 0. This also happens whenever a master reset instruction (setting CR_0 and CR_1 to a logic 1) is sent to the control register. In some applications, a programmer may use this point to clear the status register.

After the control logic inside the ACIA has been reset, then the μP can send a binary pattern to the control register to program the device. Bits 0 and 1 now have an entirely different function. They determine the rate at which the serial data is sent and received by the ACIA. For example, if a 0,1 binary pattern is sent to CR_1 and CR_0, respectively, then the ACIA is programmed in the divide-by-16 mode. This means that the transmit and receive clock frequencies are divided by 16. This function allows the ACIA to have its internal clock circuitry operate at a frequency 1/16 of the external clock frequency. Section 13.14 discusses the relationship between these pulses.

Bits 2, 3, and 4—Word Select Bits: Bits 2, 3, and 4 determine the character format for transmission or reception by the ACIA. These bits establish:

1. The number of data bits (7 or 8),
2. The type of parity (even, odd, or none),
3. The number of stop bits (1 or 2).

Since there are 3 bits involved, there are eight possible combinations ($2^3 = 8$) from which the programmer can choose, as shown in Table 13.4. The last column in the table includes one start bit because the 6850 automatically begins all transmissions with a start bit and must first receive a start bit to recognize incoming serial data.

Bits 5 and 6—Transmitter Control Bits: These two control bits provide for the following three functions, all of which deal with transmitting data:

1. To send (enable) or not to send (disable) an interrupt request signal to the μP when the ACIA has transferred data from the transmit data register to the transmit shift register.
2. To set the logic state of the request-to-send ($\overline{RTS}$) line,
3. To transmit a break level (a series of spaces).

TABLE 13.4 | Word Select Bits

Control Bits			Number of Data Bits	Type of Parity	Number of Stop Bits	Total Number of Bits (Including One Start Bit)
CR_4	CR_3	CR_2				
0	0	0	7	Even	2	11
0	0	1	7	Odd	2	11
0	1	0	7	Even	1	10
0	1	1	7	Odd	1	10
1	0	0	8	None	2	11
1	0	1	8	None	1	10
1	1	0	8	Even	1	11
1	1	1	8	Odd	1	11

For the first function, if an interrupt signal is sent from the ACIA to the μP, then the μP knows that it can send new data to the transmit data register. There also is another method for the μP to determine if the transmit data register is empty and can receive new data. This second technique involves having the μP first check a particular bit in the status register. This bit and the entire status register are covered in the next section, and the procedure for checking the status bit is covered in Section 13.13.1.

Bits 5 and 6 of the control register also determine the logic level of the request-to-send line. The $\overline{RTS}$ line is a control line to a modem or other peripheral equipment. It is used by the ACIA when the μP wishes to transmit data and must know if it is okay to do so. (The ACIA is also capable of receiving a return handshake signal, the $\overline{CTS}$ signal.) The $\overline{RTS}$ line has an active low state; that is, when this line is low, the μP through the ACIA is requesting to send data.

When the μP has completed its transmission, a break signal is usually sent. A break signal is a transmission of logic 0s.

The binary patterns for control bits 5 and 6 are summarized in Table 13.5.

Bit 7—Receive Interrupt Enable (RIE) Bit: This bit enables or disables interrupt requests being sent to the μP from the receiver section of the ACIA. A logic 1 means

TABLE 13.5 | Transmitter Control Bits

Control Bits		Logic Level on $\overline{RTS}$	$\overline{IRQ}$ Signal Transmission to μP	Break Level Transmission to μP
CR_6	CR_5			
0	0	L	No	No
0	1	L	Yes	No
1	0	H	No	No
1	1	L	No	Yes

that an interrupt request signal will be sent to the μP whenever the receive data register is full or whenever there is a low-to-high transition on the data carrier detect ($\overline{DCD}$) line. A logic 0 disables interrupts from being sent to the μP from the receiver section. *Note:* A logic 0 in the RIE bit does not stop the transmitter section or any other peripheral interface device from sending an interrupt request to the μP.

As you will study, there is a second method for the μP to determine if the receive data register is full. This second method is covered in Section 13.13.2.

13.12 | STATUS REGISTER

The status register (SR) is an 8-bit read-only register. It indicates the condition of six internal activities and two external activities. This register is addressed by the μP using the chip select lines (CS_0 and CS_1 are high and $\overline{CS_2}$ is low), register select line (RS is low), and the read/write line (R/$\overline{W}$ is high). Each bit within the status register is labeled as shown in Figure 13.12. The logic state (0 or 1) of each bit indicates a particular condition. The remaining portion of this section explains the function of each bit.

Bit 0—Receive Data Register Full (RDRF) Bit: This status bit indicates whether or not the ACIA's receive data register has new (current) or old data in it. When data is transferred from the receive shift register to the receive data register, this bit goes to a logic 1. This indicates that the contents of the receive data register are current. When this happens, the $\overline{IRQ}$ bit (bit 7) also gets set to a logic 1 and remains set until the μP reads the contents of the receive data register. The RDRF bit gets cleared to a logic 0 under any one of the following three conditions:

1. After the μP reads the contents of the receive data register (*Note:* In this situation, the receive data register is a source register; therefore, the data in it is not lost by the μP reading it.),

FIGURE 13.12 | Status Register with Bit Names for the 6850 ACIA

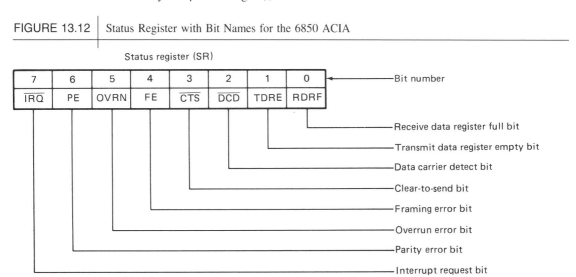

2. If the $\overline{\text{DCD}}$ line goes high, indicating that the data in the receive data register is not current,
3. When a power-on condition occurs.

Bit 1—Transmit Data Register Empty (TDRE) Bit: This bit gets set to a logic 1 when the contents of the transmit data register have been transferred to the transmit shift register. This logic state indicates that the transmit data register is ready to receive new data from the μP. When this bit gets set to a logic 1, the $\overline{\text{IRQ}}$ bit (bit 7) also gets set to a logic 1 and remains set until the μP sends new data to the transmit data register.

The TDRE bit gets cleared to a logic 0 if any of the following conditions occur:

1. If the transmit data register is full with current data and this data is waiting to be transferred to the transmit shift register,
2. If the clear-to-send ($\overline{\text{CTS}}$) line goes high (When the $\overline{\text{CTS}}$ is high, the ACIA does not transmit data; therefore, the μP should not send new data to the transmit data register.),
3. When a power-on condition occurs.

Bit 2—Data Carrier Detect ($\overline{\text{DCD}}$) Bit: As previously mentioned, the data carrier detect line indicates the presence or loss of a modem's carrier signal. The $\overline{\text{DCD}}$ status bit of the ACIA allows the μP to obtain this information. When the $\overline{\text{DCD}}$ input line goes high, it causes this status bit to go to a logic 1 and the RDRF bit to a logic 0. Also, if the receive interrupt enable, RIE, bit (bit 7 of the control register) is set to a logic 1, then the $\overline{\text{IRQ}}$ status bit (bit 7) goes to a logic 1, sending an interrupt request signal to the μP. A logic 0 in bit 2 indicates that the modem's carrier signal is present.

Bit 3—Clear-to-Send ($\overline{\text{CTS}}$) Bit: The $\overline{\text{CTS}}$ status bit continuously reflects the state of the clear-to-send input line (pin 24). This line is used by a modem or other peripheral equipment to indicate that it is ready or not ready to receive data from an ACIA. A logic 1 indicates a not ready condition.

When the $\overline{\text{CTS}}$ input line goes high, the following occurs:

1. The $\overline{\text{CTS}}$ status bit goes to a logic 1.
2. The TDRE bit (bit 1 of the status register) goes to a logic 0.
3. The $\overline{\text{IRQ}}$ bit (bit 7) goes to a logic 0 so that the ACIA's interrupt request line is inhibited.

When the $\overline{\text{CTS}}$ input line is low, it causes the $\overline{\text{CTS}}$ status bit to go to a logic 0, which is used as a signal by the ACIA that data can be transmitted.

If the $\overline{\text{CTS}}$ input line is not used, it must be wired low. The logic state of this bit is not affected by a master reset.

Bit 4—Framing Error (FE) Bit: This bit is set or cleared when data is transferred from the receive shift register to the receive data register. The FE bit is set or cleared for the entire time the data is present in the receive data register. A logic 1 indicates that received data is missing the first stop bit. This condition can be caused by a synchronization error, faulty transmission, or a break (all spaces) command.

A logic 0 indicates that the data is properly framed. Also, a high on the $\overline{DCD}$ input line or a master reset causes this status bit to go to a logic 0.

Bit 5—Overrun Error (OVRN) Bit: The overrun error bit indicates whether one or more pieces of data were received but not read from the receive data register. A logic 1 indicates that data has been received but not read by the μP prior to new data being received.

A logic 0 indicates one of the following conditions:

1. No overrun error has occurred.
2. An overrun did occur but the μP has read the receive data register.
3. The $\overline{DCD}$ input line has gone high.
4. A master reset has occurred.

Figure 13.13 shows when the OVRN bit is set and cleared. *Note:* For the OVRN bit to be cleared to a logic 0, the μP must read the status register and the receive data register a second time. The last valid character is character 1. Character 2 (and any other characters) is lost.

Bit 6—Parity Error (PE) Bit: This bit indicates whether the number of logic 1s agrees or disagrees with the preselected odd or even parity. A logic 1 indicates a parity error; that is, the number of 1s in the received data does not agree with the preselected parity choice. This error bit is set as long as the data is present in the receive data register.

A logic 0 indicates that no parity error has occurred. The parity error flag bit also is cleared to a logic 0 for any of the following conditions:

1. The next character that is transferred from the receive shift register to the receive data register has no parity error.
2. The $\overline{DCD}$ input line goes high.
3. A master reset has occurred.

FIGURE 13.13 | Overrun Error Timing Diagram (Redrawn with permission of Motorola Incorporated, Austin, Texas)

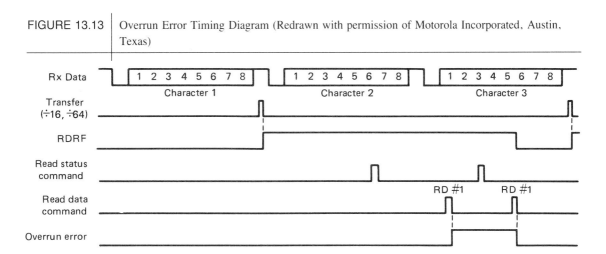

Bit 7—Interrupt Request ($\overline{\text{IRQ}}$) Bit: The $\overline{\text{IRQ}}$ bit is set to a logic 1 from three sources—the transmitter, receiver, or loss of carrier.

1. Transmitter: If the transmitter interrupt enable is active (see control bits 5 and 6), the μP is sent an interrupt request when the TDRE status bit goes to a logic 1.
2. Receiver: If the receive interrupt enable is active (see control bit 7), the μP is sent an interrupt request when the RDRF status bit goes to a logic 1.
3. Loss of carrier: If the receive interrupt enable is active and the $\overline{\text{DCD}}$ input line goes high, an interrupt request signal is sent to the μP.

A logic 0 indicates no interrupt request. The $\overline{\text{IRQ}}$ status bit is cleared to a logic 0 by any of the following conditions:

1. The μP writes a character to the transmit data register.
2. The μP reads a character from the receive data register.
3. A master reset has occurred.

Note: The logic state of the $\overline{\text{IRQ}}$ status bit is the complement of the logic level of the interrupt request line.

13.13 | TRANSMIT AND RECEIVE ROUTINES

After the ACIA is initialized, it can be used to send or receive serial data. In most systems, both the transmission and reception of data are done by subroutines. The following flowcharts and programs are taken from Motorola's *Application Note AN–754*.

13.13.1 | Transmit Routine

Figure 13.14 shows a flowchart for a μP sending data to an ACIA. The μP must first check the TDRE bit (bit 1) of the status register. If this bit is a logic 1, the data can be sent to the ACIA's transmit data register. The ACIA will automatically move the data to the transmit shift register and it will be transmitted over the transmit data line.

If the TDRE bit is a logic 0, the μP cannot send new data to the ACIA. This bit is a logic 0 whenever the transmit data register is full and/or the $\overline{\text{CTS}}$ line goes high. Therefore, the μP must check the $\overline{\text{CTS}}$ bit (bit 3) of the status register to know if it should go back to read the status register or jump to an error program. In our previous examples, the ACIA has been wired at locations 6000 and 6001. The address for the status register is 6000 and the address for the transmit register is 6001. In the following subroutine program, consider that the ASCII character is being held in accumulator B before there is a jump to the subroutine.

```
NEXTCH: LDA A $6000      Load status register.
        ASR A
```

	ASR A	Shift TDRE bit into C flag.
	BCS TXDATA	Check TDRE bit.
	ASR A	
	ASR A	Shift $\overline{CTS}$ bit into C flag.
	BCC NEXTCH	If C = 0, branch back to NEXTCH.
	BR ERROR1	$\overline{CTS}$ is high, branch to an error program (not shown).
TXDATA:	STA B $6001	Move accumulator B to the transmit data register.
	RTS	Return from subroutine.

13.13.2 | Receive Routine

A flowchart for the μP to receive data from an ACIA is shown in Figure 13.15. Similar to the transmit routine, the first step in a receive routine is to load the status register. In this application, the RDRF bit (bit 0) of the status register must be checked. When this bit is a logic 1, the μP must check the framing error, overrun, and parity error bits before the character is read. If the RDRF bit is a logic 0, then either the receive data register is not full or the data carrier detect line has gone high. Therefore, the μP must check the $\overline{DCD}$ bit before jumping back and rereading the entire status register.

Once again, consider that the ACIA is wired at addresses 6000 and 6001. Using Figure 13.10 as a guide, the status register is at the first location and the receive data register is at the second location. For this example, the status register is at address 6000

| FIGURE 13.14 | Flowchart for a Transmit Data Subroutine (Redrawn with permission of Motorola Incorporated, Austin, Texas) |

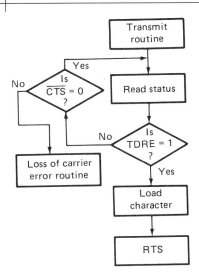

FIGURE 13.15 | Flowchart for a Receive Data Subroutine (Redrawn with permission of Motorola Incorporated, Austin, Texas)

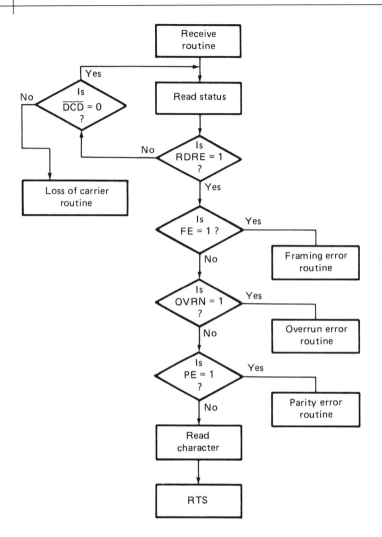

and the receive data register is at 6001. The following subroutine program satisfies the flowchart of Figure 13.15 and is reprinted with permission of Motorola.

NEXT1:	LDA A $6000	Read status register.
	ASR A	Shift RDRF bit into carry flag.
	BCS FRAM	If C = 1, branch to FRAM.
	ASR A	

	ASR A	Shift $\overline{DCD}$ bit into carry flag.
	BCC	If C = 0, branch to NEXT1.
	BR ERROR2	If C = 1, branch to error routine for loss of carrier (not shown).
FRAM:	ASR A	
	ASR A	
	ASR A	
	ASR A	Shift FE bit into carry flag.
	BCC OVRN	If C = 0, branch to OVRN.
	BR ERROR3	Framing error, branch to framing error routine (not shown).
OVRN:	ASR A	Shift OVRN bit into carry flag.
	BCC PAR	If C = 0, branch to PAR.
	BR ERROR4	Overrun error, branch to overrun error routine (not shown).
PAR:	ASR A	Shift PE bit into carry flag.
	BCC RXDATA	If C = 0, branch to RXDATA.
	BR ERROR5	Parity error, branch to parity error routine (not shown).
RXDATA:	LDA B $6001	Move receive data register to accumulator B.
	RTS	Return from subroutine.

13.14 | BIT RATE GENERATOR

As previously stated, the ACIA has two clock lines—Tx Clk and Rx Clk. If serial data is to be sent and received at the same rate, these lines are tied together and wired to a master clock line (see Figure 13.16A). If the rates are not the same, two clock lines are needed (see Figure 13.16B). Remember that the ACIA has an internal divide network set by control bits 0 and 1 (see Table 13.3) that divides the Tx Clk and Rx Clk frequencies. The Tx Clk and Rx Clk frequencies are referred to as external clock frequencies. The external clock frequency can be determined by the following equation:

$$\text{External clock frequency} = \text{ACIA's divide ratio} \times \text{Baud rate} \qquad (13.5)$$

EXAMPLE

13.4   Consider that data is to be transmitted and received at 1200 baud and the ACIA's divide ratio is set to $\div 16$. Calculate the Tx Clk and Rx Clk frequencies.

Solution:
Since transmission and reception are at the same rate, Equation 13.5 has to be applied only once:

$$\text{External clock frequency} = 16 \times 1200 = 19,200 \text{ bits/s}$$

EXAMPLE

13.5   Consider that data is to be transmitted at 2400 baud but received at 4800 baud. The ACIA's divide ratio is ÷ 16. Calculate the Tx Clk and Rx Clk frequencies.

Solution:

Since the baud rates are different, Equation 13.5 must be applied twice:

$$\text{Tx Clk frequency} = 16 \times 2400 = 38,400 \text{ bits/s}$$
$$\text{Rx Clk frequency} = 16 \times 4800 = 76,800 \text{ bits/s}$$

FIGURE 13.16 | Connecting a Bit Rate Generator to a 6850 ACIA

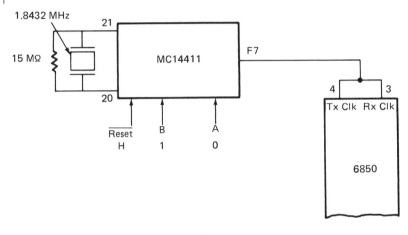

A.

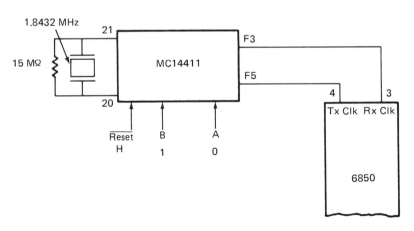

B.

In order to provide different external frequencies, a clock source for the ACIA is needed. Such a device is Motorola's MC14411 CMOS bit rate generator. The pin assignments and block diagram for this device are shown in Figure 13.17. The MC14411 provides 16 communication clock rates at one time. It is also programmable so that the clock rate range can be changed. Table 13.6 lists the clock rates for a 1.8432 MHz crystal connected between pins 20 and 21, as shown in Figures 13.16A and B. These figures also show how the bit rate generator can be connected to the ACIA for Examples 13.4 and 13.5. In these figures, the generator's rate select inputs are set to ×16.

TABLE 13.6	Output Clock Rates for the MC14411 Bit Rate Generator

Rate Select		
B	A	Rate
0	0	× 1
0	1	× 8
1	0	× 16
1	1	× 64

Output Number	Output Rates (Hz)			
	× 64	× 16	× 8	× 1
F1	614.4 k	153.6 k	76.8 k	9600
F2	460.8 k	115.2 k	57.6 k	7200
F3	307.2 k	76.8 k	38.4 k	4800
F4	230.4 k	57.6 k	28.8 k	3600
F5	153.6 k	38.4 k	19.2 k	2400
F6	115.2 k	28.8 k	14.4 k	1800
F7	76.8 k	19.2 k	9600	1200
F8	38.4 k	9600	4800	600
F9	19.2 k	4800	2400	300
F10	12.8 k	3200	1600	200
F11	9600	2400	1200	150
F12	8613.2	2153.3	1076.6	134.5
F13	7035.5	1758.8	879.4	109.9
F14	4800	1200	600	75
F15	921.6 k	921.6 k	921.6 k	921.6 k
F16*	1.843 M	1.843 M	1.843 M	1.843 M

*F16 is buffered oscillator output.

Source: Reprinted with permission of Motorola Incorporated.

FIGURE 13.17 | Pin Assignments and Block Diagram for MC14411 Bit Rate Generator (Redrawn with permission of Motorola Incorporated, Austin, Texas)

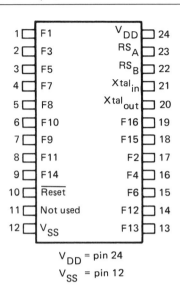

V_{DD} = pin 24

V_{SS} = pin 12

A. Pin Assignments

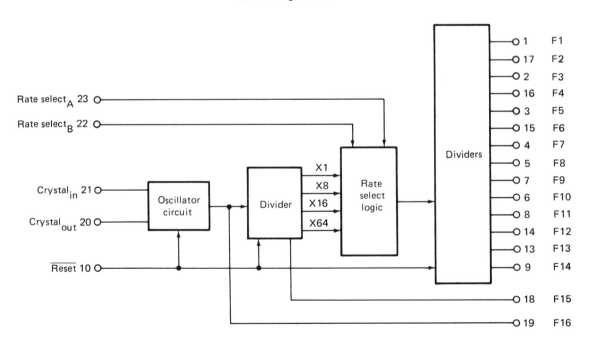

B. Block Diagram

13.15 | SUMMARY

This chapter introduced the concept of serial data transmission and why it is a convenient way to send digital data between a μC and peripheral equipment. Since data between μC components is by parallel transmission, there is a need for an interface chip to convert parallel-to-serial and serial-to-parallel data. The MC6850 asynchronous communication interface adapter, ACIA, is such a device. Similar to other peripheral interface chips, the ACIA is programmable. A programmer using the ACIA's control register can set the rate at which serial data is sent and received by the ACIA. The ACIA's status register indicates when new data can be sent or received by the μP and if incoming serial data contains a parity, a framing, or an overrun error. As with other interface chips, the ACIA "frees up" the μP to execute the main program while the ACIA communicates with the relatively slow operation of peripheral equipment. The term *baud* refers to the rate at which serial data is transmitted. Tables 13.1 and 13.2 list typical operating baud rates so that you can compare the number of bits being transmitted and the time per bit. The μP needs to know when to send or receive another byte of data from the ACIA. There are two ways for the μP to know an interrupt request or a software polling routine. An interrupt request technique is usually straightforward. Software polling routines are given in Section 13.13.

PROBLEMS

13.1 What are the two types of serial transmission?

13.2 What name is used to identify the idle state?

13.3 Is synchronous communication "character" framed or "block" framed?

13.4 Draw the serial bit stream for each of the following alphanumeric characters: (a) P, (b) 3, (c) 7, and (d) M. Use a 7-bit data format, even parity, and one stop bit.

13.5 Determine the number of characters per second for baud rates 110 through 2400. Refer to Table 13.1 if the character is formed by using only 6 data bits instead of 7 bits.

13.6 Name the write-only registers in the 6850.

13.7 Is data sent by the μP to the transmit data register or to the transmit shift register of the ACIA?

13.8 Can data be transmitted and received at the same time at different baud rates by the 6850?

13.9 What function does double buffering provide on the transmit side of the ACIA?

13.10 To what does the phrase "stripped away" apply?

13.11 What types of errors does the 6850 detect upon receiving serial data? How is an error recorded in the ACIA?

13.12 Are the logic levels on the transmit data line TTL or RS232C compatible?

13.13 Why should the ACIA's RS line be wired to address bus line A_0?

13.14 Identify what the following abbreviations represent: (a) $\overline{CTS}$, (b) $\overline{RTS}$, and (c) $\overline{DCD}$.

13.15 If the $\overline{CTS}$ and $\overline{DCD}$ lines are not used, why do they have to be wired to a low logic level?

13.16 Which bits of the control register reset the 6850?

13.17 What is the function of bits 2, 3, and 4 of the ACIA?

13.18 Identify the binary pattern that must be stored in the control register for the following conditions: (a) divided-by-16 mode; (b) 7 data bits, even parity, and one stop bit; (c) send an interrupt request to the μP when the transmit data register is empty; and (d) send an interrupt request to the μP when the receive data register is full.

13.19 Name each bit of the status register.

13.20 What are the three conditions that clear the RDRF bit?

13.21 What are the three conditions that clear the TDRE bit?

13.22 Which bit of the status register indicates that one or more pieces of data were received but not read from the receive data register?

13.23 What are the three sources for setting the interrupt request bit in the status register?

13.24 Consider that data is to be transmitted at 1200 baud, but received at 4800 baud. Show how the MC14411 bit rate generator can be connected to the ACIA. The ACIA is programmed for a divide-by-64 mode.

14 | CRT Controller 6845

14.0 | INTRODUCTION

The past decade has seen a tremendous growth in the use of low-cost video monitors. They are used in almost all μC systems to display information going into or coming out of the system. Unless a hard copy is needed, there is no need for a printer; the video monitor and accompanying keyboard are all the peripheral equipment required in many systems. The monitor is a CRT (cathode ray tube) that is similar to the unit used in TV sets. In fact, many home computer systems are designed to be used with TVs. Although the principles of operation of all CRTs are the same, they do not perform the same. High-performance, flicker-free, and low-cost computer terminals are a necessity.

Since CRT technology is well established and in wide use, there is not much room for price reduction. Therefore, to bring down the price of a video monitor system, the electronic circuitry surrounding the CRT must be reduced. To meet this need, LSI technology has reduced the number of IC chips previously used. The principle chip in video monitor systems is referred to as a *CRT controller*, like Motorola's MC6845.

Figure 14.1 shows a block diagram of a CRT controller board. The 6845 relieves the μP from the tedious task of addressing a block of memory called the display RAM buffer and outputting its contents. In most applications, the data stored in the memory buffer is in ASCII format. As you will see in Sections 14.5 and 14.6, the ASCII data will be used as an address to look up a dot matrix in the character ROM generator. The contents of the ROM generator are what actually are shifted out to the CRT monitor. The 6845 also synchronizes the ROM generator and provides the horizontal and vertical sync pulses to the display unit. Before introducing the 6845 CRT controller and the character ROM generator chips, let's begin by describing the basic operation of raster scan displays and how characters are generated on a screen.

14.1 | PRINCIPLES OF RASTER SCAN DISPLAYS

Anyone who is studying μPs probably has used an oscilloscope to measure voltage waveforms. In some experiments, you probably had to switch the x axis time per centimeter knob to x volts per centimeter, thus allowing you to make an $x-y$ plot of two input

FIGURE 14.1 | Block Diagram of a CRT Controller Board (Redrawn with permission of Motorola Incorporated, Austin, Texas)

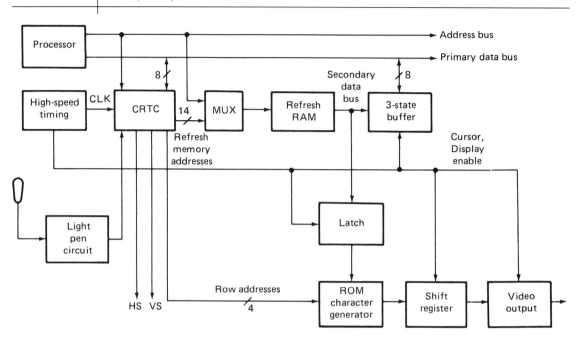

voltages. One input voltage controlled the voltage on the horizontal deflection plates of the CRT, while the other voltage controlled the voltage on the vertical deflection plates. This type of display is usually referred to as either an $x-y$ plot or a vector display. However, most alphanumeric displays and broadcast TV sets use the raster scan method of displaying information on a CRT instead of the vector method. The *raster method* implies that the data to be displayed onto the screen is displayed by the CRT's electron beam scanning across the screen at a fixed rate, then repeating the sweep on the next successive horizontal scan lines. Scan lines are equidistant from one another, and there are usually 262 or 525 lines per display. As the electron beam sweeps across a scan line, the beam intensity is modulated so that the CRT's screen coating is illuminated or not, thereby creating images on the screen. Raster scan displays produce high-quality results and their cost has decreased tremendously in the past decade, two reasons for their popularity in μC systems. There are two types of raster scanning—noninterlace and interlace.

In *noninterlace scanning*, the electron beam starts in the upper left-hand corner, moves across the screen and returns. During the return trip, the electron beam is blanked (turned off). This round-trip is called one *horizontal scan line*. The electron beam is moved down to the next scan line and the process is repeated. Many alphanumeric monitors have a total of 262 scan lines. After the electron beam finishes the last row, the beam is returned to the upper left-hand corner to repeat the first scan line. In noninterlace scanning, there is only one field per frame and each scan line is refreshed at the line frequency (for example, 50 or 60 Hz). See Figure 14.2 for an example of the electron beam sweep pattern.

An *interlace scanning* system requires the electron beam to make two complete sweeps of the screen. On the first sweep, the beam starts in the upper left-hand corner and ends in the middle of the bottom row, at which time the vertical retrace occurs. See Figure 14.3A for the pattern of the first sweep. On the second sweep, the beam starts in the middle of the first row and ends in the bottom right-hand corner, as shown in Figure 14.3B. Now, during this vertical retrace, the electron beam is brought back to the upper left-hand corner. Both fields are combined to produce one complete display, as shown in Figure 14.3C. An advantage of this system is higher density resolution per character. The disadvantage is that the refresh rate is halved. Assuming a 60 Hz line frequency, the refresh rate is 30 Hz.

The interlaced scanning technique is used by broadcast television. For a standard American TV, there are 525 scan lines in the interlaced mode. Since TV scenes contain large white areas, they usually appear flicker free. However, when TVs are used to display alphanumeric characters, quite often there is an annoying flicker because characters are small and vertical alignment is very critical. The solution to the flicker problem is to use a CRT monitor with a long-persistence phosphor. As we might expect, long-persistence phosphors do have disadvantages: (1) The spot (when the electron beam strikes the phosphor a small area is lit) is not as sharp, and (2) there is a tendency for the phosphor to "burn." Therefore, if a design requires many characters to be displayed and an interlaced scanning technique is to be used, then the designer should try several different monitors having different phosphor coatings to find the best one for the optimum readout.

14.1.1 | Single-Character Display

As previously mentioned, in raster scan displays, characters are created on the screen by turning on and off the electron beam at precise intervals. When the beam is "on," the

---

FIGURE 14.2 | Electron Beam Sweep Pattern for a Noninterlace Display

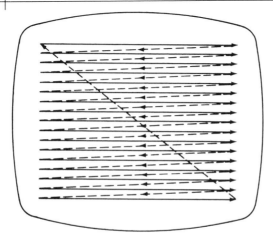

FIGURE 14.3 | Interlace Raster Scanning for a CRT Display

Scan line
number

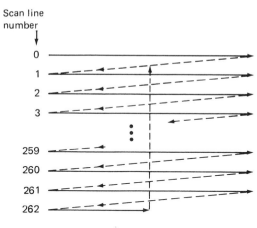

A. First Frame

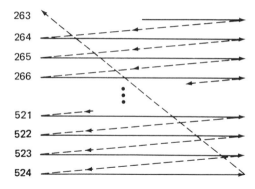

B. Second Frame

```
0    ——————————————————————————
263         ——————————————————————
1    ——————————————————————————
264  ——————————————————————————
2    ——————————————————————————
265  ——————————————————————————


259  ——————————————————————————
522  ——————————————————————————
260  ——————————————————————————
523  ——————————————————————————
261  ——————————————————————————
524  ——————————————————————————
262  ——————————————————————
```

C. Composite

electrons energize the phosphor, making it glow. When the beam is "off," no electrons strike the phosphor and hence no luminescence is created. Figure 14.4A shows all the dots illuminated in a 7 × 9 dot matrix. If the intensity of the electron beam is turned off at specific locations, then different characters can be displayed. It should be noted that the electron beam may not have to be completely turned off, but only reduced so that the phosphor is not activated. Figure 14.4B shows the letter E being displayed. As you will see later in this chapter, the characters are stored in a ROM chip similar to Figure 14.4C. A binary 1 activates the phosphor; a binary 0 does not.

Figure 14.4B shows one character. If a system is designed to have 24 character rows and 80 characters per row, there could be 1920 (24 × 80) characters displayed on the screen at the same time. Each is made from a dot matrix. How all the dots appear on the screen in the proper order will become clearer as you proceed through the chapter. At this time, let's turn our attention back to the single character of Figure 14.4B. In order for characters to be easily viewed, each character must be separated from the rest. Figure 14.4D shows there is one nonilluminated scan line above and two nonilluminated scan lines below the dot matrix. Also, on each side, there is a column with no dots. This inactive area forms a border around the character so that it can easily be viewed on the

| FIGURE 14.4 | Dot Matrix Format for a Single-Character Display |

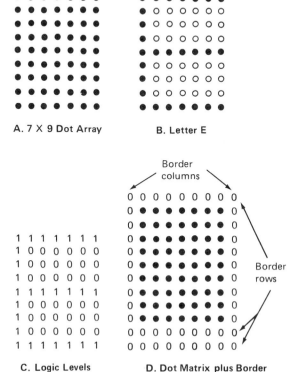

A. 7 X 9 Dot Array   B. Letter E

C. Logic Levels   D. Dot Matrix plus Border

screen. The total area (illuminated and nonilluminated) is referred to as a *character frame matrix* or *array*. Some ways that you may refer to Figure 14.4D are as a 7 × 9 dot matrix in a 9 × 12 array or a 7 × 9 font in a 9 × 12 matrix. *Note:* If the word *matrix* is used by itself, it implies the dot matrix plus the border. The word *font* is sometimes used in place of dot matrix.

14.1.2 | Character Row Display

Figure 14.5 shows a portion of one character row. The row in this system could have a maximum of 80 characters. Characters are displayed not by creating a single character at a time, but by activating or not activating the phosphor on one scan line at a time. As the electron beam moves to the next scan line, the illuminated areas (the dots) remain because of the persistence effect of the phosphor. The beam continues to move down the screen, doing all of the scan lines before returning to the top of the screen and making another sweep. Figure 14.6 illustrates how the numbers 6, 8, 4, 5 are displayed one scan line at a time. Remember, however, as the electron beam moves across each scan line, the only reason the dots remain illuminated is because of the persistence effect of the phosphor. The electron beam must return on its next sweep and reilluminate the same dots if the character is to remain displayed. Otherwise, the character will fade from the screen.

Figure 14.6 shows that if a character is housed in a 7 × 9 dot matrix, then each character is presented seven times to the CRT, once for each row. As one row of dots is finished for a character, the same numbered row for the next character must be presented

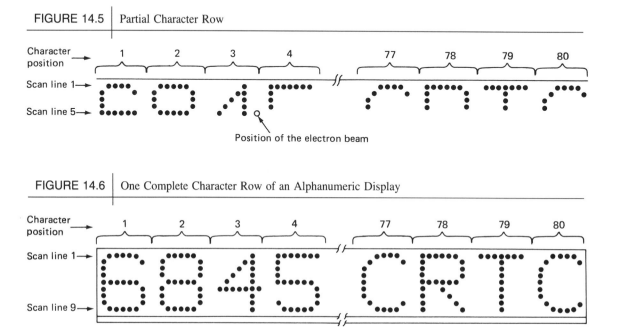

FIGURE 14.5 | Partial Character Row

FIGURE 14.6 | One Complete Character Row of an Alphanumeric Display to the CRT. Thus, you can quickly see the need for a controller to maintain synchronization. Not long ago, it took an entire PC board full of SSI and MSI parts to maintain this synchronization; now it is done by a single LSI chip such as the 6845. Although some other support chips are needed, the workhorse in this system is the CRT controller.

14.2 FEATURES AND PIN DESCRIPTIONS OF THE 6845

The 6845 is a special-purpose interface IC. It generates the necessary digital signals that permit a μP to be connected to a raster scan CRT display. The 6845 is referred to as a CRT controller (CRTC) chip. It provides video timing and refresh memory addressing. Some of the 6845's other features are as follows:

single +5 V power supply requirements,

compatibility with the 6800 and 68000 μPs,

capability for displaying most alphanumeric screen formats,

TTL input and output compatible,

hardware scroll capability,

includes light pen register,

both interlace and noninterlace scan modes available,

allows up to 16K bytes of refresh memory,

cursor format and blink rate are programmable,

up to 32 scan lines available per character row.

The 6845 controller is housed in a 40-pin dual-in-line package, as shown in Figure 14.7A. As with any peripheral interface chip, the 6845 is a link between the μP and external equipment. In Chapter 11, we showed that an interface chip can be described as having a μP side and a peripheral side. Figure 14.7B illustrates that the pins of a 6845 chip can be divided into three groups. They are the pins that link the 6845 (1) to the μP, (2) to a character ROM generator chip, and (3) to the CRT display circuitry. Let's examine each group of pins.

14.2.1 Microprocessor and Microcomputer System Interface Pins

The 6845 communicates to the μP using the bidirectional data bus and the control signals $\overline{CS}$, RS, E, and R/$\overline{W}$. The other interface lines are CLK, $\overline{reset}$, and power pins.

Data Bus (D_O–D_7): Pins D_0–D_7 are connected to the system's bidirectional data bus. They are used to transfer data between the μP and the 6845's internal registers. When this chip is not selected by the μP for a read operation, these pins are driven to their high impedance state.

Chip Select ($\overline{CS}$): When the $\overline{CS}$ pin is brought low, the device is selected to either read or write data to the μP. This pin is connected to the system's decoding logic. The

FIGURE 14.7 | Pin Assignments for the MC6845 (Redrawn with permission of Motorola Incorporated, Austin, Texas)

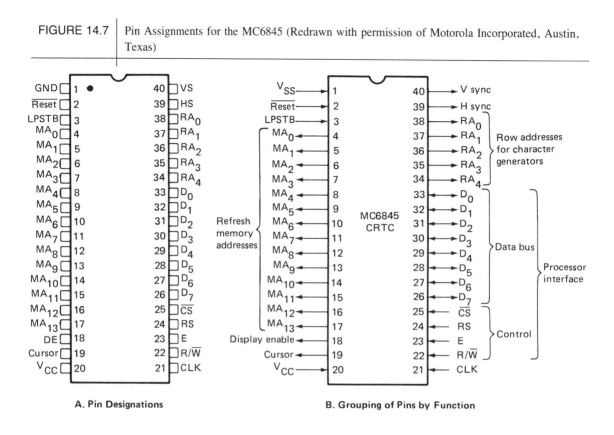

A. Pin Designations   **B. Grouping of Pins by Function**

input circuitry of the $\overline{CS}$ pin is TTL and MOS compatible. Remember the terms *read* and *write* refer to what the μP is doing and not what the peripheral device is doing.

Read/Write (R/$\overline{W}$):   This pin is connected to the system read/write line. A high logic level causes the chip's output data bus buffers to be turned on so that the 6845 can send data to the μP. The μP is sending (writing) data to the 6845 when the R/$\overline{W}$ line is brought low. Remember, a peripheral chip can only read or write data if it has been selected ($\overline{CS}$ pin low). The R/$\overline{W}$ pin input circuitry is TTL and MOS compatible.

Register Select (RS):   This pin should be connected to address bus line A_0. When the RS line is a logic 0, the μP is selecting the 6845's internal address register. When the RS line is a logic 1, the μP is communicating with one of the 6845's data registers. (The next section shows which one is selected.) As with other peripheral chips, wiring the RS pin to the A_0 line ensures the address register and data registers are in consecutive memory-mapped locations. This wiring technique makes future programming steps easier. The RS pin circuitry is TTL and MOS compatible.

Enable (E):   The signal applied to this pin is either the ϕ_2 clock pulse or a signal derived from the ϕ_2 clock pulse, such as the ϕ_2 pulse ANDed with the VMA signal. Transfer of data between the μP and the CRTC takes place on the high-to-low transition of the enable signal. This input pin's circuitry is also TTL and MOS compatible.

Clock (CLK): This pin is an input line from a dot counter. The counter establishes the rate at which characters are generated. This signal also synchronizes all of the 6845's CRT control signals. It does not synchronize the transfer of data between the 6845 and the μP; these transfers are done by the enable (E) pulse. The CLK input circuitry is TTL and MOS compatible.

$\overline{\text{Reset}}$: This pin is connected to the system's reset line. When the reset line goes low, all the internal counters are cleared to logic 0. Also, the output lines of the 6845 are set low. Thus there will be no video output signal. *Note:* Although the internal counters are cleared, the 6845's programmable registers (see Section 14.3) are not cleared. This allows the 6845 to resume operation after the reset line goes high.

Power Pins (V_{CC}, V_{SS}): The 6845 is a 5 V device; $V_{CC} = +5$ V $\pm$ 5% and $V_{SS} = $ gnd.

14.2.2 | Screen Memory Buffer and Character Generator Pins

The 6845 has memory address output pins (MA_0–MA_{13}) to access the memory buffer. This interface chip also contains row address pins (RA_0–RA_4) to be used with a character ROM generator.

Memory Address Pins (MA_0–MA_{13}): These 14 pins allow the 6845 to access 16K ($2^{14} = 16,134$) bytes of memory. This block of memory is often called the CRT memory buffer. The buffers may be designed using either static or dynamic RAM chips, and the 6845 is capable of working with either type. The output circuitry on these pins is capable of driving one standard TTL load and 30 pF.

Row Address Pins (RA_0–RA_4): These pins are connected to a character ROM generator chip, as will be shown in Section 14.5. The binary pattern on RA_0–RA_4 comes from the 6845's internal row address counter (see Section 14.3.4). These outputs can also drive one standard TTL load and 30 pF. The 6845's memory and row address counters continue during vertical retrace, thereby allowing the controller to provide refresh addresses for dynamic RAMs.

14.2.3 | CRT Monitor Control and Interface Signals

The 6845 provides horizontal and vertical sync pulses as well as a display enable signal.

H Sync Pin: The output signal on this pin supplies the horizontal sync pulse needed to determine the horizontal position of the text on the CRT display. This output is TTL compatible and should only be directly connected to monitors that have TTL input circuitry. If the monitor is not TTL compatible, then external circuitry is needed.

V Sync Pin: The output signal on this pin provides the vertical sync pulse needed to determine the vertical position of the text on the screen. This signal is either connected directly to monitors or to a video circuit that generates a composite video signal. Whichever connection is made, the vertical sync output is only TTL compatible and its ratings should not be exceeded.

Display Enable (DE): The logic state on this pin indicates the 6845 is providing an address to the memory buffer in the active display area. Usually the text that is displayed is much less than the size of the memory buffer. For example, a CRT displaying 24 rows of characters with 80 characters per row requires 1920 (80 $\times$ 24) bytes of memory. If the buffer is 16K (actually 16,384 bytes), then only 11.72% (1920/16,384) of the buffer is displayed at a time. The DE line is used to synchronize the video output to the CRT. This signal is TTL compatible with an active high state. *Note:* This signal is also an indication of when video blanking occurs, because the line goes high when there is a video output and low during horizontal and vertical retrace.

Cursor: This line indicates a valid cursor address so that the cursor dots can be displayed. It is an active high TTL signal.

Light Pen Strobe (LPSTB): The light pen strobe is an input pin; it is wired to light pen circuitry. This circuitry is an interface network between a light pen and the 6845. When there is a high signal on the LPSTB line, the 6845 saves the contents of the screen's memory address counter in an internal register. This allows the μP to retrieve this address and determine the location of the light pen.

14.3 | THE 6845's PROGRAMMABLE REGISTERS

The 6845 has 18 programmable registers, R_0–R_{17}, as shown in Figure 14.8. These registers control (1) the horizontal and vertical synchronization, (2) the number of characters per row, (3) the portion of memory buffer to be displayed, (4) the cursor format, (5) the cursor position, and (6) the type of interlace mode.

Registers R_0 through R_3 handle the horizontal format. The vertical format is handled by registers R_4 through R_7. Register R_8 sets the interlace mode, while R_9 fixes the maximum number of scan lines per character row. The starting and ending location for the cursor is handled by R_{10} and R_{11}. The starting memory buffer address is stored in registers R_{12} and R_{13}. The cursor's address register is R_{14} and R_{15}. If a light pen is used, its location is given by R_{16} and R_{17}.

Although the 6845 has 18 programmable registers, the device only requires two locations in the overall memory space. The reason for this is that the device uses an internal address register and decoder circuit, as shown in Figure 14.8. As far as the μP "sees," the address register is one memory location, and R_0 through R_{17} are the same memory location. The binary pattern held by the address register selects one of the 18 programmable registers. Therefore, two operations are required to address one of the programmable registers. The first operation is a write command whereby the μP sends the programmable register number to the address register. On the second operation, the μP can either read or write data to the selected programmable register. Let's determine how the μP communicates with a particular register.

FIGURE 14.8 | Internal Block Diagram of the MC6845 CRT Controller (Reprinted with permission of Motorola Incorporated, Austin, Texas)

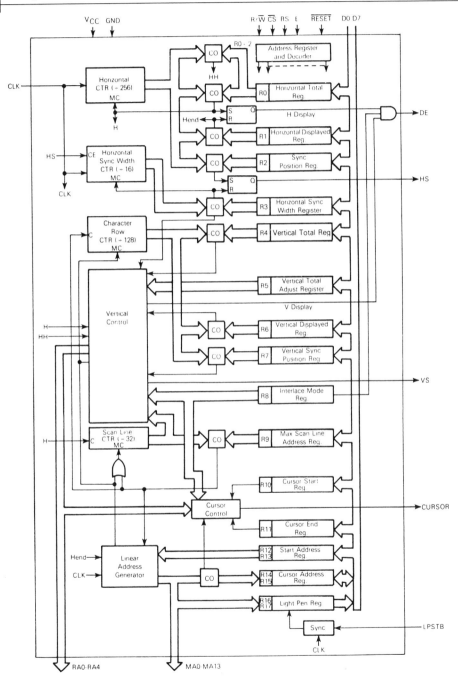

EXAMPLE

14.1 | If the 6845 is wired into a system at locations C000 and C001$_{hex}$, what programming steps are necessary to write data to register R_9?

Solution:

Consider that the data to be written is $10_{decimal}$ ($0C_{hex}$) and that we will use accumulator A.

LDA	A #09	Set up address register
STA	A C000	for register R_9.
LDA	A #0C	Data to be stored in R_9.
STA	A C001	Write data to register R_9.

A complete initialization example for the 6845 CRTC is given in Section 14.3.9.

14.3.1 | Horizontal Format Registers

Registers R_0 through R_3 are used to set the horizontal format on the CRT display. The binary patterns stored in these registers determine the total time of the horizontal sweep, characters to be displayed, the horizontal sync position, and the horizontal sync width. See Figure 14.9. There are two ways of thinking about a horizontal sweep: (1) in terms of time and (2) in terms of characters. We know it will take a certain amount of time for the electron beam to sweep across the screen, retrace, and be ready for the next scan line. This time is fixed by an external horizontal character clock generator. Once this clock generator is known for a particular system, we can treat everything in the horizontal direction in terms of characters. That is, register R_1 holds the number of characters that can be displayed in one character row. R_0 holds the total number of characters displayed and nondisplayed minus one. The nondisplayed characters are the number of equivalent characters for the horizontal blanking interval. Register R_2 holds the number of characters

FIGURE 14.9 | Horizontal Format Registers

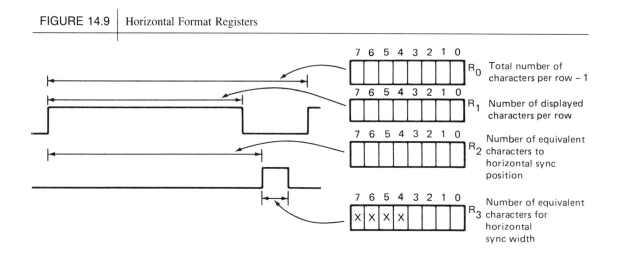

FIGURE 14.10 | Horizontal Timing Diagram

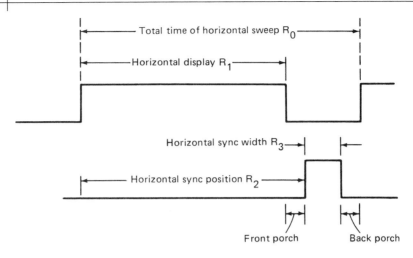

that would occur from the start of the horizontal scan until the start of the horizontal sync pulse. This value equals the number of viewed characters plus the equivalent number of characters for a horizontal sync delay (the front porch delay). See Figure 14.10. Register R_3 holds the equivalent number of characters for the horizontal sync pulse.

Let's consider an example and see what values should be stored in registers R_0 through R_3.

EXAMPLE

14.2   A Motorola M3000 CRT module is used to display an 80 × 24 screen format. The horizontal scanning frequency (f) is 15,720 Hz. The total horizontal blanking interval (t_B) is 12.72 μs. The front porch and back porch times are 2.544 μs and 5.088 μs, respectively. Determine the values to be stored in registers R_0 through R_3.

Solution:
An 80 × 24 screen format means there are 80 possible characters that can be viewed on one row. Therefore, the value to be stored in R_1 is $80_{decimal}$, or 50_{hex}. (The value 24 means there are 24 rows; this value will be used to program register R_6 in the next section.)

The total time for one horizontal scan line is given by the following equation:

$$t_{SL} = \frac{1}{f} \tag{14.1}$$

Applying Equation 14.1 yields

$$t_{SL} = \frac{1}{15,720 \text{ Hz}} = 63.6 \text{ μs}$$

Since the horizontal blanking time (t_B) is 12.72 μs, then the displayed time (t_D) for one scan line is 63.6 μs $-$ 12.72 μs $=$ 50.88 μs. The equivalent number of characters during the horizontal blanking time can be determined from the following equation:

$$\text{Number of equivalent characters} = \frac{\text{Displayed characters}}{t_D} \times t_B \qquad (14.2)$$

Applying Equation 14.2 for this example, we have

$$\text{Number of equivalent characters} = \frac{80}{50.88 \ \mu\text{s}} \times 12.72 \ \mu\text{s} = 20$$

Therefore, the value to be stored in register R_0 is 99_{decimal} $[(80 + 20) - 1]$, or 63_{hex}.

Since the total time for one scan line is 63.6 μs and the total number of characters (viewed and blanked) is 100, then the time for one character is 0.636 μs (63.6 μs/100). Thus we can solve for the equivalent number of characters that make up the three parts of the horizontal blanking interval:

$$\text{Front porch} = \frac{2.544 \ \mu\text{s}}{0.636 \ \mu\text{s}} = 4$$
$$+$$
$$\text{Horizontal sync pulse} = \frac{5.088 \ \mu\text{s}}{0.636 \ \mu\text{s}} = 8$$
$$+$$
$$\text{Back porch} = \frac{5.088 \ \mu\text{s}}{0.636 \ \mu\text{s}} = \frac{8}{20 \ \text{Total}}$$

This value checks with the previous calculation of 20 characters. The time interval for the horizontal sync pulse (5.088 μs) is calculated by subtracting the front and back porch times from the time of the blanking interval (12.72 μs $-$ 2.544 μs $-$ 5.088 μs $=$ 5.088 μs).

The value to be stored in R_2 is 84_{decimal} (80 $+$ 4), or 54_{hex}. The programmed value for register R_3 is the horizontal sync pulse width, which we found to be 8_{decimal}, or 08_{hex}. *Note:* The equivalent numbers of characters in the horizontal blanking interval are 4, 8, and 8. They are in 1:2:2 proportion, which is typical for most CRT displays.

14.3.2 | Vertical Format Registers

The values stored in registers R_4 through R_7 set the vertical format. Three of these registers (R_4, R_6, and R_7) perform functions similar to three of the horizontal registers (R_0, R_1, and R_2). The vertical refresh rate must be synchronized with the AC line frequency so that the data on the display does not have a wavy motion, which is called "swimming." The vertical refresh rate is usually 60 Hz, although it is sometimes 30 Hz in the interlace mode. For the horizontal format, the registers are programmed using characters. For the vertical format, registers R_4, R_6, and R_7 are programmed using character rows. The exception is register R_5, which is programmed with scan lines. This is so that all scan lines per frame are accounted for, thus eliminating any wavy motion. The number of scan lines per frame equals the horizontal frequency divided by the vertical refresh rate:

$$\text{Scan lines per frame} = \frac{\text{Horizontal frequency}}{\text{Vertical refresh rate}} \qquad (14.3)$$

Remember from Section 14.1.1 that a character is inside a character block. The character block allows the characters to be easily viewed on the display. The block accounts for the spacing columns between characters and the scan lines between character rows. For example, a 5×7 dot character could be housed within a 7×10 matrix; or a 7×9 dot character would be placed in a 9×12 character block.

Register R_6 is programmed with the number of character rows to be displayed. Register R_4 contains the total number of character rows per screen (displayed and non-displayed) minus one. This value equals the total number of scan lines divided by the height of the character block minus one. Only the whole number result is stored into R_4. Any fractional portion is left for the vertical adjust register (R_5). Remember, all scan lines must be accounted for.

Register R_7 determines the position of the vertical sync pulse. See Figures 14.11 and 14.12. For the 6845 CRT controller, the width of the vertical sync pulse is fixed at 16 scan lines. Example 14.3 demonstrates how to determine what values must be stored in the vertical format registers of the CRT of Example 14.2.

FIGURE 14.11 | Timing Diagrams

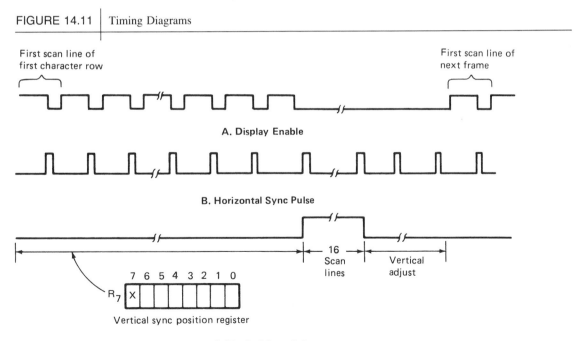

A. Display Enable

B. Horizontal Sync Pulse

C. Vertical Sync Pulse

FIGURE 14.12 | Vertical Format Registers

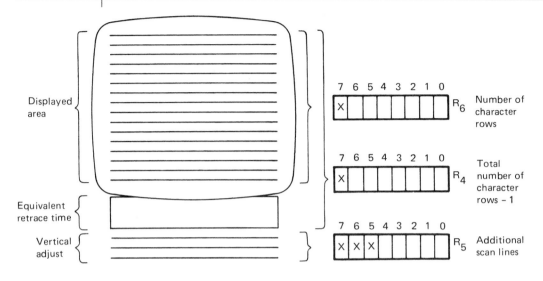

EXAMPLE

14.3 Determine the values to be stored in registers R_4 through R_7 given the following information: 80×24 screen format; horizontal scanning frequency of 15,720 Hz; vertical refresh rate of 60 Hz; and a 5×7 dot matrix housed in a 7×10 character block.

Solution:
The 80×24 format means the visual display is 80 characters per row and 24 character rows. Thus the value to be stored in register R_6 is $24_{decimal}$, or 18_{hex}.

Applying Equation 14.3 yields the following result:

$$\text{Scan lines per frame} = \frac{15,720 \text{ Hz}}{60 \text{ Hz}} = 262$$

To find the value for register R_4, first determine the total number of character rows per screen:

$$\text{Number of character rows} = \frac{\text{Number of scan lines}}{\text{Height of character block}}$$

$$\frac{262 \text{ scan lines}}{10 \text{ scan lines/character row}} = 26.2 \text{ rows}$$

Thus the value for register R_4 is $25_{decimal}$ $(26 - 1)$, or 19_{hex}. The value 0.2 means there is 0.2 of a character block $(0.2 \times 10 = 2 \text{ scan lines})$ remaining. This value is stored in register R_5.

For this example, the vertical sync position should begin immediately after the twenty-fourth character row. Therefore, R_7 should be $24_{decimal}$, or 18_{hex}. This will allow ample time for the retrace to occur. Remember, the 6845 has a fixed vertical sync width of 16 scan lines.

14.3.3 | Interlace Mode Registers

The 6845 CRT controller can be programmed for three types of interlace mode operations—normal sync, interlace sync, and interlace sync and video. It is the data stored in register R_8 that sets which mode is to be used.

In the normal sync mode, dots are written onto each scan line. During each vertical retrace, the same horizontal scan lines are traced. Thus, if the line frequency is 60 Hz, then each dot is updated 60 times per second. See Figure 14.13A. (The non-interlaced mode is the most commonly used.)

FIGURE 14.13 | Character Representations for the Different Interlace Modes and Interlace Mode Register (Redrawn with permission of Motorola Incorporated, Austin, Texas)

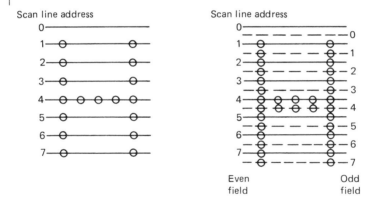

A. Normal Sync   B. Interlace Sync

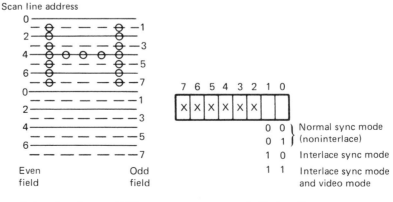

C. Interlace Sync and Video   D. Register R_8

In the interlace sync mode, the same information is written twice—on each scan line and between each scan line. This mode of operation improves resolution because the vertical lines appear to be solid. However, each dot is refreshed only 30 times per second. For some individuals, this low refresh rate can cause flicker on the CRT display. For others, it is hardly perceived, because of variations in eyesight and the CRT's phosphor coating. An example of the interlace sync mode is shown in Figure 14.13B.

In the interlace sync and video mode, the dots are written onto each scan line and between each line. This is similar to the interlace mode. The difference, however, is that the character is displayed in one-half the height. This mode permits the highest screen density. See Figure 14.13C. Figure 14.13D shows which binary pattern must be stored in register R_8 to program the device for a particular interlace mode.

14.3.4 | Maximum Scan Line Address Register

Register R_9 sets the maximum number of scan lines per character row. This value includes both the active scan lines (those on which dots appear) and the additional scan lines used for spacing between rows. Thus, register R_9 holds the height of the character block. For example, if the character block is a 7×10 matrix, then there are 10 scan lines for each row. The value $10_{decimal}$ ($0A_{hex}$) would be stored in register R_9. If the total character block is 9×12, then the value $12_{decimal}$ ($0C_{hex}$) would be stored in register R_9. The 6845 can have a maximum of 32 scan lines per character block. See Figure 14.14.

14.3.5 | Cursor Start and End Registers

The 6845 CRT controller can be programmed for different cursor formats and blink rates. Figure 14.15 illustrates different types of cursor formats commonly used on CRT displays: a square dot matrix, a single row of dots, and a double row of dots. Registers R_{10} and R_{11} are used to set the cursor.

Register R_{10} is called the cursor start register. It has two functions. First, it specifies on which scan line the cursor begins. Second, this register contains bits that determine whether or not the cursor blinks, and if so, how fast. Figure 14.15A shows which bits control the starting scan line and the bits that control the blinking function. R_{10} is a write-only register. Register R_{11}, the cursor end register, is also a write-only register. As shown in Figure 14.15B, the first 5 bits of R_{11} define the last scan line of the cursor.

If the same binary pattern is stored in both registers, the cursor will be one row of dots high. See Figure 14.15E.

FIGURE 14.14 | Register R_9 Controls the Number of Scan Lines per Row

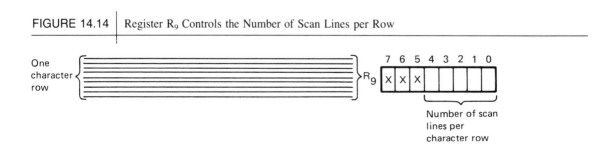

FIGURE 14.15 | Cursor Registers and Formats

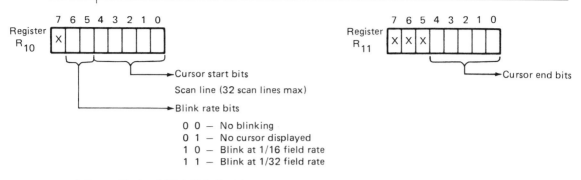

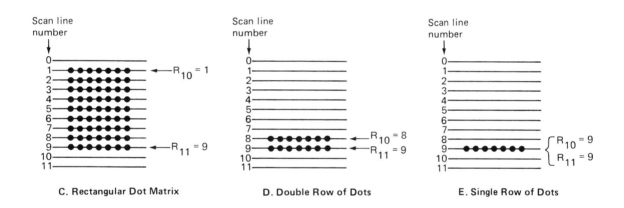

14.3.6 | Start Address Registers

Registers R_{12} and R_{13} contain the starting address of the refresh memory buffer. The contents of these registers are the first address outputted to the memory buffer after vertical blanking. The address is outputted on the 14 memory address pins, MA_0 through MA_{13}. The low address byte (MA_7–MA_0) comes from register R_{13}. The high 6 bits (MA_{13}–MA_8) come from register R_{12}. See Figure 14.16A. By changing the contents of these registers, the starting address in the refresh memory buffer is changed. This feature allows scrolling by character, line, or page.

14.3.7 | Cursor Address Registers

Registers R_{14} and R_{15} control the position of the cursor on the CRT display. Register R_{15} holds the low-order byte that will be outputted on address pins MA_7–MA_0. The high 6 bits are stored in R_{14} and outputted on address pins MA_{13}–MA_8. See Figure 14.16B. These registers are read/write registers.

FIGURE 14.16 | Memory and Cursor Address Registers

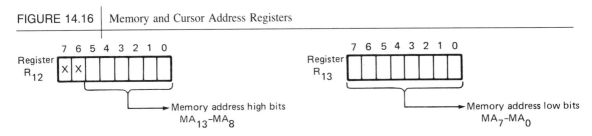

A. Memory Address Register

B. Cursor Address Register

14.3.8 | Light Pen Registers

Registers R_{16} and R_{17} are grouped as a 14-bit read-only register pair. These registers capture the address that is being outputted when a positive input signal is received at pin 3 (the light pen strobe, LPSTB, pin). The 6845 controller is designed to synchronize the asynchronous light pen signal and the refresh address timing. In order to use the light pen feature, either external circuitry must provide an interrupt to the μP or a software polling routine must be written. Registers R_{16} and R_{17} are read-only registers.

14.3.9 | Initialization of the CRT Controller

Let's assume that a 6845 CRT controller is wired into a system at location C000 and $C001_{hex}$. The memory buffer is an 8K block beginning at location 0400_{hex}. The cursor is to be a solid 5×7 dot matrix and should be in the upper left-hand corner after initialization is complete. Table 14.1 summarizes the results of Examples 14.2 and 14.3 as well as other information that must be stored in the 6845. A normal sync noninterlace mode is used.

The hexadecimal values shown in Table 14.1 are originally stored in memory locations F100 to $F10F_{hex}$. Therefore, a program must move the data at F100–F10F to the internal registers of the 6845. To complete the initialization of the 6845, let's use accumulator B as a counter and accumulator A as a temporary register in transferring data from memory to the CRT controller.

```
            LDX #$F100       Initialize X register.
            LDA B #$00       Initialize accumulator B as a counter.
NEXBYT: STA B $C000          Program address register of the 6845.
```

```
LDA A $00,X        Move one byte of data.
STA A $C001        Move one byte into CRTC register.
INX                Increment index register.
INC B              Increment counter.
CMP B #$20         Has last byte been transferred?
BNE NEXBYT         If accumulator B < 20_hex, move next byte.
RTS                Return from subroutine.
```

Note: The value 20_{hex}, at line 8, ensures that all 16 bytes of information are transferred from memory to the CRTC.

TABLE 14.1 | Initialization Data for the 6845

Register Number	Register Names	Values to Be Stored	
		Decimal	Hex
R_0	Horizontal total	100 − 1	63
R_1	Horizontal displayed	80	50
R_2	Horizontal sync position	84	54
R_3	Horizontal sync width	8	08
R_4	Vertical total	26 − 1	19
R_5	Vertical total adjust	2	02
R_6	Vertical displayed	24	18
R_7	Vertical sync position	24	18
R_8	Interlace mode	—	00
R_9	Max scan line address	10	0A
R_{10}	Cursor start	—	01
R_{11}	Cursor end	—	07
R_{12}	Start address (H)	—	04
R_{13}	Start address (L)	—	00
R_{14}	Cursor address (H)	—	04
R_{15}	Cursor address (L)	—	00

14.4 DOT FREQUENCY

The dot frequency (or dot clock) is dependent on the number of dots that must be generated on each horizontal scan line. This frequency is determined by multiplying together the dots per character block in the horizontal direction, the total number of characters per row, and the horizontal scanning frequency.

EXAMPLE

14.4 Use the data from Examples 14.2 and 14.3 and calculate the system's dot frequency.

Solution:
From Example 14.2, the total number of characters per row (displayed and blanked) is $100_{decimal}$. The horizontal scanning frequency is 15,720 Hz. From Example 14.3, the character block is 7 × 10, which means there are 7 dots on each scan line for each character. Therefore, the dot frequency is as follows:

$$\text{Dot frequency} = 7 \times 100 \times 15{,}720 \text{ Hz} = 11.004 \text{ MHz}$$

Note: The dot frequency depends on dots that make up the character block and not just the character. This is because the spacing between each character must be accounted for. The dot clock is used to serial shift the character dots out of a register to the video amplifier. Therefore, the video amplifier must have a frequency response no less than the dot frequency.

Design Example: In Examples 14.2, 14.3, and 14.4, the horizontal scanning frequency is given. However, in many designs this value has to be calculated given other information. Often a screen format, a dot matrix for the character and for the character block, and the vertical refresh rate are chosen, and the other parameters are calculated.

EXAMPLE

14.5 Consider a display that is to have an 80 × 24 screen format, a 9 × 12 character block, and a 60 Hz vertical refresh rate. Determine the horizontal scanning frequency and the dot frequency.

Solution:
Even with the given information, the design still requires the horizontal and vertical blanking intervals to be chosen. The following procedure is a step-by-step guide to determine those values and additional data that must be stored in the CRT registers:

A. Scan lines per block = 12 (store in register R_9)
B. Visual character blocks = 24 (store in register R_6)
C. Active scan lines (step A × step B) = 12 × 24 = 288
D. Choose vertical blanking = 22 scan lines
E. Total number of scan lines (step C + step D) = 288 + 22 = 310
F. Vertical refresh rate = 60 Hz
G. Horizontal scanning frequency (step E × step F) = 310 × 60 Hz = 18,600 Hz
H. Characters per line = 80 (store in register R_1)
I. Choose horizontal blanking interval in characters = 20
J. Total characters per line (step H + step I) = 80 + 20 = 100 (store value − 1 in register R_0)
K. Character frequency (step G × step I) = 18.6 kHz × 100 = 1.86 MHz

L. Dots per character block (horizontal direction) = 9
M. Dot frequency (step L × step K) = 9 × 1.86 MHz = 16.74 MHz

Note: Example 14.5 showed how to calculate the horizontal scanning, character, and dot frequencies. You still must be able to do Examples 14.2 and 14.3 to determine all the values to store in registers R_0 through R_7.

14.5 CHARACTER ROM GENERATOR

A key element to display text material is a character ROM generator. Motorola manufactures a series (MCM667xx) of ROM chips that are preprogrammed. Various sets of characters can be purchased, for example, English, French, German, Japanese, and a math symbol table. System designers can specify a custom set of symbols and have the chips programmed for unique applications. These chips are designed having 8192 bits and are referred to as an 8K horizontal scan character generator. They contain 128 characters in a 7 × 9 dot matrix and have the capability of generating descending characters. That is, they can shift characters such as g, j, p, q, and y below the baseline. Figure 14.17 shows the dot pattern for each character for the MCM66714 IC. The first

FIGURE 14.17 Dot Pattern for the MCM66714 ROM Generator Chip (Reprinted with permission of Motorola, Incorporated, Austin, Texas)

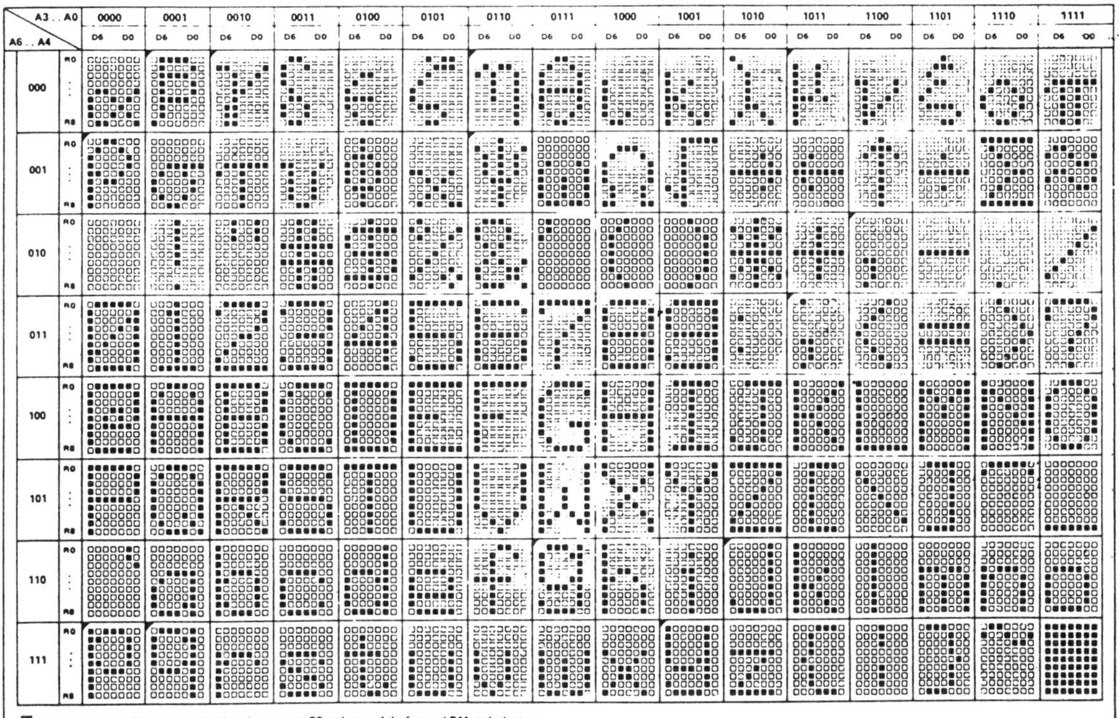

◤ = Shifted character. The character is shifted three rows to R3 at the top of the font and R11 at the bottom.

FIGURE 14.18 | Part of a CRT Controller Board

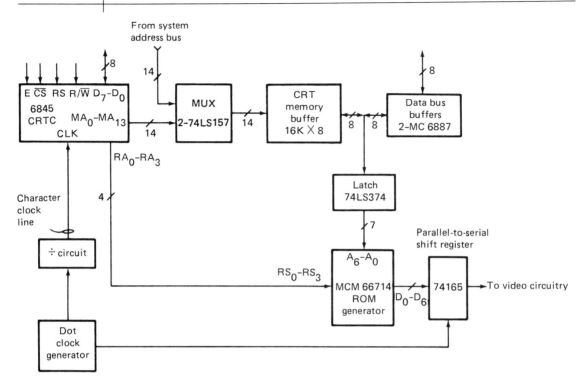

two rows in Figure 14.17 are Greek letters and some commonly used symbols. The remaining rows are English alphanumeric characters and other symbols. Row 2 (binary 010) through row 7 (binary 111) are in an ASCII matrix format. You should compare these rows with columns 2 through 7 in Figure 3.3 to prove to yourself that each character in the MCM66714 is stored at an address that is an ASCII code. This feature is an important point because the address pins of the character generator are wired to the data bus of the memory buffer. This interconnection and operation with the CRTC is shown in Figure 14.18.

14.6 | PIN ASSIGNMENTS FOR A CHARACTER GENERATOR CHIP

The MCM667xx series of character generator chips are housed in a 24-pin dual-in-line package, as shown in Figure 14.19.

Address Pins: There are 7 address input pins (A_0–A_6). A binary pattern applied to these pins selects one of the 128 characters. For the display system described in this chapter, the binary pattern comes from the memory buffer. As previously mentioned, the pattern is often in ASCII code.

FIGURE 14.19 | The MCM667xx Character ROM Generator Chip (Redrawn with permission of Motorola Incorporated, Austin, Texas)

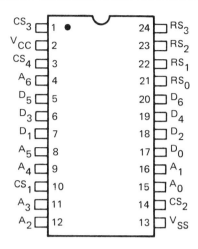

A. Pin Designations

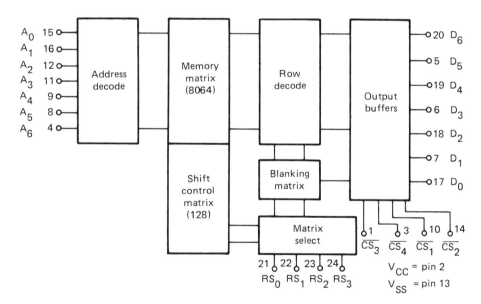

B. Internal Block Diagram

EXAMPLE

14.6 | What binary pattern must be applied to pins A_0 through A_6 to select E, p, S, 4, and D?

Solution:
From Figure 14.17, we can determine the following:

Character	A_6	A_5	A_4	A_3	A_2	A_1	A_0
E	1	0	0	0	1	0	1
p	1	1	1	0	0	0	0
S	1	0	1	0	0	1	1
4	0	1	1	0	1	0	0
D	1	0	0	0	1	0	0

Row Select Pins: The MCM667xx series has 4 row select pins (RS_0 through RS_3). These pins select one row of dots from the character matrix and output a binary pattern to pins D_0 through D_6. From Figure 14.1, you can see that this output is sent to a parallel-to-serial shift register and then to the z axis control of the video display. The binary pattern applied to the row select pins comes from the 6845 controller chip. The interconnection is shown in Figure 14.18, and the internal block diagram of a generator chip is shown in Figure 14.19.

EXAMPLE

14.7 | Consider the following binary patterns applied to MCM66714 address and row select pins. Determine the dot pattern that will be outputted on the following data pins:

A_6	A_5	A_4	A_3	A_2	A_1	A_0	RS_3	RS_2	RS_1	RS_0
1	0	0	0	1	0	1	0	1	0	0

Solution:
The pattern on the address pins selects the letter E. The pattern on the row pins selects the fourth row. See Figure 14.20. *Note:* A character's filled dots appear as logic 1s at the output pins, while unfilled dots appear as logic 0s.

FIGURE 14.20 | Output Logic Levels for Example 14.7

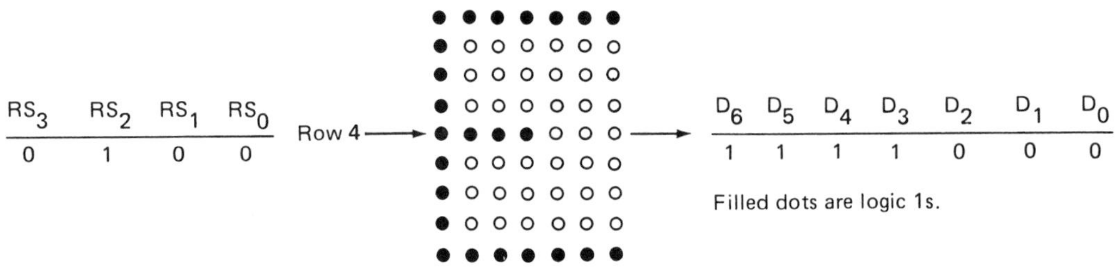

RS_3	RS_2	RS_1	RS_0
0	1	0	0

Row 4 →

D_6	D_5	D_4	D_3	D_2	D_1	D_0
1	1	1	1	0	0	0

Filled dots are logic 1s.

| FIGURE 14.21 | Examples of How Descenders Are Displayed (Reprinted with permission of Motorola Incorporated, Austin, Texas) |

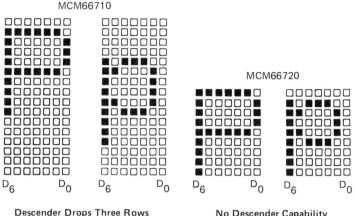

Output Pins: As shown in Figure 14.19, the MCM667xx series has 7 output pins labeled D_0 through D_6. The least significant character dot appears on D_0 and the most significant character dot appears on D_6. Although these pins are labeled the same as data bus lines, they are not connected to the data bus. The output of a character generator is connected to a parallel-to-serial shift register, as shown in Figure 14.1 and Figure 14.18.

Chip Select Pins: This series of chips has 4 chip select pins. The MCM66700, which is mask-programmable, can be ordered with logic 1, 0, or don't-care for the select inputs.

14.7 | SHIFTED CHARACTERS

Some of the ROM character generator chips in the MCM667xx series have the capability of displaying characters below the bottom line. These characters are known as descenders. Examples are the lowercase letters g, j, p, q, and y. Circuitry within the ROM chip allows descenders to be dropped three rows, as shown in Figure 14.21. Some ROM chips (MCM66720, MCM66730, MCM66734) do not contain the descender feature. If you are using a generator chip with this feature, such as MCM66714, you must program register R_9 so that there are enough scan lines per character row. Otherwise, the descending character will conflict with characters in the next row.

14.8 | SUMMARY

Most of today's general-purpose μC systems have a CRT display so that a user can view data. Images are created by an electron beam sweeping across the inside surface of the screen. This technique is called raster scanning, and we studied two types—interlace and noninterlace. The interlace method is used for high-density displays but may be susceptible to objectionable blinking. The noninterlace method is used for most applications to view alphanumeric characters. Since a CRT display is a piece of peripheral equipment, an interface chip is needed as the link between the μP and the CRT unit. Motorola's answer to this problem is the MC6845. This controller chip is programmable so it can be used both for interlace and noninterlace displays as well as for producing different data formats. Although the MC6845 is the key chip on a CRT controller card, other support circuitry is needed. Some of the necessary additional circuitry includes a character generator ROM and a memory buffer. The operation of a typical character generator ROM is covered in Sections 14.5 through 14.7. Figure 14.1 shows the interconnection of the CRT controller chip, the character generator ROM, and the memory buffer.

PROBLEMS

14.1   List the two methods of displaying information on a CRT.

14.2   List the two types of raster scanning.

14.3   Is the refresh rate for an interlace display halved or doubled from that of a noninterlace display?

14.4   How would the letter H be stored in a ROM generator chip if a 7×9 dot matrix format is used?

14.5   How many bytes of refresh memory can be addressed by the 6845 controller chip?

14.6   Which registers of the 6845 handle the (a) horizontal format and (b) vertical format?

14.7   Refer to Example 14.2. If the screen format is changed to 132×24, what hexadecimal values must be stored in registers R_0–R_3? The display and blanking times remain the same.

14.8   If the horizontal scanning frequency in Example 14.2 is increased to 18,240 Hz, calculate (a) display time, (b) front porch time, (c) horizontal sync time, and (d) back porch time. The screen format is 80×24 and a 1:2:2 proportion for the blanking interval is used.

14.9   Calculate the number of scan lines per frame if the horizontal scanning frequency is 18,240 Hz and the vertical refresh rate is 60 Hz.

14.10 Refer to Example 14.3. If the characters are formed by a 7×9 dot matrix housed in a 9×12 character block, can you display 24 character rows? Show the reason for your answer.

14.11 If the horizontal scanning frequency in Example 14.3 is 18,240 Hz, determine the new hexadecimal values that must be stored in registers R_4–R_7.

14.12 What binary pattern must be stored in registers R_{10} and R_{11} to generate the 7×9 cursor shown in Figure 14.15C with a blink rate of one-sixteenth the field rate?

14.13 The horizontal scanning frequency in Examples 14.2 and 14.3 is 18,240 Hz. Calculate the dot frequency.

14.14 Identify the alphanumeric characters that are addressed in an MCM66714 ROM generator by each of the following binary patterns: (a) 0111001, (b) 0011000, and (c) 1101011.

14.15 For each of the characters of Problem 14.14, determine the dot pattern that is outputted by the MCM66714 if the row select pins receive 0101.

15 68000 Microprocessor

15.0 INTRODUCTION

In the mid 1970s, it was a well established fact that microprocessors were here to stay. New μP applications grew at a fantastic rate. Old designs were giving way to the new μP based products and personal computers were beginning to be introduced. These products were all based on 8-bit μPs such as the 6800 μP. These 8-bit devices were originally designed to replace digital logic circuits. Therefore, the roots of these early μPs are in hardware, not software. Even their instruction sets are oriented toward hardware designers and not software programmers. Although these 8-bit μPs may seem primitive compared to today's 16- and 32-bit devices, there are still many applications where the 8-bit μPs are the best choice. Examples are in dedicated control applications (e.g., traffic light controllers, household appliances, and video games) where advanced programming is not needed. However, computer applications that primarily use high-level languages, multitasking, multiuser operations, coprocessing, and so on, require a more advanced μP. To meet these needs, Motorola designed the 68000 μP. Motorola has also introduced the 68010 and 68020 μPs. The 68010 μP has the feature of supporting virtual memory and the 68020 is a full 32-bit μP. It has 32 data lines. Since both of these μPs are object code compatible with the 68000 μP, this μP will be introduced and studied in this text.

As with any new product, designers of the 68000 μP had to make decisions and trade-offs to bring to the marketplace an advanced and competitive product. One of the major decisions that had to be made was whether the 68000 μP should only be an enhanced version of the 6800 μP or whether it should be an entirely new design. An enhanced version approach would be something like upgrading the 6800 with 16-bit registers, extending its address range, and adding some new instructions. This design choice would have the advantage of allowing programs written for the 6800 to run on the new μP, thus ensuring customers that upgrading their hardware would not render their programs obsolete. The disadvantage with simply an enhanced version is that the user, especially the programmer, is still bound by old technology. Therefore, to make use of current VLSI technology and to provide the programmer with maximum flexibility, the designers of the 68000 μP chose to introduce a totally new architecture. Thus, they were able to introduce an extremely powerful μP, yet one that is easy to program. Previously, many hardware designers found the 6800 μP easy to use; now many hardware and software designers should find the 68000 μP easy to use as well.

Chapter 2 discussed classifications of μPs. One method of classification is the width of the data bus. The width of the 6800 μP's data bus is 8 bits. Its arithmetic and logic unit is 8 bits, as is its op code size. Therefore, the 6800 μP can easily be classified as an 8-bit μP. The 68000 μP is not so easily classified. The width of its external data bus is 16 bits; it also has a 16-bit op code. Internally, however, this μP has multiple 32-bit registers. It can perform arithmetic and logic operations either on 8, 16, or 32 bits of data. The 68000 is often classified as both a 16-bit and a 32-bit μP. Most often it is referred to as a 16-bit μP because of the size of its external data bus and its op code.

In any computer system, there must be input/output ports and many I/O operations only require 8 bits. Therefore, the designers of the 68000 μP decided that it would be best to allow the 68000 to be easily interfaced with the 8-bit peripheral devices that had been designed for the 6800 μP. This decision allowed the 68000 μP to be marketed immediately and not have to wait for an entirely new line of 16-bit peripherals. It also allowed users who were familiar with the 6800 peripherals to concentrate only on the new μP. A disadvantage with this decision is that the 6800 μP and its peripheral devices are synchronous devices, and the 68000 μP is an asynchronous device. The difference is that for the 6800 μP, all data transfers are completed within a clock cycle. Data transfers to and from memory for the 68000 μP are not complete until the μP receives a data acknowledge signal. In order for the 68000 to interface directly with the 6800 peripheral devices, three control pins have been included for this specific purpose. The reason for synchronization is that the peripherals are designed for 1 to 2 MHz operation. The clock frequencies of the 68000 μP range from 4 to 12 MHz. Therefore, for the μP to know when to transfer data, synchronization is needed. Chapter 17 explains in more detail how to interconnect the 68000 with 6800 peripherals.

Table 15.1 compares many of the features of the 68000 with the 6800. The comparison of the basic types of instruction in Table 15.1 can be very misleading. The 6800 μP is listed as having 72 basic instructions, while the 68000 μP has only 56. When the 6800 μP's basic instructions are combined with its addressing modes, the result is an instruction set with a total of 197 op codes. However, when the 68000 μP's basic instructions are combined with its addressing modes, and the fact that it can operate on 8, 16, or 32 bits of data, the result is an instruction set of over 1000 op codes. Thus the 68000 is an extremely more powerful μP than the 6800.

14 modes

15.1 | PACKAGE STYLE AND PIN DESIGNATIONS

In order for the designers to incorporate all of the 68000 μP features and not have to multiplex the address and data bus lines, a 64-pin package was needed. Figure 15.1 shows both the package style and pin designations. Chapter 2 introduced the idea that a μP's pins can be grouped into functional sets—address bus, data bus, and control bus. This point is also true for the 68000 μP. However, the 68000 has so many control pins that they are further subdivided, as shown in Figure 15.1C. The following material in this chapter gives a brief description of each control pin of the 68000 μP.

TABLE 15.1 | Comparison of Selected Features of the 68000 and 6800 Microprocessors

Features	68000 μP	6800 μP
Total number of pins	64	40
Number of address pins	23	16
Number of data pins	16	8
Number of bytes of direct addressing	16M	64K
Number of data registers	8 (32 bits each)	2 accumulators
Number of address registers	7 (32 bits each)	1 X register (16 bits)
Basic types of instruction	56	72
Number of addressing modes	14	6*
Size of program counter	32 bits	16 bits
Size of status register	16 bits	8 bits
Memory-mapped I/O	Yes	Yes
Pipeline architecture	Yes	No
TTL compatible	Yes	Yes
Operates from a +5 V supply	Yes	Yes
Built-in logic to handle multi-CPU configurations	Yes	No
Operate either in a "supervisor" or "user" mode	Yes	No

*Includes the inherent and relative addressing modes.

15.1.1 | Power Pins

The 68000 μP is a +5 V device. However, +5 V must be applied to two pins (pin 14 and 49), labeled V_{CC}. The 68000 μP must also be grounded at two pins (pin 16 and 53), labeled GND.

15.1.2 | Clock Pin

Pin 15 is the 68000 μP's clock pin (CLK). This input line is TTL compatible. The 68000's internal circuitry has an "on-board" clock generator circuitry that develops all other timing signals. Presently there are five frequency versions of the 68000 μP: 4 MHz, 6 MHz, 8 MHz, 10 MHz, and 12 MHz. However, faster versions will be introduced.

15.1.3 | Address Bus (A_1–A_{23})

The 68000 μP has a 23-bit address bus labeled A_1–A_{23}. Note that there is no logical A_0 address line; it is used internally, however. The external hardware does not require an A_0 line. As shown in Figure 15.1B, the 68000 μP has a separate pin for each address line. This concept is different than for some other 16-bit μPs, such as Zilog's Z8000, Intel's 8086, and Digital's DCT–11. These μPs multiplex their address and data lines. Texas Instrument's 9900 does have separate address and data lines, but it only has 16 address lines. Therefore, the 9900 is not capable of directly addressing as many words as the 68000 μP. Fairchild and National have introduced 32-bit μPs; these devices should be compared to the 68020 and not the 68000 μP.

FIGURE 15.1 | 68000 μP Package Style, Pin Designations, and Functional Grouping of the Pins (Reprinted with permission of Motorola Incorporated, Austin, Texas)

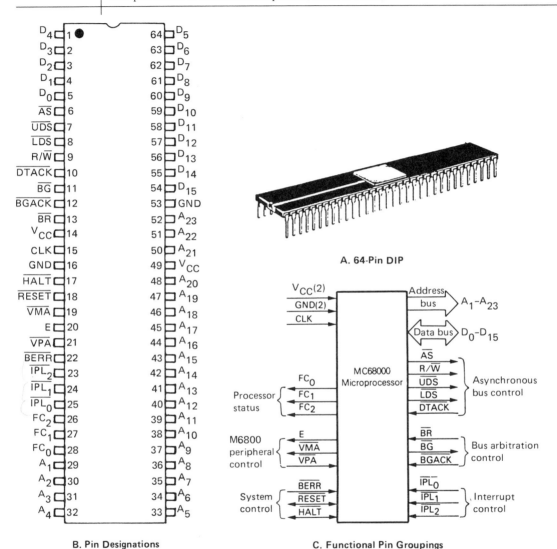

A. 64-Pin DIP

B. Pin Designations

C. Functional Pin Groupings

The 23 physical address lines allow the user to directly address $2^{23} = 8,388,608$ words (8 megawords). A word is 16 bits, or 2 bytes. Therefore, a 68000 μP is capable of addressing 16,777,216 bytes (2 × 8,388,608), or 16 megabytes (16M bytes).

The 68000 address lines are unidirectional and three-state. During an interrupt, address lines A_1, A_2, and A_3 provide information about what level interrupt is being serviced, while address lines A_4–A_{23} are set high.

15.1.4 | Data Bus (D_0–D_{15})

The 68000 μP has 16 data bus pins labeled D_0–D_{15}. Therefore, the 68000 can transfer 16 bits of data at a time between memory or an I/O device. A user of the 68000 μP should not confuse this physical limitation of 16 data pins with the μP's software capabilities. Internally, the μP is capable of performing either 8-, 16-, or 32-bit arithmetic and logical operations. To transfer 32 bits into or out of the μP requires either two read or two write operations. Like the 6800 μP, the 68000 μP's data bus is bidirectional with three-state capability. During an interrupt acknowledge cycle, an external device must place the interrupt vector number on data lines D_0 to D_7.

15.1.5 | Asynchronous Bus Control Lines

The 68000 μP has 5 asynchronous bus control pins, as shown in Figure 15.1C. They are: address strobe ($\overline{AS}$), read/write ($R/\overline{W}$), upper data strobe ($\overline{UDS}$), lower data strobe ($\overline{LDS}$), and data acknowledge ($\overline{DTACK}$). The $\overline{AS}$, $R/\overline{W}$, $\overline{UDS}$, and $\overline{LDS}$ are output signals from the μP. The $\overline{DTACK}$ is an input signal. These bus lines are used to control the flow of data between the μP and memory. These lines are referred to as asynchronous because they allow memory chips with different access times to be connected to the 68000 μP. This concept is different than for the 6800 μP. With the 6800 μP, memory chips had to have fast enough access times to conform to the 6800 μP's clock cycle (see Section 9.10). However, with the 68000 μP, the transfer of data is not complete until the μP receives a data acknowledge ($\overline{DTACK}$) signal.

Address Strobe ($\overline{AS}$): The $\overline{AS}$ line is used by the 68000 μP to output a control signal indicating that there is a valid and stable address on its address bus (A_1–A_{23}). As the bar indicates, the active state is low. Figure 15.2 is a timing diagram to show the relationship between the address bus signals and the $\overline{AS}$ signal. The $\overline{AS}$ signal is most often used by a dynamic memory controller chip to indicate that it has received a valid

FIGURE 15.2 | Timing Diagram of the Address Bus and the Address Strobe Signals

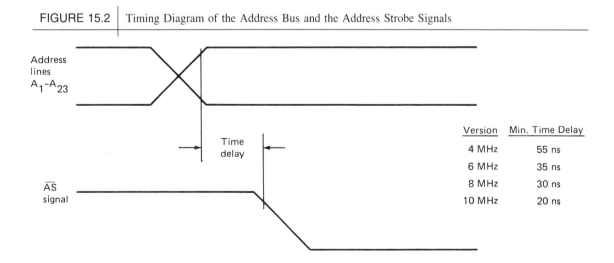

Version	Min. Time Delay
4 MHz	55 ns
6 MHz	35 ns
8 MHz	30 ns
10 MHz	20 ns

address and the controller can latch the address and begin its multiplexing operation along with generating a row address strobe signal followed by column address strobe. Chapter 17 shows how the 68000 can be connected to dynamic RAMs.

Read/Write (R/$\overline{\text{W}}$):   This control signal is similar to the R/$\overline{\text{W}}$ line of the 6800 μP because it defines in which direction the data flows on the data bus. A logic 1 indicates that the μP is reading (receiving) data. A logic 0 is the signal that the μP is writing (sending). However the 68000 μP is capable of transferring either bytes (8 bits) or words (16 bits). Therefore, the R/$\overline{\text{W}}$ line is used in conjunction with the data strobe lines to indicate on which data lines there is information.

Upper and Lower Data Strobe ($\overline{\text{UDS}}$ and $\overline{\text{LDS}}$):   These control signals indicate on which group of data lines there is valid data. The term *upper* refers to data lines D_8–D_{15}, in other words, the *upper byte* of data. The term *lower* refers to data lines D_0–D_7, the *lower byte* of data. Table 15.2 summarizes the logic states of the upper and lower data lines and the read/write line.

Data Transfer Acknowledge ($\overline{\text{DTACK}}$):   This control line is an input signal to the 68000 μP. It indicates that the transfer of data is completed. Since this signal is an input to the μP, it is controlled by circuitry either on a memory board or an I/O board. When the 68000 μP recognizes a $\overline{\text{DTACK}}$ signal during a read cycle, data is latched inside the μP and the μP can begin terminating the bus cycle. When the μP recognizes a $\overline{\text{DTACK}}$ signal during a write cycle, the μP begins terminating the bus cycle. This signal and other timing diagrams are shown in Section 15.4 (Figures 15.6–15.8).

15.1.6 | 6800 Peripheral Control Lines

The 68000 μP is an asynchronous device. The bus cycles (read or write) are terminated after the μP receives a $\overline{\text{DTACK}}$ signal. The asynchronous capability of the 68000 μP allows it to be interfaced with memory chips with varying access times. The 6800 μP, on the other hand, is a synchronous device; that is, each bus cycle automatically is terminated at the end of a ϕ_2 clock cycle. This requires that any memory chip or I/O device connected

TABLE 15.2 | Control of the Data Bus Using Data Strobe and Read/Write Lines

Operation	R/$\overline{\text{W}}$	$\overline{\text{LDS}}$	$\overline{\text{UDS}}$	D_0–D_7	D_8–D_{15}
	High impedance state	H	H	No valid data	No valid data
Read	H	L	L	Valid data	Valid data
	H	L	H	Valid data	No valid data
	H	H	L	No valid data	Valid data
	L	L	L	Valid data	Valid data
Write	L	L	H	Valid data	No valid data
	L	H	L	No valid data	Valid data

FIGURE 15.3 | Relationship between the 68000 μP's Clock Cycle and Enable (E) Signal

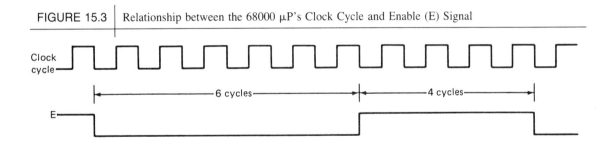

to the 6800 μP must have access times that are fast enough to meet the ϕ_2 clock cycle requirement (see Section 9.10). The peripheral I/O devices that have been designed for the 6800 μP also are synchronous devices and must conform to the same timing signals. In order to use all the peripheral devices that have been designed for the 6800 μP with the 68000 μP, the 68000 μP has three special control lines: an enable (E) line, a valid peripheral address ($\overline{\text{VPA}}$) line, and a valid memory address ($\overline{\text{VMA}}$) line.

Enable (E):   The enable line carries an output signal from the 68000 μP. It is the standard enable signal used by the 6800 μP. The signal is 0.1 of the 68000 μP's clock pulse. The E line is low for six clock pulses and high for four pulses, as shown in Figure 15.3.

Valid Peripheral Address ($\overline{\text{VPA}}$):   When this input control signal goes low, the 68000 μP has addressed a 6800 peripheral device. The transfer of data between the 68000 μP and the peripheral device coincides with the enable signal. The $\overline{\text{VPA}}$ signal is generated on the I/O board, as will be shown in Chapter 17.

Valid Memory Address ($\overline{\text{VMA}}$):   This output signal from the 68000 μP indicates to the 6800 peripheral devices that there is a valid address on the address bus and the 68000 μP internal circuitry is synchronized with the E signal. The $\overline{\text{VMA}}$ line only goes low after a $\overline{\text{VPA}}$ signal is received by the μP.

15.1.7 | Interrupt Control Logic ($\overline{\text{IPL}_0}$, $\overline{\text{IPL}_1}$, $\overline{\text{IPL}_2}$)

Not counting the reset pin, the 6800 μP has only two levels of hardware interrupt: an interrupt request and a nonmaskable interrupt request. In comparison, the 68000 μP has seven levels of hardware interrupt: level 1 to level 7. Level 1 is the lowest priority and level 7 is the highest priority. Level 0 indicates no interrupt request. These seven levels are encoded into three input pins—$\overline{\text{IPL}_0}$, $\overline{\text{IPL}_1}$, $\overline{\text{IPL}_2}$. $\overline{\text{IPL}_0}$ is the least significant bit and $\overline{\text{IPL}_2}$ is the most significant bit.

15.1.8 | Bus Arbitration Control

Like the 6800 μP, the 68000 μP's address bus, data bus, and many of its control lines have three-state capability. This feature permits another device to be a bus master. Examples of such devices are DMA (direct memory access) controllers or other μPs. The 68000 is often used in multiprocessing applications, that is, systems that link several

μPs together. In such systems, however, only one μP can be in control at a time. All other devices must relinquish control of the bus lines. There are three bus arbitration control lines used to determine which device becomes the master.

Bus Request ($\overline{\text{BR}}$):   This line is wire ORed with all other potential bus masters. When this line goes low, it is the signal to the μP that another device wishes to become the bus master.

Bus Grant ($\overline{\text{BG}}$):   This output signal line is the response to a bus request. When the bus grant line goes low, it is a signal to all other bus master devices that the processor, which is controlling the lines, will release control at the end of the current bus cycle.

Bus Grant Acknowledge ($\overline{\text{BGACK}}$):   When this line goes low, it indicates that another device has become the bus master. This line does not go to its active state until the following conditions are met:

1. $\overline{\text{BG}}$ is low. This indicates a bus grant has been received.
2. $\overline{\text{AS}}$ is high. This indicates that the μP is not using the address bus.
3. $\overline{\text{DTACK}}$ is high. This indicates that neither memory nor the I/O peripherals are using the bus.
4. $\overline{\text{BGACK}}$ is high. This indicates that no other device is in control of the bus lines.

15.1.9 | Processor Status

The 68000 has three function code (FC_0, FC_1, FC_2) output lines. These lines indicate the state (user or supervisor) as well as the cycle type that is being executed by the μP. Table 15.3 summarizes the eight possible classes. The logic levels on the function code lines are valid when the $\overline{\text{AS}}$ line is low.

The supervisor state is the higher privilege state. The S bit (Section 15.3) in the status register determines if the instruction execution is supervisor state or user state. If the S bit is a logic 1, the μP is in the supervisor state. If the S bit is a logic 0, user instructions are being executed. The 68000 μP has a few instructions that can only be

TABLE 15.3 | Function Code Outputs

FC_2	FC_1	FC_0	*State*	*Cycle Type*
L	L	L	User	Unassigned
L	L	H	User	Data
L	H	L	User	Program
L	H	H	User	Unassigned
H	L	L	Supervisor	Unassigned
H	L	H	Supervisor	Data
H	H	L	Supervisor	Program
H	H	H	Supervisor	Interrupt acknowledge

executed in the supervisor state. If a user program tries to execute supervisor instructions, a trap occurs to halt the user's program.

15.1.10 | System Control

The 68000 μP has one input and two bidirectional system control lines. The input line is used for bus errors and the bidirectional lines are for reset and halt signals.

Bus Error (BERR): This input line is used to inform the 68000 μP that an external device(s), such as memory, has not responded within an expected amount of time. The advantage of this feature is to ensure that the 68000 μP is not hung up indefinitely. The μP treats a bus error like an interrupt request. An error causes the μP to save the status information on the stack and jump to a program to analyze the cause of the error. If the HALT line and the BERR line are both low, the μP automatically retries the bus cycle.

Halt (HALT): As just mentioned, one function of the HALT line, in conjunction with the BERR line, is to signal the μP to try the bus cycle again. Another function, when this line is used by itself, is to place the 68000 μP in an inactive state. The halted state causes all control signals to be inactive and all three-state lines to go to their high impedance state. If the μP stops executing instructions—an example is a double bus fault—the μP brings the HALT line low. External logic circuitry should be able to detect this condition. A halt and reset action is a third function of the HALT line. Whenever the HALT line is used in conjunction with the RESET line, a system (μP and external devices) reset condition occurs.

Reset (RESET): Similar to the HALT line, the reset line is bidirectional. As an input line, the μP is reset to an initialization sequence by an external reset signal. The reset line is used as an output line whenever the μP decodes a RESET instruction. Therefore, external devices can be reset under programmer's control. A RESET instruction does not affect the internal state of the 68000.

15.2 | PROGRAMMING MODEL

As shown in Figure 15.4, the 68000 μP has eight data registers, seven address registers, two stack pointers, one program counter, and one status register. All the registers are 32 bits wide except for the status register, which is 16 bits. The eight data registers, labeled D_0 to D_7, are used for either 8-bit (byte), 16-bit (word), or 32-bit (long word) data operations. The seven address registers are labeled A_0 to A_6 and the two stack pointers are both labeled A_7. Any one of the data or address registers may be used as an index register. Thus, the 68000 μP has been designed for programming flexibility.

The purpose of a data register is quite different from that of an address register. Data registers usually are used to hold data temporarily before or after an ALU operation. Any ALU operation that uses data stored in an internal μP register(s) is the fastest to execute because the μP does not have to retrieve data from memory. Also, whenever data is moved or manipulated, the programmer usually needs to know the condition of

FIGURE 15.4 | Programming Model of the 68000 μP

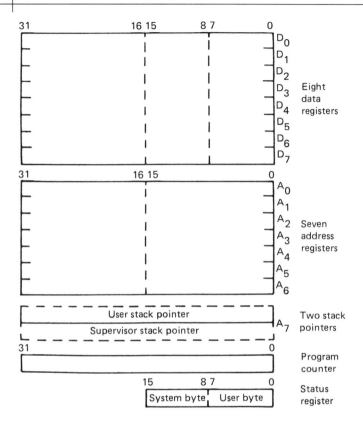

the data. This is done by setting or clearing a flag bit(s) in the status register. This bit(s) then can be used for other data calculations or checked by branch instructions.

Besides the data registers, a programmer needs another set of registers that do not affect the flag bits. These registers are address registers. The reason these registers become important is that, in the middle of data operations, an address may have to be modified. One can easily see that if an address modification changes a flag bit(s), then the programmer must be aware of this and temporarily store the status register (flag bits) before the address modification. After the modification, the programmer must restore the status register to its original condition. This temporary storage wastes time and thus slows down program execution. Therefore, within the 68000 μP, any operation that uses a data register affects one or more flag bits. Any operation involving an address register does not affect a flag bit. These registers provide great program flexibility for the user.

15.3 | STATUS REGISTER

The 68000 μP has a 16-bit status register. It is considered to be divided into two parts —the user byte and the system byte. Figure 15.5 shows this register along with the names and symbols of the bits. Note at the present time not all the bits are used.

FIGURE 15.5 | Status Register

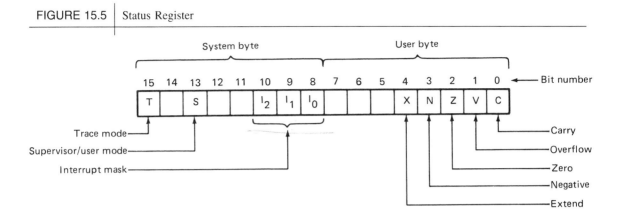

The user byte is similar to the condition code register of the 6800 μP. A user's program can only affect the status bits on the user's portion. The system status bits contain information about the system. The system bits as well as the user bits can be changed by the μP when it is in its supervisor mode.

Carry (C) Bit: The C bit is set to a logic 1 if there is a carry-out of the MSB from an add operation. The C bit is also set to a logic 1 if there is a borrow from the MSB during a subtraction operation. The shift and rotate instructions also affect this bit.

Overflow (V) Bit: The V bit is set when there is a magnitude overflow.

Zero (Z) Bit: The Z bit is set whenever the result of an operation is zero.

Negative (N) Bit: The N bit, also called the sign bit, is set whenever the result of an arithmetic operation is negative.

Extend (X) Bit: The extend bit is used in multiprecision arithmetic operations.

Interrupt Mask Bits (I_0, I_1, and I_2):   Bits 8, 9, and 10 of the status register are the three least significant bits of the system byte. These bits provide seven levels of interrupts, as shown in Table 15.4. Level 1 is the lowest priority and level 7 is the highest priority. Level 7 is a nonmaskable interrupt. Level 0 indicates no interrupt request.

The 68000 handles interrupts in the following manner: An interrupt request signal is received by the μP on its interrupt pins; then it is decoded and compared with the interrupt mask bits. If the binary pattern on the interrupt pins is greater than the binary pattern of the mask bits, then the μP stores the new interrupt level into the mask bits and then jumps to a subroutine to service the interrupt. For example, consider that the mask bits are set to 100 (level 4). The 68000 will only jump to an interrupt subroutine if a level 5, 6, or 7 is received on the interrupt pins. If the μP should receive a level 1, 2, 3, or 4 interrupt request, it will be ignored. Thus, external interrupts are blocked for levels less than or equal to the level in the mask bits. Level 7 is a special case and cannot be inhibited. It is considered to be a nonmaskable interrupt.

Before the μP jumps to an interrupt subroutine, it will set the mask bits to the new interrupt level. This operation is part of the internal procedures of the 68000 μP when an interrupt request is recognized. Interrupts are classified as part of the μP's

TABLE 15.4 | Seven Levels of Interrupt

Description	Interrupt Levels	Interrupt Mask Bits		
		I_2	I_1	I_0
No interrupt request	Level 0	0	0	0
Lowest priority	Level 1	0	0	1
	Level 2	0	1	0
	Level 3	0	1	1
	Level 4	1	0	0
	Level 5	1	0	1
	Level 6	1	1	0
Highest priority (nonmaskable interrupt)	Level 7	1	1	1

exception-processing capabilities, as are traps and traces. For complete details, flowcharts, and timing diagrams, refer to the manufacturers' data books and application notes.

Supervisor/User (S) Bit: The S bit specifies whether the 68000 μP is in its supervisor or user mode. A logic 1 is the supervisor mode; a logic 0 is the user mode.

Trace (T) Bit: The T bit is the trace bit. Normal operation for the 68000 is when this bit is a logic 0. When the T bit is a logic 1, the μP is in the trace mode. This mode allows the μP to do single-step execution of a program. After each instruction, a trap is automatically forced and the μP should jump to a debugging program. Usually, this program is designed to output the results of the μP's registers and other important data stored in memory.

15.4 | DATA TRANSFER OPERATIONS

Like any CPU, the transfer of data between the μP and memory, the μP and interface devices, or memory and interface devices involves using the address bus, the data bus, and control signals. In this section, we will see how the 68000 uses its bus lines to read and write data. Remember, this μP can transfer either single bytes or words (2 bytes) of data. In addition to the read and write cycles discussed in this section, the 68000 has one instruction (test and set) that uses a read-modify-write cycle. If you are using this instruction, you should refer to Motorola's data sheet for the 68000 μP.

15.4.1 | Read Operation

A read operation means that data is being transferred either from memory or an interface device to the μP. If the instruction is a byte read operation, the 68000 uses the A_0 internally to assert either the upper or lower data strobe lines. If A_0 is a logic 0, then the $\overline{UDS}$ line goes low. If A_0 is a logic 1, then the $\overline{LDS}$ line goes low. If the instruction is a word operation, both strobe lines go low.

Flowcharts for word and byte read operations are given in Figures 15.6A and B, respectively. The timing diagram is given in Figure 15.6C. Note how the μP must

FIGURE 15.6 | Memory Read Operation (Reprinted with permission of Motorola Incorporated, Austin, Texas)

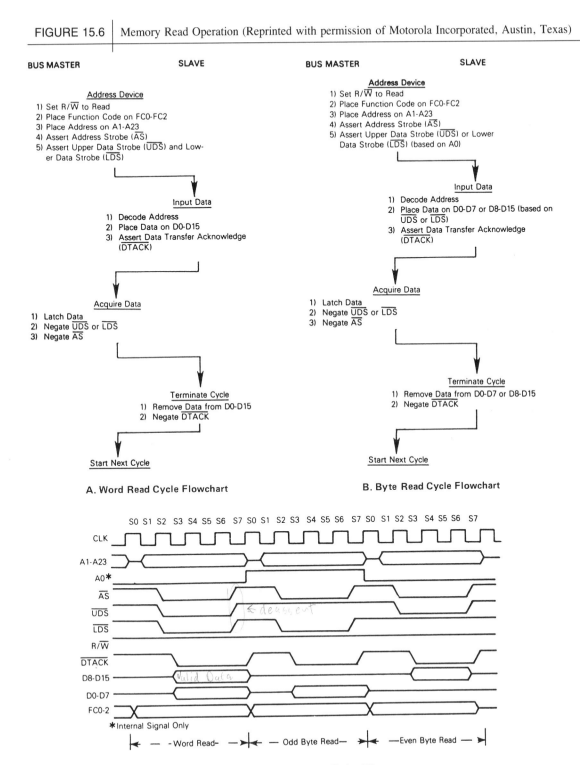

A. Word Read Cycle Flowchart

B. Byte Read Cycle Flowchart

C. Word and Byte Read Cycle Timing Diagram

first set up the address bus and control lines before the slave (either memory or peripheral device) can begin to respond. The μP must now wait for the $\overline{\text{DTACK}}$ line to go low before latching the data. From Figure 15.6C, we see that a read operation takes four clock cycles to complete. If, however, the μP has not received a low logic signal on the $\overline{\text{DTACK}}$ line in the fourth clock cycle, the 68000 will generate wait cycles until the slave responds. See Figure 15.7. We can quickly see that a problem arises if the device never responds, because the μP will remain in the wait state indefinitely. The solution to this problem is to have an external timing circuit signal to the μP that a bus error has occurred. This external timing circuit is referred to as a *watchdog* circuit.

15.4.2 | Write Operation

A write cycle operation is one in which the μP is sending data either to memory or a peripheral device. The operation is very similar to a read operation, except the R/$\overline{\text{W}}$ line is brought low. See Figure 15.8. The μP does not remove the data from the data bus until it receives an active $\overline{\text{DTACK}}$ signal, even if the μP has to insert wait cycles. Once again, the μP could be hung up if an active $\overline{\text{DTACK}}$ signal is never received. To become free, the μP must receive a bus error signal from the watchdog circuit.

15.5 | MEMORY ORGANIZATION

The designer and user of 68000 μP products should visualize memory organized as shown in Figure 15.9. As we discussed in a previous section, each byte of a word is addressable by the μP. The high-order bytes have even addresses and the low-order bytes have odd addresses. Instructions and multibytes of data can only be accessed on even addresses. These addresses are designated as n, $n + 2$, $n + 4$, where n is an even integer. If the μP tries to fetch an instruction at an odd address, an addressing error occurs so that the

$n = bytes$

FIGURE 15.7 | Read and Write Cycle Timing Diagram for the 68000 μP (Reprinted with permission of Motorola Incorporated, Austin, Texas)

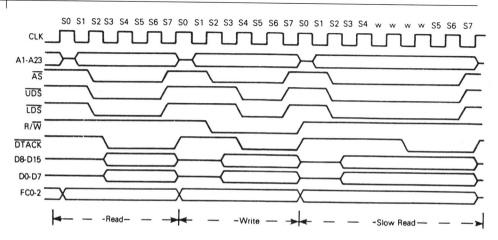

FIGURE 15.8 | Flowcharts and Timing Diagram for a Write Operation (Reprinted with permission of Motorola Incorporated, Austin, Texas)

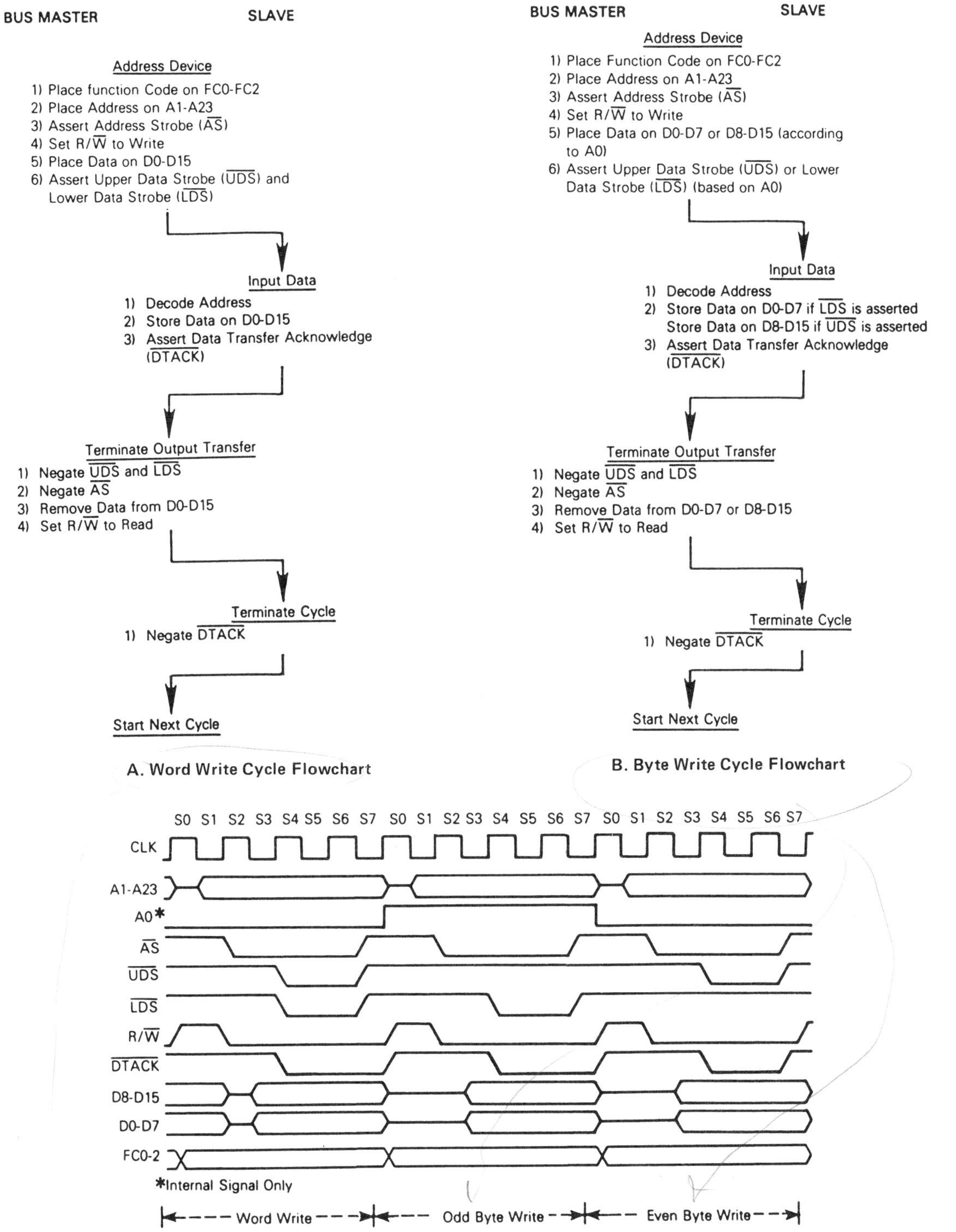

BUS MASTER   **SLAVE**

Address Device

1) Place function Code on FC0-FC2
2) Place Address on A1-A23
3) Assert Address Strobe ($\overline{AS}$)
4) Set R/$\overline{W}$ to Write
5) Place Data on D0-D15
6) Assert Upper Data Strobe ($\overline{UDS}$) and Lower Data Strobe ($\overline{LDS}$)

Input Data

1) Decode Address
2) Store Data on D0-D15
3) Assert Data Transfer Acknowledge ($\overline{DTACK}$)

Terminate Output Transfer

1) Negate $\overline{UDS}$ and $\overline{LDS}$
2) Negate $\overline{AS}$
3) Remove Data from D0-D15
4) Set R/$\overline{W}$ to Read

Terminate Cycle

1) Negate $\overline{DTACK}$

Start Next Cycle

A. Word Write Cycle Flowchart

BUS MASTER   **SLAVE**

Address Device

1) Place Function Code on FC0-FC2
2) Place Address on A1-A23
3) Assert Address Strobe ($\overline{AS}$)
4) Set R/$\overline{W}$ to Write
5) Place Data on D0-D7 or D8-D15 (according to A0)
6) Assert Upper Data Strobe ($\overline{UDS}$) or Lower Data Strobe ($\overline{LDS}$) (based on A0)

Input Data

1) Decode Address
2) Store Data on D0-D7 if $\overline{LDS}$ is asserted Store Data on D8-D15 if $\overline{UDS}$ is asserted
3) Assert Data Transfer Acknowledge ($\overline{DTACK}$)

Terminate Output Transfer

1) Negate $\overline{UDS}$ and $\overline{LDS}$
2) Negate $\overline{AS}$
3) Remove Data from D0-D7 or D8-D15
4) Set R/$\overline{W}$ to Read

Terminate Cycle

1) Negate $\overline{DTACK}$

Start Next Cycle

B. Byte Write Cycle Flowchart

S0 S1 S2 S3 S4 S5 S6 S7   S0 S1 S2 S3 S4 S5 S6 S7   S0 S1 S2 S3 S4 S5 S6 S7

CLK
A1-A23
A0 *
$\overline{AS}$
$\overline{UDS}$
$\overline{LDS}$
R/$\overline{W}$
$\overline{DTACK}$
D8-D15
D0-D7
FC0-2

*Internal Signal Only

|← --- Word Write --- →|← --- Odd Byte Write --- →|← --- Even Byte Write --- →|

C. Word and Byte Write Cycle Timing Diagram

319

FIGURE 15.9 | Word Organization in Memory (Reprinted with permission of Motorola Incorporated, Austin, Texas)

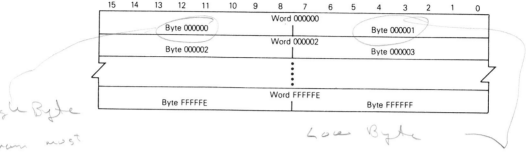

High Byte

program must start at even byte

Low Byte

bus cycle is stopped and the μP ceases whatever it is currently doing. Long words occupy two 16-bit locations and must be stored in memory at addresses designated by n, $n + 4$, and $n + 8$, where n is an even integer.

Figure 15.10 shows how data or addresses are stored in memory. The numbers within the figure indicate the order in which data is accessed. The 68000 μP supports bit data; integer data of 8, 16, and 32 bits; 32-bit addresses; and BCD (binary coded decimal) data. For integer data the rightmost bit is the LSB, and the leftmost bit is the MSB. For long words the high-order 16 bits are stored at address n, while the low-order 16 bits are stored at address $n + 2$. BCD values are stored as two digits per byte.

EXAMPLE

15.1   Show how each of the following alphanumeric characters is stored in memory: (a) 152A (hexadecimal value), (b) C4003128 (hexadecimal value), (c) EMD1 (ASCII format), and (d) 1297 (BCD value). For each case, assume that the starting address is 0500.

Solution:

	Memory Location	Binary Pattern
a.	0500	0001 0101 0010 1010 1 5 2 A
b.	0500	1100 0100 0000 0000 C 4 0 0
	0502	0011 0001 0010 1000 3 1 2 8
c.	0500	0100 0101 0100 1101 E M
	0502	0100 0100 0011 0001 D 1
d.	0500	0001 0010 1001 0111 1 2 9 7

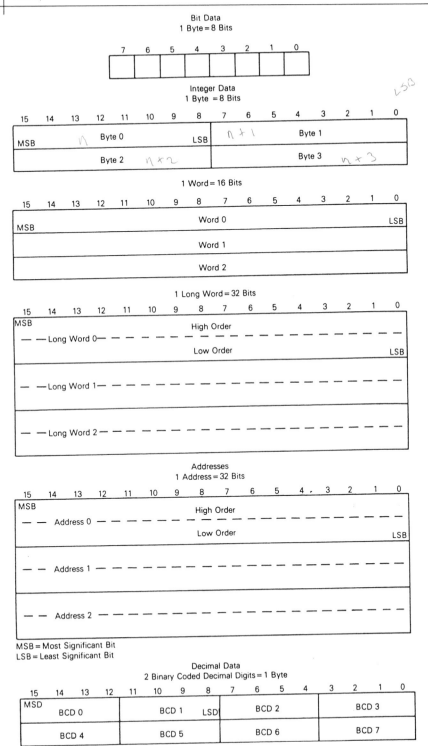

15.6 | SUMMARY

The 68000 μP is a VLSI (very large scale integration) device. It has approximately 68,000 transistors fabricated in a chip size of 246 mils by 280 mils and housed in a 64-pin dual-in-line package. Its address, data, and control lines and their purposes were introduced in this chapter. A comparison between the 6800 μP and the 68000 μP was a topic covered in Section 15.0. The 68000 μP is an asynchronous device; the idea that it can be connected to synchronous peripheral chips was mentioned and will be covered again in Chapter 17. This chapter discussed the hardware aspects of the device, leaving the instructions and address modes to Chapter 16. Some of the hardware aspects covered were the 68000's ability to directly address 16 megabytes of memory, its memory-mapped I/O system, its 32-bit data and address registers, and vectored interrupts and bus control for multiprocessor applications.

PROBLEMS

15.1 What does the phrase "enhanced version" mean when it is applied to a new μP?

15.2 How many words (16 bits) can be addressed by a μP with 16 address lines? How many bytes (8 bits) can be addressed by 16 address lines?

15.3 Is the 68000 μP an asynchronous or synchronous device?

15.4 What is the 68000 μP's total address space in (a) words and (b) bytes?

15.5 If a μP has 32 address pins, what is its total address space in (a) long words (32 bits), (b) words (16 bits), and (c) bytes (8 bits)?

15.6 Which address lines of the 68000 μP provide information about what level interrupt is being serviced?

15.7 The program counter for the 68000 μP is 32 bits wide. How many of these bits are used, and which ones?

15.8 For the 10 MHz version of the 68000, what is a typical time delay for the address strobe line to start to go from high to low?

15.9 If the interrupt request bits are set for level 3, what level of interrupts will be serviced by the μP?

15.10 Refer to Problem 15.9. If a level 5 interrupt is received, what binary pattern will be stored in bits 8, 9, and 10 of the status register?

15.11 Does an operation that uses the address registers affect the flag bits?

15.12 Can the 68000 μP read 8 bits of data from memory in fewer clock cycles than it can read 16 bits of data?

15.13 The following hexadecimal values are the contents of the status register. Determine the level of interrupt for each value: (a) 0504, (b) A210, (c) 060A, and (d) 2100.

15.14 For each of the hexadecimal values of Problem 15.13, identify whether the μP is in the supervisory or user mode.

15.15 Show how the following values would be stored in memory: (a) 14ea (ASCII), (b) 7310 (BCD), and (c) A52BC07F (hexadecimal).

CHAPTER

16 | 68000 Microprocessor Instruction Set

16.0 | INTRODUCTION

This chapter deals with the software aspects of the 68000 μP, which includes the μP's instructions and addressing modes. Section 16.3 presents some short programs to illustrate the instruction set. This chapter begins with how the fifty-six basic instructions are grouped. The addressing modes are studied in Section 16.2. To illustrate how each addressing mode operates, an example is given using a basic instruction such as the ADD instruction. The programs use absolute addresses instead of assembler labels with the intention that this will give a better insight into what is happening when each instruction is executed. In this chapter, a $ symbol before a number means it is a hexadecimal number. Also, the symbol # means the immediate addressing mode.

16.1 | 68000'S BASIC INSTRUCTIONS

The fifty-six instructions for the 68000 μP have been divided by Motorola into eight categories: (1) data movement, (2) integer arithmetic, (3) logical, (4) shift and rotate, (5) bit manipulation, (6) binary coded decimal, (7) program control, and (8) system control. Let's examine which instructions fall into each category and whether the instructions operate on bytes, words, or long words.

16.1.1 | Data Movement Instructions

One of the most common types of instructions for any μP is to move data from one location to another. In this category of instructions, the 6800 μP had load, store, push, pull, and transfer instructions. The designers of the 68000 μP have lumped all of these instructions together and refer to them simply as a *move* instruction. This instruction, along with the 68000's addressing modes, allows programmers great flexibility to manipulate both data and addresses. There is a difference, however, when a move instruction is applied to data and address operands. For example, when a move instruction is applied to data, the programmer can specify byte, word, or long word operands to be transferred. For address operands, however, the programmer only can specify word or long word operands. This procedure ensures that the μP only addresses even memory locations. In addition to the basic move instruction, the 68000 μP has more special move instructions, such as exchange registers, swap, load and push effective address, and load and unload stack. Tables 16.1 and 16.2 in the appendix to this chapter summarize the 68000's data movement instructions. (*Note:* All tables for Chapter 16 appear in Section 16.5.) The 68000 μP also has four move instructions that are grouped under "System Control Instructions" (Section 16.1.8).

16.1.2 | Integer Arithmetic Instructions

This category of instructions includes four arithmetic operations as well as compare, clear, negate, and test instructions. The arithmetic operations are add, subtract, multiply, and divide. The add and subtract instructions can be used for both address and data operations. The difference is that all sizes of operands (byte, word, and long word) are permitted for data operations. Address operations, however, permit only word and long word operands; this is because the 68000 only addresses on word boundaries.

The multiply and divide instructions can be used on either signed or unsigned operands. Two 16-bit numbers can be multiplied to produce a 32-bit product. In the division operation, the dividend is a 32-bit number and the divisor is 16 bits. The result is a 16-bit quotient and a 16-bit remainder.

Multiprecision and mixed size arithmetic use the extended instructions. These operations are indicated by an X as the last letter in the mnemonic. Remember, the extend bit (X bit) is bit 4 of the status register (see Figure 15.5). Table 16.3 in Section 16.5 provides a summary of the 68000's integer arithmetic instructions.

16.1.3 | Logical Instructions

The 68000 μP has four basic logical instructions: AND, OR, Exclusive OR, and NOT (complement). These instructions can operate on 8, 16, or 32 bits of data. Within the first three categories (AND, OR, EOR), there is a set of immediate instructions. Immediate mode instructions are useful to clear, set, or toggle (change from one logic state to the other) individual bits, in particular, those of the status register. Table 16.4 in Section 16.5 summarizes the logical instructions.

16.1.4 | Shift and Rotate Instructions

The 68000 has eight shift and rotate instructions. Like the 6800 instruction set, the 68000 has arithmetic shift instructions (ASR and ASL) and logical shift instructions (LSR and LSL). All of the shift operations use the carry and extend flag bits. Two of the rotate instructions use only the carry bit, while two other rotate instructions use both the carry and extend bits. Table 16.5 is a summary of the 68000's shift and rotate instructions.

The 6800 μP allows only single-bit shifts or rotates. However, the 68000 μP allows the contents of a register to be shifted or rotated by a specific shift count. The shift count first must be loaded into a data register. Register shifts and rotates support all operand sizes (8, 16, and 32 bits). Memory shifts and rotates are only for word sizes (16 bits), and only single-bit shifts and rotates are allowed.

16.1.5 | Bit Manipulation Instructions

There are four bit manipulation operations in the 68000 instruction set. They are bit test, bit test and set, bit test and clear, and bit test and change. These instructions can be used to sense input port lines, drive output port lines, and test register or memory bits. Table 16.6 summarizes the bit manipulation instructions.

16.1.6 | Binary Coded Decimal Instructions

The 68000 μP is capable of performing arithmetic instructions on decimal digits. The instructions are add, subtract, and negate. Each of these instructions operates on two decimal digits packed in a single byte that is stored as binary coded decimal (BCD) data. The extend (X) bit is included in the operation. In many applications, BCD numbers are many bytes wide; therefore, multiprecision operations must be performed. The 68000 is designed for this type of operation, and the zero (Z) bit reflects the state of the whole operation, not just the last byte. Table 16.7 summarizes the BCD instructions.

16.1.7 | Program Control Instructions

The 68000 μP's program control instructions include conditional and unconditional branch instructions, jump, and return instructions. Table 16.8 describes the conditional branch instructions (those instructions that require the μP first to check a flag bit before proceeding). The unconditional branch, jump, and return instructions are unconditional branch instructions and are listed in Table 16.9. This group of instructions does not require the μP to check a flag bit.

16.1.8 | System Control Instructions

This group of instructions does not exist for the 6800 μP. As shown in Tables 16.10, 16.11, and 16.12, there are three subcategories of system control instructions: privileged, trap generating, and status register. Privileged instructions only can be used by the supervisor and not by general users of the system. If the μP is not in the supervisor mode and a privileged instruction is used, the result will be a jump to the privileged violation vector (located at memory address 20_{hex}). The μP is in the supervisor mode when bit 13 of the status register is set to a logic 1. This occurs after the $\overline{RESET}$ signal line to the μP is asserted.

16.2 | ADDRESSING MODES

Addressing modes are different ways the μP can reference an operand in one of its internal registers or in memory. The 68000 has six basic types of addressing modes: (1) register direct, (2) register indirect, (3) absolute, (4) immediate, (5) program counter, and (6) implied. These basic categories are subdivided into fourteen variations that are used by the programmer. The entire set of addressing modes is listed in Table 16.13.

The programmer of assembly language routines uses the instructions and the addressing modes to write efficient software routines. However, all addressing modes are not permitted with every instruction. Therefore, careful attention to the manufacturer's literature may be required when you are writing other than basic programs.

16.2.1 | Register Direct Modes

There are two addressing modes in this category: data register direct and address register direct.

Data Register Direct: This addressing mode specifies that the operand is located in one of the data registers. The effective address register field of the instruction specifies which data register. Figure 16.1 shows how the contents of two data registers can be added. The sum is placed back into one of the data registers.

FIGURE 16.1 | Example of Data Register Direct Addressing Mode and the μP's Machine Code

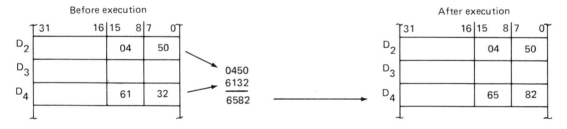

Assembler listing	Machine code in hex	Description
ADD.W D_2, D_4	D842	Add the contents of D_2 to the contents of D_4. The result is placed in D_4; the original data in D_4 is re-placed with the sum.

ADD·W [source], [destination]

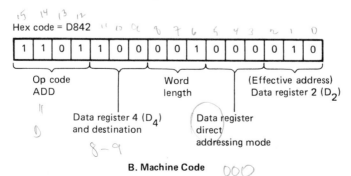

A. Data Register Direct Mode

Hex code = D842

| 1 | 1 | 0 | 1 | 1 | 0 | 0 | 0 | 0 | 1 | 0 | 0 | 0 | 0 | 1 | 0 |

Op code
ADD

Data register 4 (D_4)
and destination

Word
length

Data register
direct
addressing mode

(Effective address)
Data register 2 (D_2)

B. Machine Code

Address Register Direct: This addressing mode is similar to data register direct except that the operand is contained in one of the address registers. The effective address register field is specified in the instruction word. An example is shown in Figure 16.2.

16.2.2 | Register Indirect Modes

There are five addressing modes grouped together in this category: (1) address register indirect, (2) address register indirect with postincrement, (3) address register indirect with predecrement, (4) address register indirect with displacement, and (5) address register indirect with index and displacement.

FIGURE 16.2 | Example of Address Register Direct Addressing Mode and the μP's Machine Code

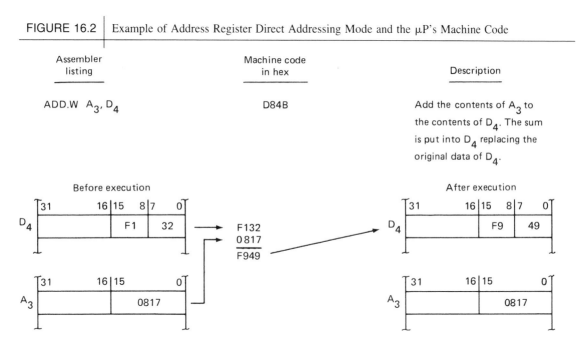

Assembler listing	Machine code in hex	Description
ADD.W A_3, D_4	D84B	Add the contents of A_3 to the contents of D_4. The sum is put into D_4 replacing the original data of D_4.

A. Address Register Direct Mode

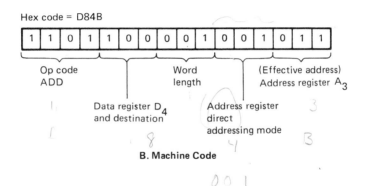

B. Machine Code

Address Register Indirect: In this addressing mode, the location of the operand is held in one of the address registers. The programmer specifies which register by placing it within parentheses. For example, (A_4) means that the contents of address register A_4 is used as a pointer to memory where the operand is located. An example is shown in Figure 16.3.

FIGURE 16.3 | Example of Address Register Indirect Addressing Mode and the µP's Machine Code

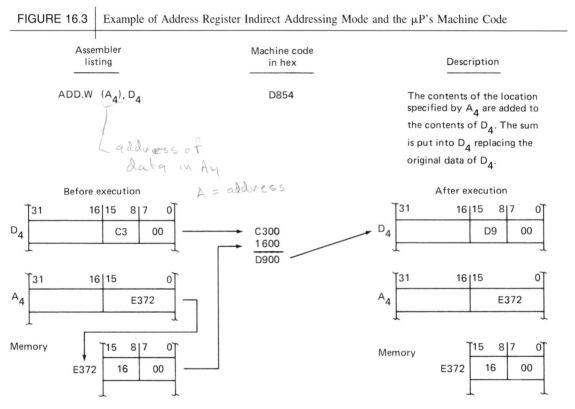

A. Address Register Indirect Mode

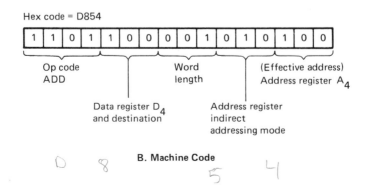

B. Machine Code

Address Register Indirect with Postincrement: This addressing mode is similar to the previous addressing mode except that, after the operand is fetched from memory, the contents of the address register are incremented. The 68000 μP has different incremental sizes depending on whether a byte, word, or long word instruction is specified. The contents of the address register are (1) incremented by one for a byte instruction, (2) incremented by two for a word instruction, and (3) incremented by four for a long word instruction.

The symbol $(A_6)+$ means that the contents of address register A_6 are used as a pointer to memory to locate the operand, after which the contents of A_6 are incremented. How much A_6 is incremented is given by the following instructions:

.B   byte instruction, increment by one

.W   word instruction, increment by two

.L   long word instruction, increment by four

Since many instructions are word length operations, the .W format is not always shown. The 68000 μP's assembler automatically defaults to word length operations. Therefore, the example given in Figure 16.4 could also have been written as ADD $(A_6)+$, D_4.

Address Register Indirect with Predecrement: In this addressing mode, the contents of the address register are first decremented. Then the contents are used as a pointer to memory. Depending on the instruction format, there are three decrement sizes: (1) decrement by one for a byte instruction, (2) decrement by two for a word instruction, and (3) decrement by four for a long word instruction.

The symbol $-(A_6)$ means that the contents of A_6 are decremented. The result is used as a pointer to memory to locate the operand. As for the postincrement procedure, the notations .B, .W, and .L following the instruction indicate how much the contents of the address register will be decremented. The default case (no notation) means decrement by two. See Figure 16.5 for an example.

Address Register Indirect with Displacement: In this addressing mode, the effective address is the sum of the contents of an address register and a displacement value. The displacement value, also called offset, is the second word of the instruction. The 68000 μP treats the displacement value as a 2's complement number. Thus, if bit 15 is a logic 0, the displacement value is positive; if bit 15 is a logic 1, the displacement value is negative. This treatment of the displacement gives a range of $\pm 32K$ bytes from the base address. Figure 16.6 shows how a displacement value of 10_{hex} is written in assembly language and how this type of addressing mode works.

Address Register Indirect with Index and Displacement: In this addressing mode, the effective address is the sum of three values: (1) the contents of an address register, (2) the contents of an index register, and (3) a displacement value. The index register can be any address or data register.

Figure 16.7 shows the format of the second word of the instruction. The second word contains the following information: (1) whether an address or data register is used, (2) which register is used for indexing, (3) how bits of the index register are used, and

FIGURE 16.4 | Example of Address Register Indirect with Postincrement and the μP's Machine Code

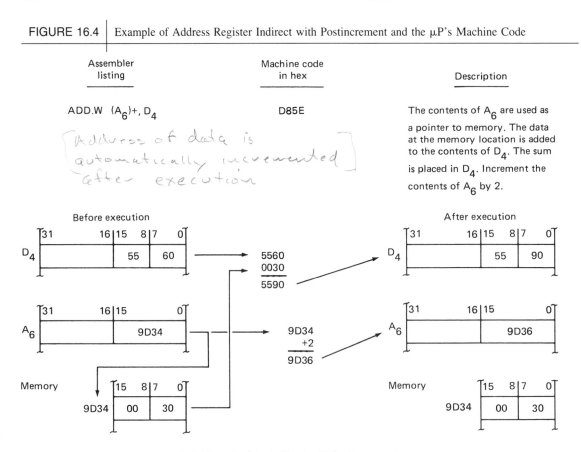

Assembler listing	Machine code in hex	Description
ADD.W $(A_6)+, D_4$	D85E	The contents of A_6 are used as a pointer to memory. The data at the memory location is added to the contents of D_4. The sum is placed in D_4. Increment the contents of A_6 by 2.

[Address of data is automatically incremented after execution]

A. Address Register Indirect with Postincrement

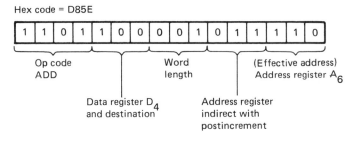

Hex code = D85E

| 1 | 1 | 0 | 1 | 1 | 0 | 0 | 0 | 0 | 1 | 0 | 1 | 1 | 1 | 1 | 0 |

Op code ADD

Word length

(Effective address) Address register A_6

Data register D_4 and destination

Address register indirect with postincrement

B. Machine Code

FIGURE 16.5 | Example of Address Register Indirect with Predecrement and the μP's Machine Code

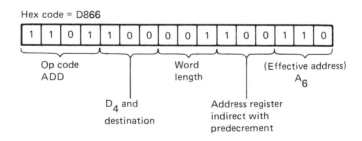

Assembler listing	Machine code in hex	Description
ADD $-(A_6)$, D_4	D866	Decrement the contents of A_6 by 2. Use the new contents of A_6 as a pointer to memory. The data at the memory location is added to the contents of D_4. The sum is placed in D_4.

Address of data is automatically decremented before execution

Before execution

D_4 | 31 ... 16|15 8|7 0 | 55 | 60

5560
0010
5570

A_6 | 31 ... 16|15 ... 0 | 9D34

9D34
-2
9D32

Memory 9D32 | 15 8|7 0 | 00 | 10

After execution

D_4 | 31 ... 16|15 8|7 0 | 55 | 70

A_6 | 31 ... 16|15 ... 0 | 9D32

Memory 9D32 | 15 8|7 0 | 00 | 10

A. Address Register Indirect with Predecrement

Hex code = D866

| 1 | 1 | 0 | 1 | 1 | 0 | 0 | 0 | 0 | 1 | 1 | 0 | 0 | 1 | 1 | 0 |

Op code
ADD

D_4 and
destination

Word
length

Address register
indirect with
predecrement

(Effective address)
A_6

B. Machine Code

FIGURE 16.6 | Example of Address Register Indirect with Displacement and the μP's Machine Code

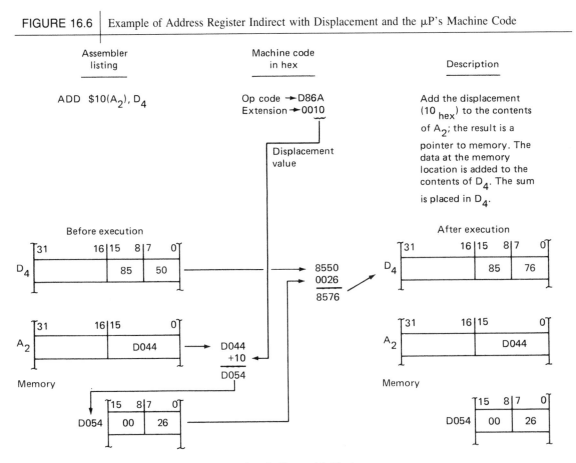

A. Address Register Indirect with Displacement

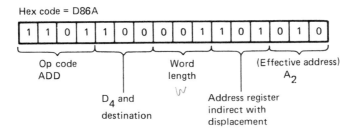

B. Machine Code

Even address = high byte
odd = low byte

FIGURE 16.7 | Format for the Second Word of an Instruction That Uses Indexing

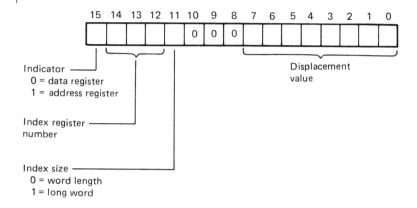

(4) the displacement value. In this type of addressing mode, the displacement value is restricted to an 8-bit signed number. If the index register is specified as word length, a 16-bit sign-extended integer is used when determining the effective address. Sign-extension notation is also used for the displacement value.

Figure 16.8 shows the example, ADD.W $2($A_2$, A_4.W), D_4. The format used by a 68000 μP assembler treats A_2 as the base address register and A_4 as the index register. Since .W follows the index register, 16 bits of A_4 are used in the calculation of the effective address.

16.2.3 | Absolute Data Modes

The two addressing modes in this category are the absolute short and the absolute long modes.

Absolute Short: In this addressing mode, the second word of the instruction is the effective address. Since a word is only 16 bits and the 68000 μP uses 24 bits for addressing, the most significant bit (MSB) is extended. This is called *sign extension* because the MSB is known as the sign bit. Thus, if bit 15 is a logic 0, the address range is from 000000 to 007FFF. If bit 15 is a logic 1, the address range is from FF8000 to FFFFFF. This addressing mode allows quick access to the first and last 32K bytes of memory, as illustrated in Figure 16.9. An example of this type of addressing mode is shown in Figure 16.10.

In the register direct and register indirect addressing modes, bits 3, 4, and 5 were used to indicate the type of addressing mode. The absolute, program counter, and immediate addressing modes use bits 0, 1, and 2, as shown in Figure 16.11. Bits 3, 4, and 5 are logic 1s.

Absolute Long: The long addressing mode requires two extension words following the operation word. This mode allows the programmer to access any location in the entire memory space. Figure 16.12 shows how a word at location 187400 is added to the contents of a data register.

FIGURE 16.8 | Example of Address Register Indirect with Index and Displacement and the μP's Machine Code for Both Instruction Words

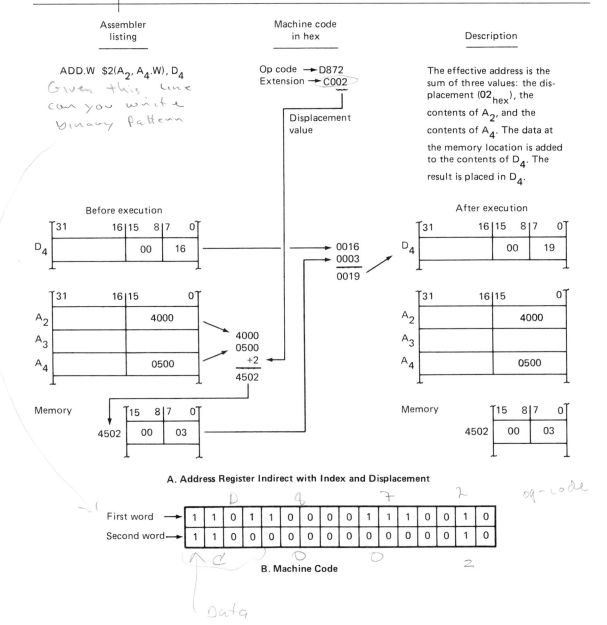

A. Address Register Indirect with Index and Displacement

B. Machine Code

FIGURE 16.9 | Memory Range for the Absolute Short Addressing Mode

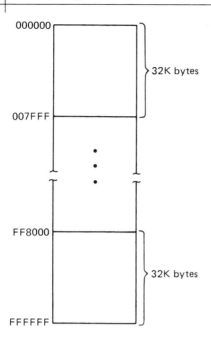

16.2.4 | Immediate Data Modes

The immediate addressing mode and the quick addressing mode are the two modes that are grouped in the immediate data addressing mode category.

Immediate: This addressing mode uses the extension word or words as an operand. The 68000 μP interprets the # sign as the immediate mode. Byte and word operations require only one extension word, while long words require two extension words. Figure 16.13 illustrates the extension word formats, and Figure 16.14 shows an example of the immediate addressing mode.

Quick: This mode is a modified version of the immediate addressing mode. The data is contained as part of the operation word. Bits 9, 10, and 11 are the data bits, as illustrated in Figure 16.15.

16.2.5 | Program Counter Modes

This addressing mode category includes two modes: program counter relative with displacement and program counter relative with index and displacement.

Program Counter Relative with Displacement: For this addressing mode, the location of the operand is calculated by adding the contents of the program counter and the extension word of the instruction. The addition is done by sign extending the 16-bit extension word.

FIGURE 16.10 | Example of Absolute Short Addressing Mode and the μP's Machine Code for the First Instruction Word

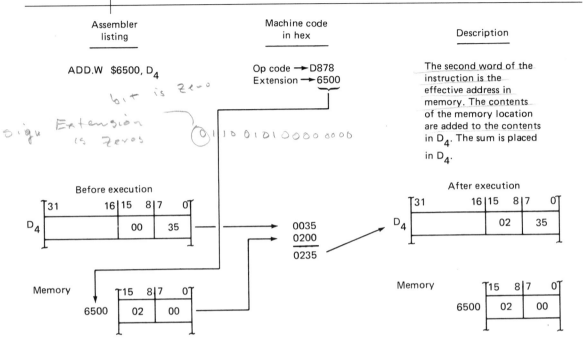

A. Absolute Short Addressing Mode

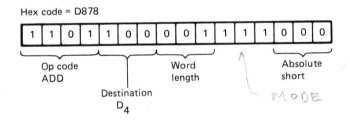

B. Machine Code

FIGURE 16.11 | Encoding Summary of Bits 0, 1, and 2 When Bits 3, 4, and 5 Are Logic 1s

15	14	13	12	11	10	9	8	7	6	5	4	3	2	1	0
										1	1	1			

0 0 0 = Absolute short
0 0 1 = Absolute long
0 1 0 = PC with displacement
0 1 1 = PC with index
1 0 0 = Immediate, or status register

FIGURE 16.12 | Example of Absolute Long Addressing Mode and the µP's Machine Code for the First Instruction Word

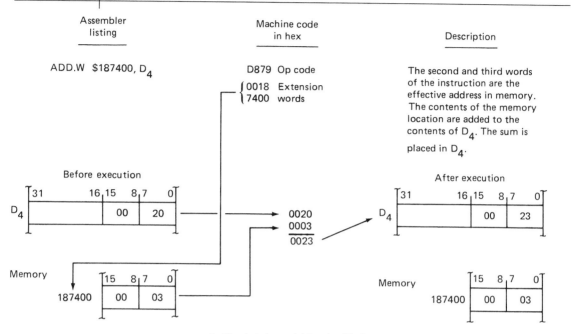

A. Absolute Long Addressing Mode

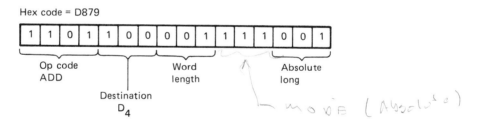

B. Machine Code

absolute long can address any
location in memory

absolute short can address
000000 - 007FFF and FF8000 to FFFFFF
uses sign extension

FIGURE 16.13 | Extension Word Formats for the Immediate Addressing Mode

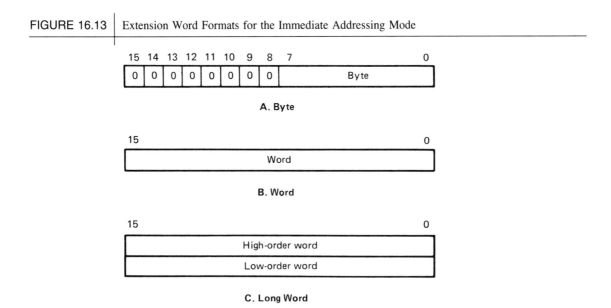

A. Byte

B. Word

C. Long Word

FIGURE 16.14 | Example of Immediate Addressing Mode and the μP's Machine Code for the First Instruction Word

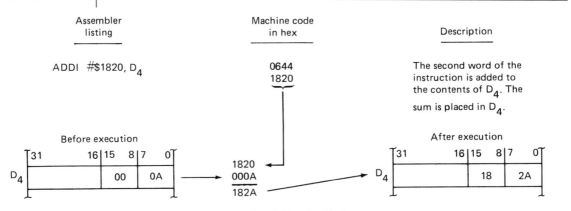

A. Immediate Addressing Mode

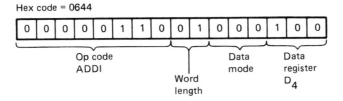

B. Machine Code

FIGURE 16.15 | Example of the Quick Addressing Mode and the μP's Machine Code

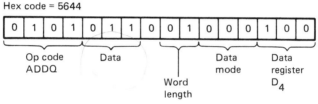

Assembler listing	Machine code in binary	Description
ADDQ #$3, D₄	0 1 0 1 011 0 01 000 100	The data at bits 9, 10, and 11 are added to the contents of D₄. The sum is placed in D₄.

Before execution

After execution

A. Quick Addressing Mode

Hex code = 5644

0	1	0	1	0	1	1	0	0	1	0	0	0	1	0	0

Op code
ADDQ

Data

Word
length

Data
mode

Data
register
D₄

B. Machine Code

The contents of the program counter is the address of the extension word. Figure 16.16 shows how the operand address is determined.

Program Counter with Index and Displacement: This address mode requires one extension word. The format of the extension word is shown in Figure 16.17. The operand address is the sum of the value in the program counter, the contents of the index register, and the sign-extended displacement value. The value in the program counter is the address of the extension word. Figure 16.17 illustrates how the operand address is calculated.

16.2.6 | Implied Mode

This addressing mode includes instructions that make implicit reference to the program counter, stack pointer (supervisor or user), or the status register. The μP knows from the op code which addresses and/or registers to use.

FIGURE 16.16 | Example of Program Counter Relative with Displacement Mode and the μP's Machine Code for the First Instruction Word

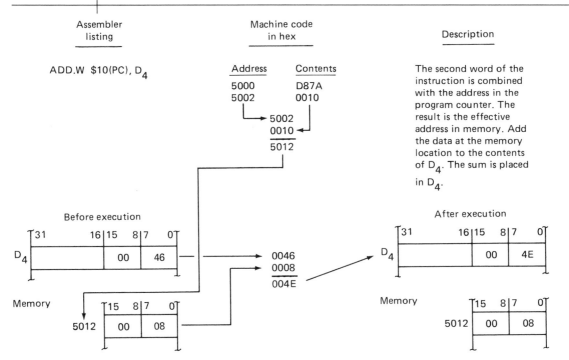

A. Program Counter Relative with Displacement Mode

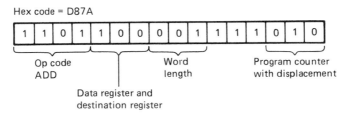

B. Machine Code

FIGURE 16.17 | Example of Program Counter Relative with Index and Displacement Mode and the Format for the Second Word of the Instruction

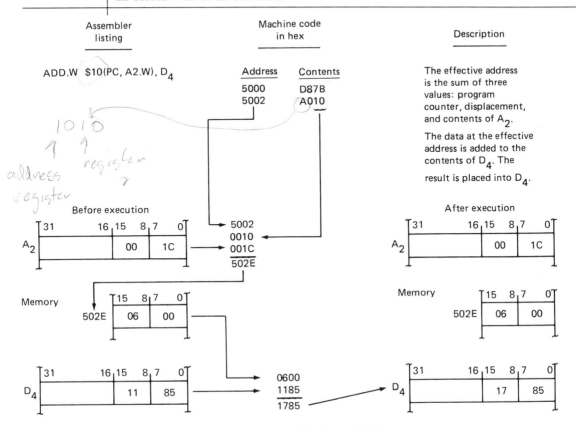

A. Program Counter Relative with Index and Displacement

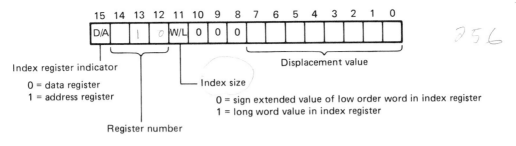

Index register indicator

0 = data register
1 = address register

Index size

0 = sign extended value of low order word in index register
1 = long word value in index register

Register number

B. Format for the Second Word

16.3 | USING THE 68000 MICROPROCESSOR INSTRUCTIONS

In Chapter 7, we used the 6800 μP instruction set to write a number of short programs for that microprocessor. This section contains seven short examples that use some of the 68000 μP instructions and addressing modes. The programs, for the most part, are written using absolute addresses instead of labels. Although this is consistent with Chapter 7, it is primarily done so the reader can concentrate on the instruction and the memory locations.

EXAMPLE

16.1

Write a program for the addition of two 16-bit numbers at locations $8000 and $8002. Store the result at location $9000. Use register D_0 for the addition.

Solution A:

```
MOVE.W $8000, D_0     Move first value into register D_0.
MOVE.W $8002, D_1     Move second value into register D_1.
ADD.W D_1, D_0        Add contents of D_0 and D_1, and place result into D_0.
MOVE.W D_0, $9000     Store sum into memory.
```

Solution A uses registers D_0 and D_1. However, the μP is capable of bringing the second value into the μP and adding it to the contents of D_0. The result is temporarily stored in D_0. Solution B shows an alternative method of adding two 16-bit numbers.

Solution B:

```
MOVE.W $8000, D_0     Move first value into register D_0.
ADD.W $8002, D_0      Add second value and contents of D_0. Result stored in D_0.
MOVE.W D_0, $9000     Store sum into memory.
```

Remember that the 68000 μP is capable of performing 8-, 16-, and 32-bit operations. Therefore, in the programs in Example 16.1, if the W suffix is changed to B or L, the μP will do 8- or 32-bit additions, respectively.

EXAMPLE

16.2

Write a program for the addition of two 64-bit numbers. Use registers D_0 and D_1 for the first value, and D_2 and D_3 for the second value. Consider that the first value is stored at locations $4000 and $4002. The second value is at locations $5000 and $5002. Store the result at $9000 and $9002.

Solution:
When data is stored in consecutive memory locations, the MOVEM instruction can be used.

```
MOVEM.L $4000, D_0-D_1     Move first value into D_0 and D_1.
MOVEM.L $5000, D_2-D_3     Move second value into D_2 and D_3.
```

ADD.L D_1, D_3	ADD $D_1 + D_3 \rightarrow D_3$.
ADDX.L D_0, D_2	ADD $D_0 + D_2 + X \rightarrow D_2$.
MOVEM.L D_2–D_3, \$9000	Store the sum into memory.

EXTEND BIT = carry bit for long words

The ADDX instruction in the program in Example 16.2 is needed to include the extend bit from the previous 32-bit addition. If the first value and the second value are held in eight consecutive locations beginning at \$4000, then the first two lines of the program can be combined into MOVEM.L \$4000, D_0–D_3.

EXAMPLE

16.3

Write a program for converting a string of 10 ASCII numbers to BCD, beginning at location \$5000. Store the BCD numbers in memory beginning at location \$6000.

Solution:

From the ASCII table of Figure 3.3, we see that if 30_{hex} is subtracted from the ASCII format, the numbers 0 to 9 are converted to BCD. This step is the key to the following program.

CLR D_0	Clear register D_0.
CLR D_2	Clear register D_2.
MOVE #9, D_2	Move count value -1 into register D_2.
MOVE A #\$5000, A_0	Move \$5000 into register A_0.
MOVE A #\$6000, A_1	Move \$6000 into register A_1.
NEXT: MOVE D_0, $(A_0)+$	Move ASCII character into D_0.
SUB #\$30, D_0	Subtract \$30 from ASCII value.
MOVE D_0, $(A_1)+$	Move BCD value into storage area.
DBRA D_2, NEXT	Branch to NEXT if not complete.

Post increment

The program in Example 16.3 assumes the eighth bit of the ASCII code is a logic 0; if the eighth bit should be a logic 1, subtract \$C0. A program that converts ASCII to BCD is usually only the first step for inputting data into the computer. The next step is to convert the BCD to straight binary. This conversion is shown in the next two examples.

EXAMPLE

16.4

Consider two BCD numbers stored at locations \$8000 and \$8002. Write a program for converting them to a single binary number. The most significant number is at \$8000. Store the result at location \$9000. Decimal 49 is stored as follows:

$$\$8000 = 04$$
$$\$8002 = 09$$

Solution:

The most significant number ($4 = 0100$) must be multiplied by $10_{decimal}$, and then the least significant number (9 $=$ 1001) is added. Let's use register D_0 for the arithmetic operations.

	CLR.L D_0	Clear register D_0.
	MOVEA.W #$8000, A_0	Move address $8000 into register A_0.
1.	MOVE.W $(A_0)+$, D_0	Move number into register D_0.
2.	MULU.W #10, D_0	Multiply contents of register D_0 by $10_{decimal}$.
3.	ADD.W (A_0), D_0	Add contents of $8002 to register D_0.
	MOVE.W D_0, $9000	Move the binary result to location $9000.

The next example shows how this program can be modified to convert a longer BCD number to binary. But first, let's examine steps 1–3 for the decimal number 49. For this example, the number would be stored as follows:

$8000 = 04$

$8002 = 09$

Step	Contents of Register D_0 after Instruction Is Executed
1.	0100
2.	101000
3.	110001

The result is $110001_{binary} = 49_{decimal}$.

EXAMPLE

16.5

Write a program for converting the four BCD numbers stored at locations $8000 to $8006 to a binary number. The most significant number is at $8000. Store the result at $9000. Decimal 4910 is stored as follows:

$8000 = 04$

$8002 = 09$

$8004 = 01$

$8006 = 00$

Solution:

Like the solution of Example 16.4, the most significant BCD values have to be multiplied in sequence by a factor of 10. For this example, and for conversion problems of longer BCD numbers, a counter is needed. Let's use register D_0 for the arithmetic operations and register D_2 as a counter.

CLR.L D_0	Clear register D_0.
CLR.L D_2	Clear register D_2.

```
              MOVEA.W #$8000, A_0     Move address $8000 into register A_0.
              MOVE #Count − 1, D_2    Count − 1 = 4 − 1 = 3.
              MOVE.W (A_0)+, D_0      Move a BCD number into D_0.
       NEXT:  MULU.W #10, D_0         Multiply contents of D_0 by 10_decimal.
              ADD.W D_0, (A_0)+       Add next BCD number.
              DBRA D_2, NEXT          Branch to NEXT unless count = −1.
              MOVE.W D_0, $9000       Store result.
              RTS                     Return from subroutine
```

The value Count − 1 to be put into register D_2 should be set up in the main program before the jump to subroutine is executed.

EXAMPLE

16.6

Write a program for the division of the 32-bit number stored at locations $4000 and $4002 by the 16-bit number stored at location $4004. Both numbers are unsigned. Store the remainder at location $6000 and the quotient at location $6002.

Solution:

```
MOVE.L $4000, D_0     Move contents of $4000 and $4002 to D_0.
DIVU $4004, D_0       Divide D_0 by contents of $4004.
MOVE.L D_0, $6000     Quotient and remainder are stored at $6000 and $6002,
                      respectively.
```

Note that when the 68000 μP executes a divide instruction, the remainder is placed in the 16 MSBs of the data register, and the quotient in the lower 16 bits of the data register. The MOVE.L instruction stores both 16 bits in consecutive word locations.

EXAMPLE

16.7

Write a program that performs the mathematical operation $N \times 2^n$ when both N and n are positive integers. Consider that N is a positive 32-bit number and n is a positive number less than $32_{decimal}$. Hence, this program raises a positive 32-bit number by 2^n. Use register D_0 to hold N and D_2 to hold n. The result is to be temporarily stored in registers D_0 and D_1 and then moved to memory locations $4500 and $4502, respectively. Consider the values N and n to be originally stored in memory locations $4000 and $4002 for N and $4004 for n. Register D_2 is used as a counter register.

Solution:

If the program is used as a subroutine, then the contents of registers D_0, D_1, and D_2 should be temporarily stored on the stack before the main portion of the subroutine. The contents of these registers must be returned before the RTS instruction.

```
              MOVE.L D_0, −(SP)     Save contents of D_0.
              MOVE.L D_1, −(SP)     Save contents of D_1.
              MOVE.L D_2, −(SP)     Save contents of D_2.
```

```
          MOVE.L $4000, D₀      Move N into D₀.
          MOVE.B $4004, D₂      Move n into D₂.
          CLR.L D₁              Clear the 32 bits of D₁.
LOOP: LSL.L #1, D₀             Shift left D₀ one bit (multiply by 2).
          ROXL.L #1, D₁         Shift carry from D₀ into D₁.
          SUB.I #1, D₂          Decrement n.
          BNE LOOP              Branch if not equal to LOOP.
          MOVE.L D₀, $4500      Store result left in D₀.
          MOVE.L D₁, $4502      Store result left in D₁.
          MOVE.L (SP)+, D₂      Restore contents of D₂.
          MOVE.L (SP)+, D₁      Restore contents of D₁.
          MOVE.L (SP)+, D₀      Restore contents of D₀.
          RTS
```

To show some of the power of the 68000 μP's instruction set, the first three move instructions could be replaced by a single move multiple register instruction. Therefore,

$$\begin{array}{l} \text{MOVE.L } D_0,\ -(SP) \\ \text{MOVE.L } D_1,\ -(SP) \qquad = \text{MOVEM.L } D_0/D_1/D_2,\ -(SP) \\ \text{MOVE.L } D_2,\ -(SP) \end{array}$$

Similarly, the last three move instructions could be rewritten as follows:

$$\begin{array}{l} \text{MOVE.L } (SP)+,\ D_2 \\ \text{MOVE.L } (SP)+,\ D_1 \qquad = \text{MOVEM.L } (SP)+,\ D_0/D_1/D_2 \\ \text{MOVE.L } (SP)+,\ D_0 \end{array}$$

When the MOVEM instruction is executed, the order of storing registers is from address register A_7 to address register A_0; then the contents from data register D_7 are transferred to data register D_0. When using the MOVEM instruction and the postincrement addressing mode, such as $(SP)+$, the order of transfer is from data register D_0 to data register D_7 and then from address register A_0 to address register A_7.

16.4 │ SUMMARY

This chapter introduced the 68000's basic instructions and addressing modes. There are fifty-six basic instructions and fourteen addressing modes. When these instructions are combined with the addressing modes and the fact that the μP can perform operations on bytes, words, and long words, there are over 1000 instructions. Although space in this text would not permit an example for every instruction possibility, there is at least one example for every type of addressing mode. These examples illustrate what happens when an instruction is executed.

The fifty-six basic instructions are grouped into eight categories: data movement, integer arithmetic, logical, shift and rotate, bit manipulation, binary coded decimal, program control, and system control. All I/O operations for the 68000 μP are done through memory-mapped I/O similar to what is done in a 6800 μP system.

Section 16.3 showed how to use some of the 68000 μP instructions in different programming applications. The programs have been written using absolute addresses to help in visualizing where data could come from in memory. Since there is no unique way of writing a program, the programs in this chapter have been written to illustrate some of the 68000's instruction flexibility.

16.5 | APPENDIX TO CHAPTER 16

TABLE 16.1 | Data Movement Instructions

Instruction	Description	Operand Size (Bits)	Operation
EXG	Exchange registers	32	Register X↔Register Y
LEA	Load effective address	32	Destination→Address register
LINK	Link and allocate	—	Address register→Stack pointer @ − Stack pointer→Address register Stack pointer plus displacement → Stack pointer
MOVE		See Table 16.2.	
PEA	Push effective address	32	Destination→Stack pointer @ −
SWAP	Swap register halves	32	Register [31:16]↔Register [15:0]
UNLK	Unlink	—	Address register→Stack pointer Stack pointer @ + →Address register

TABLE 16.2 | Variations of the MOVE Instruction

Instruction	Description	Operand Size (Bits)	Operation
MOVE	Move data from source to destination	8, 16, 32	(Source)→Destination
MOVEA	Move contents of source to an address register	16, 32	(Source)→Address register
MOVEM	Move multiple registers	16, 32	Registers→Destination or (Source)→Registers
MOVEP	Move peripheral data	16, 32	(Source)→Destination
MOVEQ	Move quick	32	Immediate data→Data register

TABLE 16.3 | Integer Arithmetic Instructions

Instruction	Description	Operand Size (Bits)	Operation
ADD	Add binary	8, 16, 32	(Source) + (destination) →Destination
ADDA	Add address	16, 32	(Source) + (destination address register) →Destination address register
ADDI	Add immediate	8, 16, 32	Immediate data + (destination) →Destination
ADDQ	Add quick	8, 16, 32	Immediate data + (destination) →Destination
ADDX	Add extended	8, 16, 32	(Source) + (destination) + X →Destination
CLR	Clear an operand	8, 16, 32	0→Destination
CMP	Compare	8, 16, 32	(Destination) − (Source)
CMPA	Compare address	16, 32	(Destination address register) − (Source)

TABLE 16.3 | Continued

Instruction	Description	Operand Size (Bits)	Operation
CMPI	Compare immediate	8, 16, 32	(Destination) − Immediate data
CMPM	Compare memory	8, 16, 32	(Destination) − (Source)
DIVS	Signed divide	$\frac{32}{16} \to 32$	(Destination)/(source) →Destination
DIVU	Unsigned divide	$\frac{32}{16} \to 32$	(Destination)/(source) →Destination
EXT	Sign extend	16, 32	(Destination) sign extended →Destination
MULS	Signed multiply	16×16 →32	(Source) × (destination) →Destination
MULU	Unsigned multiply	16×16 →32	(Source) × (destination) →Destination
NEG	Negate	8, 16, 32	0 − (destination)→Destination
NEGX	Negate with extend	8, 16, 32	0 − (destination) − X→Destination
SUB	Subtract binary	8, 16, 32	(Destination) − (source) →Destination
SUBA	Subtract address	16, 32	(Destination address register) − (source)→(Destination address register)
SUBI	Subtract immediate	8, 16, 32	(Destination) − immediate data →Destination
SUBQ	Subtract quick	8, 16, 32	(Destination) − immediate data within op code→Destination
SUBX	Subtract with extent	8, 16, 32	(Destination) − (source) − X →Destination
TAS	Test and set an operand	8	(Destination) tested→CC then 1→Bit 7 of destination
TST	Test an operand	8, 16, 32	(Destination) tested→CC

TABLE 16.4 | Logical Instructions

Instruction	Description	Operand Size (Bits)	Operation
AND	Logical AND	8, 16, 32	(Source)$\wedge$(destination) $\rightarrow$(Destination)
ANDI	AND immediate	8, 16, 32	Immediate data$\wedge$(destination) $\rightarrow$(Destination)
ANDI to CCR	AND immediate to condition code register	8	(Source)$\wedge$CCR$\rightarrow$CCR
ANDI to SR	AND immediate to status register*	16	Supervisor mode: (Source)$\wedge$SR$\rightarrow$SR User mode: TRAP
OR	Inclusive logical OR	8, 16, 32	(Source)$\vee$(destination) $\rightarrow$(Destination)
ORI	Inclusive OR immediate	8, 16, 32	Immediate data$\vee$(destination) $\rightarrow$(Destination)
ORI to CCR	Inclusive OR immediate to condition code register	8	(Source)$\vee$CCR$\rightarrow$CCR
ORI to SR	Inclusive OR immediate to status register*	16	Supervisor mode: (Source)$\vee$SR$\rightarrow$SR User mode: TRAP
EOR	Exclusive logical OR	8, 16, 32	(Source) $\oplus$ (destination) $\rightarrow$(Destination)
EORI	Exclusive logical OR immediate	8, 16, 32	Immediate data $\oplus$ (destination) $\rightarrow$(Destination)
EORI to CCR	Exclusive OR immediate to condition code register	8	(Source) $\oplus$ CCR$\rightarrow$CCR
EORI to SR	Exclusive OR immediate to status register*	16	Supervisor mode: (Source) $\oplus$ SR$\rightarrow$SR User mode: TRAP
NOT	1's complement of the destination operand	8, 16, 32	$\sim$(Destination)$\rightarrow$Destination

Note: The symbol $\sim$ means invert.   *Privilege instruction.

TABLE 16.5 | Shift and Rotate Instructions

Instruction	Description	Operand Size (Bits)	Operation
ASL	Arithmetic shift left	8, 16, 32	
ASR	Arithmetic shift right	8, 16, 32	
LSL	Logical shift left	8, 16, 32	
LSR	Logical shift right	8, 16, 32	
ROL	Rotate left	8, 16, 32	
ROR	Rotate right	8, 16, 32	
ROXL	Rotate left with extend	8, 16, 32	
ROXR	Rotate right with extend	8, 16, 32	

TABLE 16.6 | Bit Manipulation Instructions

Instruction	Description	Operand Size (Bits)	Operation
BTST	Test a bit	8, 32	$\sim$(Bit of destination)$\rightarrow$Z
BSET	Test a bit and set	8, 32	$\sim$(Bit of destination)$\rightarrow$Z 1$\rightarrow$Bit of destination
BCLR	Test a bit and clear	8, 32	$\sim$(Bit of destination)$\rightarrow$Z 0$\rightarrow$Bit of destination
BCHG	Test a bit and change	8, 32	$\sim$(Bit of destination)$\rightarrow$Z $\sim$(Bit of destination)$\rightarrow$Bit of destination

Note: The symbol $\sim$ means invert.

TABLE 16.7 | Binary Coded Decimal Instructions

Instruction	Description	Operand Size (Bits)	Operation
ABCD	Add decimal with extend	8	$(\text{Source})_{10} + (\text{destination})_{10} + X$ $\rightarrow$Destination
SBCD	Subtract decimal with extend	8	$(\text{Destination})_{10} - (\text{source})_{10} - X$ $\rightarrow$Destination
NBCD	Negate decimal with extend	8	$0 - (\text{destination})_{10} - X$ $\rightarrow$Destination

TABLE 16.8 | Conditional Branch Instructions

Instruction	Description	Displacement Size (Bits)	Operation
B_{CC}	Branch conditionally	8, 16	If condition is true, then PC + $d*\to$PC; otherwise, next instruction
DB_{CC}	Test condition, decrement, and branch	16	
S_{CC}	Set according to condition	8	If condition is true, then 1s $\to$Destination; otherwise, 0s$\to$Destination

*d is the displacement value.

TABLE 16.9 | Unconditional Branch, Jump, and Return Instructions

Instruction	Description	Displacement Size (Bits)	Operation
BRA	Branch always	8, 16	PC + $d*\to$PC
BSR	Branch to subroutine	8, 16	PC$\to -$(SP) then PC + $d\to$PC
JMP	Jump	—	Destination$\to$PC
JSR	Jump to subroutine	—	PC$\to -$(SP) then Destination$\to$PC

TABLE 16.9 | Unconditional Branch, Jump, and Return Instructions

| RTR | Return and restore condition codes | — | $(SP)+\to CC$ then $(SP)+\to PC$ |
| RTS | Return from subroutine | — | $(SP)+\to PC$ |

*d is the displacement value.

TABLE 16.10 | System Control Privileged Instructions

Instruction	Description	Displacement Size (Bits)	Operation
ANDI to SR	AND immediate to the status register	16	If in supervisor state, then $(Source)\wedge SR\to SR$; else, TRAP
EORI to SR	Exclusive OR immediate to the status register	16	If in supervisor state, then $(Source)\oplus SR\to SR$; else, TRAP
MOVE EA to SR	Move effective address to the status register	16	If in supervisor state, then $(Source)\to SR$; else, TRAP
MOVE USP	Move user stack pointer	32	If in supervisor state, then $USP\to A_n$ $A_n\to USP$; else, TRAP
ORI to SR	OR immediate to the status register	16	If in supervisor state, then $(Source)\vee SR\to SR$; else, TRAP
RESET	Reset external devices	—	If in supervisor state, then Assert $\overline{RESET}$ line; else, TRAP
RTE	Return from exception	—	If in supervisor state, then $(SP)+\to SR$ $(SP)+\to PC$; else, TRAP
STOP	Load status register and stop	—	If in supervisor state, then Immediate data$\to SR$ STOP; else, TRAP

TABLE 16.11 | System Control Trap Instructions

Instruction	Description	Displacement Size (Bits)	Operation
CHK	Check data register against upper bounds	16	If $D_n < 0$ or $D_n >$ Effective address then TRAP
TRAP	Trap	—	PC→−(SSP) SR→−(SSP) (Vector)→PC
TRAPV	Trap on overflow	—	If V flag is a logic 1, then TRAP

TABLE 16.12 | System Status Register Instructions

Instruction	Description	Displacement Size (Bits)	Operation
ANDI to CCR	AND immediate to condition code register	8	(Source)$\wedge$CCR→CCR
EORI to CCR	Exclusive OR immediate to condition code register	8	(Source)$\oplus$CCR→CCR
MOVE EA to CCR	Move effective address to condition code register	16	(Source)→CCR
MOVE SR to EA	Move status register to effective address	16	SR→Destination
ORI to CCR	OR immediate to condition code register	8	(Source)$\vee$CCR→CCR

TABLE 16.13 | Addressing Mode Groups

Addressing Modes	Example
Register direct	
Data register direct	Figure 16.1
Address register direct	Figure 16.2
Register indirect	
Address register indirect	Figure 16.3
Address register indirect	Figure 16.4
with postincrement	
Address register indirect	Figure 16.5
with predecrement	
Address register indirect	Figure 16.6
with displacement	
Address register indirect	Figure 16.7
with index and displacement	
Absolute data	
Absolute short	Figure 16.8
Absolute long	Figure 16.9
Immediate data	
Immediate	Figure 16.10
Quick	Figure 16.11
Program counter	
Program counter relative	Figure 16.12
with displacement	
Program counter relative	Figure 16.13
with index and displacement	
Implied	
Implied register	Figure 16.14

PROBLEMS

16.1 Refer to Figure 16.1 and determine the contents of D_4 for each of the following instructions:

   (a) MOVE.W D_2, D_4

   (b) MOVE.B D_2, D_4

   (c) OR.W D_2, D_4

16.2 If the instruction in Figure 16.2 is changed to ADD.B A_3, D_4, what is the result stored in D_4?

16.3 How should the instruction in Figure 16.2 be written if the result is to be put into register A_3?

16.4 Refer to Figure 16.3. If the instruction is changed to ADD.W D_4, (A_4), show the contents of D_4, A_4, and the memory location after the instruction is executed.

16.5 Determine the contents of D_4 in Figure 16.3 for each of the following instructions:
   (a)   ADD.B (A_4), D_4
   (b)   AND.W (A_4), D_4
   (c)   SUB.W (A_4), D_4
   (d)   MOVE.W (A_4), D_4

16.6 Determine the contents of D_4, A_6, and memory location 9D34 in Figure 16.4 for each of the following instructions:
   (a)   EOR.W $(A_6)+$, D_4
   (b)   ADD.B D_4, $(A_6)+$
   (c)   OR.B $(A_6)+$, D_4

16.7 Consider the instruction given in Figure 16.5 is followed by the instruction given in Figure 16.6. Determine the final result stored in D_4. The initial condition for D_4 is given in Figure 16.5. The instructions are:
   ADD $-(A_6)$, D_4
   ADD $10(A_2)$, D_4

16.8 If the instructions in Problem 16.7 are interchanged, determine the final result stored in D_4. The initial condition for D_4 is given in Figure 16.6. The instruction sequence is:
   ADD $10(A_2)$, D_4
   ADD $-(A_6)$, D_4

16.9 Consider the data given in Figure 16.8. If the instruction format is changed from .W to .B, would the final result stored in D_4 be the same? Give the reason for your answer.

16.10 For each of the following instructions, is the effective address in the first or last 32K bytes of memory?
   (a)   AND.W $4FFE, D_1
   (b)   SUB.B $940C, D_3
   (c)   MOVE.L $56F2, D_4
   (d)   ADD.W $7340, D_7
   (e)   OR.W $E000, D_2

16.11 If the extension words in Figure 16.12A are interchanged, determine the effective address.

16.12 Refer to Figure 16.13. If the instruction is changed to SUBI #$1820, D_4, determine the final result stored in D_4. After this instruction is executed, is the carry flag bit set or cleared?

16.13 What is the maximum data value that can be contained in a quick addressing mode instruction?

16.14 Which instructions use the quick addressing mode?

16.15 What is the range of the displacement for an instruction using the program counter relative with displacement addressing mode?

16.16 What is the range of the displacement value for an instruction using the program counter relative with index and displacement addressing mode?

16.17 Show how the move multiple registers instruction can be used in Example 16.1.

16.18 Refer to Example 16.3. If the program is written as a general subroutine, which instructions should be changed from using absolute values to labels?

16.19 The four BCD numbers of Example 16.5 are stored in four consecutive word locations. If the leading zeros were removed, could the four BCD numbers be stored at a single memory location? Explain the reason for your answer.

Because each memory location is 2 bytes each BCD number is 4 bits

CHAPTER

17 | Interfacing the 68000 Microprocessor

17.0 | INTRODUCTION

This chapter deals with interconnecting the 68000 μP to memory and peripherals. The 68000 normally is used in applications requiring large memory arrays. As pointed out in Chapter 9, large memory arrays are constructed using dynamic memories (DRAMs) because of their high bit capacity and low power consumption. Sections 17.1 through 17.5 discuss how the 68000 μP can be connected to dynamic memories and how they operate.

Since peripheral devices are the CPU's link to the outside world, the 68000 μP needs these interface devices. Many 68000 μP applications use the 6800 μP's peripherals, and Section 17.6 shows how these devices are used with the 68000 μP.

17.1 | MCM6665A DYNAMIC RAM

The MCM6665A is a 65,536-bit dynamic RAM. It is organized as 65,536 words × 1 bit. Therefore, by interconnecting eight of these devices, 64K of memory can be added to a μC system. This memory chip requires only +5 V to operate. Each memory cell is designed using a single transistor, and each cell has to be refreshed within 2 ms. The device is housed in a 16-pin dual-in-line package, as shown in Figure 17.1. The figure also gives the pin assignments and names.

Note that there are only eight address pins, which would usually indicate that there can be only 256 ($2^8 = 256$) memory locations within the device. Manufacturers have designed dynamic memories, however, so that each address pin is used twice. This accounts for the 65,536 ($2^{16} = 65,536$) words within the memory chip. First, a row address is sent to the memory chip through the eight address pins, and then a column address is sent to the memory chip through the same address pins. This requires a controller IC to be connected between the μP and the dynamic RAMs. Therefore, when dynamic RAMs are added to a μC system, we must consider two items that did not exist with static RAMs—a controller IC and refresh cycles.

FIGURE 17.1 | Pin Designations for the MCM6665A Dynamic RAM (Redrawn with permission of Motorola Incorporated, Austin, Texas)

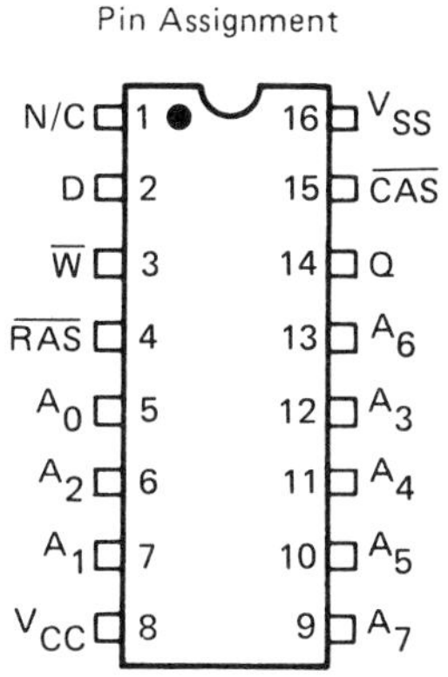

Pin Assignment

```
         N/C ⊏ 1  ⌣ 16 ⊐ V_SS
           D ⊏ 2     15 ⊐ CAS
           W̅ ⊏ 3     14 ⊐ Q
         RAS̅ ⊏ 4     13 ⊐ A_6
          A_0 ⊏ 5    12 ⊐ A_3
          A_2 ⊏ 6    11 ⊐ A_4
          A_1 ⊏ 7    10 ⊐ A_5
         V_CC ⊏ 8     9 ⊐ A_7
```

Pin Names	
A_0–A_7	Address input
D	Data in
Q	Data out
$\overline{W}$	Read/write input
$\overline{RAS}$	Row address strobe
$\overline{CAS}$	Column address strobe
V_{CC}	Power (+5 V)
V_{SS}	Ground

17.2 | DYNAMIC MEMORY CONTROLLER

Most new dynamic memory controllers are designed to be used with either 16K, 64K, or 256K dynamic RAMs. LSI technology allows controllers to be housed in 40- or 48-pin dual-in-line packages. Figure 17.2 shows a typical logic diagram for a controller. It contains (1) address latches; (2) a multiplexer; (3) an address refresh generator, also called a refresh address counter; (4) a row address strobe, RAS, decoder; (5) a column address strobe, CAS, buffer; and (6) a read/write, R/$\overline{W}$, buffer. Let's investigate how the internal parts of the controller work and how it is interfaced between the μP and memory arrays. See Figure 17.3.

Address Inputs A_0–A_7:   Often the controller chip is purchased from a different manufacturer than the μP, so the user must learn how to connect the μP to the controller. The controller's address inputs usually are labeled A_0–A_7 and are wired to the μP's lower eight address lines. Remember, however, that the 68000 does not have an A_0 line; therefore, the controller's A_0–A_7 pins are connected to the 68000's A_1–A_8 lines. When the address information on the controller's A_0–A_7 is sent to the RAM chips, it will be used by the memory chips as a row address. Remember, too, from Chapter 9, the term *row address* refers to a row of memory cells within the RAM chips.

Address Inputs A_8–A_{15}:   These address input pins are wired to the 68000's address lines A_9–A_{16}. The address information on these lines will be sent to the memory chips and be used by them to identify a particular column of cells within the memory chip.

Address Latch Enable: This pin latches the addresses coming from the μP. When the line is high, information from the μP is brought into the controller; this condition is referred to as the *transparent state*. When the latch input line goes low, all incoming information is latched. For 68000 μP operation, this pin is wired to the $\overline{AS}$ line.

FIGURE 17.2 | Typical Block Diagram of a Dynamic Memory Controller

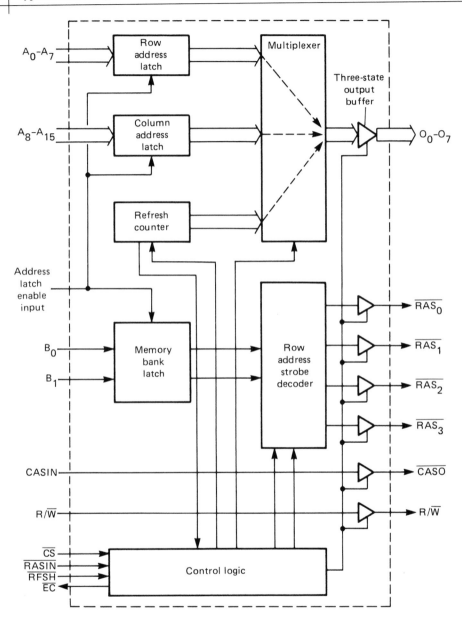

FIGURE 17.3 | Dynamic Memory System

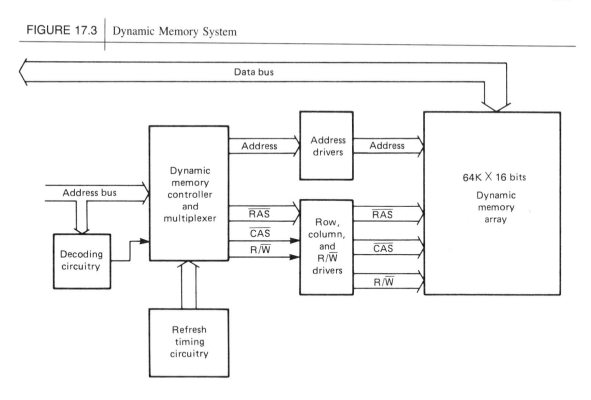

Address Outputs (O_0-O_7): These pins are the controller's outputs, which are connected to the RAM's address pins. Although these lines have output buffers, usually there are external line drivers connected between the controller and the memory chips, as shown in Figure 17.3. External line drivers provide extra drive capability. Information on the output lines comes either from the row address input latch, column address input latch, or the refresh counter.

Chip Select ($\overline{CS}$): The logic level on this pin controls the three-state capability of the address output (O_0-O_8) lines, row and column address strobe lines, and the read/write line. When the chip select line is high, all outputs are in their high impedance state. The output lines are enabled when $\overline{CS}$ is low.

Row Address Strobe ($\overline{RAS}_0-\overline{RAS}_3$): These output lines are used to select one of four memory banks. Which line goes low depends on the binary pattern on the bank select inputs, the refresh line, and the row address strobe input. See Table 17.1. Note when the refresh line and row address strobe input line go low, all $\overline{RAS}$ lines go low. This allows the same memory cell row in every bank to be refreshed at the same time. During a refresh operation, the decoder is said to change from a one-of-four to a four-of-four.

Bank Select Pins (B_0-B_1): The logic levels on these pins are decoded to select one of the row address strobe lines. See Table 17.1.

TABLE 17.1 | Row Address Strobe Function Table

$\overline{RFSH}$	$\overline{RASIN}$	B_1	B_0	$\overline{RAS_3}$	$\overline{RAS_2}$	$\overline{RAS_1}$	$\overline{RAS_0}$
H	L	L	L	H	H	H	L
H	L	L	H	H	H	L	H
H	L	H	L	H	L	H	H
H	L	H	H	L	H	H	H
L	H	X	X	H	H	H	H
L	L	X	X	L	L	L	L

Row Address Strobe Input ($\overline{RASIN}$):   During normal CPU read or write operations, one of the four row select output lines will be active when $\overline{RASIN}$ goes low. During the refresh operation, all of the row address strobe lines are active when this line is active. See Table 17.1.

Column Address Strobe Input ($\overline{CASIN}$):   During normal CPU read or write operations, an active low in $\overline{CASIN}$ causes $\overline{CASO}$ to go low. During the refresh operation, the logic level on $\overline{CASIN}$ is a don't-care condition. See Table 17.2.

Column Address Strobe Output ($\overline{CASO}$):   An active low on this line indicates to the dynamic RAMs that the information on O_0–O_8 should be latched into the RAM's column decoder. The $\overline{CASO}$ line is inhibited if the refresh line is low. See Table 17.2.

Read/Write Input and Output: Many dynamic memory controllers provide buffering for the system's read/write line. This capability also allows the R/$\overline{W}$ output signal to be synchronized with the $\overline{CASO}$ line.

Refresh ($\overline{RFSH}$):   This input line inhibits the $\overline{CASO}$ line, as shown in Table 17.2, and changes the row address decoder from one-of-four to four-of-four, as shown in Table 17.1. The $\overline{RFSH}$ line also switches the multiplexer from one of the address latches to the refresh counter. The refresh counter may be advanced (or decremented, depending on the design) whenever the $\overline{RFSH}$ line goes from low to high. In burst mode refreshing, the $\overline{RFSH}$ line is held low and the $\overline{RASIN}$ line is toggled.

End of Count ($\overline{EC}$):   A low on this line indicates that the refresh counter contains all zeros. In burst operation, this line indicates that the counter has sequenced through its count.

TABLE 17.2 | Column Address Strobe Function Table

$\overline{RFSH}$	$\overline{CASIN}$	$\overline{CASO}$
H	H	H
H	L	L
L	X	H

FIGURE 17.4 | Timing Diagram for a Read Operation of the MCM6665A

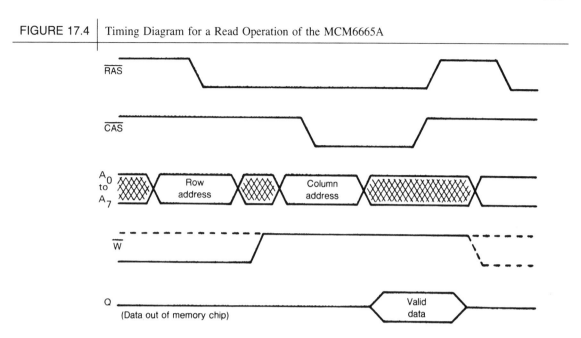

17.3 | READ OPERATION

Remember that the terms *read* and *write* always refer to the μP reading (receiving) or writing (sending) data, not to what the memory chips are doing. When the μP is reading data from memory, the memory chips are sending the data.

Dynamic memory chips receive two addresses, the row address and the column address. Which one is being received depends on the logic levels of the $\overline{RAS}$ and $\overline{CAS}$ lines. Figure 17.4 shows the timing diagram for the read operation. The figure shows that when $\overline{RAS}$ is low and $\overline{CAS}$ is high, the memory chips are receiving a row address. When both $\overline{RAS}$ and $\overline{CAS}$ lines are low, the column address is being received. With the $\overline{W}$ line high, the data becomes valid on the data bus after a specified time delay (the length of the time delay depends on the device used). The row address and column address strobe lines come from the dynamic memory controller chip.

17.4 | WRITE OPERATION

The process the μP goes through to write data to a dynamic memory is similar to the read process. The timing diagram for the write operation is shown in Figure 17.5. The exception, of course, is the logic level of the read/write line. Figure 17.5 shows that after the $\overline{W}$ line goes low, the memory chip is able to receive valid data.

FIGURE 17.5 | Timing Diagram for a Write Operation of the MCM6665A

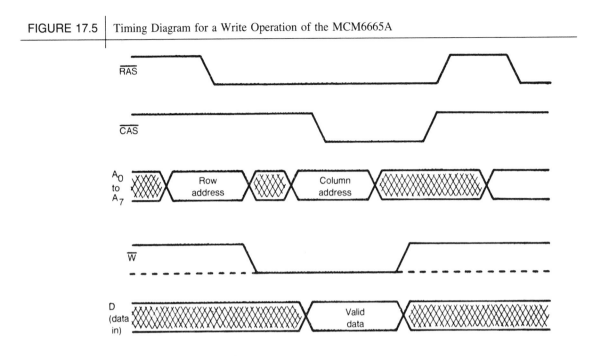

17.5 | DYNAMIC REFRESH

In order to keep the capacity of a dynamic memory cell charged to its logic state, a refresh signal is required. Each cell of the MCM6665A has to be refreshed within 2 ms. Dynamic memories are designed so that all the cells in a row are refreshed at the same time. In the MCM6665A, a row consists of 256 cells, and there are 256 rows. As a check:

$$256 \text{ cells per row} \times 256 \text{ rows} = 65,536 \text{ cells}$$

For this device, however, two rows are refreshed in one cycle. Therefore, all cells are refreshed by sequentially cycling through 128 row addresses on lines A_0 to A_6. Note that the logic level on line A_7 is not used during the refresh cycle.

There are different techniques for refreshing. One method is to have the μP wait and refresh all rows within a short period of time; this is called *burst mode refresh*. Another method is to refresh one row when the μP is not addressing memory; this is called *hidden refresh*. Although hidden refresh increases program execution time, it does require additional circuitry. Thus there is a trade-off of speed versus cost. In this text we will concentrate on the burst mode operation.

Figure 17.6 shows the timing diagram for the $\overline{\text{RAS}}$-only refresh cycle. The data-in and write are don't-care conditions and are not shown. The $\overline{\text{CAS}}$ line is high. When the $\overline{\text{CAS}}$ line is high and the $\overline{\text{RAS}}$ line goes from a logic 0 to a logic 1 and back to a logic 0, the memory device senses that a refresh cycle is to be done. The binary pattern

FIGURE 17.6 | Timing Diagram for $\overline{\text{RAS}}$-Only Refresh Cycle of the MCM6665A

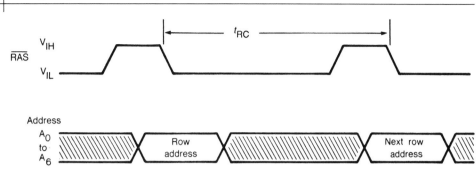

on the memory chip's address pins, A_0 to A_6, defines two row addresses. All the cells in both rows will be refreshed.

A typical cycle time, t_{RC}, is 250 ns. This is the time required to refresh both rows. Therefore, to refresh through a count of 128 takes the following time:

$$250 \text{ ns} \times 128 = 32 \text{ } \mu s$$

Thus, out of every 2 ms, these memory devices require 32 μs to be refreshed. In terms of percentage, we have the following:

$$\frac{32 \text{ } \mu s}{2 \text{ ms}} = 0.016, \text{ or } 1.6\%$$

Note: All memory chips in the system are refreshed in the same 32 μs. The remaining time, 1.968 ms (2 ms − 32 μs) or 98.4%, can be used for normal program execution. The 1.6% is the overhead for burst mode refresh, or the percentage of time lost by the μP for executing instructions.

17.6 | INTERFACING A 68000 MICROPROCESSOR TO 6800 PERIPHERALS

Many peripheral chips have been designed for the 6800 μP. Chapter 11 listed most of them. In order for the 68000 μP to gain wide popularity, it had to be easily interfaced with the 6800 peripherals. Otherwise, the 68000 would have no easy way of communicating with peripheral equipment. The problem that arose for the μP designers was that the 68000 would be an asynchronous device, while all the 6800 peripherals were synchronous devices. The difference is that for an asynchronous device, the μP automatically inserts wait states until it receives a data transfer acknowledge signal, after which it can begin the next cycle. Synchronous devices, however, require the data to be transferred within a specific time. Otherwise, the data will be lost. The advantage of an asynchronous μP is that it can begin the next cycle as soon as data has been transferred. This type of operation not only speeds up the data throughput, but also allows the μP to be connected to a variety of memory chips with different access times. Therefore, for the 68000 μP to modify its internal operation and interface easily with 6800 peripherals, the designers added three control lines. They are $\overline{VPA}$ (valid peripheral address), $\overline{VMA}$ (valid memory address), and E (enable).

The $\overline{VPA}$ signal is an input signal to the μP. It must be generated whenever a 68000 peripheral device is addressed. Therefore, external decoding circuitry used by the peripheral devices generates the $\overline{VPA}$ signal. After receiving a $\overline{VPA}$ signal, the 68000 sends out the $\overline{VMA}$ signal. The $\overline{VMA}$ signal signifies that the address on the address bus is a valid 6800 peripheral address. Now the transfer of data between the μP and the peripheral device is synchronized with the enable, E, pulse.

17.6.1 | Read Operation

Figure 17.7 shows the timing diagrams for a 68000 μP reading data from a 6800 peripheral device. The 68000's address lines are in their high impedance during state zero (S_0). In

---

FIGURE 17.7 | Timing Diagram for a 68000 μP Reading Data from a 6800 Peripheral Device (Redrawn with permission of Motorola Incorporated, Austin, Texas)

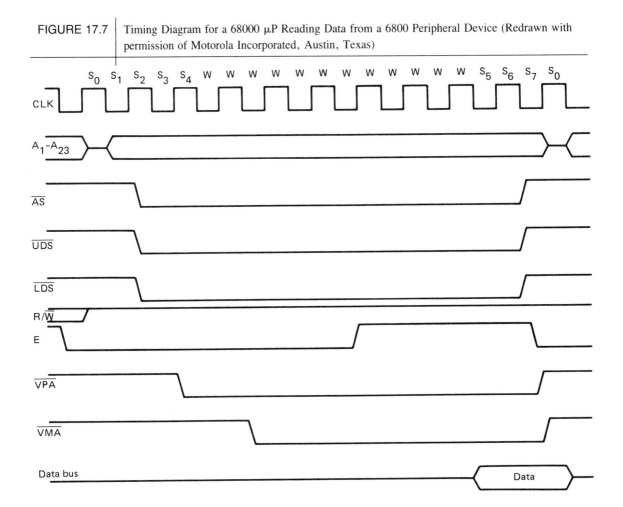

state one (S_1), the μP places an address on the address bus. During state two (S_2), the address strobe line goes low. This control signal indicates that there is a valid address on the address bus. Also, during S_2, the upper and/or lower data strobe ($\overline{\text{UDS}}$, $\overline{\text{LDS}}$) lines go low. During these states, the read/write line remains high.

The μP would now insert wait states until it recognizes either a $\overline{\text{DTACK}}$ or a $\overline{\text{VPA}}$ signal. Since we are interfacing a 68000 μP to a 6800 peripheral, most designs would have the external hardware on the I/O board return a $\overline{\text{VPA}}$ signal. The hardware circuitry that generates the $\overline{\text{VPA}}$ signal does so by decoding the address bus. This point is covered in Section 17.6.3. Note that the $\overline{\text{DTACK}}$ and $\overline{\text{VPA}}$ lines never should be low at the same time. This is because the μP would not know whether an asynchronous job is being completed or a synchronous job is being started.

After the 68000 recognizes the $\overline{\text{VPA}}$ signal and if the enable (E) line is low, the μP brings the $\overline{\text{VMA}}$ line low. If the E line is not low, or if there are not at least two clock cycles remaining before the E line goes high, the μP will wait before bringing the $\overline{\text{VMA}}$ line low. The $\overline{\text{VMA}}$ signal now can be used to generate a chip select signal to the I/O device.

During S_6, the μP latches the data. During S_7, the address and data strobe lines go high and the enable line goes low. The next half clock cycle, which is S_0 (state zero) again, is when the address bus goes to its high impedance state. Figure 17.8 shows a flowchart for the 68000 μP reading data from a 6800 peripheral device.

17.6.2 | Write Operation

The timing diagrams for a 68000 μP writing data to a 6800 peripheral device are shown in Figure 17.9. Comparing Figure 17.7 with Figure 17.9, you can see that many of the transitions occur during the same states. For example, the address bus is in its high impedance state during state zero (S_0) and a valid address occurs during state one (S_1). Similar to a read operation, the address strobe line goes low during S_2. Note however that the data strobe lines do not change; they wait until S_4. The reasons for this are that during S_3 the μP places the data on the data bus, and during a write operation the data strobe lines indicate valid data from the μP. The read/write (R/$\overline{\text{W}}$) line goes low during S_2. The flowchart for a write operation is similar to the read operation flowchart of Figure 17.8, except during S_2 the read/write line is switched low, and in S_3 data is placed on the data bus.

17.6.3 | External Decoding Circuitry

Figure 17.10 shows an address decoding circuit for the address range FF00XX to FFFFXX. The output of the NAND gate goes low only when address lines A_{16} through A_{23} are all at a logic 1. The output of the NAND gate is used for two purposes. The first is to send the $\overline{\text{VPA}}$ signal back to the μP. The second purpose is to produce a low at the A = B input of comparator #1. Now, when the logic states of address lines A_{12} through A_{15} equal the logic states of switches S_{12} to S_{15}, the A = B output of comparator #1 goes low. This low output is fed into the A = B input comparator #2. If the logic states of address lines A_8 to A_{11} and switches S_8 to S_{11} are equal, the A = B output of comparator #2 goes low. On some peripheral boards, no further decoding is necessary and the output

FIGURE 17.8 | Flowchart for a 68000 μP Reading Data from a 6800 Peripheral Device (Redrawn with permission of Motorola Incorporated, Austin, Texas)

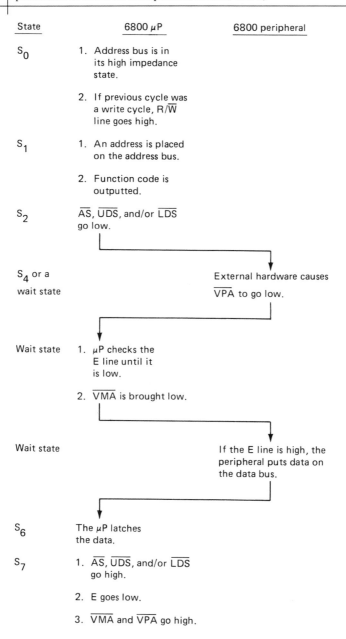

State   6800 μP   6800 peripheral

S_0 1. Address bus is in
            its high impedance
            state.

         2. If previous cycle was
            a write cycle, R/$\overline{W}$
            line goes high.

S_1 1. An address is placed
            on the address bus.

         2. Function code is
            outputted.

S_2 $\overline{AS}$, $\overline{UDS}$, and/or $\overline{LDS}$
         go low.

S_4 or a   External hardware causes
wait state $\overline{VPA}$ to go low.

Wait state   1. μP checks the
                E line until it
                is low.

             2. $\overline{VMA}$ is brought low.

Wait state   If the E line is high, the
                                        peripheral puts data on
                                        the data bus.

S_6 The μP latches
         the data.

S_7 1. $\overline{AS}$, $\overline{UDS}$, and/or $\overline{LDS}$
            go high.

         2. E goes low.

         3. $\overline{VMA}$ and $\overline{VPA}$ go high.

FIGURE 17.9 | Timing Diagram for a 68000 μP Writing Data to a 6800 Peripheral Device (Redrawn with permission of Motorola Incorporated, Austin, Texas)

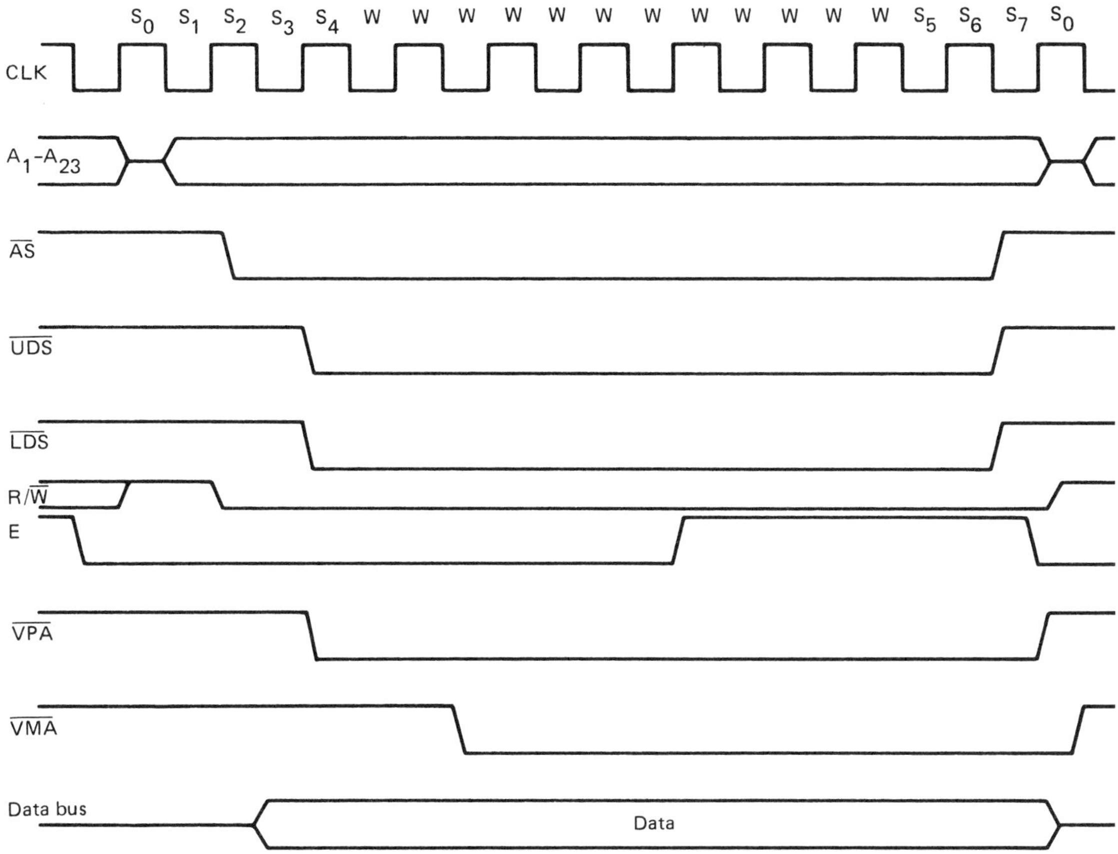

of comparator #2 is fed directly into a peripheral's chip select pin. In other systems, more decoding is necessary and the output of comparator #2 is wired to an enable pin on a decoder chip.

The circuit of Figure 17.10 is capable of selecting any one of the last 256 pages of memory. Remember that 256 pages yield 64K bytes of memory. This amount of memory may be too much to use for peripheral devices. The address range can be reduced from 64K bytes to 4K bytes by replacing comparator #1 with a four-input NAND gate, as shown in Figure 17.11. The address range is now from FFF0XX to FFFFXX.

FIGURE 17.10 | Decoding Circuitry for the Address Range FF00XX to FFFFXX

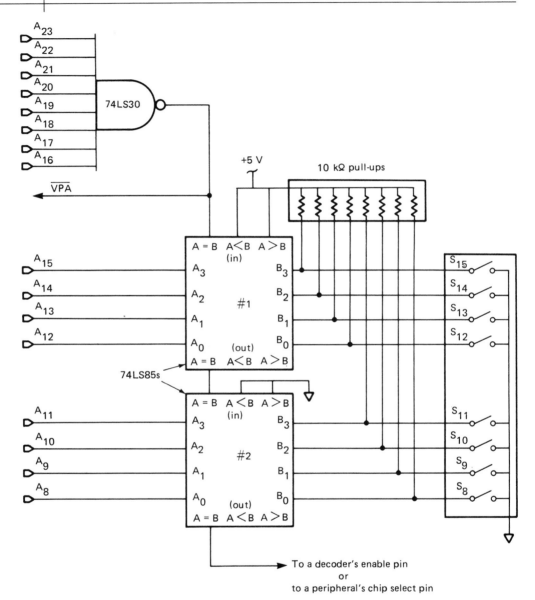

FIGURE 17.11 | Decoding Circuitry for the Address Range FFF0XX to FFFFXX

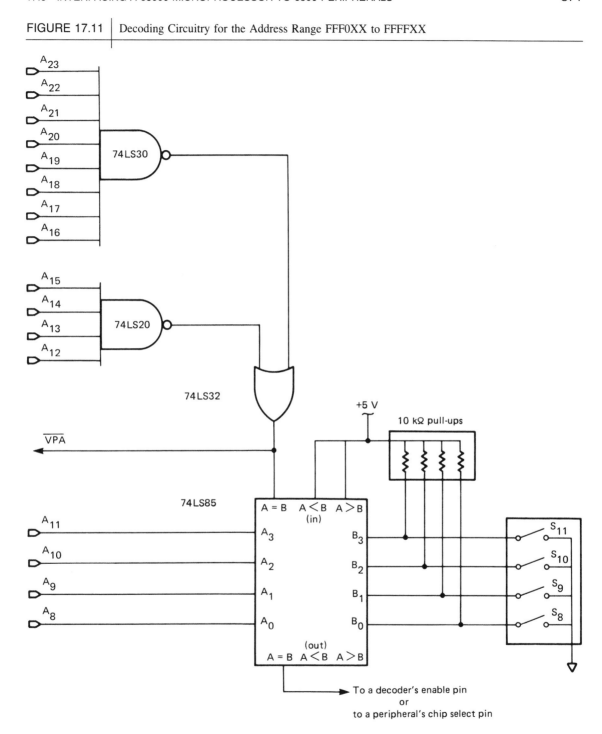

17.6.4 | 8- and 16-Bit Input/Output Ports

In some applications, such as 68000 μP connected to a full ASCII keyboard or to a 16-bit A/D/A (analog-to-digital and digital-to-analog) converter, the user would like to make use of all the μP's 16 data lines. Although the 6821 has 16 I/O lines, it has only 8 data lines. Therefore, the μP has to use two read or write operations to transfer 16 bits of data. What is needed is to have a 16-bit peripheral device or to interconnect two 6821 PIAs. By doubling the data lines, the μP's throughput is doubled because 16 bits of data instead of 8 bits can be sent at one time.

Since 6821 devices are relatively inexpensive and interconnecting them to the 68000 μP is quite easy, a low-cost, general-purpose I/O board can be built. Figure 17.12 shows how two 6821 PIAs can be interconnected to form two 16-bit I/O ports. Port A of each PIA forms one of the new 16-bit I/O ports and port B of each PIA forms the other 16-bit port, thus giving the user 32 I/O lines. In Figure 17.12, port A of each PIA and port B of each PIA can work together as a unit and be addressed together, or they can work separately and be addressed separately. Let's study how the decoding and control circuitry works.

The decoding circuitry of Figure 17.12 is wired to respond to word addresses from FFF430 to FFF436. Figure 17.13 shows how each word address is divided into two byte addresses. Figure 17.14 shows the location of the ports, data direction registers, and control registers for each PIA. Since PIA #1 is wired to the lower portion of the data bus, it occupies the odd-numbered address bytes. PIA #2 is wired to the upper portion of the data bus and thus occupies the even-numbered address bytes.

The PIAs are selected by the chip select pins, CS_0, CS_1 and $\overline{CS_2}$. Output pin 3 of the 74LS154 is wired to $\overline{CS_2}$ of both PIAs. Pin 3 goes low only when the μP outputs an address in the range from FFF430 to FFF436. The CS_0 pin on each PIA is wired to the output of a NOR gate. The inputs to the NOR gate are the data strobe and valid memory address control signals from the μP. The following examples will show how the upper and lower data strobe lines are used to select a PIA. Since CS_1 is not used, it is permanently tied to V_{CC}.

An example of the PIAs working together would be when the μP uses word addressing and sends or receives data. For example, consider Figure 17.12 and the following instruction:

MOVE.W D_4, FFF430

When this instruction is executed, the μP outputs on the address bus FFF430 and on the data bus bits 0 through 15 of register D_4. The lower 8 bits go to PIA #1, while the upper 8 bits go to PIA #2. This instruction also causes the μP to bring both data strobe lines low so that both PIAs are selected.

If the above instruction is changed to a byte instruction, only one PIA will be selected. Which PIA this is depends on the address. Table 17.3 summarizes how the μP controls the data strobe lines for byte and word instructions. Thus, when 16 bits of data are transferred to or from the PIAs of Figure 17.12, the μP must use word addressing and not byte addressing. Remember that a word address is always an even number and a byte address may be either an even or odd number.

FIGURE 17.12 | Connecting Two 6821 PIAs to the 68000 μP Bus Lines

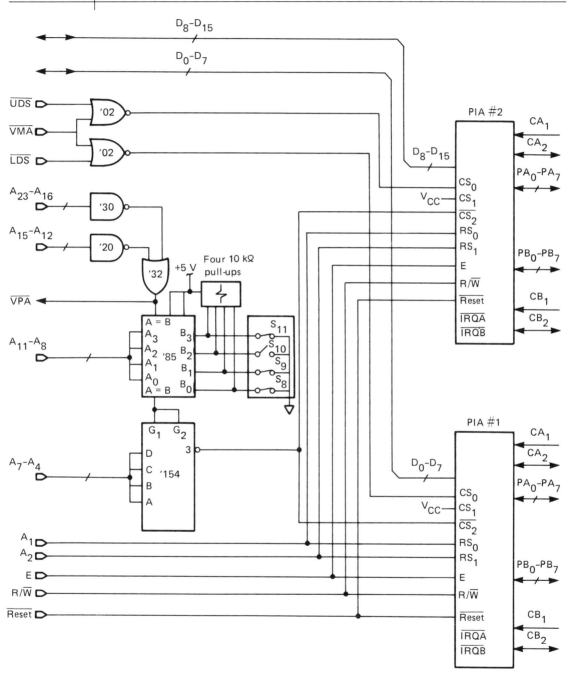

FIGURE 17.13 | Word and Byte Address Organization for the PIAs of Figure 17.12

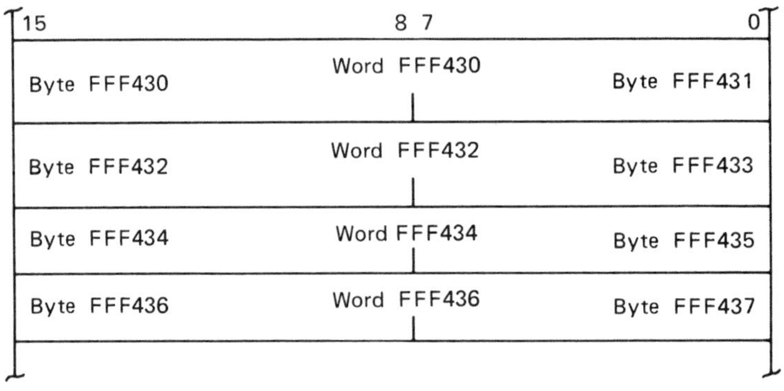

15	8 7	0
Byte FFF430	Word FFF430	Byte FFF431
Byte FFF432	Word FFF432	Byte FFF433
Byte FFF434	Word FFF434	Byte FFF435
Byte FFF436	Word FFF436	Byte FFF437

FIGURE 17.14 | Port, Data Direction, and Control Register Locations for Both PIAs of Figure 17.12

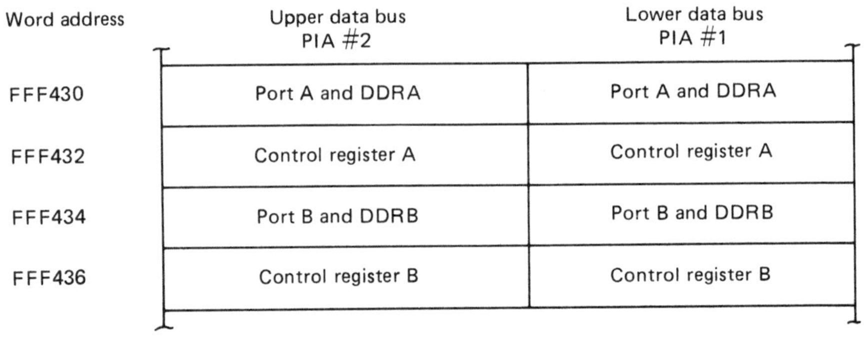

Word address	Upper data bus PIA #2	Lower data bus PIA #1
FFF430	Port A and DDRA	Port A and DDRA
FFF432	Control register A	Control register A
FFF434	Port B and DDRB	Port B and DDRB
FFF436	Control register B	Control register B

TABLE 17.3 | Byte and Word Instructions for Control of Data Strobe Lines

		Strobe Lines		
Instruction	Valid Data Bits	$\overline{UDS}$	$\overline{LDS}$	PIA Selected
MOVE.B D_4, FFF431	0–7	H	L	#1
MOVE.B D_4, FFF430	8–15	L	H	#2
MOVE.W D_4, FFF430	0–15	L	L	#1 and #2

17.6.5 | Connecting the 6850 ACIA

Chapter 13 introduced the 6850 asynchronous interface adapter, ACIA, peripheral device. This IC chip allows a μC system to transmit and receive serial data. These devices are readily available, relatively inexpensive, and easy to interconnect to a 68000 μP. Figure 17.15 shows how two 6850 ACIAs can be wired to a 68000 μP using the same decoding circuitry of Figure 17.12.

FIGURE 17.15 | Interfacing Two 6850 ACIAs to a 68000 μP

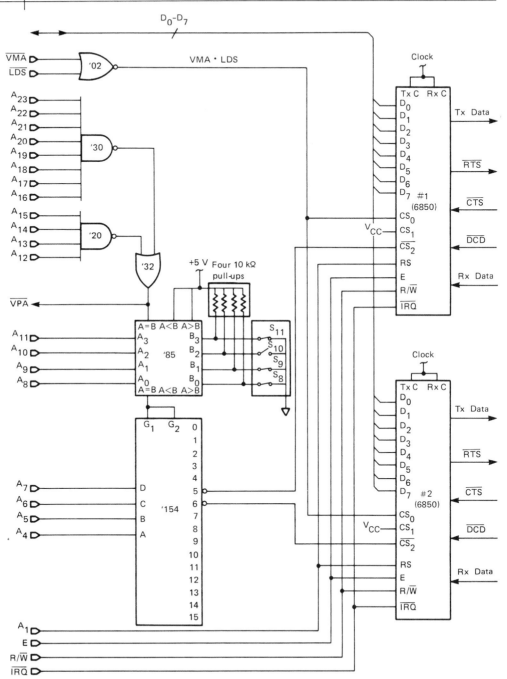

Before the devices can actually be wired, some decisions must be made: (1) Exactly where in the overall memory map should both ACIAs be located, and (2) should the devices be connected to the upper or lower portion of the data bus? To answer the first question, remember that each ACIA requires only two address byte locations. The addresses will not be in consecutive locations because the devices are connected only to one portion of the data bus. For our example, let's choose both devices connected to the lower portion of the data bus. Also, ACIA #1 is wired for address locations FFF451 and FFF453, while ACIA #2 is wired for address locations FFF461 and FFF463. Figure 17.16 illustrates where in memory the registers of the devices are located. This figure is useful for a programmer to visualize where data is located and how to obtain it. Remember, the 6850 uses the same address for two registers. It is the logic level of the read/write line that determines which register is actually addressed. Refer to Chapter 13 if you need more information on how an ACIA operates.

The decoding circuitry operation is as follows: Switches S_{11}, S_9, and S_8 are closed so that the output of the comparator goes low only when there is a 0100 pattern on address lines A_{11}, A_{10}, A_9, and A_8, respectively. Remember, for the comparator's A = B output to go low, not only must address lines A_{11} through A_8 be at the correct logic levels, but also the comparator's A = B input must be low. This input line only can go low if address lines A_{12} through A_{23} are all high and, therefore, the outputs of the NAND gates are low. The 74LS154 chip decodes address lines A_4 through A_7, and Figure 17.15

FIGURE 17.16 | Memory Map for the ACIAs of Figure 17.15

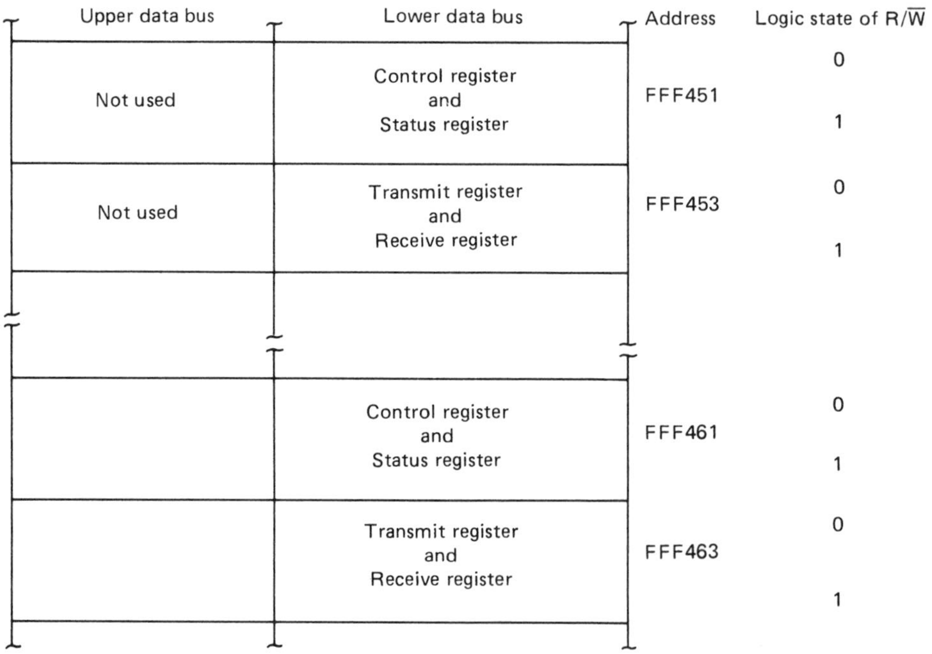

Upper data bus	Lower data bus	Address	Logic state of R/$\overline{W}$
Not used	Control register and Status register	FFF451	0 / 1
Not used	Transmit register and Receive register	FFF453	0 / 1
	Control register and Status register	FFF461	0 / 1
	Transmit register and Receive register	FFF463	0 / 1

shows which output pin is connected to each ACIA. Address line A_1 is wired to both ACIAs. In this interface scheme, address lines A_2 and A_3, are not used.

The enable (E) and the read/write (R/$\overline{\text{W}}$) lines on each chip are connected back to the 68000 μP. Although not shown in Figure 17.15, most applications would require these lines to be buffered to reduce loading effect on the μP.

After the 68000 μP receives a $\overline{\text{VPA}}$ signal, it generates a $\overline{\text{VMA}}$ (valid memory address) signal. This line goes low as does the $\overline{\text{LDS}}$ control line. When both the $\overline{\text{VMA}}$ line and the $\overline{\text{VPA}}$ line are low, the output of the NOR gate goes high. The output of the NOR gate could be wired to either CS_0 or CS_1. In Figure 17.15, it is wired to CS_0, and CS_1 is permanently tied to V_{CC}.

Operation of the ACIAs is similar to how it was described in Chapter 13; that is, the reset circuitry is released and the control register is set up. After this, the μP can monitor the status register to know when to transmit and/or receive data. Bit 0 of the status register indicates if the receive data register is full, and bit 1 indicates if the transmit data register is empty. Remember that the 6850 can be set up to send an interrupt request signal to the μP either when the transmit data register is empty or when the receive data register is full, thereby relieving the μP from constantly checking bits 0 and 1. If a modem is being used, the μP should also check the $\overline{\text{DCD}}$ bit (bit 2) and the $\overline{\text{CTS}}$ bit (bit 3) of the status register.

17.7 | SUMMARY

Since all μC systems need memory and I/O, this chapter introduced some of the principles necessary to add dynamic memory and peripheral chips to the 68000 μP. For dynamic RAMs, a controller chip is necessary. It provides the multiplexer needed for the address bus and the refresh counter. A dynamic memory controller chip also provides decoding logic for the row address strobe lines and buffering for the column address strobe and read/write lines. Designers of dynamic memory systems must consider refreshing each row of memory cells within a RAM chip every 2 ms. Two of the techniques for refreshing are burst mode and hidden refresh. In Section 17.5 an example showed a typical overhead charge for the burst mode technique.

This chapter also showed how the 68000 μP's address bus can be decoded for different memory space allocation for peripheral devices. It also showed how a $\overline{\text{VPA}}$ signal can be generated and how to use the $\overline{\text{VMA}}$ signal to enable the peripheral devices. Examples of how the 6821 and 6850 ICs can be connected to the 68000 μP were shown in Section 17.6.

| PROBLEMS

17.1 How many address pins must there be on a 256K DRAM?

17.2 If each $\overline{\text{RAS}}$ output line is used to activate a 64K $\times$ 16 bank of memory chips, determine the number of bytes of RAM in the system.

17.3 Refer to Figure 17.1. Could a 256K DRAM be housed in a 16-pin dual-in-line package?

17.4   If the refresh clock cycle is 200 ns, calculate the time to refresh a 64K DRAM. Consider the device uses 128 row refresh.

17.5   How could 64K $\times$ 1 memory chips be used to build a 32K $\times$ 8 memory system?

17.6   How is the $\overline{\text{VPA}}$ signal generated?

17.7   Refer to Figure 17.10. What changes are necessary in the decoding circuitry for an address range of 0000XX to 00FFXX?

17.8   Determine the new address range in Figure 17.11 if the 74LS20 NAND gate is replaced by (a) an OR gate and (b) an AND gate.

17.9   What has to be changed in Figure 17.12 to have the PIA's word address range from FFF490 to FFF96?

17.10 Could an interface network be designed for Figure 17.15 so that ACIA #2 has addresses FFF450 and FFF452, while ACIA #1 remains at addresses FFF451 and FFF453?

A Conversion between Decimal and Hexadecimal

Most Significant Hex Digit	Least Significant Hex Digit															
	0	1	2	3	4	5	6	7	8	9	A	B	C	D	E	F
0	0	1	2	3	4	5	6	7	8	9	10	11	12	13	14	15
1	16	17	18	19	20	21	22	23	24	25	26	27	28	29	30	31
2	32	33	34	35	36	37	38	39	40	41	42	43	44	45	46	47
3	48	49	50	51	52	53	54	55	56	57	58	59	60	61	62	63
4	64	65	66	67	68	69	70	71	72	73	74	75	76	77	78	79
5	80	81	82	83	84	85	86	87	88	89	90	91	92	93	94	95
6	96	97	98	99	100	101	102	103	104	105	106	107	108	109	110	111
7	112	113	114	115	116	117	118	119	120	121	122	123	124	125	126	127
8	−128	−127	−126	−125	−124	−123	−122	−121	−120	−119	−118	−117	−116	−115	−114	−113
9	−112	−111	−110	−109	−108	−107	−106	−105	−104	−103	−102	−101	−100	−99	−98	−97
A	−96	−95	−94	−93	−92	−91	−90	−89	−88	−87	−86	−85	−84	−83	−82	−81
B	−80	−79	−78	−77	−76	−75	−74	−73	−72	−71	−70	−69	−68	−67	−66	−65
C	−64	−63	−62	−61	−60	−59	−58	−57	−56	−55	−54	−53	−52	−51	−50	−49
D	−48	−47	−46	−45	−44	−43	−42	−41	−40	−39	−38	−37	−36	−35	−34	−33
E	−32	−31	−30	−29	−28	−27	−26	−25	−24	−23	−22	−21	−20	−19	−18	−17
F	−16	−15	−14	−13	−12	−11	−10	−9	−8	−7	−6	−5	−4	−3	−2	−1

B Data Sheets for the 6800 Microprocessor

APPENDIX
TABLE B.1 | 6800 Microprocessor Instruction Set in Alphabetic Order

ABA	Add Accumulators	CLR	Clear	PUL	Pull Data
ADC	Add with Carry	CLV	Clear Overflow	ROL	Rotate Left
ADD	Add	CMP	Compare	ROR	Rotate Right
AND	Logical And	COM	Complement	RTI	Return from Interrupt
ASL	Arithmetic Shift Left	CPX	Compare Index Register	RTS	Return from Subroutine
ASR	Arithmetic Shift Right	DAA	Decimal Adjust	SBA	Subtract Accumulators
BCC	Branch if Carry Clear	DEC	Decrement	SBC	Subtract with Carry
BCS	Branch if Carry Set	DES	Decrement Stack Pointer	SEC	Set Carry
BEQ	Branch if Equal to Zero	DEX	Decrement Index Register	SEI	Set Interrupt Mask
BGE	Branch if Greater or Equal Zero	EOR	Exclusive OR	SEV	Set Overflow
BGT	Branch if Greater than Zero			STA	Store Accumulator
BHI	Branch if Higher	INC	Increment	STS	Store Stack Register
BIT	Bit Test	INS	Increment Stack Pointer	STX	Store Index Register
BLE	Branch if Less or Equal	INX	Increment Index Register	SUB	Subtract
BLS	Branch if Lower or Same	JMP	Jump	SWI	Software Interrupt
BLT	Branch if Less than Zero	JSR	Jump to Subroutine	TAB	Transfer Accumulators
BMI	Branch if Minus	LDA	Load Accumulator	TAP	Transfer Accumulators to Condition Code Reg.
BNE	Branch if Not Equal to Zero	LDS	Load Stack Pointer	TBA	Transfer Accumulators
BPL	Branch if Plus	LDX	Load Index Register	TPA	Transfer Condition Code Reg. to Accumulator
BRA	Branch Always	LSR	Logical Shift Right	TST	Test
BSR	Branch to Subroutine	NEG	Negate	TSX	Transfer Stack Pointer to Index Register
BVC	Branch if Overflow Clear	NOP	No Operation	TXS	Transfer Index Register to Stack Pointer
BVS	Branch if Overflow Set	ORA	Inclusive OR Accumulator	WAI	Wait for Interrupt
CBA	Compare Accumulators				
CLC	Clear Carry	PSH	Push Data		
CLI	Clear Interrupt Mask				

Source: Reprinted from data sheet for MC6800 microprocessor with permission Motorola Incorporated. Phoenix, AZ

6800 Microprocessor Accumulator and Memory Operations

OPERATIONS	MNEMONIC	IMMED OP ~ #	DIRECT OP ~ #	INDEX OP ~ #	EXTND OP ~ #	IMPLIED OP ~ #	BOOLEAN/ARITHMETIC OPERATION (All register labels refer to contents)	H	I	N	Z	V	C
Add	ADDA	8B 2 2	9B 3 2	AB 5 2	BB 4 3		A + M · A	:	•	:	:	:	:
	ADDB	CB 2 2	DB 3 2	EB 5 2	FB 4 3		B + M · B	:	•	:	:	:	:
Add Acmltrs	ABA					1B 2 1	A + B · A	:	•	:	:	:	:
Add with Carry	ADCA	89 2 2	99 3 2	A9 5 2	B9 4 3		A + M + C · A	:	•	:	:	:	:
	ADCB	C9 2 2	D9 3 2	E9 5 2	F9 4 3		B + M + C · B	:	•	:	:	:	:
And	ANDA	84 2 2	94 3 2	A4 5 2	B4 4 3		A · M · A	•	•	:	:	R	•
	ANDB	C4 2 2	D4 3 2	E4 5 2	F4 4 3		B · M · B	•	•	:	:	R	•
Bit Test	BITA	85 2 2	95 3 2	A5 5 2	B5 4 3		A · M	•	•	:	:	R	•
	BITB	C5 2 2	D5 3 2	E5 5 2	F5 4 3		B · M	•	•	:	:	R	•
Clear	CLR			6F 7 2	7F 6 3		00 · M	•	•	R	S	R	R
	CLRA					4F 2 1	00 · A	•	•	R	S	R	R
	CLRB					5F 2 1	00 · B	•	•	R	S	R	R
Compare	CMPA	81 2 2	91 3 2	A1 5 2	B1 4 3		A − M	•	•	:	:	:	:
	CMPB	C1 2 2	D1 3 2	E1 5 2	F1 4 3		B − M	•	•	:	:	:	:
Compare Acmltrs	CBA					11 2 1	A − B	•	•	:	:	:	:
Complement, 1's	COM			63 7 2	73 6 3		M̄ · M	•	•	:	:	R	S
	COMA					43 2 1	Ā · A	•	•	:	:	R	S
	COMB					53 2 1	B̄ · B	•	•	:	:	R	S
Complement, 2's	NEG			60 7 2	70 6 3		00 − M · M	•	•	:	:	①	②
(Negate)	NEGA					40 2 1	00 − A · A	•	•	:	:	①	②
	NEGB					50 2 1	00 − B · B	•	•	:	:	①	②
Decimal Adjust, A	DAA					19 2 1	Converts Binary Add of BCD Characters into BCD Format	•	•	:	:	:	③
Decrement	DEC			6A 7 2	7A 6 3		M − 1 · M	•	•	:	:	4	•
	DECA					4A 2 1	A − 1 · A	•	•	:	:	4	•
	DECB					5A 2 1	B − 1 · B	•	•	:	:	4	•
Exclusive OR	EORA	88 2 2	98 3 2	A8 5 2	B8 4 3		A ⊕ M · A	•	•	:	:	R	•
	EORB	C8 2 2	D8 3 2	E8 5 2	F8 4 3		B ⊕ M · B	•	•	:	:	R	•
Increment	INC			6C 7 2	7C 6 3		M + 1 · M	•	•	:	:	⑤	•
	INCA					4C 2 1	A + 1 · A	•	•	:	:	⑤	•
	INCB					5C 2 1	B + 1 · B	•	•	:	:	⑤	•
Load Acmltr	LDAA	86 2 2	96 3 2	A6 5 2	B6 4 3		M · A	•	•	:	:	R	•
	LDAB	C6 2 2	D6 3 2	E6 5 2	F6 4 3		M · B	•	•	:	:	R	•
Or, Inclusive	ORAA	8A 2 2	9A 3 2	AA 5 2	BA 4 3		A + M · A	•	•	:	:	R	•
	ORAB	CA 2 2	DA 3 2	EA 5 2	FA 4 3		B + M · B	•	•	:	:	R	•
Push Data	PSHA					36 4 1	A · M$_{SP}$, SP − 1 · SP	•	•	•	•	•	•
	PSHB					37 4 1	B · M$_{SP}$, SP − 1 · SP	•	•	•	•	•	•
Pull Data	PULA					32 4 1	SP + 1 · SP M$_{SP}$ · A	•	•	•	•	•	•
	PULB					33 4 1	SP + 1 · SP M$_{SP}$ · B	•	•	•	•	•	•
Rotate Left	ROL			69 7 2	79 6 3		M	•	•	:	:	⑥	⑥
	ROLA					49 2 1	A	•	•	:	:	⑥	⑥
	ROLB					59 2 1	B C b7 → b0	•	•	:	:	⑥	⑥
Rotate Right	ROR			66 7 2	76 6 3		M	•	•	:	:	⑥	⑥
	RORA					46 2 1	A	•	•	:	:	⑥	⑥
	RORB					56 2 1	B C b7 → b0	•	•	:	:	⑥	⑥
Shift Left, Arithmetic	ASL			68 7 2	78 6 3		M	•	•	:	:	⑥	⑥
	ASLA					48 2 1	A	•	•	:	:	⑥	⑥
	ASLB					58 2 1	B C b7 b0	•	•	:	:	⑥	⑥
Shift Right, Arithmetic	ASR			67 7 2	77 6 3		M	•	•	:	:	⑥	⑥
	ASRA					47 2 1	A	•	•	:	:	⑥	⑥
	ASRB					57 2 1	B b7 b0 C	•	•	:	:	⑥	⑥
Shift Right, Logic	LSR			64 7 2	74 6 3		M	•	•	R	:	⑥	⑥
	LSRA					44 2 1	A	•	•	R	:	⑥	⑥
	LSRB					54 2 1	B b7 b0 C	•	•	R	:	⑥	⑥
Store Acmltr	STAA		97 4 2	A7 6 2	B7 5 3		A · M	•	•	:	:	R	•
	STAB		D7 4 2	E7 6 2	F7 5 3		B · M	•	•	:	:	R	•
Subtract	SUBA	80 2 2	90 3 2	A0 5 2	B0 4 3		A − M · A	•	•	:	:	:	:
	SUBB	C0 2 2	D0 3 2	E0 5 2	F0 4 3		B − M · B	•	•	:	:	:	:
Subtract Acmltrs	SBA					10 2 1	A − B · A	•	•	:	:	:	:
Subtr with Carry	SBCA	82 2 2	92 3 2	A2 5 2	B2 4 3		A − M − C · A	•	•	:	:	:	:
	SBCB	C2 2 2	D2 3 2	E2 5 2	F2 4 3		B − M − C · B	•	•	:	:	:	:
Transfer Acmltrs	TAB					16 2 1	A · B	•	•	:	:	R	•
	TBA					17 2 1	B · A	•	•	:	:	R	•
Test, Zero or Minus	TST			6D 7 2	7D 6 3		M − 00	•	•	:	:	R	R
	TSTA					4D 2 1	A − 00	•	•	:	:	R	R
	TSTB					5D 2 1	B − 00	•	•	:	:	R	R

(bottom condition code header) H I N Z V C

LEGEND:
OP   Operation Code (Hexadecimal).
~   Number of MPU Cycles.
#   Number of Program Bytes.
+   Arithmetic Plus.
−   Arithmetic Minus.
·   Boolean AND.
M$_{SP}$ Contents of memory location pointed to be Stack Pointer.
+   Boolean Inclusive OR.
⊙   Boolean Exclusive OR.
M̄   Complement of M.
→   Transfer Into.
0   Bit = Zero.
00   Byte = Zero.

CONDITION CODE SYMBOLS:
H   Half-carry from bit 3.
I   Interrupt mask.
N   Negative (sign bit).
Z   Zero (byte).
V   Overflow, 2's complement.
C   Carry from bit 7.
R   Reset Always.
S   Set Always.
:   Test and set if true, cleared otherwise.
•   Not Affected.

CONDITION CODE REGISTER NOTES:
(Bit set if test is true and cleared otherwise)
1   (Bit V)   Test: Result = 10000000?
2   (Bit C)   Test: Result = 00000000?
3   (Bit C)   Test: Decimal value of most significant BCD Character greater than nine? (Not cleared if previously set.)
4   (Bit V)   Test: Operand = 10000000 prior to execution?
5   (Bit V)   Test: Operand = 01111111 prior to execution?
6   (Bit V)   Test: Set equal to result of N⊕C after shift has occurred.

Note − Accumulator addressing mode instructions are included in the column for IMPLIED addressing.

Source: Reprinted from data sheet for MC6800 microprocessor with permission. Motorola Incorporated, Phoenix, AZ

APPENDIX TABLE B.3 | 6800 Microprocessor Index Register and Stack Pointer Operations

POINTER OPERATIONS	MNEMONIC	IMMED OP	~	=	DIRECT OP	~	=	INDEX OP	~	=	EXTND OP	~	=	IMPLIED OP	~	=	BOOLEAN/ARITHMETIC OPERATION	5 H	4 I	3 N	2 Z	1 V	0 C
Compare Index Reg	CPX	8C	3	3	9C	4	2	AC	6	2	BC	5	3				$X_H - M, X_L - (M+1)$	●	●	①	↕	②	●
Decrement Index Reg	DEX													09	4	1	$X - 1 \to X$	●	●	●	↕	●	●
Decrement Stack Pntr	DES													34	4	1	$SP - 1 \to SP$	●	●	●	●	●	●
Increment Index Reg	INX													08	4	1	$X + 1 \to X$	●	●	●	↕	●	●
Increment Stack Pntr	INS													31	4	1	$SP + 1 \to SP$	●	●	●	●	●	●
Load Index Reg	LDX	CE	3	3	DE	4	2	EE	6	2	FE	5	3				$M \to X_H, (M+1) \to X_L$	●	●	③	↕	R	●
Load Stack Pntr	LDS	8E	3	3	9E	4	2	AE	6	2	BE	5	3				$M \to SP_H, (M+1) \to SP_L$	●	●	③	↕	R	●
Store Index Reg	STX				DF	5	2	EF	7	2	FF	6	3				$X_H \to M, X_L \to (M+1)$	●	●	③	↕	R	●
Store Stack Pntr	STS				9F	5	2	AF	7	2	BF	6	3				$SP_H \to M, SP_L \to (M+1)$	●	●	③	↕	R	●
Indx Reg → Stack Pntr	TXS													35	4	1	$X - 1 \to SP$	●	●	●	●	●	●
Stack Pntr → Indx Reg	TSX													30	4	1	$SP + 1 \to X$	●	●	●	●	●	●

① (Bit N) Test: Sign bit of most significant (MS) byte of result = 1?
② (Bit V) Test: 2's complement overflow from subtraction of ms bytes?
③ (Bit N) Test: Result less than zero? (Bit 15 = 1)

Source: Reprinted from data sheet for MC6800 microprocessor with permission. Motorola Incorporated, Phoenix, AZ

APPENDIX TABLE B.4 | 6800 Microprocessor Jump and Branch Operations

OPERATIONS	MNEMONIC	RELATIVE OP	~	#	INDEX OP	~	#	EXTND OP	~	#	IMPLIED OP	~	#	BRANCH TEST	5 H	4 I	3 N	2 Z	1 V	0 C
Branch Always	BRA	20	4	2										None	●	●	●	●	●	●
Branch If Carry Clear	BCC	24	4	2										C = 0	●	●	●	●	●	●
Branch If Carry Set	BCS	25	4	2										C = 1	●	●	●	●	●	●
Branch If = Zero	BEQ	27	4	2										Z = 1	●	●	●	●	●	●
Branch If ≥ Zero	BGE	2C	4	2										N ⊕ V = 0	●	●	●	●	●	●
Branch If > Zero	BGT	2E	4	2										Z + (N ⊕ V) = 0	●	●	●	●	●	●
Branch If Higher	BHI	22	4	2										C + Z = 0	●	●	●	●	●	●
Branch If ≤ Zero	BLE	2F	4	2										Z + (N ⊕ V) = 1	●	●	●	●	●	●
Branch If Lower Or Same	BLS	23	4	2										C + Z = 1	●	●	●	●	●	●
Branch If < Zero	BLT	2D	4	2										N ⊕ V = 1	●	●	●	●	●	●
Branch If Minus	BMI	2B	4	2										N = 1	●	●	●	●	●	●
Branch If Not Equal Zero	BNE	26	4	2										Z = 0	●	●	●	●	●	●
Branch If Overflow Clear	BVC	28	4	2										V = 0	●	●	●	●	●	●
Branch If Overflow Set	BVS	29	4	2										V = 1	●	●	●	●	●	●
Branch If Plus	BPL	2A	4	2										N = 0	●	●	●	●	●	●
Branch To Subroutine	BSR	8D	8	2											●	●	●	●	●	●
Jump	JMP				6E	4	2	7E	3	3				See Special Operations	●	●	●	●	●	●
Jump To Subroutine	JSR				AD	8	2	BD	9	3					●	●	●	●	●	●
No Operation	NOP										01	2	1	Advances Prog. Cntr. Only	●	●	●	①	●	●
Return From Interrupt	RTI										3B	10	1							
Return From Subroutine	RTS										39	5	1	See Special Operations	●	●	●	●	●	●
Software Interrupt	SWI										3F	12	1		●	●	●	●	●	●
Wait for Interrupt*	WAI										3E	9	1		●	②	●	●	●	●

*WAI puts Address Bus, R/W, and Data Bus in the three-state mode while VMA is held low.

① (All)   Load Condition Code Register from Stack. (See Special Operations)
② (Bit 1) Set when interrupt occurs. If previously set, a Non-Maskable Interrupt is required to exit the wait state.

Source: Reprinted from data sheet for MC6800 microprocessor with permission. Motorola Incorporated, Phoenix, AZ

APPENDIX
TABLE B.5 | 6800 Microprocessor Special Operations

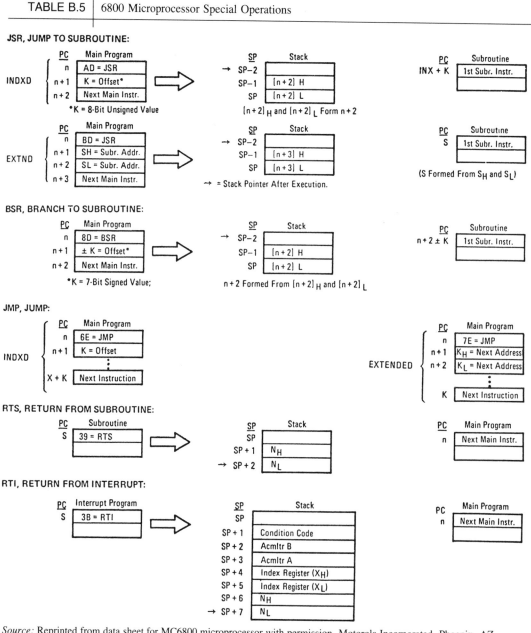

JSR, JUMP TO SUBROUTINE:

BSR, BRANCH TO SUBROUTINE:

JMP, JUMP:

RTS, RETURN FROM SUBROUTINE:

RTI, RETURN FROM INTERRUPT:

Source: Reprinted from data sheet for MC6800 microprocessor with permission. Motorola Incorporated, Phoenix, AZ

APPENDIX
TABLE B.6 | 6800 Microprocessor Condition Code Register Operations

OPERATIONS	MNEMONIC	IMPLIED			BOOLEAN OPERATION	COND. CODE REG.					
		OP	~	=		5 H	4 I	3 N	2 Z	1 V	0 C
Clear Carry	CLC	0C	2	1	$0 \rightarrow C$	●	●	●	●	●	R
Clear Interrupt Mask	CLI	0E	2	1	$0 \rightarrow I$	●	R	●	●	●	●
Clear Overflow	CLV	0A	2	1	$0 \rightarrow V$	●	●	●	●	R	●
Set Carry	SEC	0D	2	1	$1 \rightarrow C$	●	●	●	●	●	S
Set Interrupt Mask	SEI	0F	2	1	$1 \rightarrow I$	●	S	●	●	●	●
Set Overflow	SEV	0B	2	1	$1 \rightarrow V$	●	●	●	●	S	●
Acmltr A → CCR	TAP	06	2	1	$A \rightarrow CCR$			①			
CCR → Acmltr A	TPA	07	2	1	$CCR \rightarrow A$	●	●	●	●	●	●

R = Reset
S = Set
● = Not affected
① (ALL) Set according to the contents of Accumulator A.

Source: Reprinted from data sheet for MC6800 microprocessor with permission. Motorola Incorporated, Phoenix, AZ

C Data Sheets for the 68000 Microprocessor

16-BIT MICROPROCESSING UNIT

Advances in semiconductor technology have provided the capability to place on a single silicon chip a microprocessor at least an order of magnitude higher in performance and circuit complexity than has been previously available. The MC68000 is the first of a family of such VLSI microprocessors from Motorola. It combines state-of-the-art technology and advanced circuit design techniques with computer sciences to achieve an architecturally advanced 16-bit microprocessor.

The resources available to the MC68000 user consist of the following:

- 32-Bit Data and Address Registers
- 16 Megabyte Direct Addressing Range
- 56 Powerful Instruction Types
- Operations on Five Main Data Types
- Memory Mapped I/O
- 14 Addressing Modes

As shown in the programming model, the MC68000 offers seventeen 32-bit registers in addition to the 32-bit program counter and a 16-bit status register. The first eight registers (D0-D7) are used as data registers for byte (8-bit), word (16-bit), and long word (32-bit) data operations. The second set of seven registers (A0-A6) and the system stack pointer may be used as software stack pointers and base address registers. In addition, these registers may be used for word and long word address operations. All seventeen registers may be used as index registers.

MC68000L4   MC68000L6
(4 MHz)   (6 MHz)

MC68000L8   MC68000L10
(8 MHz)   (10 MHz)

MC68000L12
(12.5 MHz)

HMOS
(HIGH-DENSITY, N-CHANNEL,
SILICON-GATE DEPLETION LOAD)

**16-BIT
MICROPROCESSOR**

L SUFFIX
CERAMIC PACKAGE
CASE 746

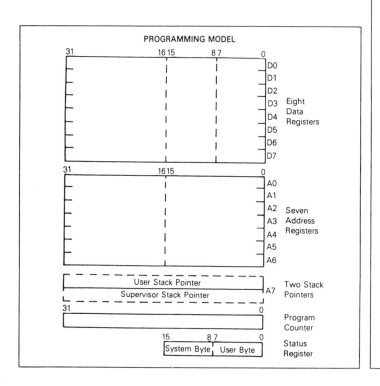

PROGRAMMING MODEL

PIN ASSIGNMENT

D4 ☐ 1 ●	64 ☐ D5
D3 ☐ 2	63 ☐ D6
D2 ☐ 3	62 ☐ D7
D1 ☐ 4	61 ☐ D8
D0 ☐ 5	60 ☐ D9
A̅S̅ ☐ 6	59 ☐ D10
U̅D̅S̅ ☐ 7	58 ☐ D11
L̅D̅S̅ ☐ 8	57 ☐ D12
R/W̅ ☐ 9	56 ☐ D13
D̅T̅A̅C̅K̅ ☐ 10	55 ☐ D14
B̅G̅ ☐ 11	54 ☐ D15
B̅G̅A̅C̅K̅ ☐ 12	53 ☐ GND
B̅R̅ ☐ 13	52 ☐ A23
V_CC ☐ 14	51 ☐ A22
CLK ☐ 15	50 ☐ A21
GND ☐ 16	49 ☐ V_CC
H̅A̅L̅T̅ ☐ 17	48 ☐ A20
R̅E̅S̅E̅T̅ ☐ 18	47 ☐ A19
V̅M̅A̅ ☐ 19	46 ☐ A18
E ☐ 20	45 ☐ A17
V̅P̅A̅ ☐ 21	44 ☐ A16
B̅E̅R̅R̅ ☐ 22	43 ☐ A15
I̅P̅L̅2 ☐ 23	42 ☐ A14
I̅P̅L̅1 ☐ 24	41 ☐ A13
I̅P̅L̅0 ☐ 25	40 ☐ A12
FC2 ☐ 26	39 ☐ A11
FC1 ☐ 27	38 ☐ A10
FC0 ☐ 28	37 ☐ A9
A1 ☐ 29	36 ☐ A8
A2 ☐ 30	35 ☐ A7
A3 ☐ 31	34 ☐ A6
A4 ☐ 32	33 ☐ A5

MAXIMUM RATINGS

Rating	Symbol	Value	Unit
Supply Voltage	V_{CC}	-0.3 to $+7.0$	V
Input Voltage	V_{in}	-0.3 to $+7.0$	V
Operating Temperature Range	T_A	0 to 70	°C
Storage Temperature	T_{stg}	-55 to 150	°C

THERMAL CHARACTERISTICS

Characteristic	Symbol	Value	Unit
Thermal Resistance Ceramic Package	θ_{JA}	30	°C/W

This device contains circuitry to protect the inputs against damage due to high static voltages or electric fields; however, it is advised that normal precautions be taken to avoid application of any voltage higher than maximum-rated voltages to this high-impedance circuit. Reliability of operation is enhanced if unused inputs are tied to an appropriate logic voltage level (e.g., either V_{SS} or V_{CC}).

POWER CONSIDERATIONS

The average chip-junction temperature, T_J, in °C can be obtained from:

$$T_J = T_A + (P_D \bullet \theta_{JA}) \tag{1}$$

Where:

$T_A \equiv$ Ambient Temperature, °C

$\theta_{JA} \equiv$ Package Thermal Resistance, Junction-to-Ambient, °C/W

$P_D \equiv P_{INT} + P_{I/O}$

$P_{INT} \equiv I_{CC} \times V_{CC}$, Watts — Chip Internal Power

$P_{I/O} \equiv$ Power Dissipation on Input and Output Pins — User Determined

For most applications $P_{I/O} \ll P_{INT}$ and can be neglected.

An approximate relationship between P_D and T_J (if $P_{I/O}$ is neglected) is:

$$P_D = K \div (T_J + 273°C) \tag{2}$$

Solving equations 1 and 2 for K gives:

$$K = P_D \bullet (T_A + 273°C) + \theta_{JA} \bullet P_D^2 \tag{3}$$

Where K is a constant pertaining to the particular part. K can be determined from equation 3 by measuring P_D (at equilibrium) for a known T_A. Using this value of K the values of P_D and T_J can be obtained by solving equations (1) and (2) iteratively for any value of T_A.

DC ELECTRICAL CHARACTERISTICS ($V_{CC} = 5.0$ Vdc $\pm 5\%$, $V_{SS} = 0$ Vdc; $T_A = 0°C$ to 70°C. See Figures 1, 2, and 3)

Characteristic		Symbol	Min	Max	Unit
Input High Voltage		V_{IH}	2.0	V_{CC}	V
Input Low Voltage		V_{IL}	$V_{SS} - 0.3$	0.8	V
Input Leakage Current @ 5.25 V	$\overline{BERR}$, $\overline{BGACK}$, $\overline{BR}$, $\overline{DTACK}$, CLK, $\overline{IPL0}$-$\overline{IPL2}$, $\overline{VPA}$	I_{in}	—	2.5	μA
	$\overline{HALT}$, $\overline{RESET}$		—	20	
Three-State (Off State) Input Current @ 2.4 V/0.4 V	$\overline{AS}$, A1-A23, D0-D15 FC0-FC2, $\overline{LDS}$, R/$\overline{W}$, $\overline{UDS}$, $\overline{VMA}$	I_{TSI}	—	20	μA
Output High Voltage ($I_{OH} = -400 \mu$A)	E*	V_{OH}	$V_{CC} - 0.75$	—	V
	$\overline{AS}$, A1-A23, $\overline{BG}$, D0-D15 FC0-FC2, $\overline{LDS}$, R/$\overline{W}$, $\overline{UDS}$, $\overline{VMA}$		2.4	—	
Output Low Voltage ($I_{OL} = 1.6$ mA)	$\overline{HALT}$	V_{OL}	—	0.5	V
($I_{OL} = 3.2$ mA)	A1-A23, $\overline{BG}$, FC0-FC2		—	0.5	
($I_{OL} = 35.0$ mA)	$\overline{RESET}$		—	0.5	
($I_{OL} = 5.3$ mA)	E, $\overline{AS}$, D0-D15, $\overline{LDS}$, R/$\overline{W}$ $\overline{UDS}$, $\overline{VMA}$		—	0.5	
Power Dissipation (Clock Frequency = 8 MHz)		P_D	—	1.5	W
Capacitance ($V_{in} = 0$ V, $T_A = 25°C$; Frequency = 1 MHz)		C_{in}	—	10.0	pF

* With external pullup resistor of 470 Ω

FIGURE 1 — RESET TEST LOAD   FIGURE 2 — HALT TEST LOAD   FIGURE 3 — TEST LOADS

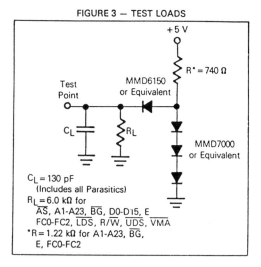

CLOCK TIMING (See Figure 4)

Characteristic	Symbol	4 MHz MC68000L4		6 MHz MC68000L6		8 MHz MC68000L8		10 MHz MC68000L10		12.5 MHz MC68000L12		Unit
		Min	Max	Min	Max	Min	Max	Min	Max	Min	Max	
Frequency of Operation	F	2.0	4.0	2.0	6.0	2.0	8.0	2.0	10.0	4.0	12.5	MHz
Cycle Time	t_{cyc}	250	500	167	500	125	500	100	500	80	250	ns
Clock Pulse Width	t_{CL} t_{CH}	115 115	250 250	75 75	250 250	55 55	250 250	45 45	250 250	35 35	125 125	ns
Rise and Fall Times	t_{Cr} t_{Cf}	— —	10 10	— —	10 10	— —	10 10	— —	10 10	— —	5 5	ns

FIGURE 4 — INPUT CLOCK WAVEFORM

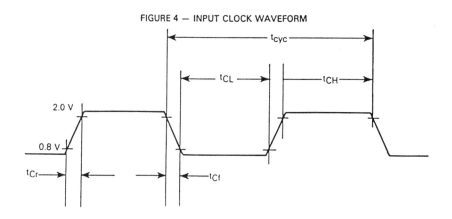

AC ELECTRICAL SPECIFICATIONS (V_{CC} = 5.0 Vdc ±5%, V_{SS} = 0 Vdc; T_A = 0°C to 70°C, See Figures 5 and 6)

Num.	Characteristic	Symbol	4 MHz MC68000L4		6 MHz MC68000L6		8 MHz MC68000L8		10 MHz MC68000L10		12.5 MHz MC68000L12		Unit
			Min	Max	Min	Max	Min	Max	Min	Max	Min	Max	
1	Clock Period	t_{cyc}	250	500	167	500	125	500	100	500	80	250	ns
2	Clock Width Low	t_{CL}	115	250	75	250	55	250	45	250	35	125	ns
3	Clock Width High	t_{CH}	115	250	75	250	55	250	45	250	35	125	ns
4	Clock Fall Time	t_{Cf}	—	10	—	10	—	10	—	10	—	5	ns
5	Clock Rise Time	t_{Cr}	—	10	—	10	—	10	—	10	—	5	ns
6	Clock Low to Address	t_{CLAV}	—	90	—	80	—	70	—	55	—	55	ns
6A	Clock High to FC Valid	t_{CHFCV}	—	90	—	80	—	70	—	60	—	55	ns
7	Clock High to Address Data High Impedance (Maximum)	t_{CHAZx}	—	120	—	100	—	80	—	70	—	60	ns
8	Clock High to Address/FC Invalid (Minimum)	t_{CHAZn}	0	—	0	—	0	—	0	—	0	—	ns
9[1]	Clock High to $\overline{AS}$, $\overline{DS}$ Low (Maximum)	t_{CHSLx}	—	80	—	70	—	60	—	55	—	55	ns
10	Clock High to $\overline{AS}$, $\overline{DS}$ Low (Minimum)	t_{CHSLn}	0	—	0	—	0	—	0	—	0	—	ns
11[2]	Address to $\overline{AS}$, $\overline{DS}$ (Read) Low/$\overline{AS}$ Write	t_{AVSL}	55	—	35	—	30	—	20	—	0	—	ns
11A[2]	FC Valid to $\overline{AS}$, $\overline{DS}$ (Read) Low/$\overline{AS}$ Write	t_{FCVSL}	80	—	70	—	60	—	50	—	40	—	ns
12[1]	Clock Low to $\overline{AS}$, $\overline{DS}$ High	t_{CLSH}	—	90	—	80	—	70	—	55	—	50	ns
13[2]	$\overline{AS}$, $\overline{DS}$ High to Address/FC Invalid	t_{SHAZ}	60	—	40	—	30	—	20	—	10	—	ns
14[2, 5]	$\overline{AS}$, $\overline{DS}$ Width Low (Read)/$\overline{AS}$ Write	t_{SL}	535	—	337	—	240	—	195	—	160	—	ns
14A[2]	DS Width Low (Write)	—	285	—	170	—	115	—	95	—	80	—	ns
15[2]	$\overline{AS}$, $\overline{DS}$ Width High	t_{SH}	285	—	180	—	150	—	105	—	65	—	ns
16	Clock High to AS, DS High Impedance	t_{CHSZ}	—	120	—	100	—	80	—	70	—	60	ns
17[2]	$\overline{AS}$, $\overline{DS}$ High to R/$\overline{W}$ High	t_{SHRH}	60	—	50	—	40	—	20	—	10	—	ns
18[1]	Clock High to R/$\overline{W}$ High (Maximum)	t_{CHRHx}	—	90	—	80	—	70	—	60	—	60	ns
19	Clock High to R/$\overline{W}$ High (Minimum)	t_{CHRHn}	0	—	0	—	0	—	0	—	0	—	ns
20[1]	Clock High to R/$\overline{W}$ Low	t_{CHRL}	—	90	—	80	—	70	—	60	—	60	ns
21[2]	Address Valid to R/$\overline{W}$ Low	t_{AVRL}	45	—	25	—	20	—	0	—	0	—	ns
21A[2]	FC Valid to R/$\overline{W}$ Low	t_{FCVRL}	80	—	70	—	60	—	50	—	30	—	ns
22[2]	R/$\overline{W}$ Low to $\overline{DS}$ Low (Write)	t_{RLSL}	200	—	140	—	80	—	50	—	30	—	ns
23	Clock Low to Data Out Valid	t_{CLDO}	—	90	—	80	—	70	—	55	—	55	ns
25[2]	$\overline{DS}$ High to Data Out Invalid	t_{SHDO}	60	—	40	—	30	—	20	—	15	—	ns
26[2]	Data Out Valid to $\overline{DS}$ Low (Write)	t_{DOSL}	55	—	35	—	30	—	20	—	15	—	ns
27[6]	Data In to Clock Low (Setup Time)	t_{DICL}	30	—	25	—	15	—	15	—	15	—	ns
28[2]	$\overline{AS}$, $\overline{DS}$ High to $\overline{DTACK}$ High	t_{SHDAH}	0	240	0	160	0	120	0	90	0	70	ns
29	$\overline{DS}$ High to Data Invalid (Hold Time)	t_{SHDI}	0	—	0	—	0	—	0	—	0	—	ns
30	$\overline{AS}$, $\overline{DS}$ High to $\overline{BERR}$ High	t_{SHBEH}	0	—	0	—	0	—	0	—	0	—	ns
31[2, 6]	$\overline{DTACK}$ Low to Data In (Setup Time)	t_{DALDI}	—	180	—	120	—	90	—	65	—	50	ns
32	HALT and RESET Input Transition Time	t_{RHrf}	0	200	0	200	0	200	0	200	0	200	ns
33	Clock High to $\overline{BG}$ Low	t_{CHGL}	—	90	—	80	—	70	—	60	—	50	ns
34	Clock High to $\overline{BG}$ High	t_{CHGH}	—	90	—	80	—	70	—	60	—	50	ns
35	$\overline{BR}$ Low to $\overline{BG}$ Low	t_{BRLGL}	1.5	3.0	1.5	3.0	1.5	3.0	1.5	3.0	1.5	3.0	Clk. Per.
36	$\overline{BR}$ High to $\overline{BG}$ High	t_{BRHGH}	1.5	3.0	1.5	3.0	1.5	3.0	1.5	3.0	1.5	3.0	Clk. Per.
37	$\overline{BTACK}$ Low to $\overline{BG}$ High	t_{GALGH}	1.5	3.0	1.5	3.0	1.5	3.0	1.5	3.0	1.5	3.0	Clk. Per.
38	$\overline{BG}$ Low to Bus High Impedance (With $\overline{AS}$ High)	t_{GLZ}	—	120	—	100	—	80	—	70	—	60	ns
39	$\overline{BG}$ Width High	t_{GH}	1.5	—	1.5	—	1.5	—	1.5	—	1.5	—	Clk. Per.
46	$\overline{BGACK}$ Width	t_{BGL}	1.5	—	1.5	—	1.5	—	1.5	—	1.5	—	Clk. Per.
47[6]	Asynchronous Input Setup Time	t_{ASI}	30	—	25	—	20	—	20	—	20	—	ns
48	$\overline{BERR}$ Low to $\overline{DTACK}$ Low (Note 3)	t_{BELDAL}	50	—	50	—	50	—	50	—	50	—	ns
53	Data Hold from Clock High	t_{CHDO}	0	—	0	—	0	—	0	—	0	—	ns
55	R/$\overline{W}$ to Data Bus Impedance Change	t_{RLDO}	55	—	35	—	30	—	20	—	10	—	ns
56	Halt/$\overline{RESET}$ Pulse Width (Note 4)	t_{HRPW}	10	—	10	—	10	—	10	—	10	—	Clk. Per.

NOTES:
1. For a loading capacitance of less than or equal to 50 picofarads, subtract 5 nanoseconds from the values given in these columns.
2. Actual value depends on clock period.
3. If #47 is satisfied for both $\overline{DTACK}$ and $\overline{BERR}$, #48 may be 0 ns.
4. After V_{CC} has been applied for 100 ms.
5. #14 and #14A are one clock period less than the given number for T6E, BF4, and R9M mask sets.
6. If the asynchronous setup time (#47) requirements are satisfied, the $\overline{DTACK}$ low to data setup time (#31) requirement can be ignored. The data must only satisfy the data-in to clock-low setup time (#27) for the following cycle.

FIGURE 5 — READ CYCLE TIMING

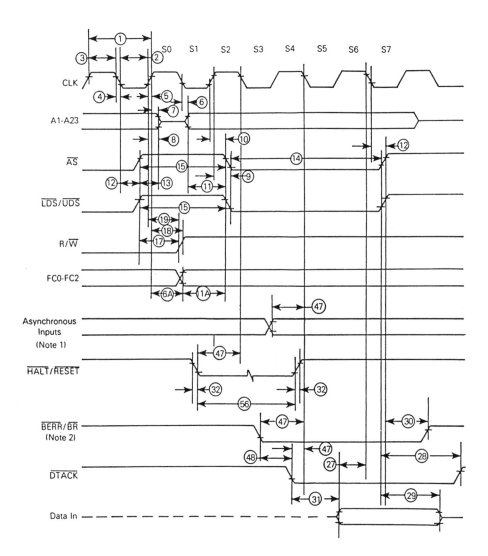

NOTES:

1. Setup time for the asynchronous inputs $\overline{BGACK}$, $\overline{IPL0}$-$\overline{IPL2}$, and $\overline{VPA}$ guarantees their recognition at the next falling edge of the clock.
2. $\overline{BR}$ need fall at this time only in order to insure being recognized at the end of this bus cycle.
3. Timing measurements are referenced to and from a low voltage of 0.8 volts and a high voltage of 2.0 volts, unless otherwise noted.

FIGURE 6 — WRITE CYCLE TIMING

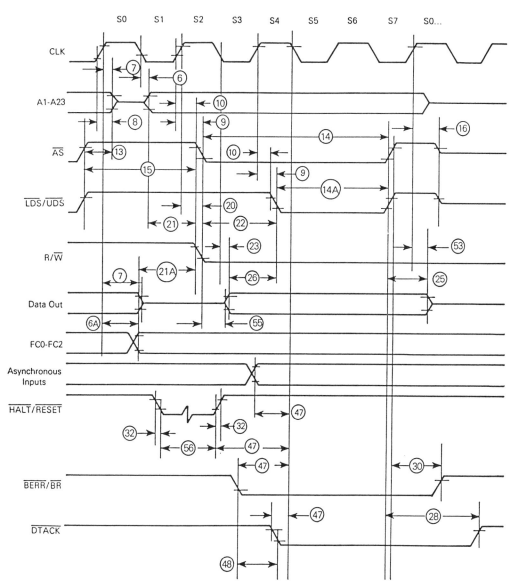

NOTE: Timing measurements are referenced to and from a low voltage of 0.8 volts and a high voltage of 2.0 volts, unless otherwise noted.

AC ELECTRICAL SPECIFICATIONS — BUS ARBITRATION(V_{CC} = 5.0 Vdc ±5%, V_{SS} = 0 Vdc; T_A = 0°C to 70°C, See Figure 7)

Num.	Characteristic	Symbol	4 MHz MC68000L4		6 MHz MC68000L6		8 MHz MC68000L8		10 MHz MC68000L10		12.5 MHz MC68000L12		Unit
			Min	Max	Min	Max	Min	Max	Min	Max	Min	Max	
33	Clock High to $\overline{BG}$ Low	t_{CHGL}	—	90	—	80	—	70	—	60	—	50	ns
34	Clock High to $\overline{BG}$ High	t_{CHGH}	—	90	—	80	—	70	—	60	—	50	ns
35	$\overline{BR}$ Low to $\overline{BG}$ Low	t_{BRLGL}	1.5	3.5	1.5	3.5	1.5	3.5	1.5	3.5	1.5	3.0	Clk. Per.
36	$\overline{BR}$ High to $\overline{BG}$ High	t_{BRHGH}	1.5	3.0	1.5	3.0	1.5	3.0	1.5	3.0	1.5	3.0	Clk. Per.
37	$\overline{BGACK}$ Low to $\overline{BG}$ High	t_{GALGH}	1.5	3.0	1.5	3.0	1.5	3.0	1.5	3.0	1.5	3.0	Clk. Per.
38	$\overline{BG}$ Low to Bus High Impedance (with $\overline{AS}$ High)	t_{GLZ}	—	120	—	100	—	80	—	70	—	60	ns
39	$\overline{BG}$ Width High	t_{GH}	1.5	—	1.5	—	1.5	—	1.5	—	1.5	—	Clk. Per.
46	$\overline{BGACK}$ Width	t_{BGL}	1.5	—	1.5	—	1.5	—	1.5	—	1.5	—	Clk. Per.

FIGURE 7 — AC ELECTRICAL WAVEFORMS — BUS ARBITRATION

These waveforms should only be referenced in regard to the edge-to-edge measurement of the timing specifications. They are not intended as a functional description of the input and output signals. Refer to other functional descriptions and their related diagrams for device operation.

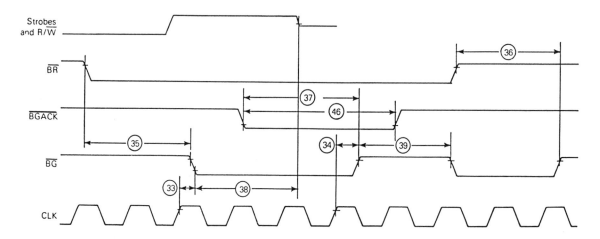

NOTES:

1. Setup time for the asynchronous inputs $\overline{BERR}$, $\overline{BGACK}$, $\overline{BR}$, $\overline{DTACK}$, $\overline{IPL0}$-$\overline{IPL2}$, and $\overline{VPA}$ guarantees their recognition at the next falling edge of the clock.
2. Waveform measurements for all inputs and outputs are specified at: logic high = 2.0 volts, logic low = 0.8 volts.

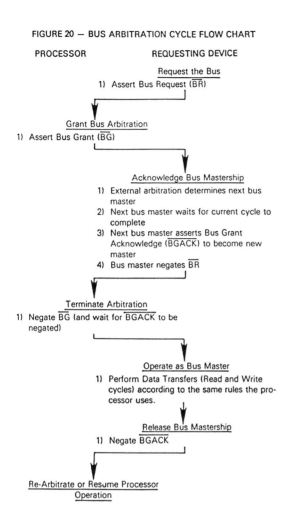

FIGURE 20 — BUS ARBITRATION CYCLE FLOW CHART

PROCESSOR   REQUESTING DEVICE

Request the Bus
1) Assert Bus Request ($\overline{BR}$)

Grant Bus Arbitration
1) Assert Bus Grant ($\overline{BG}$)

Acknowledge Bus Mastership
1) External arbitration determines next bus master
2) Next bus master waits for current cycle to complete
3) Next bus master asserts Bus Grant Acknowledge ($\overline{BGACK}$) to become new master
4) Bus master negates $\overline{BR}$

Terminate Arbitration
1) Negate $\overline{BG}$ (and wait for $\overline{BGACK}$ to be negated)

Operate as Bus Master
1) Perform Data Transfers (Read and Write cycles) according to the same rules the processor uses.

Release Bus Mastership
1) Negate $\overline{BGACK}$

Re-Arbitrate or Resume Processor Operation

Requesting the Bus. External devices capable of becoming bus masters request the bus by asserting the bus request ($\overline{BR}$) signal. This is a wire ORed signal (although it need not be constructed from open collector devices) that indicates to the processor that some external device requires control of the external bus. The processor is effectively at a lower bus priority level than the external device and will relinquish the bus after it has completed the last bus cycle it has started.

When no acknowledge is received before the bus request signal goes inactive, the processor will continue processing when it detects that the bus request is inactive. This allows ordinary processing to continue if the arbitration circuitry responded to noise inadvertently.

Receiving the Bus Grant. The processor asserts bus grant ($\overline{BG}$) as soon as possible. Normally this is immediately after internal synchronization. The only exception to this occurs when the processor has made an internal decision to execute the next bus cycle but has not progressed far enough into the cycle to have asserted the address strobe ($\overline{AS}$) signal. In this case, bus grant will not be asserted until one clock after address strobe is asserted to indicate to external devices that a bus cycle is being executed.

The bus grant signal may be routed through a daisy-chained network or through a specific priority-encoded network. The processor is not affected by the external method of arbitration as long as the protocol is obeyed.

Acknowledgement of Mastership. Upon receiving a bus grant, the requesting device waits until address strobe, data transfer acknowledge, and bus grant acknowledge are negated before issuing its own $\overline{BGACK}$. The negation of the address strobe indicates that the previous master has completed its cycle, the negation of bus grant acknowledge indicates that the previous master has released the bus. (While address strobe is asserted no device is allowed to "break into" a cycle.) The negation of data transfer acknowledge indicates the previous slave has terminated its connection to the previous master. Note that in some applications data transfer acknowledge might not enter into this function. General purpose devices would then be connected such that

FIGURE 21 — BUS ARBITRATION CYCLE TIMING DIAGRAM

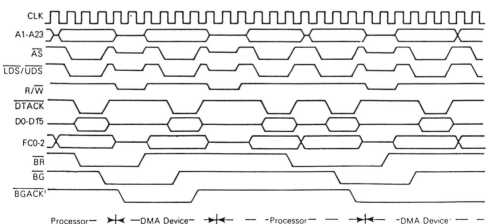

they were only dependent on address strobe. When bus grant acknowledge is issued the device is bus master until it negates bus grant acknowledge. Bus grant acknowledge should not be negated until after the bus cycle(s) is (are) completed. Bus mastership is terminated at the negation of bus grant acknowledge.

The bus request from the granted device should be dropped after bus grant acknowledge is asserted. If a bus request is still pending, another bus grant will be asserted within a few clocks of the negation of bus grant. Refer to Bus Arbitration Control section. Note that the processor does not perform any external bus cycles before it re-asserts bus grant.

BUS ARBITRATION CONTROL. The bus arbitration control unit in the MC68000 is implemented with a finite state machine. A state diagram of this machine is shown in Figure 22. All asynchronous signals to the MC68000 are synchronized before being used internally. This synchronization is accomplished in a maximum of one cycle of the system clock, assuming that the asynchronous input setup time (#47) has

been met (see Figure 23). The input signal is sampled on the falling edge of the clock and is valid internally after the next falling edge.

As shown in Figure 22, input signals labeled R and A are internally synchronized on the bus request and bus grant acknowledge pins respectively. The bus grant output is labeled G and the internal three-state control signal T. If T is true, the address, data, and control buses are placed in a high-impedance state when $\overline{AS}$ is negated. All signals are shown in positive logic (active high) regardless of their true active voltage level.

State changes (valid outputs) occur on the next rising edge after the internal signal is valid.

A timing diagram of the bus arbitration sequence during a processor bus cycle is shown in Figure 24. The bus arbitration sequence while the bus is inactive (i.e., executing internal operations such as a multiply instruction) is shown in Figure 25.

If a bus request is made at a time when the MPU has already begun a bus cycle but $\overline{AS}$ has not been asserted (bus state S0), $\overline{BG}$ will not be asserted on the next rising edge. Instead, $\overline{BG}$ will be delayed until the second rising edge following it's internal assertion. This sequence is shown in Figure 26.

BUS ERROR AND HALT OPERATION. In a bus architecture that requires a handshake from an external device, the possibility exists that the handshake might not occur. Since different systems will require a different maximum response time, a bus error input is provided. External circuitry must be used to determine the duration between address strobe and data transfer acknowledge before issuing a bus error signal. When a bus error signal is received, the processor has two options: initiate a bus error exception sequence or try running the bus cycle again.

FIGURE 22 — STATE DIAGRAM OF MC68000 BUS ARBITRATION UNIT

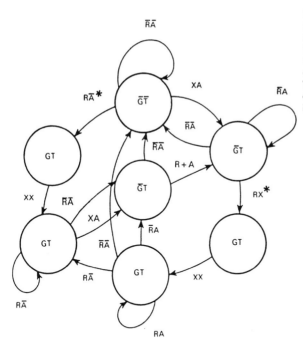

R = Bus Request Internal
A = Bus Grant Acknowledge Internal
G = Bus Grant
T = Three-State Control to Bus Control Logic
X = Don't Care

* State machine will not change state if bus is in S0. Refer to BUS ARBITRATION CONTROL for additional information.

FIGURE 23 — TIMING RELATIONSHIP OF EXTERNAL ASYNCHRONOUS INPUTS TO INTERNAL SIGNALS

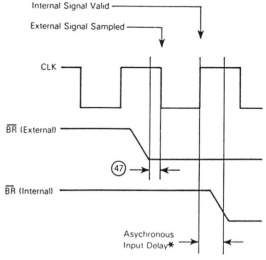

*This delay time is equal to parameter #33, tCHGL

FIGURE 24 — BUS ARBITRATION DURING PROCESSOR BUS CYCLE

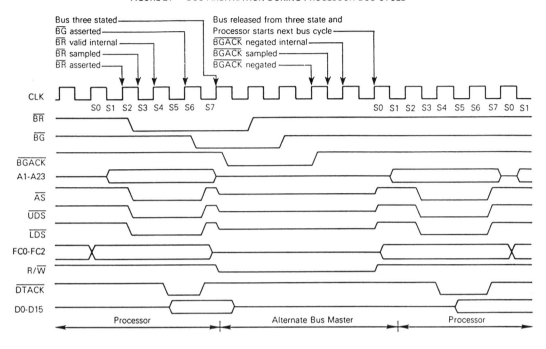

FIGURE 25 — BUS ARBITRATION WITH BUS INACTIVE

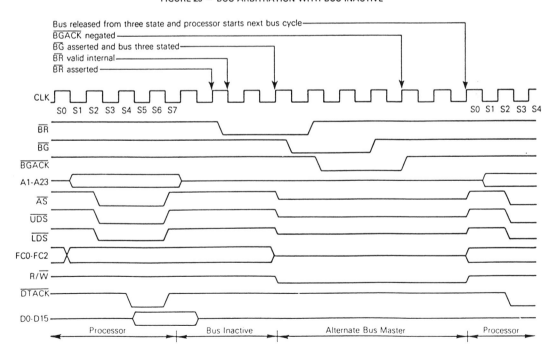

FIGURE 26 — BUS ARBITRATION DURING PROCESSOR BUS CYCLE SPECIAL CASE

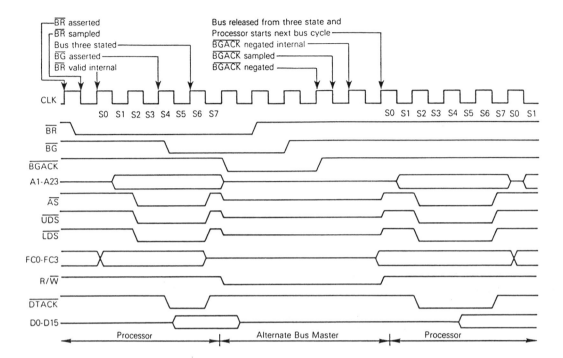

Exception Sequence. When the bus error signal is asserted, the current bus cycle is terminated. If $\overline{BERR}$ is asserted before the falling edge of S4, $\overline{AS}$ will be negated in S7 in either a read or write cycle. As long as $\overline{BERR}$ remains asserted, the data and address buses will be in the high-impedance state. When $\overline{BERR}$ is negated, the processor will begin stacking for exception processing. Figure 27 is a timing diagram for the exception sequence. The sequence is composed of the following elements.

1. Stacking the program counter and status register
2. Stacking the error information

3. Reading the bus error vector table entry
4. Executing the bus error handler routine

The stacking of the program counter and the status register is the same as if an interrupt had occurred. Several additional items are stacked when a bus error occurs. These items are used to determine the nature of the error and correct it, if possible. The bus error vector is vector number two located at address $000008. The processor loads the new program counter from this location. A software bus error handler routine is then executed by the processor. Refer to **EXCEPTION PROCESSING** for additional information.

Re-Running the Bus Cycle. When, during a bus cycle, the processor receives a bus error signal and the halt pin is being driven by an external device, the processor enters the re-run sequence. Figure 28 is a timing diagram for re-running the bus cycle.

The processor terminates the bus cycle, then puts the address and data output lines in the high-impedance state. The processor remains "halted," and will not run another bus cycle until the halt signal is removed by external logic. Then the processor will re-run the previous bus cycle using the same address, the same function codes, the same data (for a write operation), and the same controls. The bus error signal should be removed at least one clock cycle before the halt signal is removed.

NOTE

The processor will not re-run a read-modify-write cycle. This restriction is made to guarantee that the entire cycle runs correctly and that the write operation of a Test-and-Set operation is performed without ever releasing $\overline{AS}$. If $\overline{BERR}$ and $\overline{HALT}$ are asserted during a read-modify-write bus cycle, a bus error operation results.

FIGURE 27 — BUS ERROR TIMING DIAGRAM

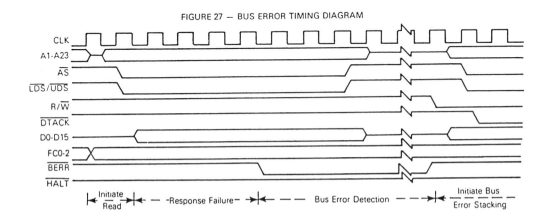

FIGURE 28 — RE-RUN BUS CYCLE TIMING INFORMATION

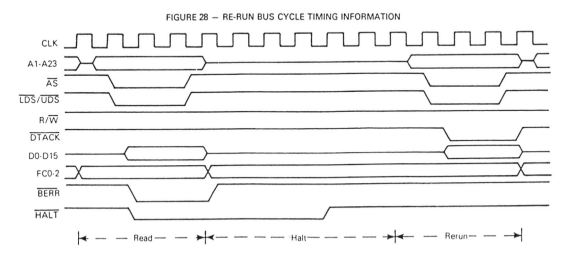

Halt Operation with No Bus Error. The halt input signal to the MC68000 performs a Halt/Run/Single-Step function in a similar fashion to the M6800 halt function. The halt and run modes are somewhat self explanatory in that when the halt signal is constantly active the processor "halts" (does nothing) and when the halt signal is constantly inactive the processor "runs" (does something).

The single-step mode is derived from correctly timed transitions on the halt signal input. It forces the processor to execute a single bus cycle by entering the "run" mode until the processor starts a bus cycle then changing to the "halt" mode. Thus, the single-step mode allows the user to proceed through (and therefore debug) processor operations one bus cycle at a time.

Figure 29 details the timing required for correct single-step operations. Some care must be exercised to avoid harmful interactions between the bus error signal and the halt pin when using the single cycle mode as a debugging tool. This is also true of interactions between the halt and reset lines since these can reset the machine.

When the processor completes a bus cycle after recognizing that the halt signal is active, most three-state signals are put in the high-impedance state. These include:

1. address lines
2. data lines

This is required for correct performance of the re-run bus cycle operation.

While the processor is honoring the halt request, bus arbitration performs as usual. That is, halting has no effect on bus arbitration. It is the bus arbitration function that removes the control signals from the bus.

The halt function and the hardware trace capability allow the hardware debugger to trace single bus cycles or single instructions at a time. These processor capabilities, along with a software debugging package, give total debugging flexibility.

Double Bus Faults. When a bus error exception occurs, the processor will attempt to stack several words containing information about the state of the machine. If a bus error exception occurs during the stacking operation, there have been two bus errors in a row. This is commonly referred to as a double bus fault. When a double bus fault occurs, the processor will halt. Once a bus error exception has occurred, any bus error exception occurring before the execution of the next instruction constitutes a double bus fault.

Note that a bus cycle which is re-run does not constitute a bus error exception, and does not contribute to a double bus fault. Note also that this means that as long as the external hardware requests it, the processor will continue to re-run the same bus cycle.

The bus error pin also has an effect on processor operation after the processor receives an external reset input. The processor reads the vector table after a reset to determine the address to start program execution. If a bus error occurs while reading the vector table (or at any time before the first instruction is executed), the processor reacts as if a double bus fault has occurred and it halts. Only an external reset will start a halted processor.

FIGURE 29 — HALT SIGNAL TIMING CHARACTERISTICS

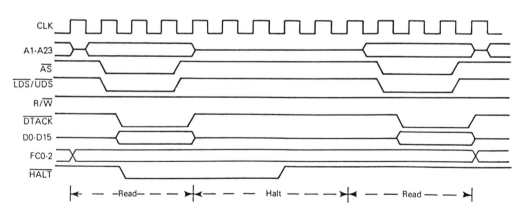

In order to properly control termination of a bus cycle for a re-run or a bus error condition, $\overline{\text{DTACK}}$, $\overline{\text{BERR}}$, and $\overline{\text{HALT}}$ should be asserted and negated on the rising edge of the MC68000 clock. This will assure that when two signals are asserted simultaneously, the required setup time (#47) for both of them will be met during the same bus state.

This, or some equivalent precaution, should be designed external to the MC68000. Parameter #48 is intended to ensure this operation in a totally asynchronous system, and may be ignored if the above conditions are met.

The preferred bus cycle terminations may be summarized as follows (case numbers refer to Table 4):

Normal Termination: $\overline{\text{DTACK}}$ occurs first (case 1).

Halt Termination: $\overline{\text{HALT}}$ is asserted at same time, or precedes $\overline{\text{DTACK}}$ (no $\overline{\text{BERR}}$) cases 2 and 3.

Bus Error Termination: $\overline{\text{BERR}}$ is asserted in lieu of, at same time, or preceding $\overline{\text{DTACK}}$ (case 4); BERR negated at same time, or after $\overline{\text{DTACK}}$.

Re-Run Termination: $\overline{\text{HALT}}$ and $\overline{\text{BERR}}$ asserted at the same time, or before $\overline{\text{DTACK}}$ (cases 6 and 7); $\overline{\text{HALT}}$ must be negated at least 1 cycle after $\overline{\text{BERR}}$. (Case 5 indicates $\overline{\text{BERR}}$

may precede $\overline{\text{HALT}}$ on all except R9M and T6E < early mask sets > which allows fully asynchronous assertion).

Table 4 details the resulting bus cycle termination under various combinations of control signal sequences. The negation of these same control signals under several conditions is shown in Table 5 ($\overline{\text{DTACK}}$ is assumed to be negated normally in all cases; for best results, both $\overline{\text{DTACK}}$ and $\overline{\text{BERR}}$ should be negated when address strobe is negated.)

Example A: A system uses a watch-dog timer to terminate accesses to un-populated address space. The timer asserts $\overline{\text{DTACK}}$ and $\overline{\text{BERR}}$ simultaneously after time-out. (case 4)

Example B: A system uses error detection on RAM contents. Designer may (a) delay $\overline{\text{DTACK}}$ until data verified, and return $\overline{\text{BERR}}$ and $\overline{\text{HALT}}$ simultaneously to re-run error cycle (case 6), or if valid, return $\overline{\text{DTACK}}$; (b) delay $\overline{\text{DTACK}}$ until data verified, and return $\overline{\text{BERR}}$ at same time as $\overline{\text{DTACK}}$ if data in error (case 4); (c) return $\overline{\text{DTACK}}$ prior to data verification, as described in previous section. If data invalid, $\overline{\text{BERR}}$ is asserted (case 1) in next cycle. Error-handling software must know how to recover error cycle.

TABLE 4 — $\overline{\text{DTACK}}$, $\overline{\text{BERR}}$, $\overline{\text{HALT}}$ ASSERTION RESULTS

Case No.	Control Signal	Asserted on Rising Edge of State		Result
		N	N+2	
1	$\overline{\text{DTACK}}$	A	S	Normal cycle terminate and continue.
	$\overline{\text{BERR}}$	NA	X	
	$\overline{\text{HALT}}$	NA	X	
2	$\overline{\text{DTACK}}$	A	S	Normal cycle terminate and halt. Continue when HALT removed.
	$\overline{\text{BERR}}$	NA	X	
	$\overline{\text{HALT}}$	A	S	
3	$\overline{\text{DTACK}}$	NA	A	Normal cycle terminate and halt. Continue when HALT removed.
	$\overline{\text{BERR}}$	NA	NA	
	$\overline{\text{HALT}}$	A	S	
4	$\overline{\text{DTACK}}$	X	X	Terminate and take bus error trap.
	$\overline{\text{BERR}}$	A	S	
	$\overline{\text{HALT}}$	NA	NA	
5	$\overline{\text{DTACK}}$	NA	X	R9M, T6E, BF4: Unpredictable results, no re-run, no error trap; usually traps to vector number 0. All others: terminate and re-run.
	$\overline{\text{BERR}}$	A	S	
	HALT	NA	A	
6	$\overline{\text{DTACK}}$	X	X	Terminate and re-run.
	$\overline{\text{BERR}}$	A	S	
	$\overline{\text{HALT}}$	A	S	
7	$\overline{\text{DTACK}}$	NA	X	Terminate and re-run when HALT removed.
	$\overline{\text{BERR}}$	NA	A	
	$\overline{\text{HALT}}$	A	S	

Legend:
   N — the number of the current even bus state (e.g., S4, S6, etc.)
   A — signal is asserted in this bus state
   NA — signal is not asserted in this state
   X — don't care
   S — signal was asserted in previous state and remains asserted in this state

TABLE 5 — $\overline{\text{BERR}}$ AND $\overline{\text{HALT}}$ NEGATION RESULTS

Conditions of Termination in Table A	Control Signal	Negated on Rising Edge of State			Results — Next Cycle
		N		N+2	
Bus Error	$\overline{\text{BERR}}$	●	or	●	Takes bus error trap.
	$\overline{\text{HALT}}$		or	●	
Re-run	$\overline{\text{BERR}}$	●	or	●	Illegal sequence; usually traps to vector number 0.
	$\overline{\text{HALT}}$	●			
Re-run	$\overline{\text{BERR}}$	●			Re-runs the bus cycle.
	$\overline{\text{HALT}}$			●	
Normal	$\overline{\text{BERR}}$	●			May lengthen next cycle.
	$\overline{\text{HALT}}$	●	or	●	
Normal	$\overline{\text{BERR}}$			●	If next cycle is started it will be terminated as a bus error.
	$\overline{\text{HALT}}$	●	or	none	

RESET OPERATION. The reset signal is a bidirectional signal that allows either the processor or an external signal to reset the system. Figure 30 is a timing diagram for reset operations. Both the halt and reset lines must be applied to ensure total reset of the processor.

When the reset and halt lines are driven by an external device, it is recognized as an entire system reset, including the processor. The processor responds by reading the reset vector table entry (vector number zero, address $000000) and loads it into the supervisor stack pointer (SSP). Vector table entry number one at address $000004 is read next and loaded into the program counter. The processor initializes the status register to an interrupt level of seven. No other registers are affected by the reset sequence.

When a RESET sequence is executed, the processor drives the reset pin for 124 clock pulses. In this case, the processor is trying to reset the rest of the system. Therefore, there is no effect on the internal state of the processor. All of the processor's internal registers and the status register are unaffected by the execution of a RESET instruction. All external devices connected to the reset line should be reset at the completion of the RESET instruction.

Asserting the Reset and Halt pins for 10 clock cycles will cause a processor reset, except when V_{CC} is initially applied to the processor. In this case, an external reset must be applied for 100 milliseconds.

FIGURE 30 — RESET OPERATION TIMING DIAGRAM

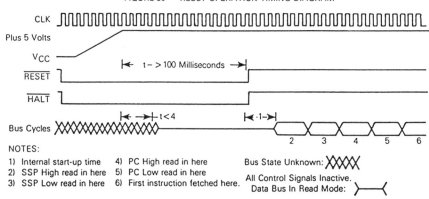

PROCESSING STATES

The following paragraphs describe the actions of the MC68000 which are outside the normal processing associated with the execution of instructions. The functions of the bits in the supervisor portion of the status register are covered: the supervisor/user bit, the trace enable bit, and the processor interrupt priority mask. Finally, the sequence of memory references and actions taken by the processor on exception conditions is detailed.

The MC68000 is always in one of three processing states: normal, exception, or halted. The normal processing state is that associated with instruction execution; the memory references are to fetch instructions and operands, and to store results. A special case of the normal state is the stopped state which the processor enters when a STOP instruction is executed. In this state, no further memory references are made.

The exception processing state is associated with interrupts, trap instructions, tracing and other exceptional conditions. The exception may be internally generated by an instruction or by an unusual condition arising during the execution of an instruction. Externally, exception processing can be forced by an interrupt, by a bus error, or by a reset. Exception processing is designed to provide an efficient context switch so that the processor may handle unusual conditions.

The halted processing state is an indication of catastrophic hardware failure. For example, if during the exception processing of a bus error another bus error occurs, the processor assumes that the system is unusable and halts. Only an external reset can restart a halted processor. Note that a processor in the stopped state is not in the halted state, nor vice versa.

PRIVILEGE STATES

The processor operates in one of two states of privilege: the "user" state or the "supervisor" state. The privilege state determines which operations are legal, is used by the external memory management device to control and translate accesses, and is used to choose between the supervisor stack pointer and the user stack pointer in instruction references.

The privilege state is a mechanism for providing security in a computer system. Programs should access only their own code and data areas, and ought to be restricted from accessing information which they do not need and must not modify.

The privilege mechanism provides security by allowing most programs to execute in user state. In this state, the accesses are controlled, and the effects on other parts of the system are limited. The operating system executes in the supervisor state, has access to all resources, and performs the overhead tasks for the user state programs.

SUPERVISOR STATE. The supervisor state is the higher state of privilege. For instruction execution, the supervisor state is determined by the S-bit of the status register; if the S-bit is asserted (high), the processor is in the supervisor state. All instructions can be executed in the supervisor state. The bus cycles generated by instructions executed in the supervisor state are classified as supervisor references. While the processor is in the supervisor privilege state, those instructions which use either the system stack pointer implicitly or address register seven explicitly access the supervisor stack pointer.

All exception processing is done in the supervisor state, regardless of the setting of the S-bit. The bus cycles generated during exception processing are classified as supervisor references. All stacking operations during exception processing use the supervisor stack pointer.

USER STATE. The user state is the lower state of privilege. For instruction execution, the user state is determined by the S-bit of the status register; if the S-bit is negated (low), the processor is executing instructions in the user state.

Most instructions execute the same in user state as in the supervisor state. However, some instructions which have important system effects are made privileged. User programs are not permitted to execute the STOP instruction, or the RESET instruction. To ensure that a user program cannot enter the supervisor state except in a controlled manner, the instructions which modify the whole status register are privileged. To aid in debugging programs which are to be used as operating systems, the move to user stack pointer (MOVE USP) and move from user stack pointer (MOVE from USP) instructions are also privileged.

The bus cycles generated by an instruction executed in user state are classified as user state references. This allows an external memory management device to translate the address and to control access to protected portions of the address space. While the processor is in the user privilege state, those instructions which use either the system stack pointer implicitly, or address register seven explicitly, access the user stack pointer.

PRIVILEGE STATE CHANGES. Once the processor is in the user state and executing instructions, only exception processing can change the privilege state. During exception processing, the current setting of the S-bit of the status register is saved and the S-bit is asserted, putting the processing in the supervisor state. Therefore, when instruction execution resumes at the address specified to process the exception, the processor is in the supervisor privilege state.

REFERENCE CLASSIFICATION. When the processor makes a reference, it classifies the kind of reference being made, using the encoding on the three function code output lines. This allows external translation of addresses, control of access, and differentiation of special processor states, such as interrupt acknowledge. Table 6 lists the classification of references.

TABLE 6 — REFERENCE CLASSIFICATION

Function Code Output			Reference Class
FC2	FC1	FC0	
0	0	0	(Unassigned)
0	0	1	User Data
0	1	0	User Program
0	1	1	(Unassigned)
1	0	0	(Unassigned)
1	0	1	Supervisor Data
1	1	0	Supervisor Program
1	1	1	Interrupt Acknowledge

EXCEPTION PROCESSING

Before discussing the details of interrupts, traps, and tracing, a general description of exception processing is in order. The processing of an exception occurs in four steps, with variations for different exception causes. During the first step, a temporary copy of the status register is made, and the status register is set for exception processing. In the second step the exception vector is determined, and the third step is the saving of the current processor context. In the fourth step a new context is obtained, and the processor switches to instruction processing.

EXCEPTION VECTORS. Exception vectors are memory locations from which the processor fetches the address of a routine which will handle that exception. All exception vectors are two words in length (Figure 31), except for the reset vector, which is four words. All exception vectors lie in the supervisor data space, except for the reset vector which is in the supervisor program space. A vector number is an eight-bit number which, when multiplied by four, gives the address of an exception vector. Vector numbers are generated internally or externally, depending on the cause of the exception. In the case of interrupts, during the interrupt acknowledge bus cycle, a peripheral provides an 8-bit vector number (Figure 32) to the processor on data bus lines D0 through D7. The processor translates the vector number into a full 24-bit address, as shown in Figure 33. The memory layout for exception vectors is given in Table 7.

As shown in Table 7, the memory layout is 512 words long (1024 bytes). It starts at address 0 and proceeds through address 1023. This provides 255 unique vectors; some of these are reserved for TRAPS and other system functions. Of the 255, there are 192 reserved for user interrupt vectors. However, there is no protection on the first 64 entries, so user interrupt vectors may overlap at the discretion of the systems designer.

KINDS OF EXCEPTIONS. Exceptions can be generated by either internal or external causes. The externally generated exceptions are the interrupts and the bus error and reset requests. The interrupts are requests from peripheral devices for processor action while the bus error and reset inputs are used for access control and processor restart. The internally generated exceptions come from instructions, or from ad-

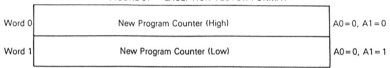

FIGURE 31 — EXCEPTION VECTOR FORMAT

Word 0	New Program Counter (High)	A0 = 0, A1 = 0
Word 1	New Program Counter (Low)	A0 = 0, A1 = 1

FIGURE 32 — PERIPHERAL VECTOR NUMBER FORMAT

D15   D8 D7   D0

Ignored	v7	v6	v5	v4	v3	v2	v1	v0

Where:
v7 is the MSB of the Vector Number
v0 is the LSB of the Vector Number

FIGURE 33 — ADDRESS TRANSLATED FROM 8-BIT VECTOR NUMBER

A23   A10 A9 A8 A7 A6 A5 A4 A3 A2 A1 A0

All Zeroes	v7	v6	v5	v4	v3	v2	v1	v0	0	0

TABLE 7 — EXCEPTION VECTOR ASSIGNMENT

Vector Number(s)	Address Dec	Address Hex	Address Space	Assignment
0	0	000	SP	Reset: Initial SSP
—	4	004	SP	Reset: Initial PC
2	8	008	SD	Bus Error
3	12	00C	SD	Address Error
4	16	010	SD	Illegal Instruction
5	20	014	SD	Zero Divide
6	24	018	SD	CHK Instruction
7	28	01C	SD	TRAPV Instruction
8	32	020	SD	Privilege Violation
9	36	024	SD	Trace
10	40	028	SD	Line 1010 Emulator
11	44	02C	SD	Line 1111 Emulator
12*	48	030	SD	(Unassigned, reserved)
13*	52	034	SD	(Unassigned, reserved)
14*	56	038	SD	(Unassigned, reserved)
15	60	03C	SD	Uninitialized Interrupt Vector
16-23*	64	04C	SD	(Unassigned, reserved)
	95	05F		—
24	96	060	SD	Spurious Interrupt
25	100	064	SD	Level 1 Interrupt Autovector
26	104	068	SD	Level 2 Interrupt Autovector
27	108	06C	SD	Level 3 Interrupt Autovector
28	112	070	SD	Level 4 Interrupt Autovector
29	116	074	SD	Level 5 Interrupt Autovector
30	120	078	SD	Level 6 Interrupt Autovector
31	124	07C	SD	Level 7 Interrupt Autovector
32-47	128	080	SD	TRAP Instruction Vectors
	191	0BF		—
48-63*	192	0C0	SD	(Unassigned, reserved)
	255	0FF		—
64-255	256	100	SD	User Interrupt Vectors
	1023	3FF		—

*Vector numbers 12, 13, 14, 16 through 23 and 48 through 63 are reserved for future enhancements by Motorola. No user peripheral devices should be assigned these numbers.

dress errors or tracing. The trap (TRAP), trap on overflow (TRAPV), check register against bounds (CHK) and divide (DIV) instructions all can generate exceptions as part of their instruction execution. In addition, illegal instructions, word fetches from odd addresses and privilege violations cause exceptions. Tracing behaves like a very high priority, internally generated interrupt after each instruction execution.

EXCEPTION PROCESSING SEQUENCE. Exception processing occurs in four identifiable steps. In the first step, an internal copy is made of the status register. After the copy is made, the S-bit is asserted, putting the processor into the supervisor privilege state. Also, the T-bit is negated which will allow the exception handler to execute unhindered by tracing. For the reset and interrupt exceptions, the interrupt priority mask is also updated.

In the second step, the vector number of the exception is determined. For interrupts, the vector number is obtained by a processor fetch, classified as an interrupt acknowledge. For all other exceptions, internal logic provides the vector number. This vector number is then used to generate the address of the exception vector.

The third step is to save the current processor status, except for the reset exception. The current program counter value and the saved copy of the status register are stacked using the supervisor stack pointer. The program counter value stacked usually points to the next unexecuted instruction, however for bus error and address error, the value stacked for the program counter is unpredictable, and may be incremented from the address of the instruction which caused the error. Additional information defining the current context is stacked for the bus error and address error exceptions.

The last step is the same for all exceptions. The new program counter value is fetched from the exception vector. The processor then resumes instruction execution. The instruction at the address given in the exception vector is fetched, and normal instruction decoding and execution is started.

MULTIPLE EXCEPTIONS. These paragraphs describe the processing which occurs when multiple exceptions arise simultaneously. Exceptions can be grouped according to their occurrence and priority. The Group 0 exceptions are reset, bus error, and address error. These exceptions cause the instruction currently being executed to be aborted, and the exception processing to commence within two clock cycles. The Group 1 exceptions are trace and interrupt, as well as the privilege violations and illegal instructions. These exceptions allow the current instruction to execute to completion, but preempt the execution of the next instruction by forcing exception processing to occur (privilege violations and illegal instructions are detected when they are the next instruction to be executed). The Group 2 exceptions occur as part of the normal processing of instructions. The TRAP, TRAPV, CHK, and zero divide exceptions are in this group. For these exceptions, the normal execution of an instruction may lead to exception processing.

Group 0 exceptions have highest priority, while Group 2 exceptions have lowest priority. Within Group 0, reset has highest priority, followed by bus error and then address error. Within Group 1, trace has priority over external interrupts, which in turn takes priority over illegal instruction and

privilege violation. Since only one instruction can be executed at a time, there is no priority relation within Group 2.

The priority relation between two exceptions determines which is taken, or taken first, if the conditions for both arise simultaneously. Therefore, if a bus error occurs during a TRAP instruction, the bus error takes precedence, and the TRAP instruction processing is aborted. In another example, if an interrupt request occurs during the execution of an instruction while the T-bit is asserted, the trace exception has priority, and is processed first. Before instruction processing resumes, however, the interrupt exception is also processed, and instruction processing commences finally in the interrupt handler routine. A summary of exception grouping and priority is given in Table 8.

TABLE 8 — EXCEPTION GROUPING AND PRIORITY

Group	Exception	Processing
0	Reset Bus Error Address Error	Exception processing begins within two clock cycles.
1	Trace Interrupt Illegal Privilege	Exception processing begins before the next instruction
2	TRAP, TRAPV, CHK, Zero Divide	Exception processing is started by normal instruction execution

EXCEPTION PROCESSING DETAILED DISCUSSION

Exceptions have a number of sources, and each exception has processing which is peculiar to it. The following paragraphs detail the sources of exceptions, how each arises, and how each is processed.

RESET. The reset input provides the highest exception level. The processing of the reset signal is designed for system initiation, and recovery from catastrophic failure. Any processing in progress at the time of the reset is aborted and cannot be recovered. The processor is forced into the supervisor state, and the trace state is forced off. The processor interrupt priority mask is set at level seven. The vector number is internally generated to reference the reset exception vector at location 0 in the supervisor program space. Because no assumptions can be made about the validity of register contents, in particular the supervisor stack pointer, neither the program counter nor the status register is saved. The address contained in the first two words of the reset exception vector is fetched as the initial supervisor stack pointer, and the address in the last two words of the reset exception vector is fetched as the initial program counter. Finally, instruction execution is started at the address in the program counter. The power-up/restart code should be pointed to by the initial program counter.

The RESET instruction does not cause loading of the reset vector, but does assert the reset line to reset external devices. This allows the software to reset the system to a known state and then continue processing with the next instruction.

INTERRUPTS. Seven levels of interrupt priorities are provided. Devices may be chained externally within interrupt priority levels, allowing an unlimited number of peripheral devices to interrupt the processor. Interrupt priority levels are numbered from one to seven, level seven being the highest priority. The status register contains a three-bit mask which indicates the current processor priority, and interrupts are inhibited for all priority levels less than or equal to the current processor priority.

An interrupt request is made to the processor by encoding the interrupt request level on the interrupt request lines; a zero indicates no interrupt request. Interrupt requests arriving at the processor do not force immediate exception processing, but are made pending. Pending interrupts are detected between instruction executions. If the priority of the pending interrupt is lower than or equal to the current processor priority, execution continues with the next instruction and the interrupt exception processing is postponed. (The recognition of level seven is slightly different, as explained in a following paragraph.)

If the priority of the pending interrupt is greater than the current processor priority, the exception processing sequence is started. First a copy of the status register is saved, and the privilege state is set to supervisor, tracing is suppressed, and the processor priority level is set to the level of the interrupt being acknowledged. The processor fetches the vector number from the interrupting device, classifying the reference as an interrupt acknowledge and displaying the level number of the interrupt being acknowledged on the address bus. If external logic requests an automatic vectoring, the processor internally generates a vector number which is determined by the interrupt level number. If external logic indicates a bus error, the interrupt is taken to be spurious, and the generated vector number references the spurious interrupt vector. The processor then proceeds with the usual exception processing, saving the program counter and status register on the supervisor stack. The saved value of the program counter is the address of the instruction which would have been executed had the interrupt not been present. The content of the interrupt vector whose vector number was previously obtained is fetched and loaded into the program counter, and normal instruction execution commences in the interrupt handling routine. A flow chart for the interrupt acknowledge sequence is given in Figure 34, a timing diagram is given in Figure 35, and the interrupt exception timing sequence is shown in Figure 36.

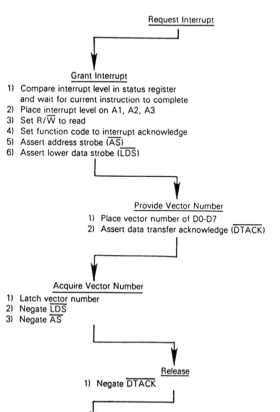

FIGURE 34 — INTERRUPT ACKNOWLEDGE SEQUENCE
FLOW CHART

PROCESSOR   INTERRUPTING DEVICE

Request Interrupt

Grant Interrupt
1) Compare interrupt level in status register and wait for current instruction to complete
2) Place interrupt level on A1, A2, A3
3) Set R/$\overline{\text{W}}$ to read
4) Set function code to interrupt acknowledge
5) Assert address strobe ($\overline{\text{AS}}$)
6) Assert lower data strobe ($\overline{\text{LDS}}$)

Provide Vector Number
1) Place vector number of D0-D7
2) Assert data transfer acknowledge ($\overline{\text{DTACK}}$)

Acquire Vector Number
1) Latch vector number
2) Negate $\overline{\text{LDS}}$
3) Negate $\overline{\text{AS}}$

Release
1) Negate $\overline{\text{DTACK}}$

Start Interrupt Processing

FIGURE 35 — INTERRUPT ACKNOWLEDGE SEQUENCE TIMING DIAGRAM

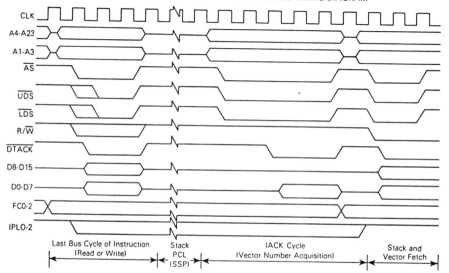

CLK

A4-A23

A1-A3

$\overline{\text{AS}}$

$\overline{\text{UDS}}$

$\overline{\text{LDS}}$

R/$\overline{\text{W}}$

$\overline{\text{DTACK}}$

D8-D15

D0-D7

FC0-2

IPL0-2

Last Bus Cycle of Instruction (Read or Write)   Stack PCL (SSP)   IACK Cycle (Vector Number Acquisition)   Stack and Vector Fetch

406

FIGURE 36 — INTERRUPT EXCEPTION TIMING SEQUENCE

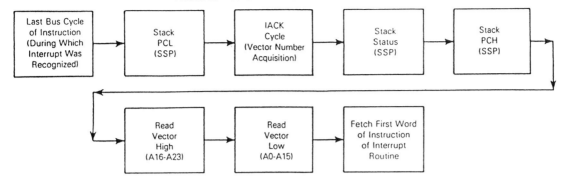

Priority level seven is a special case. Level seven interrupts cannot be inhibited by the interrupt priority mask, thus providing a "non-maskable interrupt" capability. An interrupt is generated each time the interrupt request level changes from some lower level to level seven. Note that a level seven interrupt may still be caused by the level comparison if the request level is a seven and the processor priority is set to a lower level by an instruction.

UNINITIALIZED INTERRUPT. An interrupting device asserts $\overline{VPA}$ or provides an interrupt vector during an interrupt acknowledge cycle to the MC68000. If the vector register has not been initialized, the responding M68000 Family peripheral will provide vector 15, the unitialized interrupt vector. This provides a uniform way to recover from a programming error.

SPURIOUS INTERRUPT. If during the interrupt acknowledge cycle no device responds by asserting $\overline{DTACK}$ or $\overline{VPA}$, the bus error line should be asserted to terminate the vector acquisition. The processor separates the processing of this error from bus error by fetching the spurious interrupt vector instead of the bus error vector. The processor then proceeds with the usual exception processing.

INSTRUCTION TRAPS. Traps are exceptions caused by instructions. They arise either from processor recognition of abnormal conditions during instruction execution, or from use of instructions whose normal behavior is trapping.

Some instructions are used specifically to generate traps. The TRAP instruction always forces an exception, and is useful for implementing system calls for user programs. The TRAPV and CHK instructions force an exception if the user program detects a runtime error, which may be an arithmetic overflow or a subscript out of bounds.

The signed divide (DIVS) and unsigned divide (DIVU) instructions will force an exception if a division operation is attempted with a divisor of zero.

ILLEGAL AND UNIMPLEMENTED INSTRUCTIONS. Illegal instruction is the term used to refer to any of the word bit patterns which are not the bit pattern of the first word of a legal instruction. During instruction execution, if such an instruction is fetched, an illegal instruction exception occurs.

Word patterns with bits 15 through 12 equaling 1010 or 1111 are distinguished as unimplemented instructions and separate exception vectors are given to these patterns to permit efficient emulation. This facility allows the operating system to detect program errors, or to emulate unimplemented instructions in software.

PRIVILEGE VIOLATIONS. In order to provide system security, various instructions are privileged. An attempt to execute one of the privileged instructions while in the user state will cause an exception. The privileged instructions are:

STOP	AND (word) Immediate to SR
RESET	EOR (word) Immediate to SR
RTE	OR (word) Immediate to SR
MOVE to SR	MOVE USP

TRACING. To aid in program development, the MC68000 includes a facility to allow instruction by instruction tracing. In the trace state, after each instruction is executed an exception is forced, allowing a debugging program to monitor the execution of the program under test.

The trace facility uses the T-bit in the supervisor portion of the status register. If the T-bit is negated (off), tracing is disabled, and instruction execution proceeds from instruction to instruction as normal. If the T-bit is asserted (on) at the beginning of the execution of an instruction, a trace exception will be generated after the execution of that instruction is completed. If the instruction is not executed, either because an interrupt is taken, or the instruction is illegal or privileged, the trace exception does not occur. The trace exception also does not occur if the instruction is aborted by a reset, bus error, or address error exception. If the instruction is indeed executed and an interrupt is pending on completion, the trace exception is processed before the interrupt exception. If, during the execution of the instruction, an exception is forced by that instruction, the forced exception is processed before the trace exception.

As an extreme illustration of the above rules, consider the arrival of an interrupt during the execution of a TRAP instruction while tracing is enabled. First the trap exception is processed, then the trace exception, and finally the interrupt exception. Instruction execution resumes in the interrupt handler routine.

BUS ERROR. Bus error exceptions occur when the external logic requests that a bus error be processed by an exception. The current bus cycle which the processor is making is then aborted. Whether the processor was doing instruction or exception processing, that processing is terminated, and the processor immediately begins exception processing.

Exception processing for bus error follows the usual sequence of steps. The status register is copied, the supervisor state is entered, and the trace state is turned off. The vector number is generated to refer to the bus error vector. Since the processor was not between instructions when the bus error exception request was made, the context of the processor is more detailed. To save more of this context, additional information is saved on the supervisor stack. The program counter and the copy of the status register are of course saved. The value saved for the program counter is advanced by some amount, two to ten bytes beyond the address of the first word of the instruction which made the reference causing the bus error. If the bus error occurred during the fetch of the next instruction, the saved program counter has a value in the vicinity of the current instruction, even if the current instruction is a branch, a jump, or a return instruction. Besides the usual information, the processor saves its internal copy of the first word of the instruction being processed, and the address which was being accessed by the aborted bus cycle. Specific information about the access is also saved: whether it was a read or a write, whether the processor was processing an instruction or not, and the classification displayed on the function code outputs when the bus error occurred. The processor is processing an instruction if it is in the normal state or processing a Group 2 exception; the processor is not processing an instruction if it is processing a Group 0 or a Group 1 exception. Figure 37 illustrates how this information is organized on the supervisor stack. Although this information is not sufficient in general to effect full recovery from the bus error, it does allow soft-

ware diagnosis. Finally, the processor commences instruction processing at the address contained in the vector. It is the responsibility of the error handler routine to clean up the stack and determine where to continue execution.

If a bus error occurs during the exception processing for a bus error, address error, or reset, the processor is halted, and all processing ceases. This simplifies the detection of catastrophic system failure, since the processor removes itself from the system rather than destroy all memory contents. Only the RESET pin can restart a halted processor.

ADDRESS ERROR. Address error exceptions occur when the processor attempts to access a word or a long word operand or an instruction at an odd address. The effect is much like an internally generated bus error, so that the bus cycle is aborted, and the processor ceases whatever processing it is currently doing and begins exception processing. After exception processing commences, the sequence is the same as that for bus error including the information that is stacked, except that the vector number refers to the address error vector instead. Likewise, if an address error occurs during the exception processing for a bus error, address error, or reset, the processor is halted. As shown in Figure 38, an address error will execute a short bus cycle followed by exception processing.

FIGURE 37 — SUPERVISOR STACK ORDER (GROUP 0)

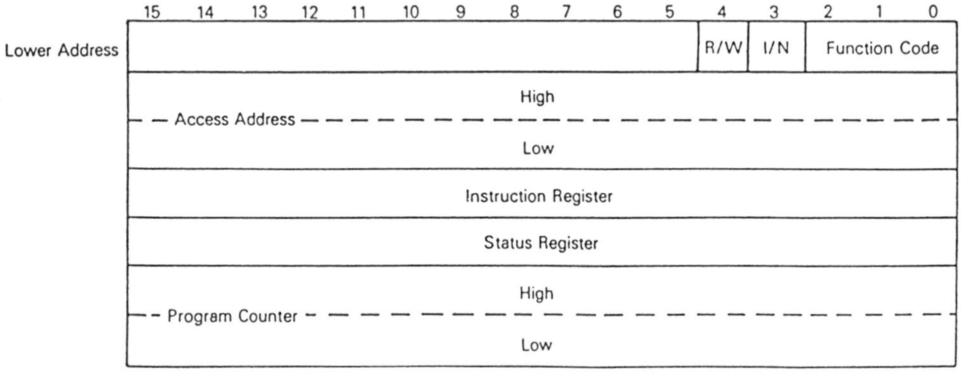

	15	14	13	12	11	10	9	8	7	6	5	4	3	2	1	0
Lower Address												R/W	I/N	Function Code		
— — Access Address — —	High															
	Low															
	Instruction Register															
	Status Register															
— — Program Counter — —	High															
	Low															

R/W (read/write): write = 0, read = 1.   I/N (instruction/not): instruction = 0, not = 1

INSTRUCTION EXECUTION TIMES

The following paragraphs contain listings of the instruction execution times in terms of external clock (CLK) periods. In this timing data, it is assumed that both memory read and write cycle times are four clock periods. Any wait states caused by a longer memory cycle must be added to the total instruction time. The number of bus read and write cycles for each instruction is also included with the timing data. This data is enclosed in parenthesis following the execution periods and is shown as: (r/w) where r is the number of read cycles and w is the number of write cycles.

NOTE

The number of periods includes instruction fetch and all applicable operand fetches and stores.

EFFECTIVE ADDRESS OPERAND CALCULATION TIMING

Table 23 lists the number of clock periods required to compute an instruction's effective address. It includes fetching of any extension words, the address computation, and fetching of the memory operand. The number of bus read and write cycles is shown in parenthesis as (r/w). Note there are no write cycles involved in processing the effective address.

MOVE INSTRUCTION CLOCK PERIODS

Tables 24 and 25 indicate the number of clock periods for the move instruction. This data includes instruction fetch, operand reads, and operand writes. The number of bus read and write cycles is shown in parenthesis as: (r/w).

STANDARD INSTRUCTION CLOCK PERIODS

The number of clock periods shown in Table 26 indicates the time required to perform the operations, store the results, and read the next instruction. The number of bus read and write cycles is shown in parenthesis as: (r/w). The number of clock periods and the number of read and write cycles must be added respectively to those of the effective address calculation where indicated.

In Table 26 the headings have the following meanings: An = address register operand, Dn = data register operand, ea = an operand specified by an effective address, and M = memory effective address operand.

IMMEDIATE INSTRUCTION CLOCK PERIODS

The number of clock periods shown in Table 27 includes the time to fetch immediate operands, perform the operations, store the results, and read the next operation. The number of bus read and write cycles is shown in parenthesis as: (r/w). The number of clock periods and the number of read and write cycles must be added respectively to those of the effective address calculation where indicated.

In Table 27, the headings have the following meanings: # = immediate operand, Dn = data register operand, An = address register operand, M = memory operand, and SR = status register.

SINGLE OPERAND INSTRUCTION CLOCK PERIODS

Table 28 indicates the number of clock periods for the single operand instructions. The number of bus read and write cycles is shown in parenthesis as: (r/w). The number of clock periods and the number of read and write cycles must be added respectively to those of the effective address calculation where indicated.

TABLE 23 — EFFECTIVE ADDRESS CALCULATION TIMING

Addressing Mode		Byte, Word	Long
	Register		
Dn	Data Register Direct	0(0/0)	0(0/0)
An	Address Register Direct	0(0/0)	0(0/0)
	Memory		
An@	Address Register Indirect	4(1/0)	8(2/0)
An@ +	Address Register Indirect with Postincrement	4(1/0)	8(2/0)
An@ −	Address Register Indirect with Predecrement	6(1/0)	10(2/0)
An@(d)	Address Register Indirect with Displacement	8(2/0)	12(3/0)
An@(d, ix)*	Address Register Indirect with Index	10(2/0)	14(3/0)
xxx.W	Absolute Short	8(2/0)	12(3/0)
xxx.L	Absolute Long	12(3/0)	16(4/0)
PC@(d)	Program Counter with Displacement	8(2/0)	12(3/0)
PC@(d, ix)*	Program Counter with Index	10(2/0)	14(3/0)
#xxx	Immediate	4(1/0)	8(2/0)

*The size of the index register (ix) does not affect execution time.

TABLE 24 — MOVE BYTE AND WORD INSTRUCTION CLOCK PERIODS

Source	Destination								
	Dn	An	An@	An@ +	An@ −	An@(d)	An@(d,ix)*	xxx.W	xxx.L
Dn	4(1/0)	4(1/0)	8(1/1)	8(1/1)	8(1/1)	12(2/1)	14(2/1)	12(2/1)	16(3/1)
An	4(1/0)	4(1/0)	8(1/1)	8(1/1)	8(1/1)	12(2/1)	14(2/1)	12(2/1)	16(3/1)
An@	8(2/0)	8(2/0)	12(2/1)	12(2/1)	12(2/1)	16(3/1)	18(3/1)	16(3/1)	20(4/1)
An@ +	8(2/0)	8(2/0)	12(2/1)	12(2/1)	12(2/1)	16(3/1)	18(3/1)	16(3/1)	20(4/1)
An@ −	10(2/0)	10(2/0)	14(2/1)	14(2/1)	14(2/1)	18(3/1)	20(3/1)	18(3/1)	22(4/1)
An@(d)	12(3/0)	12(3/0)	16(3/1)	16(3/1)	16(3/1)	20(4/1)	22(4/1)	20(4/1)	24(5/1)
An@(d, ix)*	14(3/0)	14(3/0)	18(3/1)	18(3/1)	18(3/1)	22(4/1)	24(4/1)	22(4/1)	26(5/1)
xxx.W	12(3/0)	12(3/0)	16(3/1)	16(3/1)	16(3/1)	20(4/1)	22(4/1)	20(4/1)	24(5/1)
xxx.L	16(4/0)	16(4/0)	20(4/1)	20(4/1)	20(4/1)	24(5/1)	26(5/1)	24(5/1)	28(6/1)
PC@(d)	12(3/0)	12(3/0)	16(3/1)	16(3/1)	16(3/1)	20(4/1)	22(4/1)	20(4/1)	24(5/1)
PC@(d, ix)*	14(3/0)	14(3/0)	18(3/1)	18(3/1)	18(3/1)	22(4/1)	24(4/1)	22(4/1)	26(5/1)
#xxx	8(2/0)	8(2/0)	12(2/1)	12(2/1)	12(2/1)	16(3/1)	18(3/1)	16(3/1)	20(4/1)

The size of the index register (ix) does not affect execution time.

TABLE 25 — MOVE LONG INSTRUCTION CLOCK PERIODS

Source	Destination								
	Dn	An	An@	An@ +	An@ −	An@(d)	An@(d,ix)*	xxx.W	xxx.L
Dn	4(1/0)	4(1/0)	12(1/2)	12(1/2)	14(1/2)	16(2/2)	18(2/2)	16(2/2)	20(3/2)
An	4(1/0)	4(1/0)	12(1/2)	12(1/2)	14(1/2)	16(2/2)	18(2/2)	16(2/2)	20(3/2)
An@	12(3/0)	12(3/0)	20(3/2)	20(3/2)	20(3/2)	24(4/2)	26(4/2)	24(4/2)	28(5/2)
An@ +	12(3/0)	12(3/0)	20(3/2)	20(3/2)	20(3/2)	24(4/2)	26(4/2)	24(4/2)	28(5/2)
An@ −	14(3/0)	14(3/0)	22(3/2)	22(3/2)	22(3/2)	26(4/2)	28(4/2)	26(4/2)	30(5/2)
An@(d)	16(4/0)	16(4/0)	24(4/2)	24(4/2)	24(4/2)	28(5/2)	30(5/2)	28(5/2)	32(6/2)
An@(d, ix)*	18(4/0)	18(4/0)	26(4/2)	26(4/2)	26(4/2)	30(5/2)	32(5/2)	30(5/2)	34(6/2)
xxx.W	16(4/0)	16(4/0)	24(4/2)	24(4/2)	24(4/2)	28(5/2)	30(5/2)	28(5/2)	32(6/2)
xxx.L	20(5/0)	20(5/0)	28(5/2)	28(5/2)	28(5/2)	32(6/2)	34(6/2)	32(6/2)	36(7/2)
PC@(d)	16(4/0)	16(4/0)	24(4/2)	24(4/2)	24(4/2)	28(5/2)	30(5/2)	28(5/2)	32(5/2)
PC@(d, ix)*	18(4/0)	18(4/0)	26(4/2)	26(4/2)	26(4/2)	30(5/2)	32(5/2)	30(5/2)	34(6/2)
#xxx	12(3/0)	12(3/0)	20(3/2)	20(3/2)	20(3/2)	24(4/2)	26(4/2)	24(4/2)	28(5/2)

*The size of the index register (ix) does not affect execution time.

TABLE 26 — STANDARD INSTRUCTION CLOCK PERIODS

Instruction	Size	op <ea>, An	op <ea>, Dn	op Dn, <M>
ADD	Byte, Word	8(1/0) +	4(1/0) +	8(1/1) +
	Long	6(1/0) + **	6(1/0) + **	12(1/2) +
AND	Byte, Word	—	4(1/0) +	8(1/1) +
	Long	—	6(1/0) + **	12(1/2) +
CMP	Byte, Word	6(1/0) +	4(1/0) +	—
	Long	6(1/0) +	6(1/0) +	—
DIVS	—	—	158(1/0) + *	—
DIVU	—	—	140(1/0) + *	—
EOR	Byte, Word	—	4(1/0)***	8(1/1) +
	Long	—	8(1/0)***	12(1/2) +
MULS	—	—	70(1/0) + *	—
MULU	—	—	70(1/0) + *	—
OR	Byte, Word	—	4(1/0) +	8(1/1) +
	Long	—	6(1/0) + **	12(1/1) +
SUB	Byte, Word	8(1/0) +	4(1/0) +	8(1/1) +
	Long	6(1/0) + **	6(1/0) + **	12(1/2) +

+ add effective address calculation time   ** total of 8 clock periods for instruction if the effective address is register direct
* indicates maximum value   *** only available effective address mode is data register direct

TABLE 27 — IMMEDIATE INSTRUCTION CLOCK PERIODS

Instruction	Size	op *I*, Dn	op *I*, An	op *I*, M
ADDI	Byte, Word	8(2/0)	—	12(2/1)+
	Long	16(3/0)	—	20(3/2)+
ADDQ	Byte, Word	4(1/0)	8(1/0)*	8(1/1)+
	Long	8(1/0)	8(1/0)	12(1/2)+
ANDI	Byte, Word	8(2/0)	—	12(2/1)+
	Long	16(3/0)	—	20(3/1)+
CMPI	Byte, Word	8(2/0)	8(2/0)	8(2/0)+
	Long	14(3/0)	14(3/0)	12(3/0)+
EORI	Byte, Word	8(2/0)	—	12(2/1)+
	Long	16(3/0)	—	20(3/2)+
MOVEQ	Long	4(1/0)	—	—
ORI	Byte, Word	8(2/0)	—	12(2/1)+
	Long	16(3/0)	—	20(3/2)+
SUBI	Byte, Word	8(2/0)	—	12(2/1)+
	Long	16(3/0)	—	20(3/2)+
SUBQ	Byte, Word	4(1/0)	8(1/0)*	8(1/1)+
	Long	8(1/0)	8(1/0)	12(1/2)+

+ add effective address calculation time
*word only

TABLE 28 — SINGLE OPERAND INSTRUCTION CLOCK PERIODS

Instruction	Size	Register	Memory
CLR	Byte, Word	4(1/0)	8(1/1)+
	Long	6(1/0)	12(1/2)+
NBCD	Byte	6(1/0)	8(1/1)+
NEG	Byte, Word	4(1/0)	8(1/1)+
	Long	6(1/0)	12(1/2)+
NEGX	Byte, Word	4(1/0)	8(1/1)+
	Long	6(1/0)	12(1/2)+
NOT	Byte, Word	4(1/0)	8(1/1)+
	Long	6(1/0)	12(1/2)+
S$_{CC}$	Byte, False	4(1/0)	8(1/1)+
	Byte, True	6(1/0)	8(1/1)+
TAS	Byte	4(1/0)	10(1/1)+
TST	Byte, Word	4(1/0)	4(1/0)
	Long	4(1/0)	4(1/0)+

+ add effective address calculation time

SHIFT/ROTATE INSTRUCTION CLOCK PERIODS

Table 29 indicates the number of clock periods for the shift and rotate instructions. The number of bus read and write cycles is shown in parenthesis as: (r/w). The number of clock periods and the number of read and write cycles must be added respectively to those of the effective address calculation where indicated.

BIT MANIPULATION INSTRUCTION CLOCK PERIODS

Table 30 indicates the number of clock periods required for the bit manipulation instructions. The number of bus read and write cycles is shown in parenthesis as: (r/w). The number of clock periods and the number of read and write cycles must be added respectively to those of the effective address calculation where indicated.

CONDITIONAL INSTRUCTION CLOCK PERIODS

Table 31 indicates the number of clock periods required for the conditional instructions. The number of bus read and write cycles is indicated in parenthesis as: (r/w). The number of clock periods and the number of read and write cycles must be added respectively to those of the effective address calculation where indicated.

JMP, JSR, LEA, PEA, MOVEM INSTRUCTION CLOCK PERIODS

Table 32 indicates the number of clock periods required for the jump, jump to subroutine, load effective address, push effective address, and move multiple registers instructions. The number of bus read and write cycles is shown in parenthesis as: (r/w).

TABLE 29 — SHIFT/ROTATE INSTRUCTION CLOCK PERIODS

Instruction	Size	Register	Memory
ASR, ASL	Byte, Word	6 + 2n(1/0)	8(1/1) +
	Long	8 + 2n(1/0)	—
LSR, LSL	Byte, Word	6 + 2n(1/0)	8(1/1) +
	Long	8 + 2n(1/0)	—
ROR, ROL	Byte, Word	6 + 2n(1/0)	8(1/1) +
	Long	8 + 2n(1/0)	—
ROXR, ROXL	Byte, Word	6 + 2n(1/0)	8(1/1) +
	Long	8 + 2n(1/0)	—

TABLE 30 — BIT MANIPULATION INSTRUCTION CLOCK PERIODS

Instruction	Size	Dynamic		Static	
		Register	Memory	Register	Memory
BCHG	Byte	—	8(1/1) +	—	12(2/1) +
	Long	8(1/0) *	—	12(2/0) *	—
BCLR	Byte	—	8(1/1) +	—	12(2/1) +
	Long	10(1/0)*	—	14(2/0)*	—
BSET	Byte	—	8(1/1) +	—	12(2/1) +
	Long	8(1/0)*	—	12(2/0)*	—
BTST	Byte	—	4(1/0) +	—	8(2/0) +
	Long	6(1/0)	—	10(2/0)	—

\+ add effective address calculation time

* indicates maximum value

TABLE 31 — CONDITIONAL INSTRUCTION CLOCK PERIODS

Instruction	Displacement	Trap or Branch Taken	Trap or Branch Not Taken
B$_{CC}$	Byte	10(2/0)	8(1/0)
	Word	10(2/0)	12(2/0)
BRA	Byte	10(2/0)	—
	Word	10(2/0)	—
BSR	Byte	18(2/2)	—
	Word	18(2/2)	—
DB$_{CC}$	CC true	—	12(2/0)
	CC false	10(2/0)	14(3/0)
CHK	—	40(5/3) + *	8(1/0) +
TRAP	—	34(4/3)	—
TRAPV	—	34(5/3)	4(1/0)

\+ add effective address calculation time

* indicates maximum value

TABLE 32 — JMP, JSR, LEA, PEA, MOVEM INSTRUCTION CLOCK PERIODS

Instr	Size	An@	An@ +	An@ −	An@(d)	An@(d, ix) *	xxx.W	xxx.L	PC@(d)	PC@(d, ix)*
JMP	—	8(2/0)	—	—	10(2/0)	14(3/0)	10(2/0)	12(3/0)	10(2/0)	14(3/0)
JSR	—	16(2/2)	—	—	18(2/2)	22(2/2)	18(2/2)	20(3/2)	18(2/2)	22(2/2)
LEA	—	4(1/0)	—	—	8(2/0)	12(2/0)	8(2/0)	12(3/0)	8(2/0)	12(2/0)
PEA	—	12(1/2)	—	—	16(2/2)	20(2/2)	16(2/2)	20(3/2)	16(2/2)	20(2/2)
MOVEM	Word	12+4n (3+n/0)	12+4n (3+n/0)	—	16+4n (4+n/0)	18+4n (4+n/0)	16+4n (4+n/0)	20+4n (5+n/0)	16+4n (4+n/0)	18+4n (4+n/0)
M → R	Long	12+8n (3+2n/0)	12+8n (3+2n/0)	—	16+8n (4+2n/0)	18+8n (4+2n/0)	16+8n (4+2n/0)	20+8n (5+2n/0)	16+8n (4+2n/0)	18+8n (4+2n/0)
MOVEM	Word	8+5n (2/n)	—	8+5n (2/n)	12+5n (3/n)	14+5n (3/n)	12+5n (3/n)	16+5n (4/n)	—	—
R → M	Long	8+10n (2/2n)	—	8+10n (2/2n)	12+10n (3/2n)	14+10n (3/2n)	12+10n (3/2n)	16+10n (4/2n)	—	—

n is the number of registers to move

* is the size of the index register (ix) does not affect the instruction's execution time

MULTI-PRECISION INSTRUCTION CLOCK PERIODS

Table 33 indicates the number of clock periods for the multi-precision instructions. The number of clock periods includes the time to fetch both operands, perform the operations, store the results, and read the next instructions. The number of read and write cycles is shown in parenthesis as: (r/w).

In Table 33, the headings have the following meanings: Dn = data register operand and M = memory operand.

TABLE 33 — MULTI-PRECISION INSTRUCTION CLOCK PERIODS

Instruction	Size	op Dn, Dn	op M, M
ADDX	Byte, Word	4(1/0)	18(3/1)
	Long	8(1/0)	30(5/2)
CMPM	Byte, Word	—	12(3/0)
	Long	—	20(5/0)
SUBX	Byte, Word	4(1/0)	18(3/1)
	Long	8(1/0)	30(5/2)
ABCD	Byte	6(1/0)	18(3/1)
SBCD	Byte	6(1/0)	18(3/1)

MISCELLANEOUS INSTRUCTION CLOCK PERIODS

Table 34 indicates the number of clock periods for the following miscellaneous instructions. The number of bus read and write cycles is shown in parenthesis as: (r/w). The number of clock periods plus the number of read and write cycles must be added to those of the effective address calculation where indicated.

EXCEPTION PROCESSING CLOCK PERIODS

Table 35 indicates the number of clock periods for exception processing. The number of clock periods includes the time for all stacking, the vector fetch, and the fetch of the first instruction of the handler routine. The number of bus read and write cycles is shown in parenthesis as: (r/w).

TABLE 34 — MISCELLANEOUS INSTRUCTION CLOCK PERIODS

Instruction	Size	Register	Memory	Register → Memory	Memory → Register
MOVE from SR	—	6(1/0)	8(1/1) +	—	—
MOVE to CCR	—	12(2/0)	12(2/0) +	—	—
MOVE to SR	—	12(2/0)	12(2/0) +	—	—
MOVEP	Word	—	—	16(2/2)	16(4/0)
	Long	—	—	24(2/4)	24(6/0)
EXG	—	6(1/0)	—	—	—
EXT	Word	4(1/0)	—	—	—
	Long	4(1/0)	—	—	—
LINK	—	16(2/2)	—	—	—
MOVE from USP	—	4(1/0)	—	—	—
MOVE to USP	—	4(1/0)	—	—	—
NOP	—	4(1/0)	—	—	—
RESET	—	132(1/0)	—	—	—
RTE	—	20(5/0)	—	—	—
RTR	—	20(5/0)	—	—	—
RTS	—	16(4/0)	—	—	—
STOP	—	4(0/0)	—	—	—
SWAP	—	4(1/0)	—	—	—
UNLK	—	12(3/0)	—	—	—

+ add effective address calculation time

TABLE 35 — EXCEPTION PROCESSING CLOCK PERIODS

Exception	Periods
Address Error	50(4/7)
Bus Error	50(4/7)
Interrupt	44(5/3)*
Illegal Instruction	34(4/3)
Privileged Instruction	34(4/3)
Trace	34(4/3)

*The interrupt acknowledge bus cycle is assumed
to take four external clock periods

PACKAGE DIMENSIONS

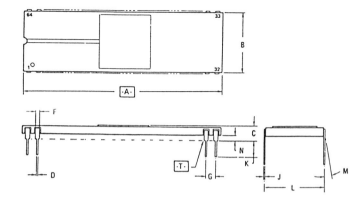

NOTES:
1. DIMENSION ⌊-A-⌋ IS DATUM.
2. POSITIONAL TOLERANCE FOR LEADS:
   ⊕ 0.25 (0.010)Ⓜ T | A Ⓜ
3. ⌊-T-⌋ IS SEATING PLANE.
4. DIMENSION "L" TO CENTER OF LEADS
   WHEN FORMED PARALLEL.
5. DIMENSIONING AND TOLERANCING PER
   ANSI Y14.5, 1973.

DIM	MILLIMETERS		INCHES	
	MIN	MAX	MIN	MAX
A	80.52	82.04	3.170	3.230
B	22.25	22.96	0.876	0.904
C	3.05	4.32	0.120	0.170
D	0.38	0.53	0.015	0.021
F	0.76	1.40	0.030	0.055
G	2.54 BSC		0.100 BSC	
J	0.20	0.33	0.008	0.013
K	2.54	4.19	0.100	0.165
L	22.61	23.11	0.890	0.910
M	—	10°	—	10°
N	1.02	1.52	0.040	0.060

CASE 746-01

Selected Answers

CHAPTER 1

1.1 Computers are machines that solve problems for people.

1.3 Digital computers solve more problems faster, easier, and with greater flexibility than analog computers.

1.5 Software means computer programs and documentation. Hardware refers to electronic components, frame, PC boards, and so on.

1.7 The transistor and the ferrite core.

1.9 Boards are assembled and tested; design time is minimized; manufacturing costs are reduced; additional boards can be purchased to expand the system; and systems can be ``tailored'' for particular applications.

CHAPTER 2

2.1 Large mainframe, mini, and micro.

2.3 Two: 0 and 1.

2.5 Bit stands for binary digit (either a logic 0 or a logic 1). Byte means 8 bits.

2.7 49,152 bytes.

2.9 I/O ports allow the rest of the μC system to communicate with peripheral equipment.

2.11 To convert a physical quantity into an electrical quantity.

2.13 To store the programs and data.

2.15 Volatile and nonvolatile.

2.17 Yes.

2.19 A bus is a wire or wires that connect the IC chips in a computer.

2.21 Bidirectional.

2.23 Accumulator.

CHAPTER 3

3.1 To reduce the possible errors in reading and writing binary patterns.

3.3 (a) C7, (b) 68, (c) F5, (d) 39, (e) A4.

3.5 (a) 1A, (b) 7B, (c) 50, (d) 1100, (e) 4000.

3.7 Page address.

3.9 Binary coded decimal.

3.11 (a) 46, (b) 99, (c) 25, (d) 68, (e) 30.

3.13 Capital letters:

M	I	C	R	O	P	R	O	C	E	S	S	O	R
4D	49	43	52	4F	50	52	4F	43	45	53	53	4F	52

Lowercase letters:

m	i	c	r	o	p	r	o	c	e	s	s	o	r
6D	69	63	72	6F	70	72	6F	63	65	73	73	6F	72

CHAPTER 4

4.1 Firmware refers to software programs loaded into a portion of memory that cannot be changed during processing.

4.3 Algorithm.

4.5 Machine language, assembly language, and high-level language.

4.7 Hex loader.

4.9 To convert an assembly language program into binary, or source code into object code.

4.11 Interpreters execute each program statement immediately every time the program is run. Compilers only execute the program after all program statements have been read and analyzed.

4.13 Assembly language programs provide faster execution, more data-handling capability, more accuracy, and less hardware.

4.15 To solve a specific problem that will be used over and over again.

4.17 A return from subroutine instruction.

CHAPTER 5

5.1 Registers, arithmetic and logic unit, timing and control circuitry, and decoding circuitry.

5.3 All of a μP's instructions.

5.5 Two.

5.7 Carry flag, zero flag, and sign flag.

5.9 The stack is an area of memory used to store temporary data.

5.11 Yes.

5.13 Op code.

5.15 No.

5.17 To move data from a memory location to a μP register.

5.19

	A Register	B Register
(a)	EC	EC
(b)	04	04
(c)	EC	04

5.21 Borrow bit.

5.23 Yes.

5.25 Compare instructions do not affect the contents of the accumulator.

5.27 Rotate instructions save data by moving the carry flag back into the register. Shift instructions destroy data because a logic 0 is always moved into the register.

5.29 Stack.

5.31 Push instruction.

5.33 Immediate.

5.35 Offset or displacement.

CHAPTER 6

6.1 Seventy-two instructions.

6.3 Three: index register, program counter, and stack pointer.

6.5 Set to a logic 1.

6.7 (a) Load accumulator A with data 04.

(b) Load accumulator A with data at location F800.

(c) Load accumulator B with data at location 0050.

(d) Load X register with data 01FF.

(e) Store accumulator A at location 0240.

(f) Store accumulator B at location of the X register + 07.

(g) Store X_H register at location C000 and X_L at location C001.

(h) Transfer accumulator B to accumulator A.

(i) Transfer CCR to accumulator A.

6.9 (a) Add accumulator B with accumulator A.

(b) Add 03 without carry to accumulator A.

(c) Add without carry data at 0200 with accumulator B.

(d) Add with carry data at 0015 with accumulator A.

(e) Subtract without carry data 10_{hex} from accumulator A.

(f) Subtract with carry data at location of the X register + 08 from accumulator B.

(g) Increment accumulator A.

(h) Increment memory location 0150.

(i) Decrement accumulator B.

(j) Decrement X register.

6.11 Accumulator A.

6.13 Yes.

6.15 N, Z, V, and C.

6.17 (a) N, Z, and V. V flag always cleared. (b) N. Z. V. and C. V and C flags always cleared.

6.19 Arithmetic shift left, ASL; arithmetic shift right, ASR; logical shift right, LSR; rotate left, ROL; rotate right, ROR.

6.21 Yes.

6.23 Yes.

6.25 Sixteen branch instructions.

6.27 Yes.

6.29 Yes.

6.31 -128 to $+127$.

6.33 Fourteen conditional branch instructions.

6.35 Increment the stack pointer.

6.37 LDS, STS, INS, DES, TSX, TXS, PSH, PUL

CHAPTER 7

7.1 LDA B $0150

ADD B $0160

STA B $0160

7.3 Yes.

7.5 No, only for accumulator A.

7.7 LDA B $1060

SUB B $0150

STA B $0160

7.9 $48_{hex} = 72_{decimal}$.

Time delay $= 2\ \mu s + (6\ \mu s)(72) = 434\ \mu s$

7.11 Equation 7.1 would be modified as follows:

$$\text{Time delay} = \overbrace{2\ \mu s}^{\text{LDA A}} + (\overbrace{2\ \mu s}^{\text{DEC A}} + \overbrace{2\ \mu s}^{\text{NOP}} + \overbrace{4\ \mu s}^{\text{BNE}}) \times \overbrace{166}^{\text{Count}_{decimal}}$$
$$= 2\ \mu s + (8\ \mu s)(166) = 1.33\ ms$$

7.13 The original contents of accumulator A.

7.15

```
                    •
                    •
                    •
               CLC
               LDA B #$0A
               LDA A #$00
               STA A $0750
     REPEAT: PUL A
               ADC A $0750
               DAA
               STA A $0750
               DEC B
               BNE REPEAT
```

CHAPTER 8

8.1 Yes.

8.3 Input lines are $\overline{HALT}$, $\overline{IRQ}$, $\overline{NMI}$, DBE, TSC, and $\overline{RES}$. Output lines are VMA, BA, and R/$\overline{W}$.

8.5 (a) Interrupt request, (b) nonmaskable interrupt, (c) data bus enable, (d) three-state control, (e) reset, (f) valid memory address, (g) bus available.

8.7 $PW_{\phi H}$ = 430 ns for ϕ_1 and $PW_{\phi H}$ = 450 ns for ϕ_2.

8.9 Three.

8.11 Yes.

8.13 Two.

8.15 Data on the data bus is irrelevant.

8.17 Yes.

8.19 Four. Decrement the stack pointer.

8.21 Yes, during clock cycles 3 and 4.

8.23

$\overline{RST}$	FFFE	FFFF
$\overline{NMI}$	FFFC	FFFD
SWI	FFFA	FFFB
$\overline{IRQ}$	FFF8	FFF9

8.25 DMA operation and single-instruction execution.

CHAPTER 9

9.1 To store information.

9.3 Bipolar and MOS.

9.5   Temporary.

9.7   Random access can refer to the way information is addressed, and to a type of semiconductor memory.

9.9   Emitter-coupled logic, ECL.

9.11 Static and dynamic.

9.13 Static RAMs are easier to use; faster; obtainable in bit, byte, and half-byte widths; and consume less power.

9.15 Bring X_2 and Y_2 to a logic 1; bring $R/\overline{W}$ line low; bring the data line low.

9.17 Dynamic RAMs have more bits per device, are less expensive, and consume less power per bit.

9.19 ROM, PROM, EPROM, EEPROM, battery backup, MBM.

9.21 No.

9.23 Block erasure.

CHAPTER 10

10.1   1024 words $\times$ 4 bits.

10.3   (a) Ten address pins (2114), (b) twelve address pins (2147).

10.5   So that the memory chip doesn't erroneously pick up data on the data bus.

10.7   At the end of the access time.

10.9   Three.

10.11 $\overline{E}$ pin, chip enable.

10.13 Advantage: less loading effect on each data bus line. Disadvantage: memory systems are built up in multiples of 4K.

10.15 Locations 3000 to 3FFF.

10.17 EXXX

CHAPTER 11

11.1   To allow the μP to communicate with peripheral equipment.

11.3   Yes.

11.5   No.

11.7   To the lowest numbered address bus lines: A_0, A_1, and so on.

11.9 D_0 to D_0; D_1 to D_1; and so on.

11.11 To synchronize all data transfers between the μP and the interface device.

11.13 Interrupt polling routine.

11.15 Address decoding, register select, timing and control, data bus buffers, internal bus, control register, status register, peripheral registers, and peripheral status/control.

11.17 High impedance state.

11.19 Status register.

CHAPTER 12

12.1 Two: port A and port B.

12.3 Five: three for chip select and two for register select.

12.5 Low.

12.7 Port A I/O lines are TTL, and Port B I/O lines are three-state.

12.9 CA_1 and CB_1.

12.11 Input lines: 0, 3, and 4. Output lines: 1, 2, 5, 6, and 7.

12.13 To select whether the μP communicates with the port or the data direction register.

12.15 (a) Port, (b) high to low, (c) control.

12.17 Wire address line A_4 to input C of the decoder chip; other inputs remain the same. See the accompanying figure.

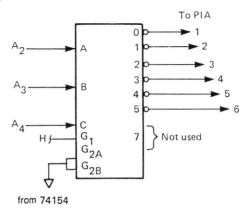

from 74154

CHAPTER 13

13.1 Asynchronous and synchronous.

13.3 Block framed.

13.5

Baud rate	110	150	300	600	1200	2400
Characters/s	12.2	16.6	33.3	66.9	133.3	267

13.7 Transmit data register.

13.9 To store the next character that is to be transmitted by the ACIA, ensuring a continuous data stream.

13.11 Framing, overrun, and parity errors. By bits 4, 5, and 6 of the status register.

13.13 So that the internal registers are in sequential memory locations.

13.15 The ACIA will not transmit data and send an interrupt request to the μP.

13.17 They determine the character format for transmission and reception by the ACIA.

13.19 Receive data register full, transmit data register empty, data carrier detect, clear-to-send, framing error, overrun error, parity error, interrupt request.

13.21 Transmit data register is full, clear-to-send line goes high, power-on condition.

13.23 The transmitter interrupt enable is active and the TDRE bit goes to a logic 1. The receiver interrupt enable is active and the RDRF bit goes to a logic 1. The $\overline{\text{DCD}}$ line goes high.

CHAPTER 14

14.1 Vector (or x–y) and raster scan.

14.3 Halved.

14.5 16K (16,134) bytes.

14.7 R_0: 164_{decimal} or $A4_{\text{hex}}$; R_1: 132_{decimal} or 88_{hex}; R_2: 136_{decimal} or 88_{hex}; R_3: 8_{decimal} or 08_{hex}.

14.9 304 scan lines per frame.

14.11 R_4: 29_{decimal} or $1D_{\text{hex}}$; R_5: 4_{decimal} or 04_{hex}; R_6: 24_{decimal} or 18_{hex}; R_7: 24–27_{decimal} or 18–$1B_{\text{hex}}$.

14.13 12.768 MHz.

14.15 (a) 0000001, (b) 1000001, (c) 1110000.

CHAPTER 15

15.1 The new μP is still capable of executing programs written for earlier μPs.

15.3 Asynchronous.

15.5 (a) $\cong$ 4.2G long words, (b) $\cong$ 8.4G words, (c) $\cong$ 16.8G bytes.

15.7 23 bits are used: A_1–A_{23}.

15.9 Levels 4, 5, 6, and 7.

15.11 No.

15.13 (a) 5, (b) 2, (c) 6, (d) 1.

15.15 (a) 8000   0011   0001   0011   0100
         8002   0101   0101   0101   0000

     (b) 8000   0111   0011   0001   0000

     (c) 8000   1010   0101   0010   1011
         8002   1100   0000   0111   1111

CHAPTER 16

16.1 (a) 0450, (b) 6150, (c) 6572.

16.3 ADD.W D_4, A_3.

16.5 (a) C300, (b) 0200, (c) AD00, (d) 1600.

16.7 5570.

16.9 Yes. The high bytes of both D_4 and memory location 4502 are zeros.

16.11 000018.

16.13 7.

16.15 65,536 ($-32,768$ to $+32,767$ from the present contents of the PC).

16.17 MOVEM.W $8000, D_0–D_1.

16.19 Yes. See Chapter 15.

CHAPTER 17

17.1 9 address pins; $2^{18} = 256K$.

17.3 Yes, by using pin 1 as an address pin.

17.5 Ground the A_{15} address pin on the dynamic memory controller. This procedure will ensure that only half of the memory cells are used.

17.7 Replace the NAND gate by an OR gate.

17.9 The output of the '154 has to be changed from output 3 to output 9.

Index